HONEY FROM A WEED

HONEY FROM A WEED

FASTING AND FEASTING IN

TUSCANY, CATALONIA, THE CYCLADES AND APULIA

BY

PATIENCE GRAY

WITH DRAWINGS BY CORINNA SARGOOD

Prospect Books

2009

Navigational Aids

The current of this book swirls to and fro between five areas of the Mediterranean. The maps on pages 14–17 show where these are.

In order of time, the places where the author and the Sculptor have lived are:

CASTELPOGGIO, a mountain village above Carrara in Tuscany

VENDRELL near Tarragona in Catalonia

APOLLONA on Naxos

LA BAROZZA in the vineyards above Carrara

above GARDA-SUL-LAGO in the Veneto

MASSERIA SPIGOLIZZI in the Basso Salento, Apulia

Abbreviations are often used to indicate a language: thus (C) for Catalan, (F) for French, (G) for Greek, and (I) for Italian. (Sal) indicates Salentine dialect words. The transcription of Greek words is not entirely systematic. It has been done in a way which helps to show how they are pronounced – as do the stress marks which appear on all of them except for monosyllables and a few proper names, e g those which have become English names also or are anglicised.

Particulars of all books referred to in the text are given in Part I of the Bibliography.

This paperback edition published in 2009 by Prospect Books, 26 Parke Road, London SW13 9NG. Reprinted 2012, 2013, 2014, 2016, 2017 (twice).

Honey from a Weed was first published in 1986 by Prospect Books.

©2009 the Estate of Patience Gray.

Drawings ©2009 the Estate of Patience Gray, except for those specified in the list of illustrations which are ©1986 Corinna Sargood.

ISBN 978-1-903018-20-0

Set in 12 on 13 point Linotype Baskerville.
Printed in Malta by the Gutenberg Press Ltd.

The cover painting is by Corinna Sargood.

For Wolfe

Man is nostalgia and a search for communion.

Octavio Paz, *The Labyrinth of Solitude*

It is through celebration that we become part
of what we perceive: the great arc of birdsong
– that runs around the world in the receding
darkness and through which we are swept into
the light of day – is as much part of the dawn
as the sun's first flash.

Norman Mommens

L'acant escolta	The acanthus listens
ecos de llunyania.	to echoes from afar.
Eternitzades,	Timeless,
altres fulles tremolen	other leaves tremble
als sons apagadíssims	to muffled sounds

Salvador Espriu, *Formes i Paraules*

Contents

Acknowledgements

ONEY from a Weed is a written proof of my affection for Tuscans, Naxians, Catalans, Apulians, among whom we have lived and worked – though they will never read it.

As far as cooking is concerned I acknowledge my debt to Irving Davis in the chapter 'Homage to a Classic Cook'. But I have also been urged on, challenged, by expectant friends – notably Wolfe Aylward, Jean Delpech, and by a 'Master of the Roast', the artist Helmut Dirnaichnèr, whose culinary prowess is indistinguishable from art.

I am in debt to Ariane Nisberg whose bracing criticism some years ago spurred me to fresh exertions. My gratitude to Alan Davidson – a St George in action – defies expression. He rescued my typescript from oblivion. By combining comment with encouragement, he inspired me to complete the work, and guided me through the kaleidoscopic changes of plant nomenclature.

I thank Ianthe Carswell for her kind permission to draw on Catalan recipes recorded in Vendrell, near Tarragona, by Irving Davis and published as *A Catalan Cookery Book* by his friend, the poet Lucien Scheler, in 1969 in Paris, in a very limited edition. The value of these recipes lies not only in their economy of means but in their authenticity.

Living in the wild, friendship operates at a distance. I gladly thank those who helped me from afar, Nicole Fenosa, Jeanne Mandello, J. L. Gili; Florá Papastávrou, Kevin Andrews, Norman Janis, Tania Midgley and my daughter Miranda; Lia Rondelli, Francesco Radino, Ugo Sissa and Chiarella Zucchi.

I particularly thank Nicolas Gray for making me laugh with his contribution to 'The Threatened Bombardment', and Antonio Lupo for laughing at me and lending me books.

It is of course entirely owing to the Sculptor's appetite for marble and stone that this work came into existence in the first place, and that I am held in the mysterious grip of olive, lentisk, fig and vine.

There is one person I cannot sufficiently thank, the Swiss painter Willi Hartung, whom we first met on Naxos. By forming over the years a magnificent collection of the Sculptor's carvings, he has enabled us to go on quietly with our work . . .

Introduction

I N the last twenty years I have shared the fortunes of a stone carver and during that time, working in silver and gold, have become a craftsman myself.

A vein of marble runs through this book. Marble determined where, how and among whom we lived; always in primitive conditions. There was not a trickle of water on tap either in the dilapidated country dwelling in the vineyards above Carrara – reached on foot up a steep muletrack – or in the spacious muleshed which served as habitation in Apollona on Naxos.

The Sculptor's appetite for marble precipitated us out of modern life into the company of marble artisans and wine-growers in Carrara and into an isolated community of 'Bronze Age' farmers on Naxos. The friendship of a Catalan sculptor and his wife and the incitement of a golden stone in a Roman quarry near Vendrell revealed – a summer long – the frugal and festive aspects of Catalan life.

The recipes in this book accumulated during this marble odyssey in the 60s, and went on accumulating when in 1970 we settled in the vaulted workspaces of a ruined sheep farm in the Salentine peninsula, exchanging marble for Lecce stone and tufa. Here, like so many others – foreshadowing the age to come – inscribed as artisans we also cultivate some acres of stony red earth.

Living in the wild, it has often seemed that we were living on the margins of literacy. This led to reading the landscape and learning from people, that is to first hand experience. This experience is both real and necessarily limited.

It is in this situation that I set out to write from personal observation and practice, underpinned by study, over a considerable period of time.

*   *   *   *   *

Good cooking is the result of a balance struck between frugality and liberality, something I learned in the kitchen of my friend Irving Davis, a bibliophile and classic cook. It is born out in communities where the supply of food is conditioned by the seasons.

Once we lose touch with the spendthrift aspect of nature's provisions epitomized in the raising of a crop, we are in danger of losing touch with life itself. When Providence supplies the means, the preparation and sharing of food takes on a sacred aspect. The fact that every crop is of short duration promotes a spirit of making the best of it while it lasts and conserving part of it for future use. It also leads to periods of fasting and periods of feasting, which represent the extremes of the artist's situation as well as the Greek Orthodox approach to food and the Catholic insistence on fasting, now abandoned.

Irving Davis had the enterprise and time during summers spent in Vendrell to write down a number of Catalan recipes which had delighted us. They were expounded in Catalan by able cooks, there and then translated into French by Nicole Fenosa, and written down by Irving in English on the spot in a little black notebook. It was my privilege to decipher this labour of love after his death.

The theme that binds this book together is not just the pursuit of marble and stone, but its location on limestone in the Mediterranean world, Italian, Greek and Catalan, a world rooted in the cultivation of the olive and the vine. The potentially shocking thing in the pages that follow is its fundament – olive oil. The difficulties of harvesting the olives makes this ever more expensive. Nevertheless, olive oil remains the basis of Mediterranean cooking, though in Catalonia and to some extent in Italy and Greece, very pure pork fat is also an important cooking medium.

It sometimes seems as if I have been rescuing a few strands from a former and more diligent way of life, now being fatally eroded by an entirely new set of values. As with students of music who record old songs which are no longer sung, soon some of the things I record will also have vanished.

The ring of hammer and chisel on marble, on stone, on wood, is the daily background of the book; morning, noon and night one is faced with a workman's appetite. The dishes I describe are the many ways in which it has and is being satisfied.

Poverty rather than wealth gives the good things of life their true significance. Home-made bread rubbed with garlic and sprinkled with olive oil, shared – with a flask of wine – between working people, can be more convivial than any feast. My ambition in drawing in the background to what is being cooked is to restore the meaning. I also celebrate the limestone wilderness.

If I stress the rustic source of culinary inspiration, it is not in opposition to the scientific. Cooking always is and always has been a partly scientific operation – in the sense that specific actions under particular conditions lead to foreseeable results. But it also presupposes aptitude, discernment and an appreciation of the intrinsic nature of different foodstuffs and awareness of the speeds at which they cook. Aptitude implies a certain skill and not a little patience and is the ally of the wish to impart to others something more than satisfaction, which can be called delight.

In my experience it is the countryman who is the real gourmet and for good reason; it is he who has cultivated, raised, hunted or fished the raw materials and has made the wine himself. The preoccupation of his wife is to do justice to his labours and bring the outcome triumphantly to table. In this an emotional element is involved. Perhaps this very old approach is beginning once again to inspire those who cook in more complex urban situations.

In my view it was not necessarily the chefs of prelates and princes who invented dishes. Country people and fishermen created them, great chefs refined them and wrote them down. In Latin countries, because of inborn conservatism, the tradition is alive and we can learn from it, that is, learning from people who have never read a book.

P.G.
Spigolizzi 1986

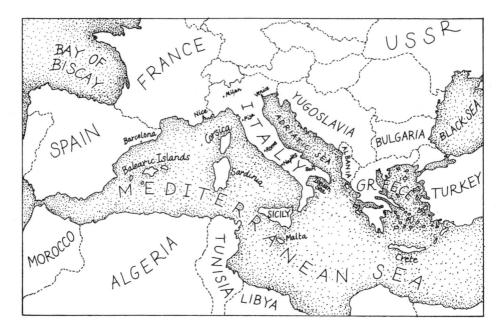

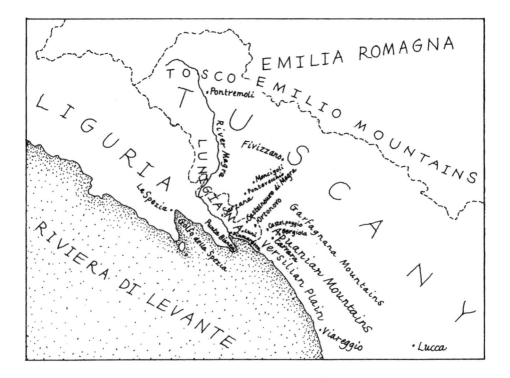

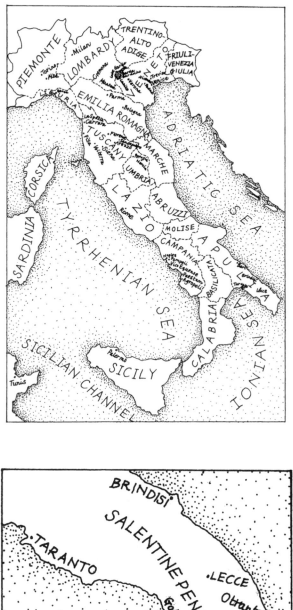

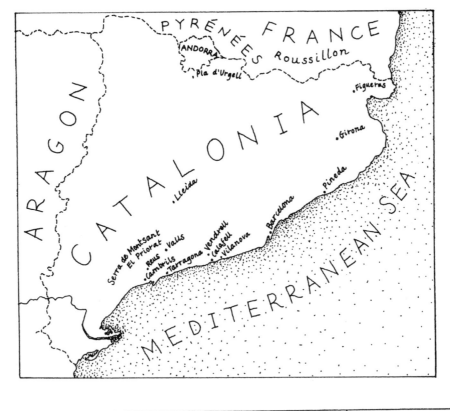

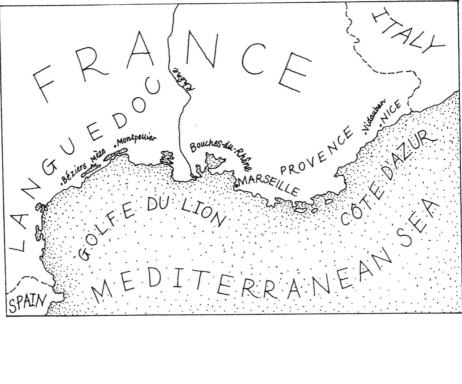

Fire

THE nature of the fire determines the procedure: you make a fire with a good draught, set between stones and oriented according to the wind, and let it burn up fiercely, fanning if necessary. When the flames have died down and the heat is at its maximum, you throw some thyme and rosemary on the glowing embers and set down the loaded grill, the meat having been anointed with oil well beforehand. You fan again and seal the meat on either side. The fire dies down a bit, the roasting proceeds at a slower rate. The searing time is short, the subsequent cooking time, once the juices have been contained, varies with the nature of what is being grilled.

Large fishes are best left unscaled, brushed with wine vinegar and oil, and cooked on a much slower braise. The fish retains its succulence; the skin and scales are then removed entire.

Out of this procedure and greatly depending on the kind of wood employed comes the real fragrance. Apple, pear, plum, apricot woods have fragrance. So do pine branches and nut woods. Sweet chestnut makes a slow smoky fire; the wood is too sappy. Fig wood is poor. Tamarisk has an unpleasant smell. Olive wood makes the most incandescent braise, and ilex is nearly as good. Dry vine cuttings are excellent for small grills, their heat being of short duration. The most fragrant fires are made from dried Mediterranean mountain scrub and the withered shrubs of the maquis – cistus, rosemary, Jerusalem sage, lentisk – which burn with the violence of a blow-torch, produce spurts of blue and emerald fire, and a smell of incense.

It is the shepherd in southern latitudes who inevitably sets the landscape on fire, the main cause of his social ostracism. He burns the maquis and mountainsides in summer to precipitate the growth of new grass for his famished flock. Artists have something in common with shepherds in that their means of livelihood is not apparent – they work for long periods with no prospect of gain, and others regard this as disreputable. It was a Salentine shepherd whose fire, advancing like a dragon across the wilderness where we were camping one summer, inadvertently destroyed my culinary reflections on the application of heat.

These notes, composed to the thrum of a guitar by firelight, at the time of losing them I thought significant . . . about copper being the best heat conductor . . . in praise of earthenware for slow cooking . . . about different intensities of heat in relation to the volume and nature of what is cooked and the type of utensil employed, both having a bearing on evaporation . . . the rapid absorption of liquor by dried staples (legumes) . . . the converse danger of drowning things in too much liquid . . . the totally different concepts of deep-frying and underfrying (*soffriggere*).

But the passage of time has turned this loss to gain. During the last two decades cooks have acquired new insights with regard to cooking. So, instead of beginning with the image of fire as destroyer, I begin with fire – borrowing Alexis Soyer's phrase – as 'gastronomic regenerator'.

Pots and Pans

THE island Greek *batterie de cuisine:* a large black pot with lid, a sieve, a frying pan, a wire grill, a wooden spoon, a pocket knife, an iron tripod and a chimney hook.

*   *   *   *   *

The nomadic cook's equipment, packed in a large grape basket and carted on muleback up the mule-track to La Barozza above Carrara: a tinned copper sole pan; an aluminium marmite with lid; a tinned copper saucepan with lid; an enamel milk pan; a glazed earthenware bean-pot; a glazed earthenware casserole with projecting handle (*padella*); an earthenware gratin dish; a colander; a cheese grater; a perforated ladle; a coffee grinder and a Neapolitan coffee-making device (*napoletana*); wooden salt and pepper mills; wooden spoons and forks; 2 French chef's knives; a *mandoline* (slicer); a funnel, a palette knife, a ladle; a polenta board and a chopping board; a wire mesh mat; a double wire grill with handles; a cake tin, a mixing bowl, a large close-grained wooden mortar and pestle. I was lucky to find an abandoned marble mortar at the top of the track.

*   *   *   *   *

Things only become history once they have disappeared. This applies to Madame Cadec's shop in Greek Street, Soho, next door to that hospitable place called Rose's, whose horsemeat steaks and dandelion salads kept a happy few well nourished long ago during the war.

Madame Cadec's shop so filled me with awe that, though I often studied from outside the beautiful terrines with hares and pheasants moulded in deep relief on their lids, and the array of chef's knives, silver hâtelets surmounted by cocks' and boars' heads, the embossed tin moulds for iced puddings in the form of pineapples and bunches of grapes, and little copper vessels and coffee grinders that filled the window, I had to pluck up courage to go inside. The tiny shop was an absolutely professional affair, it looked as if only master cooks had the right of admission. 'Established 1862' was written over the door.

Once inside, Madame Cadec occupied the foreground, an ample figure, her hair piled high and her eyes attentive to every detail behind their rimless pince-nez. Often she was too engrossed to notice one's existence. Like the captain of a minute cargo vessel she was directing the stowage and disposal of ever new consignments which arrived through the front door of the shop into a space which already seemed fully laden. Piled high from floor to roof on shelves along the walls were sumptuous pans, *marmites*, fish-kettles, vessels in cast-iron, aluminium and shining copper, lion-handled white porcelain *soupières* and glazed earthenware bean-pots and *cocottes*; even the ceiling was hung with clusters of wire contraptions for deep-frying, with ladles, wire egg baskets and salad shakers, and wooden *mandolines*.

The essential thing about this charged interior was that it contained nothing which had not a practical significance. But the quality was so superb that the function of the objects seemed to be transcended. Beautiful in themselves, they were an invocation to produce good food.

Every day this truly remarkable woman made a mid-day meal for her hard-working employees on an ancient gas stove in a minute kitchen up the creaking stairway. The Soho of which she was a queen-pin has of course vanished with Rose's and the Cafe Torino, whose atmosphere was so congenial that one used it as a bentwood haven and as an office (in Old Compton Street, on the corner site of the Colombino d'Oro, now also closed).

It is to Madame Cadec that I owe my initiation into the poetic and inspirational nature of a real *batterie de cuisine* and, years later, a debt of gratitude for an astonishing present in the form of an oval copper sole

pan. This has always been the most important object in my collection
of utensils – and one of amazing versatility.

From what one sees in many kitchens, the problem of equipment is less
what to acquire and more what to discard, starting with those battered
aluminium pans which are a handicap in any culinary adventure.
  The fact that many utensils are used as wall trophies indicates the
muddle people are in who misguidedly buy things as 'symbols' of
culinary merit. The merit lies not in the possession of the object but in
putting it to use. Equally, cooking is not to be regarded as a display of
virtuosity, it is far more vital than that.
  Besides the items already mentioned, a culinary minimum, here is a
list of additional desirable implements to be acquired with the passage
of time in accordance with the needs and size of the family and their
culinary ambitions. But I first underline the importance of having both
a wooden and marble (or stoneware) mortar in the kitchen if you wish
to carry out a number of the recipes in this book.

POTS AND PANS	an iron omelette pan an enamelled cast-iron marmite with lid solid saucepans with well-fitting lids an enamelled-iron oval casserole with lid a large copper preserving pan a *paella* (two-handled Catalan iron pan)

EARTHENWARE*	bean-pots (*pignate*, p 67)
	French earthenware lidded casseroles
	Italian earthware casseroles without lids
	  (*padelle*)
	earthenware jars, glazed inside, for storing
	  dried figs, walnuts, almonds; olives in brine;
	  dried legumes (haricot beans, peas,
	  chickpeas); *frise* (twice-baked little barley
	  and wheaten breads) – these jars, called
	  pisari in Apulia, of antique shape, derive
	  from the Greek *píthos*

STONEWARE	stoneware storage crocks for pickling tongues salting pork and *lardo*

* NOTE: before using earthenware vessels, rub them with garlic, fill them with cold water, put
in a slow oven and heat slowly. 'Proved' in this way, they will, with care, last a lifetime.

KNIVES	chef's knives, preferably French and not stainless, flexible with sharp points stainless steel vegetable knives
UTENSILS	a double grill with handles, reserved for meat asbestos or wire mesh mats (to protect earthenware) an enamelled-iron plaque a salad shaker a balloon whisk a perforated skimmer a *mezzaluna* (two-handled chopping device) a flour sieve, a flour sifter, a rolling pin a fine-meshed conical sieve a *mouli-légumes* a funnel for decanting wine, and one for oil an oil dispenser: the ideal thing is a tin vessel with a very fine spout and built-in funnel, made by tinsmiths, called *cotruba, oliera* or *orciulo* in southern Italy, *gioúmi* or *láti* in Greece, *setrill de llauna* in Catalonia

STORAGE	glass-stoppered storage jars for herbs a salt-glaze jar for sea salt glass preserving jars with hermetic closure

My Kitchens

L OOKING back I seems always to have been escaping from my kitchen into my workshop: cooking in order to work, rather than working in order to eat. But sometimes I escaped from both – into the sea, into the woods, onto the mountainside.

In Apollona there were three sources of heat. Outside the dwelling, a stone cube with an earth roof a foot thick (conspicuous survival from neolithic times), variously used as habitation, mule shed or onion store, was an outdoor hearth constructed on a stone shelf at waist level against a wall, roofed over with an escape hole for the smoke. The bricks were cemented at the precise distance to support a large black pot over a twig fire, and there was room below the shelf for stacking driftwood. This was ideal for summer, and as the sea was at the door, I was able to light a fire, start the pot with its contents cooking, plunge into the sea at mid-day and by the time I had swum across the bay and back, the lunch was ready and the fire a heap of ashes. The cool of the morning – the sun rose at 5 am – was thus kept free for working.

Indoors there was an emergency two-burner bottle gas stove on an upturned packing-case; a luxury, we brought it with us. The Apollonians used ancient paraffin stoves. Frying was done and coffee was made on the gas, including pan-roasting the coffee beans which for some reason were only to be bought 'green' in the distant port of Naxos.

In the depth of the interior was an alcove, a kind of store room, in which there was a splendid hearth with a pendant iron hook to take the cauldron. In winter this refuge was supplied with aromatic scrub from the mountain across the bay by two shepherds who used to come and warm themselves and sometimes cook a meal when one of their black goats had toppled off some precipice. We used the hearth for neolithic meals – anchovies or small bony fishes (*gópa* in Greece) grilled, on occasions when anyone went fishing, and used the cauldron when there was something of substance, dogfish or conger eel, to put in it.

In this stone-built cube was a plant bed on trestles with a mattress stuffed with leaves of asphodel, some rush-seated chairs and a table; the space defined by a central arch and the lofty ceiling of bamboo slats supported by heavy beams bearing the weight of the earth roof. Here the old lady Erýnni used to come to supervise my domestic arrangements, barter her home-preserved pork for mountain sheep's cheese, instruct me in the making of quince jam, and make sure on fast days that we were not eating meat.

*   *   *   *   *

On Naxos, the largest island of the Cyclades, the method of cooking has evolved from the existence of the one pot and the nature of the fire itself. A stick, furze, or vine-twig fire contained between stones out of doors with a good draught burns furiously for say seven minutes and afterwards dies down to a gentle heat. The island Greeks cooked their staple vegetables – potatoes, onions, okra; little marrows, onions, tomatoes; aubergines, onions, tomatoes – whatever the nature of the vegetable and its aromatic accompaniments might be, in a mixture of water and oil, roughly four parts to one part. While the fire is burning furiously, the vegetables absorb the water which also evaporates, and by the time it dies down the pot is barely simmering in a delicious liquor compounded of oil and vegetable juices. The fire has dictated the speed of the operation, the vegetables are tender, unbroken and retain their taste. (Greek cooking rather than cooking *à la grecque*, for which see page 169.)

Most of the householders in the little rockbound port had, in their courtyards, a domed bread oven lit by brushwood, vine prunings, sage and cistus. There was no baker; each family made their own magnificent loaves, mounds of corn and rye bread. Their flat rooves, piled with brushwood, looked like so many storks' nests.

*   *   *   *   *

In the kitchen at La Barozza above Carrara, that 'sombre old beautiful house' as the painter Edith Schloss described it, marooned on the saddle of an Etruscan hill, there was still the built-in tiled charcoal installation which had to be lit with little sticks of charcoal and paper. It required a lot of fanning with feather fans to set the charcoal on top alight. On this fish and meat were grilled and glazed earthenware bean pots and casseroles were set to stew, the heat being reduced when needed by sprinkling ash on the live coals.

In the hearth itself a large pot depended from a chimney hook, in which everything from polenta to wood pigeons could be cooked.

These are the traditional heat sources of Tuscan cooking, the charcoal braziers and the pendant pot, with as auxiliary the *forno di campagna* made of tin, which could be set on charcoal or in the ashes in the hearth with live braise on the lid, a kind of rustic oven: cooking between two fires (*fra due fuochi*).

But the bread oven, if it were in reach, was more often used for oven dishes. In Castelpoggio, where we lived for a time, I took, as everybody

did, things to be baked when the bread oven was losing heat. Half an hour later one went to get the 'angel bread' or *castagnaccio,* a chestnut flour confection (pp 293 and 292) and by doing so became the focus of an intense speculation – passers-by curious to know if, by merely lifting the cloth that covered it, they could judge it a success. This could have been an ordeal, of course. The baker, on whom the entire village depended for a wonderful rough bread and the vital *focaccia,* (bread dough cooked in vast shallow trays with olive oil and rosemary, sometimes with salt anchovies), fired his oven with furze cut on the mountain, gorse, maritime broom, tree heather.

But to return to the hand-painted tiles, black and white, of my Etruscan kitchen: the hand-pump fitted to the wall over the marble sink was connected with an outdoor rain cistern, but this pump had long since ceased to function. I got the water in a bucket and lowering it into the outdoor cistern had a marvellous view of the glittering Monte Sagra and the Apuanian Alps on one side and on the other a view to the Tyrrhenian through little hills, echoes of our own, their summits crowned with plumes of mimosa and dark umbrella pines. In summer we had to be excessively careful with these buckets, as the rain collected during the biennial monsoons (November, April) was used for the copper sulphate spraying of the vines.

As charcoal was expensive and cooking time was short – my workshop was down below and across the town, a Florentine tower overlooking the marble saw mills and the torrent of the Carrione – I was very glad of a little three-burner bottle gas stove which was in the kitchen.

*　　*　　*　　*　　*

Compared with these, the kitchen at Vendrell which wasn't mine was palatial and magnificent. It had a huge hearth and chimney hooks, a gas stove with an oven. It had 17th century carved fruitwood doors to the recesses in the walls. The hearth was surrounded with equally old maiolica tiles spreading their gold and there was a majestic sink.

The 'intrusion' of the gas stove meant that Anita, a classic Catalan cook, cooked some things in heavy aluminium pans which, formerly, had been prepared in the upright curved earthenware pot (*olla, caldereta*) on charcoal. But she still used this handsome vessel for cooking haricot beans, setting the pot on a low gas on an asbestos mat, and always used a shallow glazed earthenware dish (*cassola*) in the oven. There was also, of course, the huge two-handled iron *paella,* the name deriving from the Roman *patella.*

But in summer much of the cooking was done in the garden where there was a raised hearth for grilling – sardines, anchovies, mackerel, mullet – fired by a quick-burning scented scrub, and nearby a charcoal installation similar in form to the one at La Barozza, only out-of-doors. The other vital outdoor instrument was a 19th century clockwork spit.

*   *   *   *   *

As time goes by our life is simplified. Living, workplace and studios have become united. In Apulia we have cold running water from an ancient vase-like cistern carved out of the limestone, across the way, and a marble sink brought from Carrara. There is a huge hearth opening off the kitchen, a separate vaulted chamber which must, centuries ago, have been built for smoking cheeses. Cooking is done in this hearth fired by olive-wood in winter in earthenware pots (see also *la pignata,* p 67) and it is ideal for grilling, the hearth being raised.

The vaulted kitchen, a cowshed when we found it, from which we removed the seven mangers, has a four-burner bottle gas stove with an oven which has always been defective. One suspects that Italy's industrial rejects are sent specifically to Apulia. This hardly matters as our neighbour, accurately called Salvatore, lights his outdoor bread oven fairly often, and always gives me warning. He also, when the dry walling of the little courtyard, which was a sheep-pen, collapsed with age, built it again, but this time with an outdoor hearth in it with chimney. I use this for cooking in the early morning in summer when it is too hot to cook in doors. It is Salvatore's wife Teresa who has shown me some of the elements of Apulian cooking and its fundament *la pignata*, the earthenware vessel in which dried staples are cooked, cousin of the Tuscan beanpot and the Catalan *caldereta.*

*   *   *   *   *

While in the kitchen I must mention the important subject – olive oil. The best oil is of this year's making, wherever it comes from, Greece, Spain, Provence, Italy. Keeping it longer, though it becomes more refined with age, its taste vanishes. But one is often using last year's oil, because the olive trees produce only in quantity in alternate years.

I tremble to think of the adulterations in commerce. Even in oil-producing regions, people economize today by deep-frying in vegetable oil and some mix their olive oil half and half with vegetable oil for cooking. Oil is not cheap even where it is produced. But if you use it for cooking you practically renounce butter, a saving. Olive oil confers on the simplest dish a delicious flavour. This cannot be said of vegetable oils, however healthy. If you ask how much oil does one put in the bottom of a pan, it is really a question of how little? Only just enough to simmer, fry or brown the ingredients put in it. A certain thrift, a little experience and a pouring vessel with a fine spout is needed.

Virgin oil is oil which runs out of its own accord after the crushing of the olives. The usual oil is that which issues when the crushed olives are placed in tiers in the olive press between mats and pressed. Modern machinery tends to operate at tremendous pressures. Subsequently the oil is separated from the 'sordes' (deposit) in a high-speed centrifuge which spoils both its consistency and taste, over-refining it. The oil is far far better if ladled out carefully from the bin into which it has dripped after pressing, and if some of the 'sordes' get into the oil, they sink, and after a month one decants the oil into a clean receptacle, preferably made of zinc.

Never travel any distance with new oil in glass demijohns; it may still be fermenting and will crack the jar. Never put it in plastic containers. If you have to, then decant instantly on arriving at your destination.

The Macedonians, very good oil producers, say: 'Never keep oil in tin, keep it in glass demijohns and bottles.'

You judge it by taste and colour, the colour may be green or gold, but if it is too *clear*, it is suspicious, i e too old or too refined. It should naturally taste of olives.

The acidity of the oil depends on how long the olives have been left to lie on the ground in bad weather. Those with a small number of trees, as is our case, strip them in November at one go to avoid it. (See The Olive Field, page 312).

I had better tell you the worst: a household of two with a good many visitors consumes in a year at least 60 litres of olive oil, using it for cooking, in salads and for conserving.

*   *   *   *   *

The olive being as old as time, I think it appropriate here to set down Antonin Artaud's sentence from 'The Peyote Dance', which I have had on my work table for a long time:

> They [the Tarahumara] know that every step forward, every convenience acquired through the mastery of a purely physical civilization, also implies a loss, a regression.

Chopping and Pounding

Without work the vessel of human life lacks ballast.

Stendhal, *Souvenirs d'Egotisme*

THE fine chopping of aromatics is the basis of Italian and Catalan cooking. The Italian *soffritto* or *battuto*, for which there is no Anglo-Saxon equivalent, consists in the fine chopping of aromatic herbs and vegetables which, under-fried in olive oil, are the point of departure for imparting flavour to whatever is being cooked.

SOFFRITTO

The Italian *soffritto* normally consists of a little handful of fragrant herbs – parsley, dill, *sedano* (green celery, cultivated as a herb, not a vegetable, and unblanched), thyme, savory (p 331), rosemary – and aromatic vegetables – onion, leek, garlic, carrot – very finely chopped, simmered in oil before the meat, beans, fish or whatever it is, is added, the moment they begin to colour.

SOFREGIT

Its relation, the simpler Catalan *sofregit*, is based on the fine chopping of a huge white onion, achieved by skilfully slicing it with a very sharp knife geodetically in three directions, i e north-south, east-west, and then latitudinally, while holding it together and rotating it with the other hand. The fragmented outcome is simmered slowly in olive oil until it gradually acquires a golden colour, and only then are some large peeled, seeded, crushed tomatoes added, to be simmered until their liquor has evaporated. This is the Catalan prelude to cooking rice, potatoes, rock fishes, salt cod (first dipped in batter and fried), joints of chicken, rabbit, partridge, pieces of veal, in it. The slow procedure guarantees the homogeneity of the sauce.

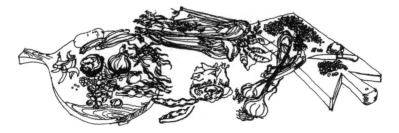

PICADA

This gives rise to the other characteristic of Catalan cuisine, which is the *picada*, a concept with no northern equivalent, a way of giving a last minute 'bite' to a dish which has been slowly simmering for a long time; and, incidentally, a solution to the use of garlic (introduced at the last moment), whose flavour in any case is spoiled by slow cooking – leaving one with a thirst.

The *picada* involves the pounding of blanched and peeled almonds, sometimes roasted, and/or hazelnuts, and/or pine kernels, with garlic and chopped parsley to a fine paste, then diluted with olive oil to liberate it from the mortar. The parsley used is the smooth single-leaved variety (p 329).

In the preparation of the *picada* the dilution with olive oil conserves the aromas released by pounding until they are imparted by coming in contact with something hot. There are naturally variations and additions to this preparation – ground black pepper, or pounded whole peppercorns; bread, soaked in milk or vinegar, or soaked and fried; roasted chilli peppers; paprika; and more rarely bitter chocolate.

The real function of the *picada* in its diverse forms is the final unification of the various ingredients and the liaison of the sauce without recourse to flour; it produces a more subtle result.

*   *   *   *   *

ALMONDS, which have been cultivated for as long as the vine, the olive and the fig – at least 7000 years – in Mediterranean regions are a basic source of nourishment. For their varieties and their Catalan, Italian and Greek names see the description on page 336.

The ancient Greeks made marzipan with ground almonds and honey. This confection was first praised by Archestratus (5th century BC) in his poem *Hedypatheia* (good food).

Almonds are fundamental to many preparations described in the *Libre de Sent Soví*, the earliest surviving collection of Catalan recipes, in which the first mention is to be found of *Menjar blanc* – where the broth of chicken and its breasts and wings fragmented are combined with almond milk, rice roasted and pounded to a powder, pounded sugar, rose-water, and are cooked in an *olla* on a charcoal braise until with much stirring it becomes a dense and uniform cream to be eaten with a spoon as fasting food. *Menjar blanc* has survived as a shadow of the above in the Ibizenkan Christmas pudding (p 297).

The prevalence of almonds in mediaeval cooking is explained by Dr Rudolf Grewe, editor of the *Sent Soví*, as a consequence of rules governing religious fasting. On fast days not only meat was forbidden but also the use of cow's and goat's milk in cooking. Milk of almonds was therefore substituted in the preparation of broths, employing fish or vegetables and spices. The Catalans were celebrated for the exquisite nature of their Lenten confections, and were highly praised in 1475 by Platina (see Bibliography), who visited them.

The earliest Italian book on cookery, *Il Cuoco Secreto di Papa Pio Quinto* by Bartolomeo Scappi, 1570, employed the flour or milk of almonds in almost every recipe. This work contained the first printed recipe for marzipan, till then made only by pharmacists.

In Lecce and Gallipoli today, in the Salento, a delicious almond paste takes the imprint of carplike fish moulds to become the centre-piece of the Christmas feast, the same paste being used in making Holy Lambs at Easter (see *Il Pesce di Natale*, p 290).

PINE KERNELS are often used with or instead of almonds in a *picada*. Although generally ignored in northern countries, their use in the Mediterranean is widespread, as is the presence of the stone or umbrella pine from which they come – see page 339, and for their function as a culinary chameleon. Pine kernels are an essential ingredient of the Ligurian *pesto*.

PESTO
The Catalan *picada* has its counterpart in the *pesto* of the Ligurian littoral – a pounded mixture of garlic, torn basil leaves and pine kernels to which grated *pecorino sardo* or parmesan is added. This is used to flavour vegetable soups, as a dressing for *past'asciutta* or *gnocchi*, and without the cheese as a fragrant sauce for poultry.

The *picada* and the *pesto* (*pistou* in Provençal) have three things in common: the pounding which liberates the flavour of herbs and garlic; the use of pine kernels as the medium for absorbing flavour, and the fragrance imprisoned in olive oil, which is only introduced at the end of the cooking so that its freshness is retained.

The *pesto* employing the scented leaves of basil (the large tender-leaved variety Grande di Genoa cultivated in open ground), is added off the fire. The *picada*, using the coarser single-leaved parsley, is put in some minutes before the dish has finished cooking, and earlier if almonds are employed.

The Greek word for BASIL, *vasilikós*, means royal. The supernatural fragrance of the basil plant grown in summer Mediterranean sun illuminates the idea of kingship like an aura. Grown on a northern window-sill, it has been known to develop a strong smell of cats. It is

not itself when dried, and rather limp and faded when preserved in
olive oil. The best way to recall the perfume in winter is to immure
some sprigs at the last moment in a cauldron of peach or quince jam;
see *la persicata* (p 311) and *kydóni glikó* (p 309). For the varieties of basil,
see page 330.

AROMAS

Basil with parsley, giant, single- and curly-leaved, mint, coriander
grown for its wonderfully fragrant leaves as well as perfumed seeds,
and the green celery cultivated as a herb in Italy and Greece are the
culinary herbs which are better cultivated than wild.

Shrubby evergreen plants like rosemary, myrtle, juniper, the various
thymes, wild marjoram (*origano*), winter savory, are infinitely more
fragrant in the wild. This also applies to the scented leaves of the bay
laurel, native in the south, where even its bark is perfumed. The fennel
seeds and fronds used in southern cooking derive from the wild plant,
having greater pungency. The sage, *Salvia triloba*, growing wild in
Greece is more delicate than *S officinalis*, the cultivated herb, and so is
wild clary, *S verbenaca*, growing on Italian mountainsides. (For more
about all these plants, see the final chapter.)

The reason is that, thriving on limestone, these herbs alter their
nature in richer damper soils; in the droughty limestone wilderness,
resort of bees and butterflies, they grow out of the rock and produce a
higher concentration of their essential oil, contained in minute sacs in
their leaves. This has a bearing on pounding which releases the aromatic
oil from leaves and seeds.

To return to the mortar and GARLIC, the vital bulb (on which see also
p 164). The origin of *aïoli* is often attributed to Virgil, even by Provençal
cooks. According to the story, one day, having lost his appetite, he was
advised to restore it by crushing some cloves of garlic and mixing the
resulting paste with breadcrumbs. It had the desired effect, as anyone
in a similar condition can prove – providing they have a pestle and
mortar.

Pounding fragrant things – particularly garlic, basil, parsley – is a
tremendous antidote to depression. But it applies also to juniper
berries, coriander seeds and the grilled fruits of the chilli pepper.
Pounding these things produces an alteration in one's being – from
sighing with fatigue to inhaling with pleasure. The cheering effects of
herbs and alliums cannot be too often reiterated. Virgil's appetite was
probably improved equally by pounding garlic as by eating it.

MORTAR AND PESTLE. Many names for mortar – *mortaio* (I), *murtaru* (Sal), *morter* (C) – derive from the Latin *mortarium*. The Greek name, *goudí*, naturally does not. Names for the pestle are: *pestello* (I), *pisaturu* (Sal), *boix* or *mà* (C).

The ideal is to have at least three mortars, each with its own pestle.

First, a small wooden mortar for grinding hot roasted chilli pepper, for juniper berries, allspice, coriander seeds, cinnamon bark, fresh or dried leaves of rosemary, thyme, and fennel seeds.

Next, a large wooden mortar, curved in at the top so that what is being pounded or emulsified doesn't spill out, is needed for the Provençal *aïoli*, the Catalan *allioli*, and for mayonnaise; for *pesto*, the *picada, salsa verde, salsa di noci*, etc.

Third, a large stoneware or marble mortar. These have a very satisfying ring and are ideal for pounding olives, tunnyfish, capers, salt anchovies for a *tapénade*; for reducing cooked salt cod to the consistency of a cream; for pounding smoked cod's roe, or the ingredients of a pâté, or for reducing dried and roasted chilli peppers in quantity in autumn, or anything in fact that will impregnate a wooden mortar.

The Catalan fishermen produce their *allioli* by crushing 8 or 9 large cloves of garlic in a marble mortar to a fine paste, then adding oil drop by drop to obtain a dense sauce (p 120). Precisely this preparation is also found in the Languedoc (in the 12th and 13th centuries under Catalan dominion), called *ail-y-oli* and used as a sauce for snails. The garlic cloves are sometimes grilled beforehand, thus obtaining a sauce rather similar in taste to the Provençal garlic mustard (*purée d'ail*), though in the latter case desalted anchovies are added. Whether fresh or grilled, the pounded garlic and oil produce a dense consistency

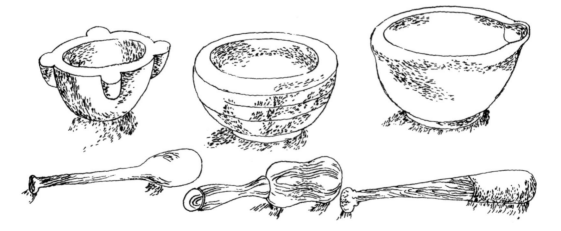

similar to mayonnaise but pale in colour. Breadcrumbs, soaked in vinegar, or a slice of bread first fried in oil, are sometimes pounded in, especially when the *allioli* threatens to disintegrate. So, at first glance, it seems as if the Catalan fishermen are harking back to Virgil.

It is my conviction that fishermen, who have always been preoccupied with gastronomy rather than the mere satisfaction of appetite, have had much to do with establishing ways of preparing food, and not always in their own ports. Who knows if the Genoese *pesto* did not first embark from the Catalan coast via Sardinia and the once Catalan town of Alghero, the Italian inspiration being the substitution of pine kernels for almonds and the far more fragrant basil for the parsley? And whether, in Provence, the famous *aïoli* was not first achieved by a Provençal who failed to reproduce the *allioli* of Catalan fishermen, cooking their fish supper on the quay at Marseille, and then saved his face with a couple of egg yolks? Failure as a source of discovery is an encouraging thought. In any case, according to Morard, the use of garlic was only generally adopted in Marseille after the plague of 1720 on account of its antiscorbutic and antiseptic properties.

As can be seen, all this chopping and pounding has much to do with health.

The Workplace

S our friend the Cuban, dark as the night itself, pursued me across the Piazza San Francesco, I could discern the Sculptor peering through the iron scrolls of the locked gate which separated him from his working studio. He was in no condition to come to my rescue.

The party in Clara's bar had begun hours too soon to celebrate the departure of a Czech sculptor. Grudgingly granted a brief leave of absence from his homeland and carrying a suitcase stuffed with salami to counterweigh his lack of Italian currency, he had come to Carrara to execute a work in marble.

His going had filled the afternoon to the brim and dusk to the eyeballs with Clara's indifferent wine. Long after he had been dragged away by his political overseer – a Czech marble agent posing as a friend – the discordant sounds of revelry spilled out into the piazza and had already made the adorable grandmother of Carlo Nicoli fasten the entrance door of the *piano nobile* with a heavy chain, the bar being so situated in the structure of the palace as to be acoustically connected.

Eventually the remaining sculptors shambled out of the courtyard with the preoccupying vision of supper at the Nicoli's. One of them was lying gurgling in the gutter, others were ripping off his overalls, a de-bagging ritually performed in this case as a quite useless attempt to recover respectability. The remnants of the party were ravaging the night air with unharmonious song.

I turned to face my pursuer, whose facial muscles were quivering, accompanied by an intermittent growling sound. The Sculptor did not heed my cry. Immobilized in front of the locked gate and separated from the work he had abandoned for the Czech's sake, he was intent on resuming it, in spite of the hour and the darkness.

Darting off in the direction of the Nicoli palace, I pushed open the heavy door and hared up the spiral staircase, pursued by the Cuban. At the top of the stair I banged on the door. Hearing me banging, hearing me call, la signora Gina courageously undid the chain and hastily admitted me to the apartment.

A change of scene has often the effect of totally quenching hilarity. In this case the transition from Clara's bar, the resort of everyman, to the first-floor precincts of 'Edwardian' respectability was as sobering as cold water. A short time after, the surviving members of the celebration

were sitting down subdued in front of a vast porcelain tureen of spaghetti at the long table in the old tiled kitchen and what, in the timorous imaginings of the grandmother had presented itself as a siege, suddenly dwindled to a muted gathering as of shame-faced schoolboys, some of whom, however expert with hammer and chisel, could not bring themselves to focus their forks on the elusive spaghetti. The evening phuttered out like a damp squib.

Before long we regained the freedom of the night outside. From across the way a party of late revellers, quarrymen perhaps, were bawling a *stornello* which fell like a vocal firework in the dark piazza.

*   *   *   *   *

You have to imagine this 19th century piazza, the buildings of stone with the stucco parts painted in chrome and bulls' blood. These colours when first applied stood up to the dazzling white of the mountains in the background; now faded, to tones of pink and gold. A stout Victorian palace rose up at the western end, looking towards the marble mountains. Adjoining it at right-angles loomed a studio of immense size built for the execution of colossal marbles.

Nineteenth century sepia photographs present the original proprietor as a Victorian Hercules in working smock and stovepipe hat holding a hammer in one hand and a toscanello cigar in the other. Looking at him, one might be correct in supposing that the cake-like decorations of the Roman Quirinale were his legitimate offspring – the gigantic blocks of marble, the material of these effusions, being conveyed into the piazza on wooden carts drawn by twenty oxen. But, in fact, he executed with countless assistants, works forty feet high for the King of Naples, celebrating the wonders of steam, engineering, commerce – the victories of progress.

Today this magnificent studio, run by Carlo Nicoli, the heroic Carlo's great grandson, is still littered with works that culminate in Victorian rhetoric – plaster casts of fig-leaved Apollos, Sabine women, vine-wreathed Bacchante, winged Mercuries, angels in demure garments, portly politicians, horsemen riding into battle, saints, goddesses, cardinals, *amorini*, and not forgetting the exquisite bust of Marie Antoinette or the Winged Victory of Samothrace. Any of these nostalgic objects can even now with the aid of the pointing machine and the pneumatic chisel be translated into marble in a matter of days.

The piazza itself was initially an extension of the workplace, sheltered by old lime trees, and across it and opposite the studio was a walled enclosure entered through wrought iron gates, and within was a long low studio, ample space for dumping marble blocks and a tap under which the workmen washed.

Though all was massive, monumental, from the beginning intruded an element of farce. The farcical clung to the piazza as insidiously as the stickiness dripped from the lime trees at flowering time. This priceless element governed the relations between workmen and employers, intruded in the execution of religious works, and often entered unwittingly into the creations of visiting sculptors like a Victorian curse.

The Nicoli great-grandfather was perhaps to blame. This hero, during working hours, was in the habit of taking his pleasure with a passing ricotta-vendor who entered the piazza singing her wares – fresh sheep's cheese wrapped in bayleaves, brought down from mountain fastnesses – and he, insisting at the same time and most particularly at the crucial moment she continue to sing them, so as not to provoke suspicion in the neighbouring palace, the balcony of which perilously overlooked the workplace; suspicion being ever the handmaid of farce.

In this studio, now humming with mechanical tools and penetrating fine dust, its owner carries on the hospitable tradition of welcoming – not dairymaids – but any scupltor, Italian or foreign, who comes to Carrara to work. We were very kindly treated by the Nicoli family, who, not only hospitable, were voluble, witty and eloquent. I shall not forget la signora Gina, standing in the doorway clasping a bunch of Parma violets we had brought her and singing *Sono pochi fiori* in an enchanting way.

Like a permanent set that changed only in the sense that the limes grew taller and the piazza's name changed from time to time to harmonize with political events, the same structures, the same running to and fro, the same labours accompanied by clamour, instructions, shouts, bursts of anger and hilarity, were for a century the constant of the working day. Only on Sundays and feast days it presented a disconsolate air of having been abandoned by the actors and their props – hammers, chisels, claws, rasps, rickety barrows, iron handling bars and paper hats – these last ephemera being made on the principle of children's paper boats out of yesterday's newspaper to keep off the dust.

There were two places of respite built into this scene, the corner bar Da Giove and the more congenial retreat Da Lino which occupied a high Dickensian room on the ground floor of the Nicoli palace with access through a little courtyard overlooking the neglected garden full of loquats, oleanders and lumps of marble.

Giove was a gloomy dispenser of raw spirits and the early morning *focaccina*, towering behind the wooden counter in an alpaca overall, supported to right and left by two sad thin-lipped women, his wife, her sister. Clara and her husband Lino had been drawn onto the scene years before to provide the midday repast of forty workmen and refreshment when they knocked off work. With the passage of time and decline in demand for statuary marbles, she had become the reluctant foster-mother of a dozen remaining workmen who had still not rebelled against a métier combining grinding labour with expert craftsmanship.

It is no wonder that laughter should so often be the other face of manual labour – and in Carrara, song. Its point of departure is the subject of the next chapter.

La Merenda

N Latin *merum* means pure, unadulterated. The word was often used in connection with wine. The Italian word *mero* stands for wine which has not been tampered with. But as such wine is bound to go to one's head if not accompanied by something to eat, it is ritually accompanied by a *merenda*. *La merenda* cannot be confused with the modern snack. The snack is snatched, *la merenda* is shared. The word implies conviviality and if anything is to be seized it is time by the forelock, an event insinuated between laying off work and the return to the polished anonymity of that little prison of perfection which is every Italian's home.

It comprises food in its simplest form – good bread and a plate of local mortadella or salame. (Mortadella originally described a smoked pork sausage of domestic manufacture, still made on farms in the Apuanian mountains.)

It is only incidental to the wine you happen to be drinking and is normally located where it is likely to be good. The wine enthusiast naturally hastens uphill after work to the vineyard of a friend in whose *cantina* in a normal year a *fiasco* of wine is to be had for a few hundred lire.

> *Vino-vinello*
> *Come sei bello!*
> *Sei nato in collina*
> *E muore in cantina*

The Tuscan is concerned with the kind of bread and the quality of the ham and, before sitting down to a glass of wine in any bar, is likely to dash round the corner to a provision shop whose owner has a reputation for selecting both. He returns with 100 grams of some fragrant and paper-thin *prosciutto crudo*, a rustic loaf and some firm tomatoes. Pulling a knife from his pocket and a little tin containing sea salt and wild marjoram (*origano*), he sits down to a *merenda* and a litre of wine with an air of self-approbation, delighted to share it with friends.

At Clara's, apart from the marble workers, the majority of the familiars were retired quarrymen. And if it sometimes seemed like an ante-chamber to death, they meanwhile were enjoying a conviviality, daily renewed, in which fooling, outbursts of wit, snatches of *stornelli* (see p 220) revealed the seed-bed of the *commedia dell'arte:* the genius for amusing each other, priceless inheritance of the poor.

In spring, snails are consumed in quantity in little bars and also frogs, requiring the skilful intervention of the bar proprietor's wife. The snails come out of the stone walls after rain and are assiduously collected in plastic bags. The frogs were imported alive from Reggio Emilia, their backs and legs being dusted with fine flour and deep-fried.

If the weather is particularly inclement (spirits low and spring retarded), a leg of young lamb, neatly fragmented, is cooked *alla cacciatora* (p 262) and eaten with the fingers. But this is much more often a daydream indulged while munching lupin seeds, the round white seeds of *Lupinus albus*, macerated in salt water to soften them, or *passatempi*, the salted seeds of the winter pumpkin (*zucca invernale*).

Wherever quails are raised, there is in spring a supply of quail's eggs, *uova di quaglia*, very pretty little eggs, a pale blue with tawny freckles. Eaten raw, they are popped into the mouth and crunched up with their delicate shells.

Italians believe that fresh eggs, in any case, are intended to be drunk, usually beaten up in a glass with a pinch of salt and some drops of lemon, and tossed back as *uova da bere*.

FORMAGGIO CON LE PERE • ewe's cheese and pears

In Tuscany in summer a delicious long-shaped pear ripens at the same time as *pecorino* matures, made by farmers in the mountains of ewe's milk in early spring and left to ripen for a few months on open shelves suspended from the ceiling in an airy room serving as farmhouse dairy.

In town these cheeses are not easy to discover. About 20 cm (8″) across, creamy within, with a pale exterior. Cheeses of larger dimensions are darker; they are coated with wood ash. In the old days when every peasant supplied the landowner with the fruits of the vineyard – loquats, lemons, oranges, pears, plums, cherries, apricots, peaches, figs – there was a saying:

Al contadino non bisogna	Don't let the peasant
far sapere quanto è buono	know how good
il formaggio con le pere	cheese is with pears

So the association of this delicious cheese and summer pears was something the *signori* wished to keep to themselves! A ridiculous presumption. Living in town, they nourished a false idea of the 'simplicity' of those working the land, who were both secret and wise.

In winter *la merenda* might well be a slab of *lardo di Bergiola* – pork fat from the pig's rump conserved in dry salt and mountain herbs, in marble basins, in this high-up village – eaten with hunks of bread and black olives. It could consist of a salt herring, grilled; or, skinned, boned, soaked in water for a while, then drained and served with finely sliced onion, olive oil, a thread of wine vinegar and black pepper. Both are thirst-provoking.

A standby at any time of year are salted anchovies, produced by Genoese and Portuguese firms in large round tins, which have a far better flavour and consistency than tinned filleted anchovies in oil.

ACCIUGHE ALLA MARINARA · marinated anchovies

200 g (7 oz) salt anchovies · ground black pepper
a handful of chopped parsley · 2 garlic cloves · olive oil

Drain and rinse the anchovies. Split each little fish, removing dorsal fin and backbone. Rinse several times, then dry. Arrange the cleaned fillets radially on a flat plate. Grind some pepper over them, sprinkle with parsley and sliced garlic. Anoint with olive oil.

An appetising start to a meal consists of a plate of these anchovies, a dish of haricot or marble beans cooked then dressed with olive oil (p 62) and a raw salad of the cultivated bulbous fennel, finely sliced.

And that reminds me of the triumphant May Day celebrations devoted to the consumption of young broad beans straight from the husk, at the moment when last year's wine comes into its own in response to the vines coming again into leaf.

A *merenda* can take place under the shade of a loquat tree on one's way up the muletrack on a summer evening, in the courtyard of a bar at a marble table, or in winter in a ruined cottage which served as an illicit wine bar; there among friends, with the vine twigs from the November pruning blazing in the chimney corner, it sometimes started off an evening of *baldoria. Baldoria* means revelry, but in this case it proved to be a feast of song. Television had not yet killed the irrepressible need to sing, at least on the hillsides above Carrara.

In a manner of speaking many loquats led to our house and it was sometimes difficult to get home without being hailed at a distance by men called Adamo, Alceste, Amleto, Attilio, intent upon delaying their own home-coming with its inevitable surrender to female despotism. *La merenda* has been invented to curtail its duration and effects.

MEZÉS. In Greece this 'something to eat at any time of day' is called *mezés* or *mezedáki.* In its most rudimentary form it consists of salty *féta* and black olives, but it can comprise a wide variety of things.

A sight that normally greets the stranger on landing in the port of Naxos is a pole festooned with the tentacles of large octopuses, supported on the backs of two rush-seated chairs and drying in the sun. The chairs are set in a surrealistic way on the very brink of the promenade, overlooking a minute island on which is planted one telegraph pole and a tiny white church.

OCHTAPÓDI • octopus

Should you enter one of the waterfront cafés in search of a glass of ouzo you will be offered with it a *mezedáki* consisting of these same tentacles, which have just been oiled, grilled and cut into small pieces, a process which brings out their unique iodized flavour.

It is common knowledge that these alarming creatures are killed by turning their 'bag' inside out. They are then bashed against the rocks to soften them. The bag is subsequently severed and usually floured and deep-fried in strips while fresh. The crown of tentacles, with their curious suckers like little craters, is peeled of its outer skin by rubbing with sea salt, then sprinkled with vinegar and hung out to dry for a few days in the full glare of solar and marine exposure.

The octopus, 'Old No-bones the Polyp' as Hesiod called it, was a powerful fertility symbol in Mycenaean times, and the little museum in Naxos contains among other wonders pale earthenware jars painted with the eight tentacles of octopuses formalized into a magic pattern; these are of Cretan origin.

ACHINÓS • sea urchins

I sometimes think that gastronomes are returning to bronze age practices. The Apollonians had no gastronomic pretensions; nevertheless, after work in the summer, they repaired with a loaf of bread and a flask of wine to a little promontory of rock frequented by sea urchins (*Paracentrotus lividus*). Picking them off the rocks underwater, they bashed in their prickle-covered shells with knife or stone, emptied them, then dipped some bread into the shell to extract their succulent orange ovaries to the accompaniment of jokes and laughter.

RESTORATIVES. The popularity of small salt fish – anchovies, sardines, pilchards – in Latin countries has much to do with heat, physical fatigue and need for restoration. These fish, even though desalted before serving, are by nature thirst-provoking; and thus induce the workman, parched by his labours, to imbibe copious draughts of water (or wine) and so restore the balance. These observations have significance in a working context round latitude 40.

MAKAPOULO
ZYMAPIKA CON

salting fish at home

A Naxian farmer used to barter a quantity of splendid onions for a fresh haul of anchovy (*gávros*) and pilchard (*sardélla*) in autumn. He then sat at his door overlooking the harbour with these two piles of fish, two large petrol cans and a sackful of sea salt culled illicitly from the rocks, salt being a state monopoly. Assisted by his children and a gallon bottle of amber wine, he pulled the heads off the fish which at the same time removed the guts, and laid the fish neatly in the petrol cans, alternating each layer with a layer of salt and finally putting a weighted board on top.

In this way he provided himself and his large family with supper throughout the winter, his wife baking a monumental bread and nightly serving with the fish a dish of home-grown beans flavoured with tomatoes and *radíkia* (wild chicory, p 194). Since everything on Naxos happened as an emergency, the salted anchovies or pilchards were never given time to soak, the result producing a colossal thirst, slaked with his own 17° wine.

Restoration is also brought about in another way – by eating something extremely sweet, which equally induces thirst – demonstrated by the Greek *gliko*.

GLIKÓ • fruit in syrup

This can be made of muscat or *rosakí* grapes, of quince, or even of very immature green walnuts (see Preserves, p 310). It often greets the traveller after a laborious journey on foot across the mountains, served with ice-cold water from the village fountain and sometimes followed by a dose of *rakí*, a powerful spirit distilled from pressed grapeskins, akin to *marc* or *grappa*.

The *gliko* is presented on a saucer with a spoon and is consumed under a fig tree in the courtyard. The lady of the house provides you with a rush-seated chair to sit on, and another on which to rest your legs. She sprinkles the courtyard floor with water from a water jar to lay the dust and cool the air, and presents you with a sprig of basil and a glass of spring water while you despatch the *gliko*.

Hospitality: to be able to discern precisely what your guests are in need of.

In a wider perspective, one should not forget the restorative powers of herbs, garlic and olive oil; see *Aigo bouido* (p 76) and its Catalan counterpart, Thyme soup (p 77). Sage, thyme and bay have similar properties and, used in infusions, they arouse appetite and restore the organism.

But one is not always in a position to select the substance of revival. On Naxos we were sometimes faced in company with delicacies chivalrously proffered on a fork which were difficult to receive with a good grace: the grilled head for instance of a small bird, the fried spleen of a goat, a very spongy substance.

SPLÍNA KE KOKORÉTSI KATSIKÍOU • grilled goat's lights

The goat's spleen is more acceptable, considered a delicacy in fact, when cut in sections and wound round with little strips of intestine, with slices of garlic inserted, sprinkled with mountain herbs and olive oil, then grilled on charcoal on wooden skewers.

However it is prepared, the antidote to the spleen is a few drops applied to it from a bottle of wine vinegar in which 50 peeled garlics have been macerating, i e garlic vinegar.

Such preparations occur wherever kid or lamb are freshly killed; above all lights must be fresh. In Apulia a very similar grill is made of lamb's pluck wound with strips of intestine and known as *gnummarieddi* (p 284).

REFRIGERIS, from the Latin *refrigero*, is the Catalan word for 'refreshment' and thus the equivalent of the Italian *merenda*. The Catalan working in the fields restores himself at mid-day with a salt herring, a hunk of bread, a bunch of muscat grapes and a trickle of wine from the porró. As the condition of the traveller in summer – exposed to heat, sights, unfamiliar smells, dust and consequent dehydration – may amount to a prostration equal to that of a man working in the fields, it is a good thing to be aware of the remedy.

Probably the most universal refreshment in summer among working men in Greece, Italy and Catalonia is a slab of bread onto which are crushed some ripe tomatoes with a garlic clove, sea salt, bathed in olive oil, most invigorating. It relies on the rusticity of the bread, the fragrance of the ripe tomatoes, the taste of olive oil for excellence, and the accompanying wine. The Catalan version is called *Pa amb tomàquet*.

Anyone with the use of a car in Catalonia should make an expedition to the mountain fastness of the Priorat, a high enclosed valley reached from Reus. The landscape is a series of little hills densely cultivated with vines, figs, apricots and almonds – against a background of fierce mountains whose lower slopes are studded with plantations of hazel nut. The terrain is pure rock, fractured with picks and mattocks, and glittering with mica. The heat of the sun reflected off the metallic rock produces the golden strength of the Priorat wines, which resemble the amber colour, taste and power of Naxian wines.

The land was worked by the inhabitants of nine villages raised on rock resembling mediaeval fortresses, who descended to their work on mule back. Sitting on the elevated shaded terrace of one of these ancient houses, overlooking the glittering countryside, breakfast at 10 in the morning began in this manner – bread, tomatoes, garlic, olive oil. The wines we tasted at this breakfast were so extraordinary that they obliterated the memory of the lunch – majestic – that followed later. I recall only the 'fig bread' served as a dessert in the shape of a little domed loaf unwrapped from its figleaves, made of pressed whole dried figs flavoured with aniseed and bayleaves. A wine more than a century old was served with it. Its alcoholic content had naturally vanished, leaving what tasted like chocolate syrup.

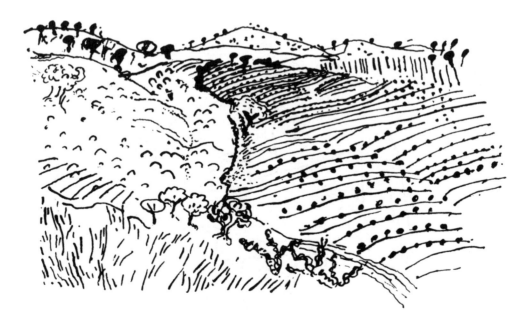

Fasting on Naxos

fools all! who never learned
how much better than the whole the half is,
nor how much good there is
in living on mallow and asphodel.

THIS is that old moralist Hesiod speaking whose pious tirades in *The Works and Days* are unwittingly echoed in the speech and behaviour of island Greeks. I take 'living on mallow' to refer not only to the edible leaves of mallow but also to the fruits of okra (*Hibiscus esculentus*), belonging to the Mallow family, indigenous Greek plants; and 'asphodel' to include besides the fleshy tuberous roots of the wild plant (*Asphodelus* in variety) and the huge bulbs of the sea squill or sea onion, *Urginea maritima*, recommended by Pliny, and still eaten in hard times, also the Alliums, which until the 19th century were classed as asphodels. The cultivation of the onion was the main Apollonian crop.

Of course Hesiod was writing about maintaining life in Boeotia. If you are poor and proud enough the half can be made to seem far better than the whole. And if you live among Greeks for long it is pride you are chiefly up against. Poverty at all times stared one in the face. It was a way of life diametrically opposed to the wishful thinking that a consumer society inspires. The Apollonians were as moralistic as Hesiod. Their village consisted of a few families each working their strips of land above the tiny harbour and in the steep valleys rising above the rocky shore, with the help of two mules and a cow.

Each household was more or less self-sufficient, their purchases being limited to paraffin for lamps and cooking, salt, sugar, soap, tobacco, flour, rice, spaghetti, coffee, and during fasting times compulsory *taramá* and slabs of *halvá*.

TARAMÁ • smoked cod's roe

As fasting food, *taramá* is cod's roe from Iceland dispensed from tins in the general store and *kapheneíon*. In non-fasting times it can be improved by pounding it with a clove of garlic, and adding olive oil and lemon juice to which black pepper is generously applied. Sometimes, to 'stretch' it, breadcrumbs are incorporated, and chopped parsley or chopped coriander leaves.

The Apollonians were shocked to find us eating *taramá* when fasting was out of season. To them it represented only an obligation and an expense.

From Advent until Christmas Eve and from Ash Wednesday until midnight on Easter Saturday the diet is reduced to the consumption of haricot beans, lentils, rice, spaghetti and weeds. The normal standbys – goat, lamb, pork, fresh cheese, eggs and often fish, as well as olive oil, are eliminated. As the diet of island Greeks was already restricted, one marvelled at their ability to deprive themselves still further. Exceptions including olive oil and olives were made for men doing heavy work, for instance in the marble quarry.

Ploughs were made indoors in autumn when it rained. Vineyards and stony terraces were cultivated with picks and mattocks. Barter was the usual form of acquisition, credit being granted against the future onion crop. The barons, who received such a blasting from Hesiod, were present in the form of lorry drivers, whose lorries derived from the smuggling of Cycladic marble goddesses, living in the fastnesses above. It was they who brought supplies of ouzo and *rakí* across the mountains from the distant port of Naxos and prevented things from being delivered by boat.

Two strangers settling in their midst were puzzling. The Greeks take nothing at its face value. A sculptor needing to be near a marble quarry – it lay just above the village – must be concealing an ulterior motive. While blocks of sparkling marble were hoisted into the studio-muleshed next door to our habitation, they greeted our desert lorry as a means of contact with the outside world, and put it to the test on urgent pretexts, local transport being confined to mules. When the brief season of summer visitors, relatives from Athens, had come and gone, they realized we were staying, decided to make the best of it, and our life with, not among, the Apollonians began.

*   *   *   *   *

The wine harvest and the sudden absence of anything to eat precipitated a new relationship. We were invited to a wedding by a man who collected shingle on the beach with two mules as transport outside our dwelling. Angelos, a patriarch with eleven children, was marrying his first-born son. As strangers we were to lend an extra dimension to the feast; something sacred still adheres to strangers. This feast involved seven enormous cauldrons of *maccheroni*, recalling the cauldrons of old, and the demise of seven goats, and was immediately followed by an invitation to Angelos's wine harvest, an appointment kept at 7 one brilliant morning on a steep hillside above the village.

Once a man has leapt into the wine-pit and sweated a whole morning treading the lustrous grapes, friendship declares itself with as generous a flow as the fiery liquid poured from the pit into the bloated goatskins for transport on muleback to the village. Angelos became our friend and benefactor. Note: women are never allowed to tread the grapes; it is thought that they would pollute the juice and deprive it of strength.

Our friend appeared with gallon bottles of his own golden nectar when last year's wine had run out. When there was nothing but corned beef and tinned squid in the 'shop' he arrived with newly dug purple-skinned potatoes, swathes of bronze onions, baskets of tomatoes, glistening aubergines and rose red grapes. Angelos never did anything by halves – which is quite different from learning 'how much better than the whole the half is'.

FASOLÁKIA • fresh haricot beans

When there was a crop of fresh haricot beans Angelos sent his daughter Kalliópe armed with a large saucepan, 2 kilos (4½ lb) of fat white beans, some fresh tomatoes, a few large onions, two big potatoes, parsley, celery fronds and basil, with instructions to give me a perfect example of how to cook them. There was only one way of doing this. Kalliópe was 16, very correctly brought up, and made me feel that piety in culinary matters was a specific for preserving life.

The beans were immersed in cold spring water in the enormous pot. Those that floated to the surface were discarded. She lit the outdoor fire in the little courtyard, boiled up the beans with a pinch of bicarbonate of soda. After cooking vigorously for twenty minutes the water was poured through a colander onto the path outside and the beans were rinsed in cold water.

She then covered the bottom of the pot copiously with olive oil, chopped up celery and parsley and put them in. She put the pot on a steady fire and proceeded to add the beans, the onions cut in rounds, the potatoes peeled and diced, the tomatoes peeled and cut up, the branch of basil, some sea salt and enough water to cover them. This done, she put on the lid, put more wood on the fire and we went down to the beach. An hour later the fire had expired, the fresh beans were tender, white, delicious and just immersed in a fragrant sauce.

The quantity, however, was so copious that at evening I took some to our neighbour who lived in a walled fruit garden across the onion fields, the old Erýnni, who, brought up with prejudice and believing them to be cooked by me and foreign in consequence, later threw them to the pig.

Angelos accompanied us to Filóti across the mountains, to acquire a wonderful green olive oil and thick amber honey. If he ever came into our high-arched room and found a mound of bread the wrong side up on the table, he pounced upon it and muttering 'that's bad' and turned it over. (Hesiod: 'Never put the wine ladle on top of the mixing bowl when people are drinking, this brings accursed bad luck with it.') 'Never drink without eating,' he'd say. We got into the habit of having something at hand at nightfall, a goat's cheese, desalted anchovies, grilled aubergines, black olives. Once he had assured himself that the utensils in which I cooked were clean, he did not hesitate to share some dish with us, provided it was not intended to quench appetite: food conceived as a stimulus to thirst. The stress on hygiene: an aspect of xenophobia – what is foreign is probably impure, an old notion. My reputation for culinary cleanliness indicated a measure of acceptance. Needless to say I had no sink. I used to wash up out of doors or in the sea close by.

Water presented a problem. Water was fetched in waterjars from the village fountain, piped from the next valley, a walk along the cliff into the next bay. This was all right and indeed a source of contact with women of the village, but it was hard on washing day. A very shallow wooden trough was used for washing at home in which one could immerse a sheet. Many women did their washing on the rocks at a little distance from the fountain. There was a taboo, almost religious, against endangering the water source, and only weeds were washed there in spring and autumn. But some people walked a long way to the river mouth with the family linen, returning with it, passing our door, balancing a tin or plastic receptacle on their heads.

During the summer there had been no difficulty about food, there being a supply of eggs, aubergines, okra, artichokes, courgettes, sweet and hot peppers, goat's milk, and in rare calm weather, fish. There were fruits, sporadically, mulberries, plums, peaches, nectarines, figs, grapes, quinces and pomegranates. We would be pressed to visit a fig or mulberry tree in the next valley and were expected to eat our fill on the spot. The island Greek has the habit of going for long periods in the fields or on foot or muleback, on a crust of home-baked bread, a hunk of hard goat's cheese and wild pears, honey sweet, stuffed inside his shirt. He then makes the most of a providential event, a ripe fruit tree, a sudden haul of fish, or the killing of a pig. This is a fundamental attitude, and only underlined by Greek Orthodox practice, whose solemn four week Advent fast and six week Lenten one, in fact, corresponded with moments when on Naxos there was hardly anything to eat. Fasting is therefore in the nature of things and feasting punctuates it with a joyful excess.

We were living in a tiny port with a single fisherman, who, besides being without a licence, was reluctant to fish unless the sea was calm. So his fishing was sporadic. But in the autumn fish were netted at night in the Ikarian Sea on a waning moon by little orange broad-bottomed caiques, which, returning, dropped anchor at Apollona.

The fish lay glistening in heaps on the burnt-orange decks. Anything larger than anchovies, sardines, bogue (*gópa*) had its price, though conger eels and dogfish (perhaps because of the difficulty in skinning these little sharks, I've tried it) were cheap. Their skin is used for abrasing ivory.

The Apollonians, standing on the quay with plate in hand, waited for the smallest fish to come ashore, the fish of size being destined for the port of Naxos. In front of this village assembly and laying myself open to instant criticism but taking courage, I sometimes begged the fishermen to unhand a larger fish, paying a price which immediately gave rise to clamorous argument. Congratulations and advice were then showered on me: the gleaming trophy must definitely be grilled, be boiled with celery, be braised.

Some of these fish were large scarlet 'goldfish' with rounded carp-like scales. Some were greenish gold with lapis-lazuli markings on the head (rainbow wrasse). There were orange whiskered gurnards, smooth moray eels (*smérna*), their brown skins marbled with yellow; there were silver flattish big-heads with yellow lateral stripes and tiny shimmering scales (*tsipoúra*); orange-red scorpion fish with coral-coloured gills fringed with sharp teeth, ferocious John Dory and little swordsmen (gar-fish).

In Apollona I first beheld these fish as wonders, and then learned to scale them, extract the gills, clean them and remove the gall, a little green sac attached to the liver, before watching their electric colours fade in the pan or on the braise. And it was here that I became convinced that, whenever possible, fish should be cooked entire.

What about the meat? In Apollona one felt that the eating of meat still had its ritual significance, that invisible thighbones were being offered to the gods. Zeus still held sway on that high peak that dominates the solid wall of mountains on the eastern side of Naxos. Meat only figured on feast days. Butchery, as we understand it, did not exist.

The signal for the feast was usually a small boy running past our dwelling on the lip of the bay, pursuing a horned goat. The carcase, freshly killed and skinned, was suspended by its Achilles tendon from a tamarisk on the village quay, and its owner hacked off portions with a blunt instrument which were then weighed on an old iron balance and rapidly seized by the contestants who stood around screaming their preferences.

There was no interval between the animal's death and its conversion into rough joints of meat, one reason why the meat was tough. The goat's meat was boiled with sage, thyme, slices of lemon, onions, carrots, celery, and was served in the invariably liquid sauce with boiled spaghetti.

The lamb was better, but at first sight the carcase was a shock. A skeleton, one realised why, seeing the flocks trotting at speed among the mountain boulders with the shepherd Apostólyi leaping after them as they nibbled the few live shoots of herbs, amongst the scrub, which had survived the sun's withering glance.

It was therefore no surprise to us when the two old peasants from up the mountain, who had rented us our lofty muleshed on the condition, inexorable, that they spend 20 days with us in July, while the old man took his annual sand-bath on the little beach, despatched a kid on a Saint's day, which they cooked and consumed in a short time between them on the seashore.

This operation bore all the aspects of a domestic crime. The guilt one feels is an old legacy from which we are saved by slaughterhouse and butcher, and which was once expunged by sacrifice. So the goat is boiled, and the kid and lamb are grilled in sections on a driftwood fire. I am speaking of what happens in Apollona. All that was left of this particular kid I found with horror and surprise next morning in the communal black pot – the unskinned head and the little furry paws.

Perhaps I should add that in the port of Naxos which had suffered the beneficial effects of four centuries of Venetian occupation, there were butcher's shops – red caverns hung with carcases and solid three-legged chopping blocks painted the colour of blood. There too, the pig entire was skilfully roasted on a charcoal spit with fragrant herbs. In the eating-houses one could eat goat which had been braised.

In Apollona we were living among the vestiges of neolithic and bronze age life: the wild almond, wild fig, wild olive and the vine which all came, if sporadically, into cultivation seven or eight thousand years ago, these staples along with wheat, rye and barley were staples still, as were the original sources of sweetness, honey, the carouba tree, wild pears, grapes, mulberry, figs. It was not hard to imagine that the same nimble flocks of long-tailed sheep and little black goats had been treading the mountain for many thousands of years, or that the acorns of ilex and dwarf kermes oaks had always been munched by little grey-skinned pigs.

In the Apeíranthos and Naxos museums the copper picks and mattocks were the precise shape of those in daily use. There were also stone and marble mortars with pebble pestles, ceremonial bronze daggers of

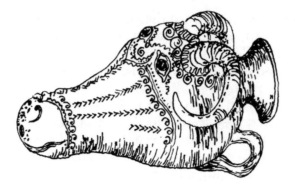

fine workmanship, marble goddesses acknowledged by all the world as wonders, as well as mysterious runic stones incised with labyrinthine spirals, and gourd-shaped cooking pots and vessels. Traces of this civilisation we found on the bare mountain above Apollona in the form of very small and delicate obsidian cutting tools, blades and minute 'leaf' obsidian arrowheads. Anyone wishing to have a closer acquaintance with these objects should examine the great work of Christian Xervos, *La Naissance de la Civilisation en Grèce*, 2 volumes and a separate volume devoted to *Les Cyclades*.

But there was also an instance of a planting method which linked the Naxians with neolithic and bronze age art. The fertile fields on the north side of the little river were entirely devoted to the onion, cultivated for export to Crete. In mid-March when the first cranes flew up the valley, the cultivation of the little fields began. Men came down from the high-up village of Komiáki on mules, sitting astride a sack of fertiliser and a sack of onion sets, shouldering their wooden ploughs with mattocks dangling from their wooden saddles. Each little dry-walled field along the river bed had first to be hoed, then the mule was harnessed to the plough and goaded up and down with grunts and cries.

After the ploughing, every man made a raised geometric pattern with the mattock; they were followed by the women, stooping and straddling the pattern while pressing in the little bulbs in rows of three. This allowed water to be channelled on either side of the raised parts on which the onions were planted, the water being piped from a distant spring. It was the Greek key pattern painted on so many Attic jars, a graphic indeed didactic reminder of the most cunning and economical way of conducting water's flow. This alone I think is a clue to understanding symbols which, long before the invention of writing, were a means of communicating knowledge.

*   *   *   *   *

In Apollona there survived a providential attitude to the sowing of a crop. A farmer planting broad beans would sow far more than his family required. Thus, if the crop were poor, there would still be plenty for his needs. If abundant, he had sacks of beans to distribute to his children's godfathers strategically stationed across the island.

During the weeks of fasting before Easter, these lavishly sown beans were eaten raw and represented the main item of diet. They were delicious but a prolonged consumption turned out to be a strain on the digestive system. At the beginning of Holy Week all hands turned to whitewashing – inside and out, and mounds of bread were baked containing eggs boiled a deep red in cochineal,* half emerging from the crust.

These breads, Easter gifts, kept us alive for three days on an iron hulk, as we wandered round the Cyclades loading sheep and goats, on our eventual way to the Piraeus. They were made with ordinary bread dough, thus different from the well known *tsouréki*, sweetened Easter breads.

During the last days of the Lenten fast nothing was cooked and, even in eating-houses in the port of Naxos, dishes prepared days before stood about for anyone who felt impelled to eat – fasting dishes like *fasolákia* and lentils.

The fast is joyfully broken at midnight on Easter Saturday, the Festival of Light, by cracking red eggs in church to accompanying shouts of *Christos Anésti* (Christ is risen) and the reply *Alithós Anésti* (It is true He has risen), followed by ritual roasting of lambs out of doors on Easter Sunday and explosions of dynamite.

---

* Cochineal is the brilliant dye derived from the scale insect *Coccus ilicis*, parasite on the shrubby Kermes oak, *Quercus coccifera*, easily recognizable by its small holly-like leaves and dwarf habit. This oak, which withstands drought, is typical of the Mediterranean region.

Beans, Peas and Rustic Soups

THE Naxian way of cooking fresh haricot beans I have described already in the previous chapter (p 55). In this one will be found the Italian and Catalan ways of cooking legumes, both fresh and dried, and some rustic soups. I insert a short essay relating to the not necessarily inevitable consequences of consuming these nutritious staples.

There is a broad dividing line in cooking between those things which are delicious in themselves – their taste has only to be revealed – and those things which, however nourishing they may be, are more properly vehicles for absorbing flavour. So one needs to cultivate a knowledge of what flavours to communicate, and an awareness of the manner in which they are absorbed, when cooking beans.

In Carrara there appeared in May beautiful pink marbled husks containing fresh marbled beans, *fagioli borlotti*, just harvested. These beans, larger than haricots, swell a great deal in the cooking and turn brown.

FAGIOLI BORLOTTI ALLA TOSCANA
Tuscan marbled beans, freshly harvested

1 kg (2¼ lb) *fagioli borlotti*	celery tops (or dandelions), chopped
¼ teaspoon bicarbonate of soda	a sprig of thyme
olive oil	*origano*
1 large sweet white onion	salt and pepper
½ kg (1 lb 2 oz) plum tomatoes	garlic cloves, sliced
fresh parsley, chopped	2 potatoes, diced
	a thread of wine vinegar

Husk the beans and put them in an earthenware pot (or heavy pan) with plenty of cold water and the pinch of bicarbonate. Bring to the boil and, after 5 minutes, strain, rinse and throw away the cooking water. This preliminary blanching is a definite ritual with regard to any bean of the species *Phaseolus vulgaris*, fresh or dried, in Italy, Spain and Greece.

Set a glazed earthenware beanpot, its bottom covered with oil, on a wire-mesh on a low heat. Slice the onion, simmer it in the oil, then add the plum tomatoes, peeled after immersion in boiling water, and crush them in the pan. Put in the parsley, roughly chopped, with the chopped celery tops (or dandelions), the thyme and the *origano*, and season. Throw in the beans and diced potatoes, simmer for 5 minutes, then cover with boiling water. Cook slowly for 1½ hours.

Strain off the excess liquor and save it for tomorrow's soup. Put the beans in a dish with a little of their sauce, sprinkle with the parsley, black pepper and garlic, and add a little olive oil and a thread of wine vinegar. Serve cold with marinated anchovies (p 45), black olives and a raw *finocchio* salad dressed with oil and vinegar.

Beans are capable of absorbing a lot of oil, being essentially dry; one must not therefore be surprised that olive oil initiates the cooking and is employed again when serving them. These beans are often cooked with vineyard weeds (see Edible Weeds, p 190). The recipe can be used for *fagioli di Spagna* (butter beans), for fresh white haricot beans, and for black-eyed beans (called *fagiolini di Sant'Anna* in Carrara), which last take less time to cook.

LA ZUPPA DI FAGIOLI • bean soup

The basis of this recipe is normally the liquor saved from cooking them with the addition of some of the beans, to which are added a few diced potatoes, chopped weeds (for example, sorrel, young dock, sow thistle, dandelions, wild spinach), a chopped carrot, water if necessary, a few tomatoes, and a handful of rice or soup pasta at the end of cooking, which results in a fairly dense soup.

But marbled or haricot beans, fresh or dried, reveal another order of excellence when cooked with the usual aromatics and a bone removed from a *prosciutto crudo*. The sumptuous taste and texture communicated to the soup is a discovery made over and over again by generations of country people, who, in the order of things, have cured with salt and lightly smoked a raw ham, then hung it in the kitchen. When the time comes to broach the ham this bone is found to be an impediment in carving it. The emergency and its removal is the inspiration of the bean soup.

Later, the cook will have her eye on the knuckle of the ham to the same end, and meanwhile will abstract a chunk of fragrant fat for *lardons*. This fat is diced, and fried, providing the point of departure for the soup, the selected aromatics being fried in the rendered fat. The presence of this innocent object in the kitchen revolutionizes, while it lasts, her culinary aspirations.

I don't pretend that every cook should endeavour to procure a ham of this kind, involving an expedition to the foothills of the Pyrenees, Bayonne, or a remote eyrie in Tuscany, when embarking on a bean soup. Drawing attention to the real thing underlines the fact that flavours must be imparted to the beans, and that the pig – whether salted, smoked, roast or in the form of sausages (preferably smoked) – or the pig's feet, tail, cheek, snout or *lardo* is the natural ally of every form of haricot, marbled, black, white or red bean which appears fresh for a season in Latin countries, and is then dried and shucked for winter. The fact that all beans take 1½ hours to cook is another reason for making sure they are absorbing delicious flavours in the meanwhile.

The Threatened Bombardment

> Let wind and water go free
> Then healthy thou wilt be

Old Wiltshire Saying

Beans are indigestible. The reasons for this indisputable fact are explained by Harold McGee on page 161 of *On Food and Cooking*.

The admirable late Victorian, Pellegrini Artusi, always so concerned for the delicate stomach, wrote in *La Scienza in Cucina*: 'It seems to me that the taste of lentils is more delicate than that of beans in general and that, as for the threat of bombardment, they are less dangerous than ordinary beans and equal to the black-eyed bean.'

Clement-Marius Morard, writing about lentils in 1886, was more pessimistic. He maintained that a frequent diet of lentils, cooked *au naturel*, produced a revolution in the organs, disturbed the head, deranged the mind, ruined the sight; a good reason for banishing lentils from the kitchen. 'But what about the partridge, the guinea-fowl, the duck, pigeon, peacock,' he exclaims, 'displaying their plump breasts in the midst of a dish of lentils, what will become of them? Will they require to be set on a mound of cabbage?'

After this flight of rhetoric, he finds the answer: 'Let us set these feathered holocausts on a soft bed of lentil purée.'

I have already referred to the practice of using a pinch of bicarbonate of soda in the initial blanching of the beans, to soften their outer skins, thus making them more digestible. This was formerly brought about by boiling the beans with a little bag of wood ash (potash), inevitably messy.

Judging by Mediterranean practice I am convinced that some of the explosive effects of the bean are offset by (1) using the recent crop, and

(2) cooking them in earthenware, and (3) after the initial blanching cooking them with wild chicory or dandelions or what Loudon called 'spinaceous' plants (goosefoots, spinach, spinach beet), which I suspect are alkaline. A handful of any of these plants, blanched for a moment or two in boiling water, is drained, squeezed, then finely chopped and added to the beans in the last quarter hour of cooking.

For the sake of interest, here is an account given to me by Nicolas Gray of the fart in English literature:

Perhaps the most notorious is the 'thunder-dent' in Chaucer's Miller's Tale, which practically blinds the importunate Absalom. This fart was of the early morning variety, not post-prandial. It is worth noting that the somewhat effeminate Absalom was described earlier as 'somdeal squaymous / of fartyng'. Rabelais resounds with rectal reverberations (*barytonant du cule*).

Of course I draw your attention to the philosophical work mentioned in the Author's Preface, volume III, chapter 20, of *Tristram Shandy* by one Didius (Dr Frances Topham) entitled 'De Fartandi et Illustrandi Fallaciis'. I imagine the fart takes up several chapters of that scholarly tome *Shakespeare's Bawdy*; and Ben Jonson was no mean practitioner of the fart as art. Sir Epicure Mammon in *The Alchemist* declares that, when Subtle has supplied him with the philosopher's stone, his court poets will 'be the same that writ so subtly of the fart'; and this is a reference to one of the most popular pieces in 17th century commonplace books, which is headed 'A Discussion in the House of Commons on the peculiar manner in which Henry Ludlow said "noe" to a message brought by the Serjeant from the Lords'. (MS Ashmole 36-7, f 131; also, dated 1607, in MS Harley 5191, f 17; versions later printed in the miscellanies – see Mennis and Smith, *Musarum Deliciae*, 1656.)

The unexpurgated Gulliver is excellent on the subject. See also E. E. Cummings, 'Poem or Beauty hurts Mr. Vinal'; Mozart's letters; Alfred Jarry's *Ubu Roi*; 'The day that Abu Hussein broke wind' in *The Thousand and One Nights*; and Charles Cotton's *Scarronides*, published in 1664, which treats of flatulence in epic form.

Casting aside the mantle of the literary archaeologist, I have some important things to say about *Scarronides*. 1. My edition (the 13th, dated 1804) has a beautiful woodcut of Aeolus, standing on a promontory, farting at the Trojan ships. The discarded stopper, like one from a decanter, lies at his feet. And Boreas is flitting about the sky, undoubtedly propelled by his own fart-jet. 2. It is a staggering notion to cool our gruel by farting on it. 3. We are on the point of discovering profound gastronomo-philosophical truths in this fart research. Homunculi, and indeed seeds of all living things, we know from the Panspermists, float about in the atmosphere, and are wafted about on the winds. According to Pythagoras, beans are souls. We know that beans are 'flatulent meat' from tradition and daily experience. And now we have the winds and farting associated by Cotton. Perhaps we might conjecture from these facts that an essential stage in the life of the Homunculus takes place in the alimentary canal – where your inert bean is, as it were, reborn and carried into the world on the winds. So plainly your cook is a very important person.

I think myself that we can take some of this last paragraph with a pinch of salt. 'Perhaps,' Nicolas concludes, 'I really ought to research into the Post Prandial Fart in 19th Century Rural Ruminative Poetry.' And

perhaps I should add, in order to bring the perils of flatulence into the
Space Age, that recent research into this matter has focussed on
astronauts (see pp 257-8 of the already cited McGee).

    A breach having been opened in this subject, every cook will recall
his/her favourite *fartiste* . . . but I would like to put in a word for Papa
Galeazzo, the 17th century priest who once stole the 'stopper' used by
the Baroness of Lucugnano in the Salento on festive occasions, replacing
it artfully with a bird whistle to startling effect in the country dance.
Lucugnano is the place where the earthenware bean-pot called *pignata*
is made.

LA PIGNATA

The slow cooking required by beans and pulses is typified in Apulian cooking in the use of this pot. Glazed inside, jug-shaped, it has two handles on one side with which to approach it to the fire. The name derives from the shape, resembling a *pigna* or pine-cone. In it are cooked the dried winter staples: haricot beans, black-eyed beans, chickpeas, peas and broad beans.

Two jars are employed: one is half-filled with the selected legume, then filled up with cold cistern water and a pinch of bicarbonate of soda is added; the other jar is to provide boiling water for filling up.

This invention permits cooking in the hearth on a very small fire indeed; the pots are placed close up to it, never on it. They require frequent attention. Both are brought up to the fire, and the pot with peas, beans or chickpeas slowly comes to the boil and cooks for, say, 20 minutes; then the water is drained away out of doors. It is refilled from the water pot, now boiling, and, with a little salt added and a broken piece of terracotta placed on it as a lid, it goes on cooking. Replenish the water pot – you'll need it to refill, as the water is absorbed and evaporates. The home-grown hard little dry peas (they have not been soaked) take about 4 hours to cook! So do the chickpeas. Broad beans, haricots and black-eyed beans take less.

This is, I believe, a method invented unconsciously by man to keep his woman occupied while he is in the fields. In the meantime she is embroidering, crocheting or knitting. An emotional element intrudes in this ancient form of cooking: the man does not feel happy, nourished or content unless *la pignata* appears on the table at least twice a week.

After these hours of attending on the little fire – wood is precious – and every 20 minutes attending to the pot, the climax comes in a last minute flurry. The peas, beans, whatever they are, are strained, but their liquor is kept. A generous amount of olive oil is heated in a pan, some hot peppers (preserved in oil, it's winter) are thrown into it, with a sliced onion, or garlic cloves, and a spoonful of *la salsa secca* (p 321), and then after a few minutes the peas or beans or chickpeas are thrown in, roasting as it were in the oil for a moment, after which is added a little of the liquor and some salt. The pan is then triumphantly set on the table with a ladle in it before the labourer, and the threatened emotional crisis gives way to satisfaction.

What remains often reappears at night, reheated in oil, with the addition when hot of 2 or 3 beaten eggs, cooked for a moment.

To see this in perspective: all these staples have been grown by him for winter consumption. The method is not only the best way of cooking

them, but the result a reward for labouring. Twenty years ago those who still insist on *la pignata* did not have anything much to eat by day except a handful of dried figs.

Throwing the peas, beans, chickpeas or broad beans into the aromatized hot oil at the end of the cooking very much resembles Catalan practice and conveys a particular 'roasted' taste to the legumes. Flavouring them not only with alliums (wild leeks are sometimes used, culled from the winter vineyard) but with the sun-dried tomato sauce is truly remarkable. But often *pomodori appesi* (p 324) are used instead, first peeled; and at the final stage wild chicory, already cooked, is often chopped and thrown in on top of the legumes. Green celery is also used. The method is always the same; the aromatics can be varied at will.

I should add that the dried broad beans, though taking less time to cook, take longer to prepare. Soaked overnight, the black skin marking the point of attachment to the pod is nipped off. This speeds the cooking and you are able to whip off some of the skins (indigestible) before precipitating them into the hot oil. These beans, excellent in taste, are flavoured with *sprunzale*, which are onion shoots (see under the Catalan *calçots*, p 163).

Here I must admit that while growing all these legumes and using them in winter I do not hover by the hearth tending the *pignata*. A Tuscan beanpot on the stove cooks them while my back is turned; I am in my workshop. Then at mid-day, in the manner described above, I precipitate the now tender legume into aromatized olive oil and achieve, I think, with no travail the same result. I also soak the peas, beans, or whatever it is overnight, and omit the bicarbonate of soda.

I will spare you an account of the cultivation of these legumes, the hoeing involved and the ardours of threshing them once the plants have dried. Peas have to be treated at once against the ubiquitous pea beetle: they are put in a receptacle in the centre of which is placed a jar containing liquid sulphur, covered with a cloth, then sealed for a few weeks. Peas, chickpeas, broad beans and haricot beans are stored in two-handled glazed earthenware pots for winter. Broad beans, dried on the roof, are often left in the husk to defend them from the broad-bean beetle.

The flat roofs of the Salento are the drying platforms (*terrazze*) of every grower. They are also observation points. People who do not read are ever reading the wide landscape and interpreting signs. No one ever goes anywhere unobserved. If this sounds like a fairy tale, remember the Princess and the Pea; her mattress was, of course, made of pea-straw, as were many Apulian mattresses till recently.

LENTICCHIE PASSATE • lentil purée

The lentil, *Lens esculenta*, belonging to the pea family, is one of the earliest forms of cultivated food, found in neolithic dwellings in Sesklo and Dimini in Thessaly and dated to 8000 years ago (see Hourmouziades in the Bibliography).

This is a recipe of Pellegrino Artusi, an example of classic Tuscan cooking.

Cook ½ kg (1 lb 2 oz) of brown lentils, unsoaked, in slightly salted water with a knob of fresh butter, until they are tender but not broken (in earthenware, if possible). Then pass them through a sieve.

Chop finely a small onion, some parsley, *sedano* (celery grown as a herb) and a carrot. Put this *battuto* in a pan with 50 g (2 oz) of butter, brown the aromatics, then add a ladleful of stock, or liquor from cooking a *cotechino* (see p 230), skimmed of its surface fat. Simmer for 10 minutes. Use this to flavour the lentil purée, which should remain stiff. I sometimes add the juice of half a lemon.

One of the best things to serve with the above-mentioned *cotechino*, but also with a *zampone*, a pigeon, pheasant or partridge.

CIGRONS GUISATS • stewed chickpeas

We are told in books that chickpeas, *Cicer arietinum*, are of Spanish origin. They are also native to Apulia and Sicily. Confirmation of this is to be found in the 'Capitulaire De Villis', an order promulgated by Charlemagne's son, Louis the Pious, in the year 795, with regard to plants to be cultivated in the royal domains; chickpeas occur in this plant list under the name *cicerum italicum*.

Gathered fresh in May, though no one will believe it, they are a short-lived delicacy, brilliant green, growing two to a pod; eaten raw they have a refreshing taste of lemon. Cooked in a dish of rice they delight the eye. But, as the May sun in southern latitudes quickly dries them, they are imagined, even by Italians, to be born brown and born dry.

In Catalonia this winter staple, valued for its nutty flavour as well as for its nourishment, has mercifully received a preliminary cooking by the market ladies. However, I give the recipe starting from scratch.

½ kg (1 lb 2 oz) chickpeas	*for the picada (all to be finely ground*
bicarbonate of soda, a pinch	*together in the mortar)*
olive oil	8 peeled and pounded almonds
1 onion, finely hashed	a few pine kernels
chopped parsley	sea salt
1 large ripe tomato, peeled	more chopped parsley
1 teaspoon flour	garlic
salt and black pepper	

Soak the chickpeas overnight with a pinch of bicarbonate of soda. Rinse and simmer them in an earthenware pot, adding a little salt. Cook for 3 hours, more if need be, then drain and keep some of the liquor.

Heat some oil in a pan, put in the onion and some chopped parsley. When the onion begins to colour, add the tomato, crushing it. Simmer, then add the flour and stir while it thickens. Dilute with a few spoonfuls of chickpea liquor. Put in the chickpeas, some black pepper, and add the *picada*. Simmer on a low flame for 10 minutes. Serve for lunch.

In northern Italy, chickpea flour is used to make appetizing *pizze*, thin as flannel, in Carrara called *Calda! Calda!* The name arose from boys carrying them in covered baskets, shouting their piping hot wares, along the rocky torrent of the Carrione, down which the famished quarrymen returned at evening on foot from the marble mountains.

In the market, a thick pancake called *panizza*, the size of little crumpets, were sold to be taken home to grill or fry. Made like *polenta* but with chickpea flour instead of maize flour, then poured to a specific thickness on a board and punched into rounds when cold.

In the Salento, chickpeas are often soaked overnight, then roasted in the bread-oven on a metal tray before bread-making. Crunched hot as a *passatempo* while waiting for the bread to come out. A neolithic way of dealing with recalcitrant grains, seeds, legumes.

'FAVA E FOGLIA'
purée of dried broad beans with wild chicory

½ kg (1 lb 2 oz) broad beans · olive oil · onion shoots · mint
wild chicory · strips of *pancetta* (salt belly of pork)

Cook the dried broad beans in the usual way in the hearth in the *pignata*, or on the stove in an earthenware pot. Strain when tender, reserving the liquor. Slip off the outer skins.

Cover the bottom of a pan with olive oil and cook in it some finely sliced *sprunzale* (onion shoots, p 164) or wild leeks, then add some leaves of mint and the beans, with a little of their liquor. Cook on a gentle heat till they dissolve, then beat to a purée with a fork. Season.

Serve the purée, which should be rather stiff, with wild chicory which has been washed, boiled, drained, then tossed in a frying pan in which you have first fried some little strips of *pancetta*.

NOTE. Dried beans minus their outer skins exist in commerce. Oddly enough one cannot achieve a smooth purée with these packaged beans. Just a warning.

'PISCIMMARE' · 'fish at sea'

Ironic Salentine name for a fish-less breakfast.

The labourer the night before has supped on a dish of *piselli secchi* (p 67), cooked in the *pignata*, and a dish of rape (p 163). When he rises at dawn in autumn to go fishing or shooting before starting work at 7, his wife hastily puts a pan on the fire, heats some olive oil, then throws in some dried chilli peppers, 2 or 3 tomatoes (*pomodori appesi*, p 324) and then the remaining peas followed by the rape.

He eats it with some home-baked bread and knocks back a glass of wine. (For a quarryman's breakfast, see *Pista e Coza*, p 145).

R u s t i c   S o u p s

We used to stay in a high-up village above Nice where only stony mule paths connected it to the dust road meandering round the ravines below. This inaccessibility made food relatively dear except for the things that the inhabitants, who were gardeners, grew.

As everyone went to work at 4 a.m. in summer, the main activity at other times of day was the game of *boules* carried on on any path which had been left uncobbled, where the village petered off onto the mountainside.

The mediaeval village lay like a curled snail shell at the foot of a great *baou* on a pyramid of fertile earth deposited by centuries of erosion of the lion-coloured mountain above, and overlooked an expanse which stretched from the Alpes Maritimes to the mountains of Esterel.

Madame Baudouin's dwelling on the ramparts contained a 'room' roofed over but open to the south and west, used for drying thyme,

sage, rosemary, lavender and wild origano, as well as haricot beans and figs in autumn. It was used for the preservation of geraniums in winter, the springtime packing of carnations and Provençal roses for market, and the despatch of orange flowers to a perfumery in Grasse. She rented it as a kind of outdoor living-room with cooking stove and sink, in conjunction with an adjoining room that contained an ancient bed, a feather mattress, a large wardrobe and an engraving of the *Sacré Coeur*. In this gardener's paradise there naturally were in early summer vegetables in abundance, peas, haricots verts, little courgettes, broad beans, baby carrots, sweet white onions with their green shoots and new garlic.

LA SOUPE AU PISTOU

This Provençal soup, Genoese by birth, is a dense concoction of vegetables given further substance by fresh *nouilles* and/or rice, a celebration of the time of year when everything is tender, sweet and fresh, to which the *pistou* (Italian *pesto*) is added. In this village it was Gruyère, not *pecorino sardo* or parmesan, that was incorporated. Here is the principle:

olive oil
1 sweet white onion
a handful of rice
haricots verts ⎫
broad beans ⎬ a handful of each
peas ⎭
a few young carrots
2 or 3 small courgettes
3 new potatoes

a handful of fresh *nouilles*

for the pistou:
3 cloves of new garlic
3 or 4 branches of basil
a few pine kernels
1 tablespoon of olive oil
2 tablespoons of grated Gruyère

Put a little olive oil in a pot on a low heat, add the chopped onion and the rice, then the haricots verts (topped, tailed and broken in two), the broad beans sliced in two, the peas, carrots and courgettes, and the potatoes, diced. Sweat for a few minutes, add water to cover and boil quickly for 10 minutes, covered. Put in the *nouilles* and cook for another 5 minutes. Turn off the heat. Add the well-pounded *pistou*.

This was the summer evening meal. The soup is sometimes made even more dense by adding an egg beaten with lemon juice, onto which some of the soup liquor is poured, stirred while it thickens, then poured back into the pot. But in this case the cheese is omitted from the *pistou*.

ZUPPA DI ACETOSA • sorrel soup

In Italy a very tender, large-leaved sorrel, *Rumex scutatus* (p 197), appears in vineyards and waste places in February-March. This plant, a perennial, is easy to cultivate. A favourite Victorian kitchen garden plant in England, it can be grown easily from seed.

Gather a handful of sorrel, wash it, and roughly chop it. Put a large knob of butter and a little olive oil in the bottom of an enamelled iron pan. Simmer in it for a few minutes a large chopped onion and 2 or 3 large potatoes, diced. Sprinkle with salt and ground pepper, cover with water and boil rapidly. When the potatoes disintegrate, throw in the sorrel. Cook for a few moments. A refreshing soup.

Sorrel makes a good accompaniment for poached and baked fish; simmered in butter it rapidly acquires the consistency of a sauce. Cooked for a few moments in butter, it is good added to an omelette before folding it. It can also be cooked with monk's rhubarb, *Rumex patientia*, another Victorian favourite: use 1 part sorrel to 4 parts monk's rhubarb.

ZUPPA DI PISELLI SECCHI • pea soup

Use dried split peas, which don't need soaking and cook quickly.

½ kg (1 lb 2 oz) split peas
a pig's trotter severed lengthwise in two
a bayleaf • salt and black pepper
ground mustard seed diluted in a little vinegar
a little butter • a large onion • 2 potatoes • 2 leeks
chopped parsley or coriander leaves • little croûtons

The pig's trotter will be improved by pickling in brine beforehand; see my recipe for *Lingua salmistrata* (p 275) and Jane Grigson's *Charcuterie and French Pork Cookery*.

Immerse the pig's trotter and the peas in cold water in a pan, bring to the boil and skim. Put in the bayleaf and the seasoning, cover and cook slowly for an hour. In another pan simmer in butter the chopped onion, the diced potatoes, the leeks chopped fine, till they soften. Then transfer from the other pot the cooked peas and their liquor, by now more or less a purée, and simmer together for 20 minutes. What meat you can find on the trotter can be cut up small and put into the soup.

Sprinkle with the chopped parsley or coriander leaves and serve with little croûtons fried in pure pork fat. The soup should be dense.

ZUPPA DI ZUCCA INVERNALE • pumpkin soup

The winter pumpkin has a gnarled greenish yellow exterior and hour-glass form, much cultivated in Italy, Greece, Catalonia. These pumpkins weigh about 2 kilos (4½ pounds), but can be much larger; they are wonderful orange colour inside and sweet. Fine-grained, not fibrous. With half such a pumpkin you can make a winter soup and with the rest an unusual preserve (p 308). See also Vegetable Heritage (p 167).

half a pumpkin • olive oil • an onion
2 large potatoes • 1 leek • a branch of thyme
½ teaspoon ground ginger • 300 g (11 oz) cooked chickpeas
salt and pepper • chopped parsley • butter • juice of a lemon

Peel the pumpkin with a sharp knife, cut it into segments about 2.5 cm (1") thick, and then into neat cubes. Discard the seeds and fibres.

Put some olive oil in the bottom of the pot, slice up the onion and simmer without browning, on a wire-mesh mat. Peel and dice the potatoes, slice the leek. Put these vegetables into the pot in which the onions are simmering, sweat a few minutes, add the thyme and hot water to cover. (If you pour on cold water, the pot will crack.) Season with ginger and add the cooked chickpeas and salt and pepper.

In an hour the pumpkin will have dissolved into a cream. Crush the potatoes against the side of the pot, sprinkle with chopped parsley, add a spoonful of butter and the juice of a lemon, and serve.

nettle soup

Early spring is a good time to go out with a basket, a pair of gloves and a pair of scissors to gather nettle tops (*Urtica dioica*). Still tender, their sting is at a minimum. At home, put them in a colander and pass under the cold tap.

Put some beef dripping in a pan on a low heat. Chop up 2 or 3 potatoes and an onion, simmer them in the dripping, then pour on water to cover and add a teaspoon of tomato purée, salt, pepper and a little milk. Raise the heat. Chop up the nettles with your gloves on. Crush the potatoes against the side of the pan, then throw in the nettles and cook for a few minutes.

The nettle is *ortica* in Italian and *ortiga* in Catalan. In Puglia they sometimes find their way into a dish of pasta: *Pasta colle ortiche*.

MINESTRA DI ERBE PASSATE • a green vegetable purée

2 or 3 little lettuces	*aromatics:*
a small crisp cabbage	a small head of *sedano* (green
a bunch of spinach beet	celery) or celery tops
2 large handfuls of fresh spinach	a small carrot
a large knob of butter	a few fronds of dill
3 tomatoes, roughly chopped	some basil
1 potato, peeled and diced	or (failing dill and basil)
salt and pepper	some sorrel

Remove the biggest ribs from the beet, wash and roughly slice up all the greenstuff on a board, put it in a large bowl with water. Chop up the aromatics and simmer them in butter till they begin to colour. Put in the undrained greenstuff, with the tomatoes and potato, add salt and pepper and boil up, stirring. When the greens have reduced in volume, cover with hot water and cook briefly till tender, then pass through a sieve.

Stir some fresh butter into the purée and, if you like, a little thick cream. Serve with grated parmesan.

R e v i v e r s

I return to the beneficial effects of herbs, garlic and olive oil. There is a saying: *l'aigo bouido, saouvo la vido.*

AIGO BOUIDO • 'boiled water'

The Provençal life-saver applying to physical debility, hangover and liver complaints is *aigo bouido* – which is water, slightly salted, boiled with 2 crushed cloves of garlic and 2 sprigs of sage (*Salvia officinalis*, or *S sclarea*, which is clary) and a spoonful of olive oil. (Two or 3 bayleaves can be added, or substituted for the sage.)

Boiled for 15 minutes, this infusion is strained and poured slowly into a plate in which a fresh egg yolk is sitting, the yolk being stirred as the aromatized water is poured on, which has the effect of slightly thickening it. An ancient remedy, prescribed for delicate children by Clement-Marius Morard in his *Manuel Complet de la Cuisinière Provençale*, but equally applicable to grown-ups.

SOPA DE FARIGOLA • thyme soup

The Catalan counterpart of the preceding recipe, thyme soup, is favoured by shepherds who naturally have the thyme to hand. A branch or two of dried thyme (many herbs gain in pungency from drying) is infused in boiling water and poured over some thin slices of bread soaked in olive oil. An egg can be broken on top of the bread before pouring on the infusion.

This sounds like an echo of the soup of pounded garlic and wild thyme which Thestylis, a country girl, brewed for the reapers wearied by the scorching heat, in Virgil's second Eclogue.

Passing through a Provençal village with a bunch of thyme in hand (*Thymus capitatus*, the most pungent of all thymes growing in mountainous and maritime situations), I met an old man who stared at it with such intensity that I asked him why. He drank every morning of his life an infusion of this wild thyme in a thin sugar syrup. Was it good for a hangover, I asked. It does me good, he said.

This proves to be an excellent soporific taken at night, but without the sugar.

Sage, thyme, bay have similar properties, as I have said in La Merenda. One should make more use of these restoratives. The Greeks make an infusion called *faskómilo* with the dried leaves of sage (*Salvia triloba*), a more delicate herb than *S officinalis*. The Greek infusion of fresh mint leaves served in glasses with slices of fresh lemon and honey or sugar is an indispensable reviver in hot weather, as anyone can prove by trying it. Drink it hot.

Another life-saver: the Italian *spremuta di limone*, sometimes served in bars, the juice of fresh lemons with sugar and iced water, as is the rarer but stupendous lemon water ice.

In this connection, Greek women seldom travel any distance without sucking lemon rinds.

Cantarem La Vida

THE Catalan sculptor Apel.les Fenosa focusses attention on the flowering moment – his figures transfixed in clay give the illusion of unfurling. They emerge from the hollow form of leaves, or leafy foliations break like ruffled wings from women's outstretched arms. The leaf woman, high as a man's hand, takes many shapes. These delicate apparitions, lightly borne like a fine breeze on a stifling summer day, always show the trace of thumb and finger pression, of the conjuring hand that shocks them into life. Creatures of an instant, they stand in the cellar below the house at Vendrell; in the semi-dark they seem like a race of natural beings, flower-figures, figure-flowers, and echo the tremulous soaring notes of the oboe in old Catalan airs, cadences light as bird-song.

'In this way,' Daniel Abadie has written, 'Fenosa belongs to those oracles of old, who awakened from their dream could not, anymore than we can, provide the key, and it is the voice of the oaks of Dodona which we hear, for the last time perhaps, in the vegetal murmur of his sculptures.'

The antique world vibrates in Fenosa's work and confirms the feeling that the Catalans remain closest to it in spirit. In Homer's time a king could go out to plough his land and build his bed of giant timbers. The old roots are being severed, but in Vendrell one could perceive them: Anita, a Catalan peasant woman preparing the age old dishes, was in her bearing like a queen. Confronting Fenosa's work we are snatched back into our Mediterranean cradle, where startled – like Nausica and her maids – we confront the vision of Odysseus.

The Portal del Perdó is a palace of many rooms and part of it is a 14th century tower which forms an arched entrance into the town-village. I slept on a mattress of hay in this tower on a remarkable 16th century bed. It was more a throne than a bed. I thought of the mysterious house as 'the palace of the thousand and one beds' – it contained carved, painted and gilded beds, gothic beds, baroque beds and papier mâché inlaid with mother-of-pearl four-poster beds. I used to lie on the hay mattress and listen to the carts tinkling and rattling under the wide arch below, rumbling like chariots, at four o'clock in the morning as the men of Vendrell rode out to the dustblown fields.

In the palatial empty room there was nothing but the great bed on which I lay and a studded leather chest. A gilded sun shone down from the summit of the painted head-board in which a little landscape was

immured. From one window I looked out on the *sgraffiti* swags, pyramids and garlands half-effaced on the street front, and the shell-encrusted mouldings above the long windows. Further up the street I could see an Easter palm trophy bleaching on an iron balcony. My scarlet damask quilt seemed to float on the old tiled floor, blue fleur-de-lys enclosed in elongated hexagons. The walls, washed a pale ochrous pink, were slashed at window openings by the pale dazzle of the sky.

On the morning of the *Festa Major* I was awoken by the sound of oboes and drums. Wandering already through the streets were a gigantic papier-mâché King and Queen towering above a little group of masked grotesques. A dozen beribboned stick-dancers and a band of devils were darting about the village, to the accompaniment of a thin thread of sound like goat music, which seemed to come from all sides and from nowhere.

No one knows how long the men of Vendrell have been building their towers. It happens there, in Vilanova and in Valls. But I have since seen 16th century engravings of the 'human towers' mounted in the Piazza San Marco in Venice.

About thirty men and boys collect in the little *plaça* by the church at 2 o'clock. They are dressed in faded shirts glowing in varying shades of red, with black cummerbunds tightly wound and white trousers. Their feet are bare. The sun is formidable and overhead. They are surrounded by intent participants and every balcony in the *plaça* is tightly wedged.

They start discussing the tower they are going to make, while tying and untying the spotted handkerchiefs round their heads. The man with the final say is the master tower builder. That year he was in prison and had to be released for the feast. The men start practising grips and holds, then some congeal into a knotted group very densely packed. The men in the middle of the group stretch up, arms aloft to minimise the foot and body space they take. The core of the tower is made of close-packed bodies with brawny arms entwined like ropes. Stouter men move in on this hard core to be the 'corner-stones'. They are encircled by others who act as 'flying-buttresses'. Four sturdy men climb up on the backs of the 'corner-stones' and plant themselves on these men's shoulders, grasping each other round the neck. The supports throw up their elbows, clasp the young men's ankles and steady them against their heads. The buttress men stretch up their arms and lean on the young men's calves.

When the first storey of the tower is made, the musicians begin their plaintive rising tune, an air like a gleam of hope, on the oboes, underpinned by drums. Lighter youths immediately begin to scale the living structure, using the men's calves as footholds and the small of their backs. As the next storey appears, the structure starts to vibrate with the strain, and smaller boys begin to shin up the edifice in dreadful haste. They have further to climb, the tower trembles and shakes. Finally two little boys, like drain-pipe rats, scurry up to the summit to deliver a Roman salute, before they slide down again, their teeth chattering.

At the moment of completion the musicians play a sudden high-sounding tune of triumph and then a falling accompaniment in a minor key as the tower crumbles storey by storey. Breathless, gasping and trembling, the smaller boys are caught in the outstretched arms below and safely brought to earth.

The whole creation and destruction of this living architecture takes a few minutes. It is a double-fisted Catalan gesture of solidarity and improvisation – the hard core of anarchism.

Anyone wishing to approach the Catalan spirit should search for the Catalan poet Raimon's first recording (Raimon, *disc antològic*, C.M. 62, Edigsa, Barcelona), and hear him sing *Cantarem la vida*.

* * * * *

One summer we escaped from marble dust and Carrara and drove in the desert lorry across the Bouches-du-Rhône, sleeping in lavender fields, to Vendrell to stay once again with Fenosa and his wife Nicole.

In the Portal, life is conducted in the old Catalan way. Presenting its magnificent formal facade to the narrow cinnamon-coloured street, it conceals within a secret garden enclosed within high walls, reached by flights of steps descending from a loggia, open and arcaded on two sides. Into this summer living space intrude the orange trumpets of bignonia, huge fronds of palm and the staring tiger-faces of passionflowers. Fenosa's workplace is in the cavern opening on the mysterious garden.

Beyond the fountain and the papyrus plants stands an old fig-tree which casts a dense shade at mid-day over a table made of old maiolica tiles, and further on is an outdoor kitchen, its hearth built against the high wall for grilling and nearby a charcoal installation.

Nicole went to the market every day and returned with an enormous

basket laden with just those things, carefully calculated, for the day. In that climate in summer, food perishes within a few hours.

Lunch always began with fresh green tomatoes, sliced raw onions and salt anchovies (p 45), followed by a wonderful *paella* or fresh sardines or little mackerel or red mullet, prepared by Anita and grilled on the outdoor fire, a fierce incendiary of aromatic scrub. Salad, cheese and pyramids of purple figs completed the meal. Here under the tree one realized how much more refreshing was a trickle of wine from the *porró* than a draught of wine from a glass.

It was the simplicity, the frugality of these meals, combined with the perfection of the raw materials and the loving care with which Anita prepared them that inspired Irving Davis to begin his collection of Catalan recipes.

Here frugality mysteriously combined with liberality epitomized the old Catalan way of life, so that – exposed to the rigours of a climate with its extremes of heat and cold – the provision of food took on the quality of life-restoring, rather than the satisfaction of appetite. This 'intensity' is reflected in the building of 'human towers', in the summons of the *sardana*, in which everyone, however young, however old, took part, and is the background against which one must imagine people eating the same dish of beans and potatoes every night in summer. Wherever a spirit of independence flowers, austerity and fellowship combine.

We often ate this dish, *Patates i mongetes*, at night and sometimes *Patates vídues* (widowed potatoes), or *Espinacs amb panses i pinyons* (pp 87 and 166). One evening three fishermen from Calafell invaded the kitchen to make the fabulous meal described by Irving Davis (p 112).

On feast days, Fenosa with great ceremony prepared a leg of lamb, stuck it with garlic cloves and sprigs of rosemary, impaled and mounted it on the late 19th century cast-iron mechanical spit: a lesson in roasting a large piece of meat slowly out of doors, over a fire of olive wood, laid and well lit beforehand, to achieve the incandescence of a braise. It took more than an hour to cook, and during this time he applied libations of olive oil and wine vinegar to it by means of a twig of thyme.

Fenosa took us to Tarragona where a silversmith, naked to the waist, fused for me a superb piece of silver. Anita lent us her barn outside the village to work in – the delight being to do one's own work in different surroundings. The Sculptor worked the golden stone from the Roman quarry in which Casals had once played.

*   *   *   *   *

I think it appropriate here to set down Anita's paella.

Anita's *PAELLA*

This requires a two-handled iron *paella*, far more capacious than a frying pan, to make it in – a large area of evaporation being vital to the perfect cooking of the rice. You need:

> half a chicken, neatly severed into small pieces
> the rib bones separated from 3 or 4 pork chops and chopped in two
> 2 small cuttlefish cleaned and sliced into rounds
> ½ kilo (1 lb 2 oz) of fresh mussels, scrubbed, washed, bearded
> 4 *langoustines* (*Nephrops norvegicus*, large prawns with claws)
> 1 coffee cup of hard-grain rice per person and 3 times its volume of water
> 6 or 7 soupspoons of olive oil
> 2 or 3 onions, hashed
> ½ kilo (1 lb 2 oz) tomatoes
> a handful of new peas or *haricots verts*, topped, tailed, broken in two
> 7 or 8 saffron threads, immersed for a few minutes in warm water

Brown the pieces of chicken in olive oil in the *paella*, on a hot flame, turning them about, (reserving two soupspoons of olive oil for later). Remove them from the pan, and brown the pork ribs in the same oil. Remove these and fry the sliced cuttlefish. Remove them and fry the *langoustines* and put them aside.

Prepare the *sofregit* (p 31) by browning the finely hashed onions slowly in the *paella*. After 10 minutes, add the peeled tomatoes, crush them. Simmer slowly for 20 minutes, time for it to soften and reduce.

Meanwhile put a pot on the fire, and for four people, pour in 12 coffee-cups of water, salt it, bring to the boil and put in peas or beans, boiling for 10 minutes with the lid on.

Add the saved oil to the *sofregit*, by now a homogeneous sauce. Raise the heat and put in 4 coffee-cups of rice. Fry briskly, stirring all the time with a wooden spoon, while the rice absorbs the oil in the sauce.

Then add the saffron and the water, now turned yellow, and pour on the boiling water and peas or beans. Put all the fried ingredients into the *paella*, distributing them, add the mussels, and from now on do not stir the rice. Cook for 20 minutes, fast at first, then moderating the heat as the liquor is absorbed and evaporates. But, as soon as the mussels open, pick them out, discard the empty shells and return the shells containing the mussels to the *paella*, a minute or two before bringing it to table.

The rice, pale gold, is fragrant, the grains separate, with the various elements distributed in it, appetizing morsels.

The principle once grasped, the ingredients can be varied, but usually pork, chicken, shellfish and crustaceans are included.

Potato Dishes and Egg Dishes

T must now be known by many people that the potato is of Peruvian rather than of Virginian origin, however much one clings to childhood's Raleigh story.

It arrived around 1570 in Spain in the wake of Pizarro's conquest of Peru; and was already cultivated in parts of Italy in the early 1580s, as reported by Clusius.

The story of a plant introduction is like a very involved detective story and I therefore refer you to the dramatic 'search' in the newly reissued work of Salaman, *The Economic and Social Influence of the Potato*, and particularly to Chapter IX, 'The Introduction to Europe: the Raleigh and other legends'.

Where Great Britain is concerned, Salaman, after following abortive Drake and Hawkins clues, discovers Raleigh to be the culprit, of which we, naturally, were convinced already.

Thus it appears that Loudon, in his *Encyclopaedia of Gardening*, was correct in saying that the potato was first imported by Sir Walter Raleigh to his estate (Youghal) near Cork, from Virginia in 1584 (even if one of his henchmen stole it from ship's stores on Drake's ship); that it came quickly into cultivation in Ireland and reached Liverpool considerably later, and was only commonly grown in England in the 18th century.

At first the English treated it like sweet potatoes (*Ipomoea batatas*) as a 'delicacy', the tubers being roasted and steeped in sack and sugar, or baked with beef marrow and spices; it was also candied. The source of this information is Parkinson, *Theatrum Botanicum*.

At the end of the 17th century potatoes were spoken of rather slightingly in gardening books: 'They are much used in Ireland and America as bread and may be propagated with advantage to poor people.' In London and Wise's *Compleat Gardener*, 1719, they were not mentioned at all.

PATATES I MONGETES • potatoes and French beans

The traditional evening meal in summer of Catalan peasants, this is also called *verdura*. When the French beans grow too big, cabbage is substituted.

2 large potatoes per person
a large handful of French beans • 1 large onion
olive oil • salt

Peel and cut the potatoes into four, put them in an earthenware bean-pot in water, bring to the boil, add salt. Top and tail the beans. Ten minutes after the water boils, put them in, with the onion cut in two. Boil for 15 minutes more, strain and serve. Each person helps himself to olive oil from the *setrill*, in this case a small glass bottle with a fine spout.

PATATES VÍDUES • 'widowed' potatoes

1 kg (2¼ lb) firm potatoes
1 large onion
olive oil
2 big tomatoes
1 teaspoon sweet paprika pepper
a bayleaf
salt

for the picada:
4 grilled almonds
1 soupspoon of pine kernels
1 peeled clove of garlic

Peel the potatoes and slice them thinly. Hash the onion minutely, brown it in a heavy pan in olive oil, then add the peeled tomatoes. Crush them in the pan, cook them for 5 minutes and put in the paprika pepper and the bay-leaf. Add the potatoes, just cover them with cold water, add salt, bring to the boil and simmer gently for 15 minutes, covered.

Pound the *picada* to a paste in the mortar, dilute with a little of the potato liquor, and pour it into the pan. Cook for another 15 minutes uncovered, by which time the liquor should have reduced into a sauce, the potatoes remaining unbroken.

Both the above recipes were given to Irving Davis by Anita Simal Llonch. I use them often.

POMMES À L'HUILE
potatoes seasoned with alliums and olive oil

Boil or steam in their skins, without overcooking, 1½ kilos (3¼ lb) of potatoes, then drain and peel them. Chop finely as much as you like of onions, shallots, garlic and parsley, and put them in a wide pan with a wineglass of olive oil on a low heat. (You are not going to fry the alliums, they should be almost raw.) Cut up the potatoes roughly and add them to the pan, with salt and plenty of ground black pepper. Turn them about in the oil and alliums with a wooden fork and serve hot with a boiled *cotechino* or *zampone* (p 230) or with grilled smoked sausages; have plenty of red wine to drink with them.

PATATE AL LATTE E BURRO
potatoes cooked with milk and butter

In May and June a delicious sweet white onion appears in Italian markets, freshly pulled and sold in little bunches, the stalks green, good for this dish.

2 sweet white onions	salt and ground black pepper
2 tablespoons of olive oil	grated nutmeg
½ kg (1 lb 2 oz) new potatoes	50 g (2 oz) butter
milk to cover	chopped parsley or coriander
	leaves

Slice the onions in rounds into a pan in which the olive oil is heating, slice the peeled potatoes ½ cm (1/5″) thick and put them in on top. Just cover with milk, add salt, and cook quickly with the lid off. Add a little ground black pepper and grated nutmeg.

When the potatoes are almost cooked, about 10 minutes, and some of the liquid has evaporated, add the butter, lower the heat and by further evaporation and absorption the potatoes will soon be bathed in a creamy sauce. Sprinkle with chopped parsley or coriander leaves and serve.

TORTA DI PATATE
potato *torta* – neither cake, nor flan, nor tart

Don't start making this delicious *torta* until you have dried a stale white loaf in the oven to the point when it can be crushed to a powder by rolling a bottle over it on a hard surface. This is called *pangrattato* or *pane grattugiato*. In Italy there is a shortcut to preparing it, in the south, in the form of *taralli* which are dry baked biscuit rings (often flavoured with fennel seeds); in the north, various forms of *grissini*, biscuit-like sticks instantly crushable.

1 kg (2¼ lbs) potatoes	1 tablespoon sugar
a little salt	2 tablespoons grated parmesan
50 g (2 oz) butter	or *pecorino*
¼ litre (9 fl oz) milk	100 g (3½ oz) *lardo*, salt pork, diced
3 fresh eggs	and lightly browned
grated nutmeg	olive oil
	pangrattato (see above)

Peel and boil or steam the potatoes. Drain and mash immediately. Put them in a pan on a low heat, beating in the butter, then adding the hot milk. Beat to a cream, take the pan off the fire and whisk in the eggs. Add nutmeg, sugar, parmesan, and finally the *lardo*.

Oil a baking tin and sprinkle the bottom and sides with fine crumbs, which will adhere. Transfer the purée to the tin, smoothing it very lightly with a spatula, oil the top and sprinkle densely with more crumbs. Bake in a moderate oven for 45 minutes. Heat a large flat dish and place it face down on the tin, then reverse it.

This Neapolitan dish which I came across years ago at Vico Equense in Campania was served nicely browned (after a grey mullet cooked *al forno*) and cut in large slices like a cake.

PASSATO DI PATATE • potato purée

It will be clear to any cook that if one reduces the eggs to two in the recipe above, forgets to crush the breadcrumbs, and omits the *lardo*, what will emerge is a potato purée, which in itself is an excellent accompaniment to poached fish, roast saddle of hare, a *daube* of beef, or braised pheasant (p 245). Serve hot.

potatoes in the oven

A dish that might occur to anyone in possession of a *mandoline* and an earthenware casserole.

Oil or butter the casserole. Very finely slice a kilo (2¼ lb) of potatoes into it, paper thin. Sprinkle with a little salt, sliced garlic, powdered marjoram, as you go along. Just cover with milk – it will take at least ¾ litre (27 fl oz) – and strew with knobs of butter or, if you have it, goose fat.

Cook for at least an hour at the top of a moderate oven. The potatoes will emerge with a golden crust, a good accompaniment to roast goose or roast chicken. If in an economical mood, cover the surface with rashers of streaky bacon instead of butter or goose fat, to make a modest supper dish.

PATATE AL FORNO
potatoes cooked in the outdoor bread oven

The traditional feast day accompaniment to roast baby lamb seasoned with oil and rosemary in Apulia.

Peel and slice 1½ kilos (3¼ lb) of potatoes ½ cm (1/5″) thick. Rinse and dry them in a clean cloth. Take a large oven tin or *tiella* (aluminium square baking dish) and oil it fairly liberally. Place the sliced potatoes in layers on the tin, sprinkling each layer with drops of oil, a little thyme or winter savory, salt, and garlic if you like. Sprinkle the surface with a little more oil and, failing the bread oven, bake in a hot indoor oven near the top. In about 45 minutes they should be cooked and golden.

AVGÁ KE PATÁTES • eggs and potatoes

In remote Cycladic outposts where travellers arrive in summer, the proprietor of the *kapheneíon* (bar) is prepared to produce, often reluctantly, a severely restricted bill of fare during these halcyon days.

Its main cornerstone is *Avgá ke patátes*, which is basically a pan of chips over which is poured at the last moment a diluted and often limited ration of raw beaten egg. But you might also meet a plate of beans, varied occasionally by boiled goat and spaghetti or, in calm weather with fried octopus, like rubber rings, or fried anchovies; and sometimes on feast days an unexpected superb fish soup.

Through a long winter during which the proprietor relinquished all culinary pretensions and limited himself to dispensing ouzo and *ráki* like medicine and supplying mouldy bread, one was left to make what one could of a few staples and something more of eggs and potatoes, transforming the humdrum into a sumptuous dish.

4 large firm purple-skinned potatoes · olive oil
thyme · savory · salt · cloves of garlic · 4 eggs
chopped parsley · ground black pepper

Cover the bottom of a heavy frying pan with olive oil and heat it slowly while peeling and slicing very finely with a *mandoline* the large potatoes. When the oil begins to smoke, throw in the sliced potatoes, spread them evenly, sprinkle with the salt and herbs, raise the heat and cover with a large lid. In about 7 to 8 minutes the potatoes should be golden-brown on the underside and have cohered.

Turn the whole thing carefully with a spatula, sprinkle the cooked side with salt and some slices of garlic, then cook on the other side. After 7 minutes pour on the beaten eggs to which you have added a little salt, some chopped parsley, and some pepper. Tilt the pan to spread the egg evenly over the surface, prod the potatoes here and there to let the heat penetrate the egg. This takes only a few moments; the eggs should not be completely set. Divide in two and serve.

LA FRITTATA · a rustic omelette

When Dirce gave me my first lesson in Castelpoggio, the *frittata* was cooked in an earthenware casserole with projecting handle, *la padella*, which I now think is the direct descendant of the ancient Roman *patella*, of similar form, of which examples survive in bronze. (*The Roman Cookery Book*, cited under Apicius in the Bibliography, has a photograph showing one found at Pompeii.)

In those days, earthenware was expendable, being incredibly cheap, and it didn't matter when it inevitably cracked. It was a good medium because it retained the heat from the frying operation and cooked the egg mixture to perfection on the subsequently lowered gas. Unlike a French omelette, the cooking is slowed up once the eggs are in; this is anyway a more substantial dish.

A *frittata* can be made with any vegetable you like – diced potatoes, onions, red peppers, artichoke hearts, aubergines, wild asparagus, hop shoots, new shoots of old man's beard, or those of blackberry or smilax, or with the bulbs, already boiled and sliced, of the tassel hyacinth (see the Edible Weeds chapter). The next recipe serves as example.

FRITTATA DI ZUCCHINI

Wash, dry and dice 3 or 4 zucchini (courgettes) and a small onion. Pour a little olive oil into an omelette pan, and fry the zucchini and onion on a quick fire until they brown, tossing them often, adding a minimum of salt.

Beat 4 eggs in a bowl with a little salt, pepper, and some finely chopped parsley, and add a dessertspoon of *pane grattugiato* (crushed crumbs from oven-dried bread) and a dessertspoon of grated parmesan.

The egg mixture is poured over the browned contents of the pan, and the heat reduced. In a few minutes the *frittata* will almost have set.

Take a large plate, lid, or board, cover the pan, and reverse the *frittata* onto it. Then slide it back into the pan. Both sides should be brown. Serve at once, or let it cool and eat it on a picnic.

The best *frittate* are made with wild asparagus shoots, sliced up and fried, their colour turns from bronze to brilliant green. In every case the vegetable element is sliced or diced, and browned, before the eggs are poured in. There is an exception, of course; in making a *frittata* with garden peas, the peas, already cooked, are incorporated in the egg mixture.

LA TRUITA • the Catalan omelette

The Catalan omelette accommodates a diversity of vegetables like the Italian *frittata*, but is often folded and presented in the French way. Taking small artichokes as an example, the prickly Sicilian kind or the unprickly more rounded Roman kind: peel back their outer leaves (they're tough), then slice off one third of each artichoke at the top and leave a few centimetres of stem which you then trim. Slice each artichoke in half vertically, remove the little choke if there is one, with your thumbnail, then slice each half into four equal sections. Immerse in acidulated water for a few minutes, then drain dry and throw the sections into hot oil in a pan; they quickly brown. Beat up 3 eggs, season, pour into the pan, stir, and fold as for a normal omelette.

Haricot beans (already cooked), raw peppers sweet or hot, onions, boiled roots of chicory and scorzonera are all treated in the same way, as is the already mentioned and much prized wild asparagus.

The Guardian of the Temple

THE secret of cooking is the release of fragrance and the art of imparting it. Fragrance: the bay laurel, *Laurus nobilis*, a sacred tree, how brightly, how fiercely it burns. Gather its dark-leaved branches in summer if you can. Sweet the influence of rosemary, its ungainly shrubby stems bursting with pale lilac flowers. Pungent the mint trodden underfoot on the way to the orchard. Peppery and sweet the scent of wild marjoram, *origano*, self-drying in July on droughty limestone hillsides; lemon-scented the clumps of wild savory, poor man's pepper, producing its minute snapdragon flowers in August, picked by quarrymen on their way down from the quarry. Irresistible the bunches of herbs sold in the market place by an old man who bothers to gather them, shrubby sprigs of thyme nibbled by hares in high pastures and green-leaved sage, and clary. Holy the Byzantine perfume of coriander leaves and seeds, recalling the smell of incense burning in a Greek chapel perched on the spine of a bare mountain. Passer-by, grasp the invitation proffered by fennel flowers and seeds on brittle stalks leaning out from the hillside. Savour the strange sweet taste of juniper berries, blue-black, picked in September on a chalk down where nothing much else will grow. Wander through the maquis in spring when shrubby sages, thyme, rosemary, cistus, lentisk and myrtle are in flower. Inhale the fragrance of the wilderness.

I would like to transport you to the house of Maurin Bacciagalupo, the guardian of the temple of Diana at Luni. In front of his door on the plain of Luni stands the skeleton of the Roman temple. Maurin's threshing floor is divided from it only by the twisted branches of an immeasurably old vine. Looking west you see the great extent of Tyrrhenian Sea at a distance and the long line of hills which terminates in the promontory, the Punta Bianca. Looking eastwards, are the high Apuanian mountains, in springtime still capped with snow, behind which barrier lurk the mysterious backlands of the Lunigiana. On the lower slopes the mountain villages adhere to their mountain background like lumps of coral.

Maurin used to keep seven bulls. He was a bachelor as befits the guardian of this temple. In his house was a spacious kitchen with red brick floor, the high ceiling made of beams, whitewashed. There was a big hearth, a bottle gas stove, a table, chairs, a settle. Behind the settle

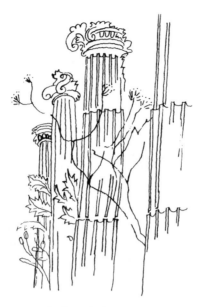

was an array of copper and aluminium pans suspended from a wooden framework on the wall. At the window was a stone sink, the drinking water kept in a large terracotta Tuscan bowl with a glaze of green marbling inside. The water was drawn from the well outside. The cheese was kept in the kitchen drawer out of the way of the cats, and the bread in the bread chest. The *cantina* across the passage was well stocked with wine, both white and red.

This man had always lived on the farm within sight of the sea and in touch with the sea breeze. The house was exposed to the moon's rise and the sun's set. He had the lilting speech of the Genoese. He had reduced his diet to a very few things because he refused to touch anything which was not genuine. This eliminated bread baked in an electric oven, industrially confected sausages and salami, cheese which had been artificially matured, wine which had been tampered with.

He prepared the meal with deliberate movements and a certain solemnity. The pasta was cooked in an enormous aluminium cauldron in a great quantity of boiling water, salted of course with sea salt. When it was *al dente* he strained it through an impressive colander at the sink, and then placing an ample white china bowl on the kitchen table, at which we were already sipping his delicious white wine, he poured in the pasta, then the sauce, and with great deliberation turned the spaghetti about with two forks to distribute the sauce. The fragrance of this sauce, whether it was a *pesto* or made of fresh tomatoes slowly simmered with garlic and herbs, was not only communicated to the pasta but to his guests. *Beato te!* Maurin.

Past'asciutta and
Pasta in Brodo

ASTA is the name for the infinite variety of forms resulting from working durum wheat-flour and water into an elastic paste or dough. When eggs are incorporated it becomes *pasta all'uovo*.

Past'asciutta is the name for the many ways of accommodating freshly boiled pasta in an appetizing sauce. The basis of this sauce may be fish, crustaceans, molluscs; flesh, fowl, game; the innards of newly killed lambs; *pancetta* (salted cuts from the stomach of the pig); a selected mushroom, vegetable or weed; the indispensable tomato; ricotta (ewe's milk cheese); or olive oil and sliced garlic.

Pasta in brodo places the emphasis on preparing a perfectly delicious broth in which, at the last moment, the pasta – delicately stuffed for festive occasions, or, simply, in the form of shells, stars, wheels, butterflies or other diverting shape – is cooked for a few minutes to give it substance. This is more often served at night.

A piquant grated cheese normally, but not always, accompanies both preparations.

Pasta al forno differs from the above in that the pasta, of a more resistant kind – macaroni, *penne, zite, cannelloni, lasagne* – is partly cooked, strained and quenched under the cold tap, before being distributed in layers in an oiled oven dish (earthenware, heavy-gauge tin or zinc), each layer being enriched with a prepared sauce and elements previously fried, with grated cheese and sliced mozzarella. The top receives more grated cheese, fine crumbs, sometimes a decoration of, say, desalted anchovies and stoned black olives. Lubricated with a thread of olive oil or curls of butter, the dish is set in a hot oven to combine its flavours and form a golden crust.

In Apulia this feast-day dish goes into the outdoor bread oven on bread-making day, which often coincides with the morning of a *festa*. As the heat of the oven is all-enveloping, *pasta al forno* receives initially, to prevent it from drying out, a more liquid sauce, and more highly flavoured, than is the norm for *past'asciutta*, and richer ingredients.

Freshly made pasta has a far greater ability to absorb flavour than the packaged kinds. Allow 150 g (just over 5 oz) per person. For dry pasta, 100 g (3½ oz) is ample. Fresh pasta takes less time to cook;

thrown into boiling salted water, it is ready when it rises to the surface. In either case, keep testing and strain the pasta the instant it reaches the *al dente* stage.

Whereas the cooking of the pasta needs only a few minutes, the preparation of a good sauce for *past'asciutta* takes time. Although there are exceptions, such as *Spaghetti colle acciughe* (p 100) and *Spaghetti colla ricotta* (p 101), it is erroneous to imagine that the whole operation can be completed in 10 minutes.

TRENETTE AL PESTO • narrow ribbon pasta with *pesto*

For the *pesto* you need a pestle and mortar and:

a bunch of basil	2 tablespoons olive oil
sea salt	2 tablespoons of grated *pecorino*
2 or 3 cloves garlic	*sardo* or parmesan
a handful of pine kernels	

Wash the basil, strip off the leaves and tear them in pieces. Pound the peeled garlic cloves with a little salt in the mortar, add the pine kernels and pound again. Put in the basil, pound some more. When all is reduced to a molecular state, add the olive oil and stir in the grated cheese.

Serve with fresh *trenette* or *tagliatelle*, cooked *al dente*.

Variations of this pesto occur well beyond the limits of the Ligurian coast where it originates. South of La Spezia, this dressing is sometimes achieved by chopping the ingredients finely instead of pounding them. Sometimes walnuts, especially in autumn when newly gathered, are used instead of pine kernels.

In speaking of fresh *tagliatelle*, I do not mean that you have necessarily made it yourself. In many towns there are *pastificii* where pasta is made daily in great variety and displayed. It is inspiring to visit a *pastificio* in Lucca, for example, and examine the delicately made confections for *past'asciutta* and *pasta in brodo*. These shops are situated in the vicinity of the Roman amphitheatre; this magnificent space is ringed round with old houses of varying sizes fitted into the husk of the amphitheatre and thus reminding one more of Canaletto than of Piranesi. For many years the interior space was enlivened by the presence of the wholesale vegetable market.

When in Venice, find your way to the garden restaurant of Locanda Montin (behind the Accademia, near San Trovaso) and sitting in an ivy-clad arbour begin the meal with *Malfatti alla panna*. These little 'badly made' envelopes of pasta stuffed with ground breast of chicken and lamb's sweetbreads are cooked like ravioli for a few moments in boiling water, are whisked out with a perforated ladle when they rise to the surface, and immersed in a cream sauce flavoured with nutmeg. This restaurant of grateful memory, and one-time haunt of D'Annunzio, has always been the patron of hungry artists; evidence of this are their teeming works which line the walls indoors.

FETTUCCINE ALLA PANNA • ribbon pasta with cream

Without having to find out if you are capable of making well these *malfatti*, cream can be used in dressing *fettuccine*, the Roman name for *tagliatelle*. For 4 people:

600 g (1 lb 6 oz) of fresh
   ribbon pasta made with eggs
50 g (2 oz) butter
half a sweet white onion, hashed
100 g (3½ oz) finely chopped
   presalata (salt rolled belly of
   pork) OR breast of chicken,
   cooked in butter and finely
   chopped

grated nutmeg
salt and ground black pepper
a handful of new peas, blanched
parsley, finely chopped
2 cloves of garlic, finely chopped
2 tablespoons of grated parmesan
½ litre (2 cups) of cream

Put the butter in a large pan and simmer the onion in it without browning. Add the chopped *presalata* or breast of chicken, some grated nutmeg, a little salt, pepper, and a few minutes later the blanched peas. Pour in the cream. Simmer on a very low heat, stirring with a wooden spoon; it will slightly thicken.

   While making the sauce, boil a cauldron of water, salt it, and cook the *fettuccine* for a few minutes. When they are barely cooked, strain them and add them to the cream sauce. Turn the pasta about with a wooden fork so that it becomes totally immersed, still on the lowest possible heat. Stir in the finely chopped parsley and garlic, sprinkle with black pepper and grated parmesan, and serve immediately.

I am not proposing recipes for the Tuscan *tordelli*, a form of *tortellini* (morsels of fine pasta rolled round thimblefuls of delicately ground and flavoured meat stuffings), because they require a manual dexterity normally found in makers of lace. Such skills can be acquired by imitation, rather than from a book.

FETTUCCINE COLLA SALSA DI FUNGHI
ribbon pasta with fungi sauce

Use *Boletus edulis* (*porcini*) or *Amanita caesarea* (*ovoli*), these fungi being the undisputed best. *Ovoli* when immature look like orange eggs; see Fungi and Michelangelo (p 208).

400 g (14 oz) ribbon pasta	olive oil
400 g (14 oz) fresh fungi	1 dessertspoon *salsa secca* (p 321)
(see above)	or tomato concentrate
1 small onion	a small glass of red wine
1 clove of garlic	1 cup reduced veal or chicken
fresh parsley	stock
fresh mountain savory	butter

Trim the stems of the fungi at the base, and clean them by wiping with a damp cloth. Chop them finely on a wooden board with a stainless steel knife. Then peel and chop the onion and garlic clove, chop the parsley and savory, and simmer all these aromatics in olive oil in a little earthenware pot. Add the tomato conserve, and after a few minutes put in the chopped fungi, shake them about in the oil, and add the wine and stock. Cook uncovered for 20 minutes, when it should achieve the consistency of a sauce. Towards the end add a knob of butter.

Boil the ribbon pasta in salted water, strain and serve on heated plates, with the sauce poured into the centre of each plate.

SPAGHETTI CON AGLIO E BURRO
spaghetti with garlic and butter

There is no pasta dish simpler than this. Nevertheless, there are, as always, two schools of thought as to how to incorporate the garlic.

The Mantuans believe that some cloves of garlic should be sliced and fried for a few moments in hot olive oil till they colour slightly. With garlic, the moment between browning and burning is brief. So, retrieved by the expert from the pan, the fried garlic is used with the addition of fresh butter to flavour the spaghetti cooked *al dente*; with or without chopped parsley and with or without parmesan.

The other school of thought cherishes the fragrance which emanates from sliced cloves of fresh garlic, particularly when it is newly pulled in June, coming in contact with hot spaghetti in a heated white china bowl in which a tablespoon of olive oil is warming. In this case, butter is lavishly added, and chopped parsley or basil, with plenty of parmesan mixed in.

SPAGHETTI COLLA SALSA DI POMODORI
spaghetti with tomato sauce

In Apulia, where I suspect a fresh tomato sauce is made daily in summer in every household, there is a perforated tin utensil, rectangular in form, for sieving the sauce, called *mattareddha* (dialect), found in weekly markets. To make a good tomato sauce, you need:

1 kilo (2¼ lb) fresh plum tomatoes	parsley, chopped
olive oil	some dried *origano*
1 sweet white onion, chopped	a bayleaf
some fronds of *sedano*	a few drops of wine vinegar
(celery grown as a herb)	sea salt
	1 teaspoon of sugar

Cover the bottom of the pan with olive oil, put in the chopped onion, the *sedano*, parsley and *origano*. Simmer for a few minutes without browning (*soffriggere*), then put in the tomatoes, which have been gently squeezed under water to release some of the pips, and the bayleaf, the wine vinegar, the salt and sugar, and cook slowly on an asbestos mat, covered. After 40 minutes, pass through a sieve and, if it has not the consistency of a sauce, reheat and reduce; then pour it over the spaghetti. Serve with grated *pecorino* or *caciotta*.

SALSA CRUDA DI POMODORI • uncooked tomato sauce

When tomatoes are newly ripe (early July), it is a pleasure to make an uncooked sauce, as follows. Pour boiling water on a kilo (2¼ lb) of firm ripe tomatoes in a bowl. Drain after 1 minute, quench with cold water and peel them. Remove the seeds and chop the flesh.

Pound in a mortar 2 or 3 cloves of garlic with a little salt, and pound in a seared, skinned and seeded hot green pepper. Pound in some leaves of basil and add the chopped tomatoes and a little olive oil. Apply this dressing (unheated) to the hot pasta the moment it has been drained, and put into a piping hot dish. This is refreshing. No cheese is added.

SPAGHETTI COLLE ACCIUGHE
spaghetti with salt anchovies

Use a fine grade of spaghetti called *spaghettini*. For 4 people, boil 400 g (14 oz) of this pasta in plenty of water and don't overcook. Wash 100 g (3½ oz) of salt anchovies in cold water, split them and remove the spine, fins etc. Wash again and chop them on a board. Put them in a small pan on the fire with plenty of olive oil and some ground black pepper. Don't overheat the oil. When it is hot, add 50 g (2 oz) of butter,

a hot pepper conserved in oil (p 317) and a very little tomato sauce. Stir with a wooden spoon. The anchovies vanish in the sauce.

Strain the *spaghettini* and put it in a heated tureen, pouring the sauce over it and distributing it by turning the *spaghettini* with two forks. Add some finely chopped parsley and garlic if you like.

SPAGHETTI COLLA RICOTTA
spaghetti with fresh ewe's cheese

In recent years at Spigolizzi a shepherd grazed his flock of sheep and a few goats on the rocky sloping land where nothing can be grown. Inevitably the sheep damage the dry-stone walls and the goats nip off the shoots of the semi-wild fig trees which produce delicious little fruits. This resulted in his coming along with rush baskets of placatory ricotta, particularly fragrant because made with a mixture of ewe's milk and goat's milk.

You eat half the ricotta fresh for lunch with plenty of black pepper and a dish of weeds or spinach. At night, you boil spaghetti in the usual way and when it is *al dente* strain it rapidly, keeping a small amount (say, a large wineglass for 2 people) of the hot liquor. This liquor is then put in the bottom of a large heated dish. The ricotta is added and, being stirred with a wooden spoon, quickly turns into a dense sauce. Chopped parsley and black pepper are put in, and a few whiskers of nutmeg, and then the hot spaghetti, which is turned with two forks to imbibe the sauce. A fragrant dish.

The sheep and goats are milked at 3 in the morning, and the ricotta is made in a cauldron in the hearth at dawn. For more about ricotta, *lu quagliatu* in dialect, see *The Land of Manfred* by Janet Ross, chapter XII.

PASTA AL FORNO • macaroni in the oven

I give the Apulian version, which is far easier to make than to explain; something to prepare at early morning when the bread oven is being fired, but you can put it in a domestic oven. Its peculiarity is the presence of minute *polpette*, meat balls, dispersed in the pasta.

800 g (1¾ lb) of *penne rigate* or *rigatoni* (short-textured macaroni)	*for the polpette:* ½ kg (1 lb 2 oz) of twice-minced horse meat (or lean beef)
200 g (7 oz) *prosciutto crudo* or *coppa*	a garlic clove
2 hard-boiled eggs	a few capers
a mozzarella cheese	salt
½ litre (18 fl oz) fresh tomato sauce, reduced	a dessertspoon of olive oil 2 fresh eggs
½ litre (18 fl oz) concentrated chicken stock	thyme chopped parsley
2 bayleaves	a brandy glass of red wine
1 soupspoon olive oil	a heap of very fine baked crumbs
2 tablespoons grated *pecorino*	1 dessertspoon olive oil
2 tablespoons grated parmesan	

Boil a cauldron of water, salt it, and cook the *penne* so that they are not quite *al dente* (i e undercooked), strain in a colander and pass rapidly under the cold tap.

Then make the *polpette*. Pound the garlic, add the capers and some salt, pound again. Liberate with the oil and add to the minced meat in a bowl. Pound the mixture. Then work in the raw eggs. Sprinkle with thyme and chopped parsley and pour in the wine.

Cover a board with crushed dried crumbs, and roll morsels of the mixture to form tiny balls (like marbles) in the crumbs to cover them. Fry them in a pan in very hot oil, shaking the pan, until brown, then drain on kitchen paper. You will have 50 *polpette* or more. Keep half of them for a *merenda*. Roll up the *prosciutto crudo* and slice it into pieces, then separate them. Peel and slice the hard-boiled eggs. Halve the mozzarella and slice the halves. Combine the tomato sauce with the chicken stock and simmer with the bayleaves.

Take a capacious earthenware dish, pour a little olive oil on the bottom, roll it round the sides, sprinkle with some fine crumbs, then put in some of the pasta, some meat balls, some slices of mozzarella, *prosciutto* and egg slices. Sprinkle with *pecorino*, add more pasta and carry on in the same way until the dish is filled to the top. Then pour on the sauce and cover the top with grated crumbs, and with the parmesan.

In this way you form a 'lid' over which is poured a thread of oil, or if you prefer crown it with flakes of butter; it has to form a golden crust. Put it in the middle of a hot oven for 30-40 minutes. You can tell when it is cooked by the aroma. Leave for 10 minutes, once taken from the oven, after which you can cut it like a cake.

LA SALSA DOPPIA • the double sauce

You can still see the huge salt-glaze dishes made in Grottaglie in which the pasta for the family was poured, dressed and then despatched, each member attacking it with a fork. Ancient practice, found equally among Cycladic Greeks – the fork was your own, the communal plate was smaller. In the Salento this custom has vanished, except perhaps among old wild countrymen, still snaring, cooking and eating badger and foxes. But the manner of presenting the pasta remains the same; it must present a splendid aspect, the colour deep red. The sauce and grated cheese are applied in the big dish in layers, then carefully mixed. Fairness must prevail.

Nowadays, whether the dish is made of *penne rigate* (a form of macaroni) or of home-made *orecchiette* (little ears) of home-grown wheat, freshly milled, the sauce must still be definitively red.

For 6 or 8 people, a litre bottle of *la salsa* (p 319) is poured into a pan in which are simmering in olive oil, chopped onion, or onion shoots, and 2 hot peppers. This, the basic sauce, goes on cooking while the pasta is prepared. Meanwhile, in addition, some just picked plum tomatoes are peeled, squeezed to expel some seeds, then simmered in oil in another pan with garlic and fresh basil leaves.

The hot pasta, drained, is poured into a large heated dish, alternated with the basic sauce and grated *pecorino*. Then all this is mixed. The separately cooked plum tomatoes are laid on top, giving it yet more colour and freshness. More grated *pecorino* then crowns the dish.

There is a gleam in our neighbour Teresa's eye when we're sitting down to a meal with her and Salvatore, and she says: *Ho fatto la salsa doppia* (I've made the double sauce). I doubt whether this double sauce has ever been recorded, yet it exists, but probably only where the summer fields are gleaming with the new tomato crop.

SPAGHETTINI COI PISELLI • fine spaghetti with peas

An early summer Venetian dish. It is only worth making with very fine
pasta and perfectly fresh young peas. For 4 people:

400 g (14 oz) *spaghetti*	salt
1 kilo (2¼ lb) new peas	leaves of mint
100 g (3½ oz) fresh butter	curls of butter
1 sweet white onion, finely chopped	

Shell the peas and blanch them in boiling water for 2 minutes. Strain,
and reserve their liquor. Melt the butter slowly in a pan, then put in the
chopped onion. Simmer for 5 minutes, then put in the peas, salt, mint
leaves, and a very little of the pea liquor.

Boil the *spaghetti* rapidly in plenty of salted water for 4 or 5 minutes,
strain and put into deep soup plates. Spoon the peas into the centre of
the pasta on each plate, with some of the sauce, and crown each centre
with a curl of butter. No parmesan with this.

PASTA IN BRODO • pasta in broth

This is the portmanteau phrase for any broth made of concentrated
stock of *vitellone* (between veal and beef) and marrow-bones, or of a
chicken carcase and veal bones, cooked with aromatics, which, being
strained and reheated for the evening meal to boiling point, has one or
two handfuls of soup pasta thrown into it and is then cooked for 5
minutes.

Pasta in brodo also refers to far more delicate creations, when on feast
days *tordelli, tortellini, agnolotti,* ravioli, *malfatti,* etc are cooked in such a
broth. In this case the little envelopes or rings of pasta enclosing
fragrant stuffings preponderate, i e there is more pasta than broth.
Always served with grated parmesan or *pecorino sardo,* almost equally
piquant.

On special occasions the *brodo* is made with *la gallina,* a two-year old
hen which has been roaming about in the back garden and naturally
produces a far more delicious broth. The bird is cooked in a capacious
pot of water, which is scrupulously skimmed while coming to the boil
and boiling, after which the aromatics – onion, carrot, celery, fennel,
salt – are added, then simmered for at least an hour. This broth is
strained in a colander through a clean cloth, and returned to the pot;
when boiling is re-established, a shell pasta is cooked in it. The hen,
hastily cut up – flurry is a concomitant of Apulian hospitality – is
served after the soup. This represents only the first cannonade in an
Apulian feast, on Easter Sunday, by tradition.

ORECCHIETTE CON LA RUCOLA • 'little ears' with rocket

A Salentine dish. Use wild rocket, *Eruca sativa* (or broccoli heads or heads of rape). Gather the plants when small, wash them well and throw into a pan of salted boiling water. Cook the *orecchiette* in another pan and drain when they are *al dente*.

Cover the bottom of a frying-pan with olive oil, add 2 hot peppers, 2 peeled cloves of garlic, sliced, and cook for a few minutes. Put the well-drained pasta and the rocket in the pan, stir with a wooden fork, mixing all together, and serve very hot with a piquant grated cheese.

Origins of Pasta

I didn't realise until the other day that the origins of pasta date at least from Roman times, though I had never been convinced by the Marco Polo story – that he brought it back from China – this rings too much like Venetian *campanilismo* (a form of blowing one's own trumpet).

An un-named journalist writing in the *Gazzetta del Mezzogiorno* reminded us that in Horace's Satire I.6, had we read it, we would have found him describing the joys of returning home to a 'tureen of leeks, chickpeas and *lagani*' (*Ad porri et ciceris refero laganique catinum*), a dish which survives in the Salento today in the form of *cece e lasagna, cece e ttria, cicere e ttria*, and *cicerittria*. One imagines that Horace's domestic slaves were Apulians, Venosa his town of origin being just across the border in Lucania; he had affection for Apulia and its industrious people.

I rapidly looked up *lagano* in Gerhard Rohlfs' magnificent *Vocabolario dei dialetti salentini* and found *lagana*. It denotes in the Salentine Greek dialect (*griko*) a sheet of pasta from which lasagne (Greek: *láganon*) are cut and made with a *laganaturu* (rolling pin). These words occur where *griko* survives, in the villages of Zollino, Sternatia, Calimera, Martano, Castrignano dei Greci, Melendugno, and Corigliano d'Otranto.

LAGANELLE

Laganelle, deriving from the rolled out pasta (*lagana*), are a rustic form of *tagliatelle*, 1½ cm wide, sometimes 2 cm, made with unrefined *grano duro* (hard wheat), home grown, very filling. The sheet of pasta is well worked, well rolled and well stretched, then floured and rolled for slicing. The resulting strips are unravelled and left to dry on floured wood or marble. You need:

500 g (1 lb 2 oz) of *grano duro* flour
3 eggs · a tablespoon of ground sea salt
a little tepid water · a *mezzaluna* for cutting
a rolling pin

Pour the flour in a mound on slab or board, make a hole in the centre and pour in the eggs, salt, and a dash of tepid water. Work into a dense paste, adding a little more water if it doesn't seem sufficiently elastic. Divide the mass into two, work each again, dust with flour and roll out into two even sheets. Sprinkle each sheet lightly with flour again, roll them up and from each roll cut 1½ cm strips with the *mezzaluna*. Unravel the strips and twist them, if you like, round a wooden knitting needle. Lay each strip or coil on a floured board to dry.

Set a cauldron of water to boil. Should you still feel like attempting the Horatian dish, then, armed with 2 cloves of garlic, 6 small leeks finely chopped and ½ kilo (1 lb 2 oz) of cooked chickpeas (p 69), some chopped parsley, olive oil, salt, and a lemon, proceed as follows:

Take a heavy pan, cover the bottom with olive oil, add the peeled garlic and the sliced leeks, simmer them till they soften, then add the chickpeas. Cook, shaking the pan, for a few minutes so that the oil impregnates the chickpeas, pour in a little of the liquor in which the chickpeas were cooked and the juice of a lemon.

Put salt into the boiling cauldron, and half the *laganelle* (the rest can be used in a more conventional way next day). In a few minutes they will be *al dente*; strain at once and add them to the leeks and chickpeas, mix well and turn into a heated earthenware tureen. Sprinkle with parsley and serve.

The leeks in this dish are wild, growing in olive fields and vineyards. Such dishes are for labouring men. On the same page of the *Gazzetta* was a not altogether startling heading: 'They [the Italians] gulp down a thousand calories too many every day.'

Horace, as usual, was pointing out the delights of the simple life.

In Sternatia, *laganelle* become *lavanedda*; in Calimera *lanedda*, so that in this village *ruittia ce lanedda* is the dish's dialect name.

According to Rohlfs, the *griko* dialects of these Salentine villages in the neighbourhood of Maglie have retained elements of ancient Greek, vanished elsewhere, which point to their origins as Homeric rather than Byzantine.

Light has been thrown on this subject of contention by a delightful man, Dr Giuseppe Toma of Maglie, who has traced the origins of certain surviving traditions to do with Holy Week – with neighbourly services to the bereaved (*parasómia*) and with the traditional form of mourning the dead – right back to the *Oedipus Rex* of Sophocles, the drama relating to Homeric times.

So one might suppose that the origins of pasta are, after all, not Roman but ancient Greek, and that it came to the Salento even before Taranto was founded by the Spartans in the 8th century BC.

When I suggested this to an Italian friend, a schoolmaster, he looked worried and said: 'Then what Marco Polo imported must have been Chinese *spaghetti*.' But I'm grateful to the unknown journalist for taking me back to Horace.

For a less 'provincial' view of pasta origins see Charles Perry's 'The Oldest Mediterranean Noodle: a Cautionary Tale' in *Petits Propos Culinaires* 9, 1981, and 'Notes on Persian Pasta' by the same author in *PPC* 10, 1982; a complex linguistic story.

But, sticking to local matters, which are also revealing, in the Salentine dish mentioned already, named *cicere e ttria*, *cicerittria*, etc (chickpeas and ribbon pasta), the word *ttria*, a rustic form of *tagliatelle*, derives also from an ancient Greek word, *itria*. *Tria* (*ttria*) is given in Rohlfs' work as '*tagliatelle* mixed with chickpeas, ritually served on 19 March, the day of San Giuseppe'.

Apart from the square or oblong sheets of pasta (*lagane*) used as a rule for *pasta al forno*, and the *laganelle* or *ttria* (rustic *tagliatelle*), you find a rustic form of *maccheroni* in which equal little strips of pasta are briskly rolled round the oiled steel ferule of an umbrella called *minchialeddi*, *minchiareddi*, *pizzicarieddi*. These are sometimes cooked together with *orecchiette*, which are little wafers of pasta moulded round the thumb to form 'little ears', the sauce settling in the depressions. A limited artisan production now finds its way into the grocers' shops in towns and villages in the Salento. But these pasta forms are basically domestic, the province of female adepts who take a pride and pleasure in creating this form of sustenance; an instance of creativity in a very ancient tradition, as I have shown.

C Queſtion de amoꝛ.
Agoꝛa nueuamente
impꝛeſſo: con algu
nas choſas añadidas.

⬥♡ Año.M.D.xlv. ❤⬥

Homage to a Classic Cook

I T is more illuminating to have as friend a gourmet who is a classic cook than to study innumerable books.

Irving Davis, when I first met him, was shocked that I had had the temerity to write on cooking before I knew him. On that occasion he engaged me in a searching discussion about fungi and finding that I had studied the subject at first hand, thereby passing a 'test', he invited me to dinner in Brunswick Square.

He had cooked a *canard à l'orange*. 'My cooking days are over,' he remarked in the face of this tangible testimony to the contrary. The aroma alone of this golden creature before it had been lifted out of the cast-iron enamelled casserole belied this statement.

His sense of perfection found complete expression in cooking. This had, in the remoter past, led to his flinging an 'imperfect' creation, another duck, out of the window in the presence of several expectant guests. This bird got inadvertently hitched onto a drainpipe, several storeys up, and had eventually to be rescued by the Fire Brigade on account of neighbourly complaints – it being high summer at the time.

At Irving's table I learned the full poetic meaning of the word 'classical', in which all forethought, selection, trouble, timing – the mechanics of creation – were erased by the disarming simplicity of the outcome, precipitating pleasure and delight.

Here was reflected that diametrically opposite conjunction of liberality and frugality which characterized his way of life, and which, incidentally, is the master-key to the art of cooking. His dishes were invocations to the ideal; his method of presenting them a celebration of his Mediterranean past. That began at the age of 23 when he and Pino Orioli opened a bookshop together in Florence in 1911. The effect was a kind of alchemy by which the past became manifest, and made me feel, in knowing him, I held the key to that lost Bohemia where Boris Koutzoff, Orioli, Douglas, Lawrence, Furbank, Beerbohm, were creatures of substance, not of reminiscence.

These 'memorable' meals were always served in the kitchen, in Brunswick Square and later at New End. I say memorable, but do I really remember them? I still see the fragile Venetian glasses into which superb clarets were liberally poured from a brittle Venetian glass decanter, and sparkling Vouvray and smoky Clos de Vougeot. I remember a single rose planted in a green Verdicchio bottle on the

mahogany table; the Chinese fish plates gaping from the dresser, the kitchen walls lined with gastronomic prints and the magnificent 'Symposium of the Gods' engraved in 1575 by Diana Mantovana from Giulio Romano's frescos in the Palazzo Te, summer palace of the Gonzaga family at Mantua, representing not a conference but a feast.

It is more difficult to recall the sequence of the dishes. The meal began simply, something prepared beforehand, so that the cook's attention could be focussed on the main event: a salad of marble beans, *fagioli borlotti*, with *ventresca di tonno* and leeks cooked *à la grecque*; or a salad of fennel, *finocchio*, with a plate of marinated anchovies; fresh asparagus, or a *peperonata*; young artichokes, or a sorrel soup, the sorrel picked in the back garden.

It proceeded on occasion with a *matelote* of eels, a *turbot à la crème*, or a lobster, followed by a salad with an admirable dressing and delicious little goat's cheeses brought back from Paris. I remember a sequence of roast birds, pheasants, grouse; braised partridges; boiled *zamponi*, *cotechini*, these last served with *pommes à l'huile*.

Between feasts he fasted.

He set as rigorous a standard of veracity in culinary matters as he practised in cataloguing books. This delightful man was equally at home in French, Italian, Latin and ancient Greek. We sometimes set off on expeditions, prompted by nostalgia for Italy and his distant past, and once in the wake of Douglas and Orioli to the 'foot' and 'heel' in search of the surviving traces of Magna Graecia. This journey was undertaken before the roadways southwards had been dreamed of, accompanied by George Gissing's *By the Ionian Sea* and Lenormant's *La Grande Grèce* and *Voyage à travers l'Apulie et la Lucanie*. As it turned out, we had little time to read; my education was pursued in conversation. Irving, having the classics by heart, was often regaling me with lines from Horace, Ovid, Athenaeus and Petronius.

Indistinguishable from an elderly Italian professor, by which appellation he was always addressed, he demonstrated the virtues of white wine in lieu of breakfast and the restorative effects of *grappa* and *Fernet Branca* in mitigating the hazards of corkscrew turns negotiated in a tiny Fiat across the mountain wildernesses of Basilicata (old Lucania). Our route was strewn with the discarded stubs of appalling Tuscan cigars. It was a shock to him that even in the south, the dusky wineshops had become so few and far between. But confidence was restored when, reaching the wine-growing country of Apulia, superb and quite unknown white wines were to be found in village *alimentari*. (Alas! this is no longer the case.)

Like the Catalan wine of the Priorat, the Apulian wine is of such strength that it is acquired to reinforce weaker wines, for the manufacture of aperitifs, or drunk on the spot. One comes at last to realise that the soil produces by natural alchemy the kind of wine that exactly corresponds to and offsets the rigours of its particular climate. Naxos in the Cyclades, the Priorat in Catalonia, the Apulian Salento produce wines of similar intensity (17 degrees) which drunk in situ are life-giving, but transported to a milder climate simply knock you out. Of course, then, I never dreamed that one day I would be responding to these rigours, living in Apulia, by making our own wine.

Irving was sufficiently eccentric to arrange his book-buying forays to coincide with the season of new peas in Florence and young asparagus, and installed himself at Sabatini's to enjoy them. Eccentricity: living according to priorities established by one's own experience.

The purchase of old manuscripts in Italy was dovetailed with the acquisition of virgin olive oil from some book collector whose cellar was as well stocked as his library, which conjunction shows that bibliophiles are inveterate gastronomes. Casks of wine and supplies of matured wine vinegar formed part of the negotiations.

It was thanks to him that I met some members of the rare world of booksellers and entered their shrines: Tamaro Damarinis, a Neapolitan octogenarian, a great collector, and Lucien Scheler, poet and publisher of Eluard in Paris. But I think especially of Galanti, a wonderful emaciated figure, whose sad face reminded me of Italy's early 19th century revolutionaries. His house at Auteuil had practically disappeared beneath static piles of priceless books. They had invaded every room, corridor of the apartment, the bath, the kitchen and what must have once been the *salon*, with the inevitability of an alluvial deposit, a lava flow. Only in one corner of Madame Galanti's bedroom could one discern the signs of normal habitation in the form of a pedestal table and two Louis XV chairs on one of which she sat, marooned, an ample Flemish figure. The books had imperceptibly curtailed the prosecution of every domestic function, leaving her staring at the clock which marked the moment of release for lunch at a nearby restaurant. Galanti, meanwhile, was unearthing incomparable treasures from underneath the bed, and then, opening an antique wardrobe, revealed a magnificent collection – not of hats – but of volumes fantastically bound by an art nouveau bookbinder.

I mention these legendary figures because there is a connection between the search for authenticity in the written and printed word and the search for it in culinary matters. The optimism which makes a book collector believe that there still is a first edition copy of Dante to be discovered also informs his approach to food – an unquenchable belief in the possibility of unprecedented experience, all part of a search for perfection. And I sometimes think that underlying his very real attachment to the Fenosas and Catalonia was a secret longing to unearth a manuscript copy hitherto unknown of the 14th century collection of recipes called 'Libre de Sent Soví', or a manuscript of the *Libre del Coch* of Robert de Nola, first printed in 1520 in Barcelona.

This is the appropriate place to record Irving Davis's historic account of the feast at Vendrell, 'the meal to end all meals' with which he terminates his *Catalan Cookery Book*, illustrated with exquisite engravings by Nicole. This event, which recurred every year, I have had the good fortune to experience twice; it took the fishermen hours of inspired labour. They arrived in the shadowy kitchen in the late afternoon with a huge basket of fish and octopus and an outsize marble mortar, and punctuated their efforts with frequent recourse to the *porró*. By the time night fell, the dishes emerged in a haze of garlic and merriment.

The Feast of the Three Fishermen of Calafell

'There are three courses: First the potatoes and fish with the *allioli* sauce. This is called the fishermen's *romesco*.
Next the dish of rice called *arrossejat* is served.
And lastly for the third course the octopi, called in Catalan *pops*.

'Four pounds (2 kilos) of rock fishes (the names of most of these fishes are unknown in England, one is the *rascassa* familiar to visitors to the Mediterranean, the others are *corballs, rata, esparrall, sàlvia*), two pounds (1 kilo) of very ripe tomatoes, two pounds of rice, eight pounds of potatoes, four heads of garlic, one pound of onions, four hot chilli peppers (dried), a slice of bread, two pounds (1 kilo) of small octopi.

'First of all take a plane to Barcelona, then drive to Calafell, then find your fishermen and go with them about four o'clock to Villanova and get them to choose the fish as it is landed.

When you return home get the fishermen to clean the rock fish and cut them up into pieces, put them in a basin and salt well. Clean the octopi thoroughly and remove their ink. Peel and cut the potatoes into slices about an inch (2½ cm) thick, cut the onions moderately fine. Peel the garlic and the tomatoes.

'First course: The Fishermen's *romesco*. In a large upright saucepan (*marmite*) brown twelve cloves of garlic in oil: as soon as the garlic is brown put in two of the chilli peppers, opened but whole from which you have removed the seeds. After two or three minutes add the slice of bread. While the bread is browning remove the peppers and the cloves of garlic and pound very fine in a mortar. When the bread is browned put it in the mortar and reduce to a fine paste. Add to this mixture a very small glass of white wine. Continue stirring and fill the mortar with water. Now add the contents of the mortar to the *marmite* making sure that the oil is smoking hot. If the bread has absorbed too much oil, add some more. Add three more mortarfulls of water.

'Here I should say that in Catalonia a mortar is far larger than those usually found in England. Allow this mixture to boil hard. Now put in the potatoes, cook hard for ten minutes and then add the rock fish and six minutes later the *picada crua*, which is made in the following manner:

'Pound two hot chilli peppers (seeded) in the mortar, add ten cloves of garlic and when finely pounded add a small glass of water. Put this mixture into the pan six minutes before the contents have finished cooking. Take the pot off the fire.

'Prepare an *allioli* sauce to be served with the fish and potatoes. Pound twelve cloves of garlic very finely, add two drops of water, and stirring continually in one direction gradually add olive oil. When the oil begins to thicken add five drops of vinegar and continue to stir adding oil until the mortar is filled with this thick garlic mayonnaise. It seems incredible that one can make a mayonnaise without eggs but the Catalan fishermen can. [Here I must interpolate that it is not only Catalan fishermen who can do this; anyone can do it, once they know it is possible. P.G.] Now pour the *allioli* into a sauce-boat and add to it about the same quantity of water which is first used to rinse out the mortar before incorporating it to thin the sauce.

'Second course: *Arrossejat*. Take a wide but not too deep pan (a *paella* in fact) put in some oil, slice up two large onions and cook them lightly, add the rice, not washed and let it cook very slowly stirring all the time until it has absorbed the oil and begins to turn a golden brown. Then add the liquor from the first pot in which the potatoes and rock fishes have cooked. This quantity of sauce should be sufficient to cook the rice but if you have any doubt add a little water, always remembering that one cup of rice requires three cups of liquid. Add a soup-spoonful of *allioli*. Cook for twenty minutes stirring often. The rice should not be overcooked and must be quite dry.

'Third course: White *pops* [curled octopus: *Eledone cirrosa*]. In a pot boil a pint of water, throw the octopi into the pot and cook them for half an hour with the lid half off. Strain them. In another pot add oil and cook the remainder of the chopped onions allowing them to brown well, then add the peeled and crushed tomatoes; as usual reduce the sauce and in it cook the octopi for about half an hour.

'Wash the meal down with *porró* after *porró* of local white wine and ask your fishermen to sing some of the songs of Catalonia. This is the last recipe in my book and is a meal to end all meals.'

Irving's book was published in 1969. Now, with the aid of Alan Davidson's fish catalogue in *Mediterranean Seafood* we can get these fishes sorted out.

CATALAN	SCIENTIFIC	ENGLISH	FRENCH	ITALIAN	GREEK
rascassa	*Scorpaena scrofa*	scorpion fish	rascasse	scorfano	scórpena
corballs	*Umbrina cirrhosa*	corb	ombrine	ombrina	mylókopi
rata	*Uranoscopus scaber*	star-gazer	boeuf, rat	pesce prete	lýchnos
esparrall	*Sargus annularis*	annular bream	sparaillon	sparaglione	spáros
sàlvia	*Trachinus radiatus*	weever	vive rayée	tracina raggiata	drákena

No one will be surprised that the meals we remember more clearly consisted of fishes grilled on little fires laid on the rocks at nightfall, lit up, by moonlight, by summer lightning and the phosphorescent shine on the dark sea.

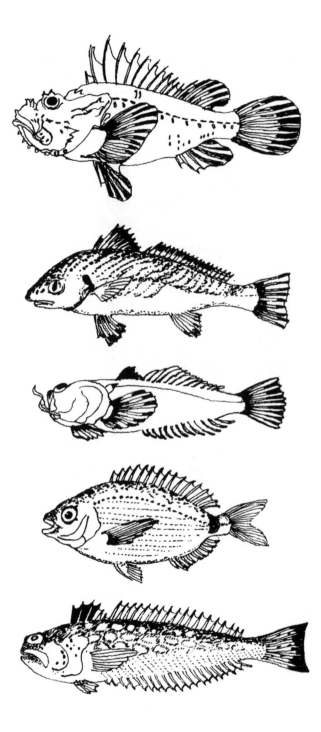

Fish, Shellfish, Crustaceans
Smoked and Salt Fish

THOUGH tempted to underline the difference between rock prawns and sand prawns and to describe how the former are employed in a risotto, and to speak of the delight of cooking full-grown scorpion fish and extraordinary John Dory (savage in appearance, delicate in taste), I have, with a very few exceptions, confined myself to giving simple ways of cooking Mediterranean fish of modest dimensions, acquired at modest cost.

Each fish for which a recipe is given has its own heading. The first name given is Catalan (C) or French (F) or Greek (G) or Italian (I), according to where I came across the method of cooking them. Then comes the English name if there is one. Names in the other languages are given in the lower part of the heading, after the scientific name.

CERNIA IMPERIALE (I) • grouper

Epinephelus guaza • family SERRANIDAE
mérou (F) • anfós (C) • rophós (G)

I shall sing the praises of this fish. Hauled out of the Ionian Sea at nightfall, from a tiny rowing boat, when the water has faded to aquamarine, it is often more than a metre long, with an enormous armour-plated head, a marine monster patterned with rust red, vermilion, bronze, gold. Quite apart from its taste, its appearance designates it as 'imperial', and qualifies it for the fate described under 'An Apulian Bachelor' (p 301).

CERNIA NERA (I) • grouper

Epinephelus caninus • family SERRANIDAE
mérou noir (F) • anfós (C) • rophós (G)

The first time I cooked a *cernia* we were camping on a beach in autumn: a little black *cernia*, impulsively acquired from a fisherman. There was no alternative but to make a fire between stones and grill it. A young man from a nearby village began to interest himself in the proceedings, fanning the fire to hasten the braise, made of scrub and pine branches gathered in the dunes.

He was shocked at the thought of grilling it. It ought, he said, to be prepared in a sauce of onions, plum tomatoes and herbs, cooked in olive oil. Impossible! We hadn't got a pan. Abashed I cleaned the fish in the sea, oiled it and, once on the grill, applied some more oil from time to time with a twig of rosemary. The young man politely withdrew and left us to eat the fish with our fingers. A very delicate fish with a taste of lobster. But one could see what he meant, it fell apart into succulent morsels.

A fish for grilling must have substance; it is the imperial *cernia* which is cut into steaks and grilled, in the same way as *pesce spada*, swordfish; that is, seasoned, oiled and set on the grill over glowing braise.

BESUC (C) · red bream

Pagellus centrodontus · family SPARIDAE
dorade commune (F) · occhialone (I) · lithríni (G)

The Catalan method of preparing this fish was shown to me by Jeanne Mandello in Barcelona.

BESUC AL FORN · red bream cooked in the oven

a red bream weighing 1½ kg (3½ lb)
salt and pepper · olive oil · 1-2 garlic cloves · a lemon
1 large onion · 3 or 4 medium potatoes
thyme · summer savory · 3 tomatoes · an oven plaque

Scale and empty the bream, then sever the gills with a sharp knife and extract them without damaging the head. Put it on a board and make three neat incisions with a knife transversely in the thickest part of the fish on one side, as far as the backbone. Put salt, a little oil and a slither of garlic in each slit, then close with a slice cut from a lemon to fit. Sprinkle with salt, pepper and olive oil when you have set the fish on an oiled enamel plaque ready for the oven.

Slice the large onion into very thin rounds and lay them on the plaque round the fish. Slice the potatoes about ½″ thick and lay them on the onions. Sprinkle with thyme, savory and a little salt. Peel the tomatoes, squeeze out the pips, lay in pieces on the potatoes, sprinkle with oil. Put the plaque fairly high in the oven, preheated and hot, and bake for ¾ hour. The vegetables cook in the oil and juices released by the fish.

PESCE IN BIANCO • fish poached with aromatics

Delicate fishes, delicate in taste and substance – like the black *cernia* and red bream described above, the *dorade grise* which has no English name, the *pagro dentice* (dentex, sea bream) and *spigola*, which is sea bass – can be poached with aromatics – thyme, bayleaves, parsley, celery, fronds of fennel, coriander (fronds or seeds), a slice of onion, a small carrot – with a glass of white wine or wine vinegar, the juice of a lemon and a slither of its zest, a tablespoonful of olive oil and sufficient water to immerse the fish in a covered pan. This is brought slowly to the boil, then barely simmered till tender, and left to cool in its liquor.

Serve with an *aïoli* sauce, with *allioli* (see recipes below), or simply with oil and lemon slices. Two more sauces follow which are good with fish.

The Italian green sauce, *salsa verde*, is excellent with poached fish, whereas the second version of *romesco*, the Catalan fisherman's sauce (p 121), is suitable for fishes grilled or roasted.

AÏOLI

Aïoli is achieved in the same way as mayonnaise, but first crush 4 or 5 peeled garlic cloves in the mortar with a little sea salt to a fine paste, then add two drops of water before introducing the egg yolk, and the olive oil drop by drop. (Two egg yolks are capable of absorbing about ½ litre / 18 fl oz of olive oil.) Acidulate with a little wine vinegar; or, if you prefer, with lemon juice, but in this case delay its application until the last minute or it will blanch the colour of the sauce, a dense lustrous yellow.

ALLIOLI

Allioli is the Catalan sauce discussed in 'Chopping and Pounding' (p 35) and illustrated in 'The Feast of the Three Fishermen of Calafell' (p 113). This sauce, most welcome in hot weather, is at its best when garlic is freshly pulled (i e not yet dried) in June. The heads of garlic are sometimes grilled beforehand in the ashes of a wood fire, unpeeled.

Using a marble mortar, pound seven or eight peeled garlic cloves with sea salt to a perfect pulp. Add two drops of water, stir again and begin pouring the olive oil drop by drop. You will obtain a dense pale sauce. Stir in a few drops of wine vinegar.

This sauce sometimes receives, once the garlic has been pounded, the addition of a few spoonfuls of white breadcrumbs, previously soaked in wine vinegar, then squeezed, and pounded; or a substantial slice of bread fried in oil, then pounded in. In both cases finely chopped single-leaved parsley is added and similarly pounded.

This produces a pungent paste which is then diluted with the juices of a fish baked in the oven and further lubricated with olive oil and lemon juice. The sauce is served in the mortar to accompany the baked fish.

Perhaps here I should recall Josep Pla's remark: Mayonnaise is to *allioli* as lamb is to lion.

The Greek version of *allioli* is called *skordaliá*.

SALSA VERDE • green sauce

a handful of fresh parsley • a clove of garlic
a dozen capers • 2 anchovies, desalted and filleted
a slice of bread pared of its crust and soaked in wine vinegar
black pepper • olive oil

Finely chop the parsley. Pound the peeled garlic with the capers and anchovies in the mortar; add the soaked bread, squeezed of excess vinegar; and pound again. Chop the parsley, pound it in, then season with black pepper, and liberate the mixture by adding several dessert-spoons of olive oil, stirring. Used not only with poached and grilled fish, but with boiled meats – see *Il bollito misto* (p 274).

This sauce is of extremely antique origin and crops up in diverse forms in ancient manuscripts: in the Catalan *Sent Soví* as *jurvert* or *salsa vert*; in 'Le Petit Traité de 1300' as *Savor verte*; in Le Viandier (ms Sion) as *Saulce vert*; in 'The Forme of Cury' as *Verde Sawse*; and in Robert de Nola as *Jolivertada* and *Salsa verda*. I have this from the learned notes of Dr Rudolf Grewe, editor of the *Sent Soví*.

Here is a recipe (CLXVI) from the *Sent Soví* I have roughly deciphered:

To make *jurvert* [ie parsley or green sauce] take parsley and sweet marjoram and sage and mint; and cut them fine and pound them well. And put in two cloves of garlic and toasted bread, soaked in vinegar, and hazelnuts and walnuts and yolks of egg. And when it is well pounded, moisten with a jet of oil and then with vinegar. And then add honey or cooked grape must, according to use.

Dr Grewe is not sure whether the egg yolks are raw or previously boiled, nor whether this sauce is 'emulsified' or merely mixed. A mystery one will solve by making it.

ROMESCO • the Catalan fisherman's sauce

One can say that *romesco* is a development of the Catalan *sofregit* (p 31) in which fish (and meat) are normally cooked, but far more and more varied ingredients are used. So in the first recipe you are going to prepare the sauce in which fish of substance are to be cooked after being generously sliced.

The variations of this sauce are legion, secrecy surrounds the method and there is no common agreement among fishermen or cooks about its creation. The annual *romescada* at Cambrils near Tarragona is in fact a kind of challenge to fishermen to produce the 'best' *romesco*. Four thousand people may turn up to participate in the contest (as onlookers) and a white night is spent by restaurateurs to prepare for the multitude. The master *romesco*-makers set to work, crouching over their mortars, at little stands in the dazzling April light, engulfed by an excited throng.

FIRST RECIPE. Select any one of the following fish: *orada* (gilt-head bream), *rap* (angler-fish), *remol* (brill), *llobarro* (sea bass), *rajada* (ray). Clean the fish and slice into generous pieces.

a good slice of bread • olive oil • 3 cloves of garlic
3 or 4 large tomatoes, grilled on a woodfire, then peeled and seeded
12 grilled almonds • a large glass of golden wine
a soupspoon of paprika • a very little hot chilli pepper powder
a teaspoon of wine vinegar

Put a little oil in a pan and fry the slice of bread. Pound this bread in a large marble mortar, then add each ingredient listed above in the order given, reducing everything in turn to a fine smooth paste. The golden wine should preferably come from the Priorat – see p 51.

Put the fish slices in a shallow pan. Then empty the contents of the mortar into the pan in which the bread has fried, and cook in the oil for one minute, stirring hard. Cover the fish slices with this sauce and cook for 20 minutes or so on a slow fire.

SECOND RECIPE. Here is another version, employed as a sauce for a fish grilled on a wood fire or cooked by oiling it and putting on the top of the hot range (Aga or similar) to 'roast' on both sides. This is *Peix a la planxa*.

Suitable fish: *salpa* (French *saupe*, Italian *sarpa*); *mujol* (grey mullet); *gall* (John Dory); *peix espasa* (swordfish) grilled in slices.

> 40 grilled almonds · 3 cloves of garlic grilled in wood-fire ash
> a small slice of raw onion · 1 *carquinyoli* (a hard dry biscuit)
> 1 teaspoon of sweet paprika · chopped parsley
> a little hot red chilli pepper powder · 1 teaspoon of wine vinegar
> 3 or 4 tomatoes grilled on the wood fire · olive oil

Put all these ingredients except the oil in a large mortar in the above order, and pound energetically so that each is reduced to a molecular state. Bind with olive oil and stir the sauce with a wooden spoon. Serve in the mortar to accompany the grilled or roast fish.

The paprika, *pimentón*, is made from sweet pimento peppers, usually the kind called *pebrots de romesco*.

ZUPPA DI PESCIOLINI DI SCOGLIO · soup of little rockfish

If you have ever contemplated the bright eyes, the spines, the scales, the colours – rose-red, vermilion, bronze, black, viridian – of freshly caught little rockfish piled on a platter on a fishmonger's stall and wondered what you'd do with them, this is what people in the Salento do:

1 kg (2¼ lb) rockfish	some green celery and
3 peeled cloves of garlic	parsley leaves
a handful of peeled and	some fronds of fennel
seeded plum tomatoes	some sprigs of basil
1 hot green pepper halved	a bayleaf
and seeded	2 glasses of water
olive oil	salt

To deal with the rockfish, about 8-10 cm long, you need a pair of scissors. Each fish is carefully scaled and gutted, the spiky gills are snipped out, and the fierce little spines which are fins are removed with the scissors. This is rather fiddly. The fish are then washed.

The garlic is browned in olive oil in a heavy pan, and then removed. The tomatoes are torn in pieces and dropped into the oil with the green pepper. While they cook, the leaves of celery, parsley, fennel, basil and the bayleaf are roughly torn (not chopped) and go into the pan, followed by the water and the salt. The pot is simmered for 10 minutes with the lid on, then left to cool. The little fishes are then put in, raising the heat to bring the liquor quickly to the boil, are boiled vigorously for 3 minutes, then simmered for a further 7 minutes, with the lid on.

Served in a large dish in their strained liquor, aromatic and not much of it. You eat the delicious but bony fishes with your fingers and mop up the liquor with bread.

Is this infanticide? Are these rosy scorpion fish of a dwarf kind like the brownish *Scorpaena notata* (see *Mediterranean Seafood*, p 146) which also appear on the fishmonger's platter or, if left in the sea would they grow up?

This question applies to the red gurnards, weevers, diminutive bream, star-gazers and rainbow wrasse, included in this soup, child-size. I can only say that the people of the Salento (like the Naxians) regard what is small as 'theirs', and indeed turn up their noses at larger fish.

The prevailing custom for rockfish of more respectable dimensions is to cook them in the way described above but increasing the aromatics and the amount of liquor. The ensuing broth is used to flavour the tomato sauce for ribbon pasta.

In my view this is sacrificing the essential (quintessential) taste of this broth to the concept of substance. The Sculptor is not of this opinion. Those who hold, as he does, the opposite view should turn to Alan Davidson's above-mentioned book for a number of refined pasta dishes based on fish, molluscs and crustaceans.

PUPIDDU, PUPILLU, ZERRO (I) • picarel

Spicara smaris • family CENTRACANTHIDAE
gerret (C) • marída (G)

That these tiny fish (3″ long, 7½ cm) are prized in the Salento is perhaps due to the ancient Greek connection. That they are caught in shoals at Leuca and therefore need conserving, explains the *a scapece* method of preparing them. They are the offspring of the picarel and their second name derives from Latin: *pupillus* = little orphan.

The Presicce fishmonger is convinced that *pupiddi* are the females of the *vopa* (bogue, p 129), but everything points to his being wrong, including their more pointed noses.

See the Venetian *Sardoni in saor* (p 128) for the probable origin of the method of conserving them.

PUPIDDI A SCAPECE • marinated picarel

1 kg (2¼ lb) picarel
flour • olive oil • 3 tablespoons of white crumbs
2 cloves of garlic • a bunch of mint
a beaker of white wine vinegar (enough to souse the fish)
salt • 5 or 6 saffron 'threads'

The fish are not gutted. Wash, drain and dry them, then shake in white flour. Fry them in hot oil, drain on absorbent paper and set them in an earthenware dish, interspersed with the white crumbs. Peel and chop the garlic very fine, and chop the mint. Put both these in a pan with the wine vinegar, a little salt and the saffron 'threads', bring to the boil, infuse for a few minutes, then pour this liquor over the fish and put the dish in a cool place till next day, covered.

At Leuca and Gallipoli in autumn they are prepared in quantity in wooden tubs and sold on Saints' Days, but, as saffron is expensive, they now are coloured with turmeric (see under Saffron, p 334). Like *Sardoni in saor*, the Venetian dish (p 128), they keep for at least 10 days.

Neapolitan words for marinating fish: *ascapecia, schibbeci, scabeci*. Calabrian: *schipeci*. Catalan: *escabetx*. These peculiar words derive from the Arab *iskebêğ* and antique Arabic *sikbâğ* (= marinated meat). I learn this from Gerhard Rohlf's *Vocabolario dei dialetti salentini*. It is confirmed by Dr Rudolf Grewe in his notes in the *Sent Soví*, where three recipes occur for treating fried fish with *escabeyg*, with *esquabey*. In mediaeval times the dish was much more highly seasoned, and sometimes the marinade was sweetened with honey, the dish always served cold. In the *Libre del Coch* of Robert de Nola the method recurs: item 211, *Bon Escabelx*, in which it is declared that the ideal fish to submit to the procedure is *pagell* (pandora) or *déntol* (dentex, sea bream).

CEFALO (I) grey mullet		CEFALO DORATO (I) golden grey mullet
Mugil cephalus	family	*Mugil auratus*
llissa, mujol (C)	MUGILIDAE	alifranciu (C)
képhalos (G)		mixinári (G)

Grey mullet, also called *muggine* in Italian, are probably the most inexpensive of the fish of size, being very common in the Mediterranean. There is no better way of cooking them than by roasting over a slow braise. The procedure is illustrated in the next recipe.

CEFALO SULLA BRACE • grey mullet on the braise

The fish should weigh at least 1 kilo (2¼ lb). Leaving on the scales, you remove the gills from the head and, making a small incision in the stomach, draw out the gut. Replace the liver in the cavity after removing the sac of gall, and put in a frond of rosemary. Pour over the fish on a dish a small quantity of wine vinegar, red or white, and a little oil.

Put a grid on a tripod over a glowing fire, lay the fish on it and cook for 5 minutes on either side. Turn again and baste by dipping a twig of rosemary into the vinegar and oil and brushing the fish with it. The fire having died down a little by now, cook for another 10 minutes on each side (30 minutes in all), basting from time to time. Place on a board; the skin and scales can be removed entire by lifting with a spatula. Serve with olive oil and lemons, or with *salsa verde* (p 120).

If by good fortune you see that the *cefalo* has a golden spot beside its eye and a sheen faintly golden instead of the silver found in the ordinary grey mullet, pounce upon it. The golden grey mullet has more substance and a far better taste, probably from frequenting deeper waters. The *cefalo dorato* arrives in shoals in the Ionian in late September in search of warmer shallow water in which to spawn, drawn from the deeper Adriatic by the presence of freshwater springs along the coast from Leuca to Gallipoli (see Congedo, *Salento Scrigno d'Acqua*, in the Bibliography). These fish have the most delicious roe.

Cook them as above, first removing the roe. Put this in a strainer, plunge into boiling water, quench with cold water, remove the membrane and put the roe into a mortar with 2 pounded cloves of garlic and a little sea salt. Pound together, then add the juice of a lemon, stirring, and a little olive oil. This makes a perfect sauce for the roast fish. You can add to it very finely chopped parsley or coriander leaves if you wish.

LAVARELLO (I) • houting (or whitefish)

Coregonus lavaretus • family COREGONIDAE

Lavarelli are the southernmost representatives of this species, which is found in many parts of Europe, mainly in lakes but also venturing out into the Baltic Sea. Members of the family are known collectively as 'whitefish', and are related to the salmon family.

In Italy *lavarelli* are inhabitants of Lago di Garda, but they are also found in the lakes of the Haute Savoie, where they are called *lavarets*. Gertrude Stein and Alice B. Toklas, lodging in the Hotel Pernollet at

Belley for several summers; ordered these fish every night (writers thrive on monotony). Gertrude Stein had a horrid little black dog called Byron, I have no doubt that she fed it on *lavarets*. I have a very high opinion of Gertrude Stein: in *The Autobiography of Alice B. Toklas* she succeeded in painting an altogether convincing picture of Picasso, Braque and Matisse in their youth in Paris. I delight in what she has to say about métier.

LAVARELLI SULLA GRATICOLA

La graticola is a grid-iron but it can also mean a grill. Roman grid-irons (Latin *craticola*) were found in several hearths in Pompeii; they had probably already been one of the conveniences of the Iron Age.

I mention these delicacies, and this way of cooking them, as so many people visit the Italian lakes and may wish to search them out; a delight of inns round Lago di Garda, they are grilled whole on magnificent olive wood fires, set on raised hearths under monumental chimney-pieces and achieve an incandescence when there is neither flame nor smoke.

The fish are served with the marks of the iron grill on their delicate skin, their flesh is pink, and they are accompanied by Garda olive oil, fresh lemons and, separately served, a golden slab of grilled polenta (p 225).

sardines · SARDELLE E ACCIUGHE · anchovies

Sardina pilchardus	*Engraulis encrasicolus*
family CLUPEIDAE	family ENGRAULIDAE
sardina (C) · sardélla (G)	anxova (C) · gávros (G)
sarda, sardina (I)	acciuga, alice (I)

To return to more frugal themes: Byron to Trelawney: '. . . you scorn my lenten fare, but come back soon, I will despatch my salad and sardines, and then we will discuss a bottle of hock and talk over matters . . .'

Fresh sardines and gleaming anchovies provided the fundament of Mediterranean fish markets, both in terms of quantity and modest price. (Their numbers have declined in recent years, which is reflected in their price.) When they were abundant they were 'too cheap' to be found in restaurants; one had to penetrate into a *vini* or an *osteria* for working men, often combined with an eating-place near a fish market, to find them. You enter a crowded bar, thread your way through the vociferous male company and seek refuge in a farther room where oil-cloth covered tables promise restoration. Here sardines or anchovies are served which have been cleaned, dried, 'shaken in flour and rapidly deep-fried, then sprinkled with salt; served with hunks of bread in a basket, a bottle of wine vinegar being plonked on the table and a *quarto di vino* (¼ litre of rough red wine).

At the fishmonger's the sardine is recognized by its blue-green sheen, its large papery scales, and 'stubby' appearance. The anchovy, more slender, more pointed nose, blue-black its back and silvery its sides, has smaller, far more fragile scales. If sardines or anchovies don't positively shine, don't buy them.

SARDINES ABRUSADES • grilled sardines

I give the Catalan version, being less familiar. You need: a double grill with handles, 200 g (7 oz) of sardines per person, thyme, rosemary, olive oil.

Behead, gut, scale the little fish, preferably under a running tap. Then run your thumb down each cavity and with a pinching movement gingerly draw out the backbone, starting at the head end, so that you can open the fish out without splitting it in two. You stop short of the tail. A little practice and this operation is simplicity itself. Dry on absorbent paper. Then sprinkle the exposed area with powdered thyme, rosemary and a few drops of oil.

Set the prepared fish neatly within the double grill, folded and secured. Grill rapidly over the flames of an outdoor fire for a few minutes on each side. Serve with oil and wine vinegar for those who want them.

Fresh anchovies can be grilled in exactly the same way.

ACCIUGHE ALLA MARINARA • anchovies another way

200 g (7 oz) anchovies per person • olive oil
the juice of a lemon • chopped parsley • salt and pepper

Prepare the anchovies the same way as for *Sardines Abrusades* (above). Cover the bottom of a large frying pan with olive oil, put in the fish (unfloured), sprinkle each one with black pepper and chopped parsley and very little salt, squeeze the juice of the lemon over them and simmer very gently in olive oil. The flesh will turn white.

Remove them with a spatula and fan them out on a large dish on which you have placed two or three fig leaves.

SARDONI IN SAOR • marinated sardines

This is the poor man's *matafame* (hunger-killer) to be found in *rosticcerie*. A Venetian way of temporarily conserving fish, which are sold from little stalls in winter in Venice, Vicenza, Padua and Treviso with a comforting slab of polenta. It probably originated from the ancient Roman discovery that hot vinegar poured over fried fish conserved it. Versions of this process are found in many parts of the Mediterranean (see *Pupiddi a scapece*, p 124) and the method, even if originally Roman, seems to have been transmitted by the Moors.

The Venetian recipe was demonstrated with some ceremony to us by the Mantuan painter Ugo Sissa — men take cooking very seriously, especially when they are gastronomes. Having underlined the importance of the candied peel, he placed the earthen dish outside on a shaded window-sill. Three days went by before we were allowed to enjoy this dish together.

As the sardines improve with keeping, you make more than will be eaten at one sitting.

1 kg (2¼ lb) fresh sardines • flour • olive oil
2 large onions • ½ litre red wine vinegar
a few pine kernels and a few seedless raisins
a piece of candied lemon peel, chopped

Leaving the heads on, clean and scale the sardines, dry them and shake them in flour. Cover the bottom of a heavy pan with olive oil, heat it, and gently fry the fish so that they turn golden. Put them in an earthenware dish, having first drained them.

Slice finely the onions in rounds and simmer them in the oil until they are transparent. Pour in the red wine vinegar, already heated to boiling point, add the pine kernels, raisins and candied peel.

Pour this hot over the sardines, cover the dish and put it in a cool place. Leave to marinate for two or three days, time for the fish to imbibe the liquor, and turn them over once or twice.

Serve with a salad of red chicory (*rosso di Treviso*, p 167).

Very small eels are cooked whole in exactly the same way.

The Catalan version, *Sardines en escabetx*, varies in that the sardines are not floured before frying, and the less exotic seasoning consists of bayleaves, paprika, unpeeled garlic cloves, to flavour the wine vinegar. It is also applied to pilchards, sprats, smelts, tiny eels.

VOPA · bogue

Boops boops · family SPARIDAE
boga (C) · gópa (G)

Just as in Apollona in Naxos, when the caique sailed away with the fish of size, the inhabitants were left with a plate of bony little fishes, so in Apulia I find a deep-seated conviction that the small fish, sardines, anchovies, *vope*, and the minute rockfish are the 'destiny' of working people. The fish of size are something they ignore, their names, their nature and how to cook them. This is confirmed in village markets in summer, where a crowd of people, mostly men, are gazing at a great variety of fish but not acquiring them. Poverty, a tradition now reversed, has severely limited both their choice and their approval, although, strangely enough, they spend fortunes on meat as a symbol of prosperity.

The bony bogue is painstakingly scaled, cleaned, its gills are removed, it is washed, dried, and shaken in flour, then deep-fried.

It is also grilled, and sometimes is prepared *in sughetto*, that is cooked in a little oil and water with celery leaves, a few peeled and seeded tomatoes, garlic, salt, taking a few minutes only, and served cold.

VOPE CON PATATE
bogue (or anchovies, sprats) with potatoes

½ kg (1 lb 2 oz) of *vope*, cleaned, scaled, fins snipped off
say, 8 small waxy new potatoes, sliced ½ cm thick
olive oil · salt and pepper · a little grated nutmeg
2 small glasses of white wine and 2 of water

Pour a little oil on the bottom of a wide pan, put in the sliced potatoes, sprinkle them with salt and pepper and a little grated nutmeg, and pour over them a few drops of oil. Place the cleaned *vope* on top. Sprinkle a little more oil on the fish, salt and pepper, then pour in the wine and water. Cover the pan and set on a low heat.

In 10 minutes or so the potatoes are tender, most of the liquor has been absorbed and the fish are cooked but unbroken. The sign is that their protuberant eyes are white.

Anchovies and very small mackerel can be cooked in the same way. The best *vope* come from Italy's Land's End, Santa Maria di Leuca, once the sanctuary of the White Goddess. For 'the most comprehensive and inspired account' of this Divine Being, see page 70 et seq in *The White Goddess* of Robert Graves. Divinity has many aspects; in one of them she is Io, the Moon Cow, and gave her name to the Ionian Sea.

VERAT (C) • mackerel

Scomber scombrus • family SCOMBRIDAE
sgombro (I) • scoumbrí (G)

Catalans regard the sardine as the best fish to come out of the Mediterranean in spring and most particularly in the second half of April, which is also the season of new peas. But, of the so-called blue fish, all distinctly oily, the mackerel, though less esteemed, is the most nutritious and is at its best in June and July.

VERAT

I must emphasize that the mackerel used for *verat* are small and superlatively fresh, blue-black. Cooked by Anita in the garden at Vendrell:

Clean, decapitate and carefully open out the fish (as described on p 127), removing most of the backbone but leaving 3 cm or so at the tail end. Lay the opened fish on a board and sprinkle each with paprika, black pepper, salt, sliced garlic and chopped parsley. Squeeze lemon juice over them, cover them and leave them for two hours before grilling. Grill on a fierce fire, using a hinged double grill, on both sides for a few minutes. Served on their own, followed by a green salad.

COZZA (I) • mussel

Mytilus galloprovincialis • family MYTILIDAE
musclo (C) • mýdi (G)

Eating mussels raw is an Apulian addiction and, long before the rocky little Ionian coastline had been transformed by summer villas, on summer evenings crowds of people, entire families, congregated round little bivouacs made of bamboo, to consume them with bread and wine. Inheritance from mesolithic times (see Apropos of a Salt Herring, p 149).

Mussels can no longer be eaten raw. They are often cooked to flavour spaghetti, or can be used with prawns in a risotto. There is a delightful way of preparing them – which every Apulian woman knows – which I learned from the proprietor of the *Pesce Fritto* at Taranto, made with mussels, large, delicate, of a wonderful orange colour, dragged from the Mare Piccolo.

COZZE AL FORNO • stuffed mussels in the oven

9 or 10 mussels per person
a clove of garlic • finely chopped parsley • olive oil
2 tablespoons of grated parmesan
a cupful of *pangrattato* made by drying a stick of white bread in
the oven and rolling it with a bottle to a fine powder

Put the crumbs into a bowl and add a handful of chopped parsley, the garlic hashed fine and the parmesan.

Wash, scrub and beard the mussels, put them in your widest pan with the lid on and shake over a very hot flame. They should open in 3 or 4 minutes; discard the ones that don't open.

Take them out, remove the upper shells and set the shells containing the mussels on an oiled oven dish, freeing each mollusc from its shell by a quick jab with a sharp knife. Filter the rendered liquor to eliminate any residual sand and moisten the breadcrumbs with it, so that they are moist not soggy. Cover the mussels in their shells with this preparation, sprinkle each shell with a few drops of oil, then put into a hot oven to brown for a few minutes, or under the grill.

This dish is served at the beginning of a festive meal and is often followed by lamb or kid roasted in the oven and served with sliced golden 'roast' potatoes, the result of cooking them in olive oil in the same hot oven.

MUSCLOS • a Catalan dish of mussels

2 kg (4½ lb) of mussels
3 tablespoons olive oil • 2 onions • 3 ripe tomatoes
½ coffeespoon paprika • a clove of garlic • parsley • salt and pepper

Something simple to make and serve cold on a summer evening.

Wash, scrub and beard the mussels. Change the water several times. Put them into a large pan, cover and shake it on a hot flame. When they have opened, take them off the fire, discard the upper shells, and arrange the mussels in their half-shells on a large flat white dish. Strain and reserve the liquor.

Prepare a *sofregit* by heating the olive oil in a pan, hash the onions very fine and slowly brown them in the oil. Add the tomatoes peeled and crushed, simmer for half an hour on a low heat while the liquor from the tomatoes evaporates. Then pour a little of the liquor from the mussels into this sauce and add the powdered paprika, black pepper, and garlic and parsley finely chopped. Taste before adding salt, if need be, and pour this sauce over the mussels.

CALAMARS (C) · squid

Loligo vulgaris · family LOLIGINIDAE
calamaro (I) · kalamári (G)

THE CATALAN WAY: for 4 people have 1 kg (2¼ lb) squid, also soda water, flour, olive oil.

Clean the squid in a bowl of water. Pull out the heads with their crown of tentacles, and discard what is thus drawn from the 'bag' (body) by severing at the neck. Fish out the rest of the contents of each 'bag', the ink sacs and the transparent cartilage. Then peel off the fine purplish outer skin which covers them. Pinch out the eyes and 'beak' from the heads. Throw away the water and rinse the cleaned squid. Then cut the bags into rings and the head and the tentacles into pieces. Moisten them with a jet from the soda siphon. Shake in a cloth in flour and throw them into very hot olive oil in a frying pan and cook till golden, 6 or 7 minutes. Drain and serve with lemon slices.

POLIPETTI, MOSCARDINI, FRAGOLINE DI MARE, SEPPIOLE (I) • little cuttlefish

Sepiola rondeleti • family SEPIOLIDAE
sipió (C) • soupítsa (G)

I sometimes see the portly and immaculate form of a *carabiniere*, renowned as a dedicated *buongustaio* (gourmet), bending over the tiniest cuttlefish on the fishmonger's slab to examine these delicacies before buying them; they look rather like bleached sea anemones.

Clean them thoroughly under water in a bowl (see *Calamars*, above). Prepare an appetizing *sughetto* (little sauce) with a chopped white onion complete with shoot, simmer it in olive oil – it quickly softens. Then add some fronds of parsley or celery, torn apart, two or three tomatoes (peeled, seeded, then fragmented) and a slither of lemon zest. Then put in the tiny cuttlefish with a small wineglass of white wine and one of water. Cook on a lively heat for say 10 minutes, then leave to cool in their juice. Eat them with bread and black olives for lunch.

POLPO, POLIPO (I) • octopus

Octopus vulgaris • family OCTOPODIDAE
pop, pops (plural) (C) • ochtapódi (G)

Octopuses, a pleasure to cook if they come straight out of the sea, where their bags may have already been emptied by a thoughtful underwater fisherman. Make sure, then remove the eyes and 'beak'.

A daunting object. What do you do?

A Milanese diver's view: a small octopus weighing 1 kilo (2¼ lb) does not need beating. Wash it and put it in a solid pot, barely cover with cold water, secure the lid and boil rapidly for no more than seven minutes. Take it out. Rub off the outer pinkish skin with a little sea salt, rinse, then chop the tentacles into neat pieces and slice the bag. Simmer for 15 minutes with aromatics (see *Polpo in umido*, below) and serve cold as a *primo piatto*. Thirst provoking.

A Salentine diver is absolutely certain that no water is required for the preliminary cooking, it provides its own. You put it in an earthenware pot and simmer, covered, very slowly for half an hour (it exudes its own juice which then evaporates). Shake from time to time. Take it out, peel it, chop it up and proceed as below.

Octopuses of size are normally bashed on the rocks. The fisherman turns the bag inside out, thus emptying it, and holding it dashes the tentacles against the rocks. Should an unbeaten octopus arrive in the kitchen, you rub it on a ribbed old-fashioned washboard before putting it in the pot. Cook as above and cut it up. If the octopus is fresh, both these ways work.

POLPO IN UMIDO • octopus cooked with aromatics

Having adopted one or other of the methods outlined above for dealing initially with the octopus, prepare some aromatics: two or three peeled garlic cloves; chopped fronds of wild fennel; coriander leaves if you grow the plant, otherwise parsley and celery leaves. Add a few coriander seeds; two or three peeled tomatoes, seeded; and half a green hot pepper, seared and seeded. You don't need salt.

Heat some olive oil in a heavy pan, throw in the aromatics, simmer for a few minutes, then add a glass of white wine and a glass of water, put in the cut up octopus and a tablespoon of wine vinegar. Cook fairly rapidly for ¼ hour; taste a piece and, if it is not yet sufficiently tender, simmer for a while longer on a low heat, then leave to cool and serve. An excellent dish in very hot weather.

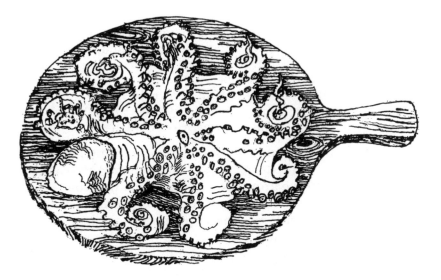

PSARÓSOUPA TOU KYRÍOU MANÓLYI
Kyrío Manólyi's fish soup

When speaking rather gloomily of culinary prowess in remote Cycladic outposts (p 90), I mentioned the feast day occurrence of 'an unexpected superb fish soup'. This is it, as made in Apollona by the owner of the quayside café.

It is a simple way of cooking fish and vegetables in one utensil, the customary large black pot, and results in a soup which has been thickened with raw egg yolks and the juice of a large fresh lemon, served hot in deep soup plates, and a platter of fish with vegetables, which follows.

The reluctant fisherman, Kapetánios, having excelled himself on such occasions, supplied Manólyi with grey mullet (*képhalos*), sea bass (*lavráki*), red gurnard (*capóni*) and John Dory (*Christósparo*). These fish, scaled and cleaned, went whole into the pot. Some substantial slices of conger eel (*mougrí*), moray eel (*smérna*) unskinned, or skinned and cleaned dogfish (*skyláki*, commonly caught at all times) were thrown in on top.

For 4 people you would need at least 2 kilos of whole cleaned fish selected from the fish mentioned above, plus some slices of unskinned and cleaned conger eel or moray eel which lend a certain unctuousness to the broth. It is the use of various different fish that makes it so good. The other ingredients:

vegetables:	2 onions, 1 celery heart, 4 large potatoes, 4 carrots, ½ kg (1 lb) peas, 3 tomatoes (peeled and seeded)
aromatics:	a handful of finely chopped coriander leaves, a sprig of thyme
seasoning:	salt and black pepper
the liquor:	a glass of strong Naxian wine (golden), 4 tablespoons of olive oil, 1½ litres (54 fl oz) water
for the soup:	3 egg yolks, juice of a large fresh lemon

Put the olive oil in the bottom of a large pot or marmite, neatly slice up the vegetables (reserving the peas), simmer them in the oil, then put in the cleaned fish, add the aromatics, and pour on the wine.

Bring the water to the boil in a separate pan, pour it onto the fish in the large pot, season with salt and pepper, raise the heat to bring the pot to the boil, then reduce the heat and cover. Poach gently for 20 minutes. After 10 minutes have passed, put in the peas.

Strain off the broth into another pan, holding back the contents with the lid. Then slide the fish and vegetables onto a large dish. Beat up the egg yolks with the lemon juice in a basin, then, while stirring, pour in a cupful of hot broth. Return the thickened liquor to the pan containing the broth, stirring continuously, but off the fire. Serve at once, and present the fish and vegetables on their platter at the same time.

ASTAKÓS (G) • spiny lobster

Palinurus mauritanicus • family PALINURIDAE

Three of these giants were hauled out of the deep by sponge-divers (*sfungarádes*) from Kálimnos who came sponge-fishing round Naxos during the fortnight of calm weather (halcyon days) in November, in a tiny vermilion boat.

These spectacular creatures (about 50 cm long) were individually thrown into an iron cauldron of sea water and cooked (40 minutes) on a large tripod over a fire lit on Apollona's quay.

There is probably nothing in the crustacean world more delectable. At this improvised feast to which we were improbably invited, there were no forks, no knives, no plates, no sauces. The spiny lobsters, clawless and resplendent, were torn apart with the fingers at the *kapheneíon* table, to the shocked astonishment of the *kapheneíon* proprietor and passing Apollonians, and accompanied with bread and a 4-litre bottle, encased in wicker, of Apollonian wine that the Sculptor had had the foresight to bring along.

DATTERO DI MARE (I) • date-shell

Lithophaga lithophaga • family MYTILIDAE
dàtil de mar (C) • solína (G)

Datteri bear a cursory resemblance to very large dates on account of their shape and rich brown colour (mother-of-pearl within). These bivalves whose structure resembles the mussels but which are 8-10 cm long have a very delicate taste and are eaten raw (with or without lemon juice) or are made into a soup. They inhabit the interstices of a calcareous rock formation from which they can only be extracted by fracturing the lumps of stone with a hammer, once raised from the deep, and so they are expensive.

But I give the recipe imparted by the amiable cook at Il Pilota at Fiumaretta at the mouth of the Magra, because it can be applied as well, with good effect, to mussels. La Spezia and Porto Venere are well-known for these sea fruits, but magnificent *datteri* are also to be found in Naples, Taranto and Gallipoli, exposed in the fish markets of the ports in beautiful salt-glazed earthenware dishes from Grottaglie.

ZUPPA DI DATTERI • date-shell soup

'Take plenty of single-leaved parsley, green celery (*sedano*), an onion, a small carrot, some leaves of rosemary, a clove or two of garlic, and a chilli pepper, and chop them all very fine. Cook this *soffritto* gently in oil in a large pan until it begins to brown, then add pepper, a dessertspoon of tomato purée diluted in a very little water, and a large glass of white wine. Reduce this a little by raising the heat, then throw in 1 kilo (2¼ lb) of *datteri* which have been well washed, and with the lid on cook rapidly for a few minutes until they open. Remove the pan from the fire.

'In another pan, fry some slices of bread in oil, then rub the slices with cut garlic. Ladle the *datteri* with a large perforated ladle onto a handsome white porcelain dish, put the hot fried bread round them and strain the steaming liquor over the dish.'

I add one comment. Don't try to prepare the fried bread in advance. It is only when the hot liquor meets the hot garlic bread that the delicious aroma of this marine dish is released.

SOGLIOLA (I) • sole

Solea vulgaris • family SOLEIDAE
llenguado (C) • glóssa (G)

SOGLIOLA AL VINO BIANCO CON UVA MOSCATA
sole in white wine with muscat grapes

One likes to make the best of materials to hand, in this case small soles fished from the Tyrrhenian, dry white wine and muscat grapes from the vineyard at La Barozza. One sole per person and 30 g (1 oz) of butter per fish. The grapes are peeled and pipped, a handful; salt and pepper.

Cut the heads off the fish, a slanting cut, clean them and strip off the skin from both sides by raising it a little where the head is severed with a sharp knife, and using a swift tearing movement – quite easy if you grasp the sole with a cloth. Leave on the lateral fins; their gelatinous nature contributes to the sauce.

Sprinkle the soles with salt and pepper and put them in a sole pan with the butter and wine, about ¼ litre for 4 small soles. Simmer on a lively heat, basting them by tilting the handle of the pan while the liquor evaporates. Add the grapes.

At a certain moment the wine, the butter and the juices of the soles unite into the consistency of a perfect sauce. Culinary miracles happen by evaporation. Serve at once.

ROSPO (Venetian) · angler-fish

Lophius spp · family LOPHIIDAE
rap (C) · vatrachópsaro (G)

The angler-fish, frogfish, toadfish, sea devil, *baudroie* in French, is a monster with a terrifying head which often reaches the fish stall without it; hence *coda di rospo*, the toad's tail, a favourite Venetian dish grilled and served with mayonnaise or poached and served with olive oil and lemon.

SOPA DE RAP · angler-fish soup (Catalan)

Acquiring the fish entire, as is normal at least in Barcelona and the Salento, one can eat the tail at night and serve the soup next day. Ask the fishmonger to sever the hideous head (to be used for soup), remove the gills, then chop the head into three sections; this saves domestic trouble. For four people the fish should weigh 1½-2 kilos (3½-4½ lb) entire.

Wash the head sections and put them in the fish pan covered with water. In another pan prepare a *sofregit* by simmering in olive oil a finely chopped large onion, then add a large tomato, peeled, seeded and cut up. Cook this sauce for 20 minutes, then pour it into the fish pan. Bring to the boil and cook rapidly for 30 minutes. Strain the broth into another pan, let it cool, and in this cook the tail of the fish; i e bring to the boil, boil vigorously for 10 minutes, then simmer for 15 minutes covered. Leave the fish to cool in the broth, then strain it, reserving the liquor, and serve it with oil and lemon juice (or mayonnaise) and new potatoes.

You are left with the broth and the cooked head. Remove the white meat from the head, chop it up and pass it through the *mouli*. Put the result into the broth, add a slice of bread per person, bring to the boil and boil vigorously for 5 minutes, stirring continuously with an egg whisk. This results in a fairly dense soup. You can add a *picada* of pounded garlic and parsley if you like.

The perfect way of cooking the angler-fish tail is the Provençal *Baudroie à la bourride*, a poetic dish and powerful restorative in hot weather. And, having so far restrained myself from describing the perfections which only the French can achieve, and as the garlic is here enshrined not just to set the palate on fire but to restore the organism in high summer – the grand reviver for those knocked out by the Lion sun – I give the recipe:

BAUDROIE À LA BOURRIDE • angler-fish *à la bourride*

One hot July when we were investigating the marble quarries of Béziers in the Languedoc we came by chance upon the little port of Mèze, situated on an inland sea surrounded by oyster parks and mussel beds, and fell exhausted into the restaurant Au Pescadou on the quay.

The *baudroie* was a fish of size, the tail weighing well over a kilo. Sliced into substantial sections, it had been initially cooked in a casserole with a sliced onion, a branch of thyme, a bayleaf and slither of orange zest, with just enough hot water to cover, and salt and pepper, for 10 minutes.

Meanwhile an *aïoli* (p 119) had been prepared containing six cloves of garlic pounded to a pulp before proceeding with the liaison of two egg yolks and olive oil, added drop by drop, stirring, in a mortar. Half the *aïoli* was put aside on ice to chill, while the rest was used as the basis of the *bourride*. This was achieved by adding two further egg yolks to it and then pouring some of the hot liquor in which the fish had cooked through a sieve onto it, stirring.

The fish slices were then immersed in this sauce for a few minutes in a pan sitting in a *bain-marie* on a low heat. Once impregnated with the sauce, they were transferred to an oval dish, white, the sauce then poured over them, very fragrant but by no means thick. A little tumulus of the chilled *aïoli*, dense and golden, was set on top of each fish slice, and some little croûtons fried in butter were set in the dish.

One was faced with the delicious impact of hot (lobster-like) fish, hot garlic and chilled *aïoli*. Copious draughts of red wine of the Languedoc were drunk with it.

A *bourride* can also be made with turbot or halibut.

Smoked and Salt Fish

Then came a puzzling object, hot, dark brown in colour, and smelling strongly of
smoke; it might be the mummified remains of a fish that has crawled up some
chimney by mistake. I scraped a fragment of this anatomical specimen and found
it strange to the taste but not bad; not at all bad.

Kippers and haddocks nowadays are for me one of the delights of England, and
I wish certain friends in that country, instead of sending me stupid novels to read,
would hollow out the printed text with a chisel and then insert a kipper or two.
How grateful I would be!

G. Orioli, *Adventures of a Bookseller*

Thus speaks Irving's friend and colleague, inspiring for a moment or
two an acute bout of nostalgia with regard to kipper, bloater, haddock
– vanished breakfasts – and indeed for buckling, trout, mackerel, eel,
angler-fish, brisling, salmon, salmon trout and cod's roe, so deliciously
smoked, as found in northern climes.

As up to now no friend of ours has acted on Orioli's suggestion, we
fall back gratefully on salt herrings in winter, which are lightly smoked
as well as salted and come in wooden boxes from Holland and Portugal.

If I mention *boutargue* here, the specially prepared and smoked roes
of the grey mullet, about which much is written, this delicacy does not
penetrate alas to remote Salentine outposts.

So I heartily recommend the salt herring, *l'aringa* (I), *l'arengada* (C),
which was once the poor man's staple in Italy and Catalonia, now the
poor man's staple no longer, but still a vital element in winter fare and
imperative for those with chest troubles. See Apropos of a Salt Herring
(p 148) for how to grill them.

They are excellent too when marinated, that is decapitated, skinned,
split, filleted, soaked in cold water for an hour or so, then drained, dried
and immersed in olive oil, seasoned with black pepper and finely cut
rounds of raw onion. The female roes can be prepared separately,
soaked longer being rather salt, then made into an ersatz *taramá* with
garlic, parsley, olive oil, lemon and dried grated crumbs all pounded in
the mortar, and eaten with *taralli* (p 328). When buying salt herrings,
you ask for those with female roes, *l'aringa con le uova*.

I hardly need to add that salted anchovies and salted sardines,
unsmoked, conserved in large tins, are an all-the-year round standby.
The work entailed in conserving them – in wooden barrels towards the
turn of the last century – is eloquently described by the Sicilian writer
Verga in his novel *I Malavoglia*.

fasting food

Not many people today know why Mr Pickwick set out on the 22nd December with a huge cod insinuated into the fore-boot of the Muggleton Telegraph en route for Dingley Dell. The cod was success-fully disinterred on arrival at the Blue Lion in the presence of the fat boy, who, handing the reins to Sam Weller, promptly went to sleep beside it, his head pillowed on a barrel of oysters, once these vital supplies had been transferred to Mr Wardle's chaise. This giant cod, mysteriously never mentioned again, we must presume was destined to be the central element in the dinner on Christmas Eve, traditionally a night of fasting.

Salt cod is still served in Italy on Christmas Eve (*La Vigilia*), and was the main feature in the Friday if not the Wednesday fast all through the winter. But its connection with fasting is now overlaid by a general appreciation of salt cod as a source of nourishment, not only in Italy but also in Spain and France. Its 'imperishable' nature is important in countries where many people live in remote mountain places, to which fresh fish does not penetrate.

STOCCAFÍSSO (I) •	BACCALÀ (I)
wind-dried cod	dried salt cod
peixopalo, estocfix (C)	bacallà (C), baccaliáros (G)
morue sèche (F)	morue blanche (F)

STOCCAFÍSSO and BACCALÀ are both cod, but being subjected to different curing processes, produce two entirely different tastes, textures and appearances.

STOCCAFÍSSO is a rigid stick-like object, gutted and dried on the pebbled shores of Norwegian fiords by the north wind, and in Iceland and Newfoundland. In the Veneto you see these fish in winter, sometimes a metre long, in wooden tubs looking like gnarled bâtons in an umbrella stand. Hard, dried, desiccated by exposure, yellow as stained parchment, it needs to be beaten, unsoaked, with a hammer to shreds before soaking for, say, twelve hours, changing the water often; or, alternatively, it must be soaked for several days. Often one or other procedure has been performed by the grocer. The first method facili-tates its incorporation with olive oil in a dish called *Baccalà mantecato* (*mantecare* = to whip) which is the Venetian version of the French *brandade*. (Misunderstandings arise because the word *baccalà* is indis-criminately used to describe both stockfish and salt cod in Italy, just as the word *morue* is often used for both in France.) The fact is that stockfish is particularly suited to both these preparations, French and Italian, rather than salt cod which is fibrous by nature – though either can be used. See Elizabeth David's *Italian Food* for the Venetian version.

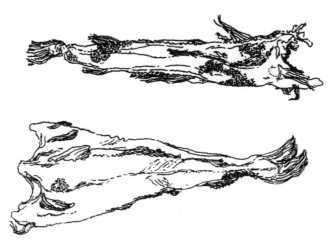

Morard in his *Manuel de la Cuisine Provençale* makes the difference patently clear, and gives the two different methods, both fairly strenuous but decidedly worthwhile, applying to Norwegian stockfish and to salt cod. He celebrates the former in a poem beginning:

Voyez cette morue à la couleur jaunâtre
Qu'un gaillard marmiton ne cesse de la battre
De son Pilon à longue mature

His final words on this subject: 'The *morue* suitable for the *brandade* is the one which is very hard, dry and remarkable for its yellow colour. Its substance lends itself with astonishing success to the preparation of the *brandade* and it would be superfluous to employ it for any other culinary preparation.'

In spite of this I mention here two rather anarchic stockfish recipes.

STOCCAFÍSSO AL FORNO • stockfish in the oven

In Carrara, stockfish was often prepared without beating – perhaps because the inhabitants had grown fearful of damaging their newly acquired plastic-topped tables. So, after soaking (7 days) the fish was poached, then flaked, and slowly cooked in earthenware in the baker's oven with olive oil, onion, parsley, celery, fragments of hot chilli pepper (dried), sliced potatoes, a glass of white wine and a little wine vinegar, a rather potent dish.

Clara who years before used to make it in quantity for 40 marble workmen on Saturdays, continued to make it on Mondays throughout the year, and could be seen returning with her covered dish from the nearby baker's oven to her undaunted clientele – a select band of marble workers – in the Piazza San Francesco. Lunchtime conversation often harped on the possibility of Clara extending her culinary vocabulary, which was confined to *past'asciutta*, *pasta in brodo*, *zuppa di fagioli*, *la trippa*, *baccalà marinato*, and *stoccafisso al forno*, which vied in indigestibility with another dish fortunately more rarely executed, *muscoli ripieni*, which last is a curiosity, the mussels being stuffed with herbs and sausage meat. Clara's cooking was far outstripped by her kindness of heart, on which account her clients cleaved to her.

PISTA E COZA • 'pound and cook'

Recalling my reference to 'vanished breakfasts', here is an authentic Carrarese one. In this town there were still some old quarrymen left, whose working day for 40 years began at 3 o'clock in the morning by making breakfast, before walking up the mountains to the quarries, carrying their boots to save the leather, with a *fiasco* of wine and a *merenda* tied in a bundle. A retired quarryman called Catossi had a great reputation as a *gran' mangiatore*, a real gourmand, and this is what he cooked.

Getting up in the dark, he took his stonemason's hammer and banged that recalcitrant object, a *stoccafisso*, unsoaked, to shreds on the marble kitchen table. He then pounded some tomatoes, parsley and garlic in a mortar, threw the shredded stockfish and pounded *odori* (the aromatics above) into a large earthenware casserole (*padella*), added a liberal quantity of olive oil (no water), and simmered it until all liquid was absorbed. He ate it with a slab of polenta. The colossal thirst this induced he slaked with alternate glasses of water and *grappa*.

What then is BACCALÀ? It is North Atlantic cod, salted and pressed in layers; this cod remains white and its tissues bear a closer resemblance to fish than to leather. It has a less powerful smell and takes less time – 24 hours – to soak. But it comes in several orders of excellence and thickness.

According to Stendhal, a subject 'wrapped in mystery' (see his letter of 7 May 1840 to Monsieur Thiers, written at Civita Vecchia where he was Consul). He declares that the French would never be able to compete with the salt cod supplied to Rome, Umbria and the Papal States by the English, unless they found some means of introducing alum, as did the English, into the salting process. The importance of this trade – its season October to April, as now – is evident from the

figure given by Stendhal of 1,724,000 kilos for English salt cod landed
in 1836 at the port of Rome, Civita Vecchia. In 1838, for the first time,
138,000 kilos of French *morue* arrived from Newfoundland at this port;
the universal opinion was that it had a more agreeable taste, but didn't
keep – the English salt cod prepared with salt and rock alum remained
rigid until June, but heat and humidity were fatal to the French *morue*,
which went soft.

This might possibly explain the extraordinary withered aspect of the
baccalà reaching Apulia, as compared with the magnificent golden
specimens, perhaps lightly smoked, to be found in the mountains
behind Naples, for instance at Sant'Agata dei Goti in Sunday markets,
and also the superb *bacallà* on sale even in late summer in the markets
of Vendrell and Tarragona, French imports perhaps. Salentine cod
must have been withered with alum.

BACALLÀ A LA LLAUNA
salt cod cooked in the oven in an earthenware dish

One of the best ways of preparing salt cod, using the thickest upper part
of the fish. In Catalan *llauna* means tin, but *llauna* paradoxically is also
the name of a shallow but robust earthenware dish of antique form
with a curved base, used here.

8 pieces of *bacallà* weighing about 1 kilo (2¼ lb)
flour · olive oil
5 cloves of garlic · 1 kilo (2¼ lb) of fresh tomatoes
2 more cloves garlic · parsley

Soak the cod the day before (unless sold already soaked, as in Catalan
markets), changing the water several times. Cut into neat pieces about
7 x 5 cm (3" x 2"). Rinse them and dry them, dust with flour and fry in
very hot olive oil for about 5 minutes on each side, to brown them, then
remove from the pan. Chop the 5 peeled garlic cloves and quickly
brown them in the same pan, then add the tomatoes peeled and
crushed. Cook until their liquor has evaporated.

Lightly oil the *llauna* or other earthenware dish, put in the pieces of
cod, cover with the sauce and cook uncovered in a moderate oven for
half an hour. Before serving, sprinkle the dish with a *picada* of finely
hashed garlic and parsley. Very simple, very good.

The Italian equivalent of this, *Baccalà marinato*, has less garlic. Green
celery, parsley and hot chilli peppers finely cut are used in the *soffritto*,
simmered in olive oil, as the point of departure for the tomato sauce.
The frying process is the same, in very hot oil.

BACCALÀ STUFATO CON LATTE • salt cod cooked in milk

Salt cod is excellent cooked in milk. For 4 people you need:

1 kilo (2¼ lb) salt cod	¾ litre (27 fl oz) milk
1 or 2 bayleaves	grated nutmeg
5 or 6 large potatoes	a little oil from a jar of preserved
1 large onion	chillis
olive oil	garlic, finely chopped
origano (wild marjoram)	parsley, finely chopped
ground black pepper	2 hard-boiled eggs
	12 black olives

Cut the fish across into two or three pieces, put these in water in an earthenware pot, skin side up, and soak for 24 hours. Change the water once or twice.

Cook the pieces of fish in an earthenware vessel with plenty of water, starting from cold, with 1 or 2 bayleaves. Do not let the water boil, as boiling would toughen the fish. Once it is steaming, simmer for 5 minutes, then take the pot off the fire and leave to stand for half an hour. Drain, remove the grey skin and the bones, and flake the fish.

Peel the potatoes and onion, and slice them to the thickness of a coin. Put some olive oil in the bottom of pan (the sole pan is good for this), put in a layer of potatoes and onion, then a layer of flaked fish, and repeat. Sprinkle with *origano* and black pepper, barely cover with milk, and simmer until the potatoes are cooked; by this time a good deal of milk will have been absorbed or will have evaporated, and what remains will have acquired a creamy consistency. Add a little grated nutmeg and a few drops of oil from the chilli jar (see *peperoncini sott'olio*, p 317) at this point, and some finely chopped garlic and parsley at the end of the cooking. Sliced hard-boiled eggs and black olives, unstoned, can be added. (Stoned olives stain the pale cream colour of the dish.)

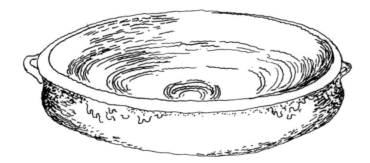

Apropos of a Salt Herring

THE discrepancy between what is happening in the world today and what I describe as going on in obscure places prompts me to take a long look backwards, rather than to plunge into an examination of changes affecting food habits. These changes could more properly be viewed as ethnocide even when euphemistically called progress. So I turn to another discrepancy which often strikes the cook – the time some dishes take to prepare and the reckless speed with which they are consumed.

In the wonderful book of Elio Vittorini, *Conversazione in Sicilia*, written in the winter of 1936-7, the salt herring cooking on a charcoal brazier in the mountain dwelling of La Concezione, Silvestro's heroic mother, defies this experience. It is the centrepiece of one chapter only, while its subsequent despatch by mother and son, meeting after a lapse of fifteen years, occupies a further three. While it cooks the pungent smell of the modest but nourishing object evokes a whole string of childhood memories in which broad beans (an indigenous plant in Sicily, Apulia, Greece), cooked with sowthistle and a dish of lentils (the first legume to be found in early neolithic sites in Thessaly) flavoured with onions, dried tomatoes, *lardo*, and rosemary, rise up from the past like subterranean suns. But for the mother the fundament remains: braised salt herring in winter, roast peppers in summer. These are what she has always eaten with a great deal of olive oil and a lot of bread – and olives, of course, and sometimes pork in autumn, if they had happened to raise a pig near a plantation of Indian figs.

Once this herring is on the table, having been carefully skinned, cleaned, boned and richly soused in olive oil, memories intensify, proliferate. A '*dolce*' reappears out of the mists of time called *mosticcioli di fichi d'India*; this rather dubious fruit, the prickly pear, is deprived one supposes of its ubiquitous seeds, and the resulting scarce pulp is fermented, then worked with flour to make little festive cakes punctuated with almonds, pine kernels and pistachios. This is no doubt a distant relation of the Apulian *mostacciuolo* sold at every festa, scented with cinnamon and coated with thin chocolate after baking.

With regard to the prickly pear there is a saying: 'You suffer three times. Once when picking them, once when eating them, then afterwards!' In fact, when eaten to excess (which often happens as they induce in late summer a passionate desire in some people to 'eat their fill' – they count them and exclaim: '59 fruits!') a virtually indissoluble ball forms in the lower intestine. On the positive side – three of four fruits carefully picked with a couple of vine-leaves as glove, and skilfully peeled with a knife, are a specific cure for colic. In winter, chilled by the north wind, they are a delicacy.

In recalling dishes which appeased the children's hunger in the mountainous deserts of central Sicily where Silvestro's father was a railway worker, over the by now despatched herring, mother and son rediscover the essence of that time, which was also the essence of now (when the book was written), that is hunger and poverty. The famished children, it transpired, caught and ate cicadas, one of the oldest insects in the world. After the first ten days of the month, when the railwayman's wages had been spent, the family lived like everyone else, including the workers in the sulphur mines, on what they could gather: snails (source of protein) and wild chicory, *Cicoria selvatica*, promoting their digestion. Snails are prepared in various ways, the mother declares: boiled; in a garlic and tomato sauce; or floured complete with shell and fried (you resolutely suck the shell and finally suck out the content).

Reflecting on this conversation, it dawned on me that the traces of mesolithic life, some thirteen thousand years ago, are here today in Sicily and in Apulia, where not only are the delicate flint and fossil-shell instruments of these food gatherers to be found in the wild, but

where also survives a genuine passion for gathering molluscs, marine and terrestrial and edible weeds. This alone makes what has happened in the last twenty years with regard to 'progress' seem insignificant.

In the Salento after the slightest shower of rain in autumn, men, women and children search for snails among the stones, each with a plastic bag; indeed, also with a torch at night, when the snails perambulate.

On the shores of the Ionian, men can be seen digging up sea-snails and bivalves at the water's edge where there is sand, and prising minute limpets off the rocks, together with several kinds of succulent *alghe marine*, edible sea-weeds. Further out, frog men equipped with floating crates are collecting sea urchins and among the rocks are prickly mounds of discarded urchin shells, bearing witness to their instant consumption. (Only the females yield their delicate reward, the orange eggs forming a small five-pointed star on the base of the shell, which is broken into with a knife and emptied of its débris in the sea.)

Food Gathering

OOD gathering is the instance, *par excellence*, of time spent procuring and preparing something to eat out of all proportion to the time spent in consuming it. But this engrossing subject is and is not a long way from snails and indeed frogs as gastronomic specialities.

A friend of ours, a painter, evolved an excellent spaghetti sauce with certain landsnails (*cozze di terra*) as a base, which in summer collect on the long wands of wild fennel on uncultivated land. He goes out early to collect them, as people come from distant villages inspired by a similar ambition. If you happen to be passing, they hasten to assure you that they are collecting snails as a diversion, that is, not from need.

CHIOCCIOLA	COZZA DI TERRA (I)	MARRUNE, COZZA CECA (I)
common snail	land snail	vineyard/Burgundy snail
Helix aspersa *H melanostoma*	*Cepaea nemoralis*	*H pomatia*

cargol (C) · salingári (G) (both general names)

Going into any self-respecting Salentine kitchen in autumn you are likely to find a shining aluminium, lidded, pan in which these treasures are undergoing an initial purging. This is achieved by sprinkling over them a handful of flour or bran (*la crusca*), and for two or three days scrupulously removing their excrement and dusting them again with flour or bran. They then fast for a day and are ready to cook.

Preliminaries: wash them and put them in a pan of cold water for an hour; they partially emerge from their shells. Put the pan, covered, on the fire and cook rapidly at first, then reduce the heat for another half hour. In this way they are easy to extract; the snout (*il muso*) remains out. The vineyard snail, large, brown, takes longer to cook.

When Silvestro's mother speaks of them as 'boiled', she means cooked as above, then eaten with bread, olive oil, salt. They can also be simmered briefly in a thin tomato sauce flavoured with garlic and *sedano* (green celery), the procedure followed by the painter for his spaghetti sauce. This in fact is the way the tiny marine bivalves called *vongole* (plural) are prepared and served with spaghetti: *Spaghetti alle vongole*, a popular dish, in which the tiny clams appear with or without their shells.

COZZA ALLA PANNA

Helix operta
municedda (Sal) · attuppatedda (Sic)

This is another species of snail, highly considered because (1) they have a more delicate flavour, and (2) they do not have to be purged or fasted, since in early summer they begin to form a covering by exuding a lot of bubbly foam, which hardens and becomes white (*la panna* = cream). They fall asleep underground. In August you need a mattock (*zappa*) to dig them out, and you have to know where to dig – in vineyards and near stone water cisterns. These snails are of oval form, of medium size, golden brown, with a beautiful logarithmic spiral structure. They are also reared intensively commercially, and very costly when bought.

There are four Apulian ways of consuming these delicacies:

¶ Crack the tender shell and eat them raw.

¶ Remove the white covering, throw them into hot olive oil for a few minutes, then eat them hot with a little salt.

¶ Put them as they are into the hot ashes of a wood fire and after a few minutes rake them out, wipe and eat them.

¶ Remove the white crust with your fingers or a knife, grill them on a fine wire mesh over a wood fire and serve hot with a sauce made of pounded garlic, chopped parsley, thickened by the addition of olive oil, drop by drop, stirring.

A fifth way, more dramatic, is practised in Roselló and in Llofriu in the Empordà, Catalonia, at the annual Cargolades (snail feast). Vineyard snails, *cargols de les vinyes*, are starved for several days, a different approach, then set close together on a heap of straw. The straw is set alight and the snails are retrieved from the ashes by jabbing them with sharply pointed sticks, and at once dipped into a *vinagretes endimoniades* (literally 'devilled vinaigrette', i e containing pounded garlic and hot chilli peppers), eaten with bread and washed down with wine.

To conclude with snails: the smallest snails (*cozze piccine, pintuliddi*), white with a fine black spiral, are found growing on sea-thistles at the beach. Our neighbour Teresa insists that these have the best flavour, and sometimes help her pick them. One might think they would be the most fiddly to extract. You don't extract them – they are cooked for

a quarter of an hour, a tiny hole is made opposite the orifice with a pointed instrument, and you suck them out, a convivial occupation for a summer evening. Teresa serves these sometimes in a scarce sauce (oil, tomatoes, garlic, celery leaves) as an evening *merenda* with Salvatore's wine, sitting under the vine.

To anyone interested in these revelations and reading Italian I recommend a perusal of Daniele Dolci's *Racconti Siciliani*, in which a youth Rosario (p 23) describes, *a viva voce*, the three main types of snail and the methods of gathering them according to their diverse habits, the season and the weather. The method is Aristotelian; it stems from close observation. This age-old cultural heritage has nothing to do with literacy, though the reader can turn to the Elder Pliny (molluscs) and to Dioscorides (plants) for reassurance.

Rosario's discourse perfectly illustrates the skill and knowledge required in food gathering. He discusses the collecting of edible weeds for market, the catching of river eels and river crabs; how to prepare frogs for sale (this is certain to repel Anglo-Saxon readers). Oddly enough, he does not mention fungi; but he patiently collects capers which grow wild among the stones in western Sicily, as I did on Naxos and do in the Salento. You gather the incipient flower buds, the smaller the better, every other day at the end of May and the beginning of June. See page 330 for how to conserve them.

With regard to edible weeds, Rosario claims that they belong to five or six different species. This may be encouraging for beginners, but in fact it is a tremendous understatement; see the chapter on Weeds. Later, however, he lists the kinds as seven: *cicoria*, wild chicory; *cavolicedde*, crucifers; *giri*, the dandelion tribe; *vurrane*, borage family; *cardelle*, various kinds of thistle; *finocchi*, wild fennel; and *sparagi di roveto*, the tender shoots, purple, of the bramble.

In Rohlf's dictionary of the Salentine dialects I was not surprised to find that the largest entries refer to these primordial food sources: snails have 65 entries, diverse names for the basic species and their varieties. Frogs have 33 names. *Cicoria selvatica* has 31 names. Fungi have 27. Marine molluscs have 63 dialect names referring to about 30 species. This proves their fundamental value as food, as well as my contention that eating habits in Apulia and Sicily are founded on mesolithic food gathering.

I think one can say that the mesolithic people who, after the retreat of the ice-cap, produced a completely new range of flint tools to cope with this newly discerned supply of molluscs, marine and terrestrial, were pioneers in gastronomy. Their artefacts are not only small, often

minute, but also made with incredible skill – fish hooks, *mezzalune*, tiny
blades to prise open the reluctant bivalves, refined points to tease out
the land and sea snails; flint arrow-tips, both pointed and cutting
(tranchets) to let fly at little birds, robin redbreasts, larks, goldfinch,
which I regret to say are still the prey of the army of shotsmen in
autumn.

As craftsmen we are particularly drawn to tools, so it is not surprising
that the Sculptor, one autumn day, discovered a mesolithic site not far
from Spigolizzi, hitherto ignored, from which we subsequently gathered
on open ground a whole armoury of mesolithic instruments. This site
is just opposite the rustic dwelling of our friend the painter, which
hangs on the edge of a deep ravine containing caves, a running stream
harbouring river eels, which flows on underground to the nearby sea,
in other words the ideal spot for food-gatherers then and now.

Should anyone be anxious to know how to prepare frogs, the study
of items 503, *Ranocchi in umido*, and 504, *Ranocchi alla fiorentina*, in
Artusi's *Scienza di Cucina* is an excellent guide.

As for small river eels, *anguille*, they are gutted, cleaned and cut
unskinned into 7 cm slices, then impaled lengthways, alternated with
bayleaves, on thin hardwood spits and roasted over a hot wood fire,
basted with oil until the skin is crisp and brown, then eaten with the
fingers at a long table out of doors with bread and strong red wine.

La Piazzetta

ARRARA, a little industrial town hemmed in by the Apuanian Alps, once mistaken by Lady Blessington for an 'earthly paradise' as she looked down at it from the summit of la Foce, while the coachman eased the horses, was, when we lived there, still small enough to be invaded in the month of May by the honey smell of acacia flowers, drifting down from wooded hills.

The mountains streaked with white morraines, when seen at a distance and in the sun, glitter like cascades. Marble is dynamited or sawn from the mountain face and sliced by elicoidal wires out of the crests. The white cascades are the crushed surplus which served as 'slides' down which the blocks of marble were perilously run on wooden rollers. They now form the uneasy bed of hairpin access roads.

The market – the clamorous heart of the old town – was sited near the 12th century Duomo in an enclosed space lovingly called by the inhabitants *la piazzetta*. It was not only a delight to the eye but an olfactory reminder of the wealth of fragrance daily pillaged from the earth. It was ruled by very old ladies instinct with avarice; they laid out their wares on trestle tables. In winter they warmed themselves with live charcoal in little iron buckets called *caldanin*, meaning 'warm the child'. In summer these ladies kept cool by placing a large cabbage leaf on their heads. They had an inexorable curiosity about one's private life and were only at peace when – over the years – they had identified and commented on all members of the family tree.

*   *   *   *   *

Obituary: in the name of progress, the city's heart has since been transplanted to the periphery and carries on in a hygienic modern structure.

*   *   *   *   *

The *piazzetta* was surrounded by butchers' shops whose counters were raised on marble pedestals so high that it was impossible to examine the meat. This was a reflection on the legendary poverty of the Carraresi and their supposed rapacity.

The pork butchers were both more appealing and more frequented, hung with hams on ceiling hooks, festoons of sausages, fresh and smoked for boiling, along with *cotechini* and *zamponi*. On accessible counters basins were displayed of whipped pork fat mixed with herbs for flavouring bean and chickpea soups; blood sausages, dark red and white, made that morning, with pigs' trotters, tails, tongues, faggots wrapped in caul, and blocks of *lardo*, accompanied in the background by an almost continuous felling of pork chops.

In the alleys which served as approach to the *piazzetta* poulterers displayed guinea fowl as a matter of course, dressed quails sprigged with sage and rosemary, rabbits, hens and, in the hunting season, game.

The fishwives were located in an alley at the bottom of the market where fresh fish – the port was only 7 kilometres away – were piled quite carelessly on wooden tables. This alley resounded with frenzied shouting. There was always a feeling of a battle won retreating from the fray with fresh sardines or anchovies, mackerel, river trout, or little soles, grey mullet. I sometimes succumbed to rock prawns or fell for the deceptive sea cicada so-called not only for the 'snapping cricket-like noise' they make underwater, but because they resemble the empty carapace the real cicada leaves behind when it is metamorphized from the beetle stage and acquires wings.

What really took the eye and titillated the nose was the freshness of the vegetables in the centre of the *piazzetta*, their abundance and variety. In summer there was every reason to live on tender vegetables, delicious salads, cheese – mountain ricotta arrived at dawn swathed in beech or bayleaves – and fruit, with fish or poultry occasionally.

The winter vegetables were a revelation: little artichokes on their

succulent stems, the grizzled roots of salsify and the black roots of scorzonera; tender spinach, succulent spinach beet, crisp young cabbages (*la verza*); orange winter pumpkins; beautiful cauliflowers with spiral inflorescences, some creamy white, others green or purple, which are Sicilian, and a dwarfed variety crossed with broccoli (*cavolo broccolo*); winter salads deriving from the wild *Cichorium endivia*, the tousled kind with a blanched heart, and *scarola* also blanched and very crisp. The cultivated forms of *Cichorium intybus* were there in great variety, including its delicious bitter white root, sold in clusters as *cicoria di radice*; a gigantic dark green leaf-chicory like overgrown dandelions, *cicoria 'Catalogna'*; and the blanched Belgian chicory. These are all ideal accompaniments to pork, as is *radicchio rosso*, the red bitter salad with its pared root, a form of *C endivia*.

Some of these vegetables came by road from Sicily in winter and from the plains of Naples and Bari. The plain of Versilia from the river Magra stretching south to Viareggio was intensively cultivated, often between rows of vines, but I must admit that at the time I was so new to this spectacle of vegetable vigour that I did not study its origins. I was too busy chasing the postman who, a former jeweller, was the elusive man who melted small slabs of gold and larger ones of silver for me in his spare time; I daily repaired from the market to my workshop.

In those days I had to come to terms with the Carraresi, with their nature and dialect. If Tuscan vegetables are sweet and have an aromatic savour, English vegetables are grown for substance. Italian conversations in the same way are delightful effluvia, which quickly evaporate. In England you get the equivalent of substance – an argument. The nature of the Italians resembles earthy emanations; in England what you have is 'character'. The consequence of this, both in human beings and in fruit and vegetables, is a passion for youth and freshness, for grasping what the season has to give at the precise moment; this lends an ardour to daily living and eating.

The feeling of the mountains was never far away: retired quarrymen sold bunches of herbs they had gathered there. In summer great baskets of bilberries and small ones of wild strawberries appeared. In autumn, fresh cranberries, fungi and chestnuts were brought down from the Spanish chestnut woods. In this way a dialogue between town and country was maintained, but also appointments kept between townsmen and freshly milled maize-flour in outlying farms. Those *borse*, leather bags, carried by everyone always turned out to contain not papers, but some rich find, golden *polenta* flour, a mountain sheep's cheese, a rustic *mortadella* . . . In those days it was still possible to feel that the Carraresi were definitely in touch with the 'earthly paradise'.

Vegetable Heritage

 OR I am he who hunted out the source of fire, and stole it, packed in pith of a dry fennel stalk.

Prometheus Bound
Aeschylus

The vegetables treated here follow the growing cycle through the year, beginning in autumn. The first name given is the Italian, unless otherwise indicated.

FINOCCHIO · bulbous (or Florence) fennel

Foeniculum vulgare var *dulce* · family APIACEAE (formerly UMBELLIFERAE)
fonoll (C) · márathon (G)

It was in the hollow pith of the giant fennel, *Ferula communis*, that Prometheus concealed a lump of live charcoal broken from the torch he lit at the fiery chariot of the sun, defying Zeus, and brought fire to mankind: a sacred plant, the fire bearer.

Robert Graves says in *Greek Myths*: 'The mythic importance of Marathus (fennel) lay in the use made of fennel stalks for carrying the new sacred fire from the central hearth to private ones after their annual extinction.'

The wild form of *F vulgare* (till recently classified separately as *F officinalis*, to indicate its use by apothecaries and its health-giving properties) grows vigorously, with the giant fennel, in droughty calcareous situations all round the Mediterranean and can be sown from seed. It is these seeds which are used in cooking and conserving, being far more fragrant than the cultivated kind. The fronds are used in delicate fish stuffings, in soups, and – along with thistles, dandelions, etc – in a Tuscan dish of boiled weeds in spring.

Finocchio, the bulbous fennel, whose aromatic swollen stem is a winter vegetable, is a valuable and easily cultivated plant; it is earthed up to blanch it. It is often served whole and without dressing to conclude a meal; it clears the palate. It can be finely sliced and dressed with oil and wine vinegar and served as a salad. As a vegetable it is boiled, fried, braised. In the 19th century in Italy this aromatic vegetable, along with aubergines, was only eaten by Jews, says Artusi, thus proving their gastronomic perception.

TO BRAISE FENNEL. Slice each well-washed stem vertically into two pieces. Blanch for 5 minutes in boiling salted water, drain, then simmer in a heavy pan with olive oil or butter. Grate some *pecorino sardo* or parmesan over the fennel while it is cooking, then turn the pieces and sprinkle with more of the same. Both sides should brown. This takes about 15 minutes. Add some *pomodori appesi* (p 324), which are small, and cook for another few minutes. Serve on its own.

CAROTA • carrot

Daucus carota • family APIACEAE
pastanaga (C) • karóto (G)

Cooking practices are reflected in market ladies' offerings of aromatics: you find in Tuscany a little bunch of *odori* already prepared for the *soffritto*, the point of departure in cooking many things. The bunch consists of two carrots, two or three slender leeks (sometimes wild ones, sometimes the long slender *lungo d'inverno*), some stems of single-leaved parsley and some of *sedano* (celery grown for its leaves and not blanched – the familiar blanched celery is *sedano da coste*); and sometimes spring onions; all to be chopped and simmered in oil before being used in the cooking of rice, beans, birds, game, fish.

This is to say that carrots play a modest role as an aromatic rather than a vegetable in Italian cooking and are normally of modest size. But in one village, Corsano, in the Salento they are grown to remarkable dimensions – survival of a priapic rite. Here they are called *la pastinaca* rather than *carota* and are rather pale in colour. On the feast of Santu Pati the engaged youths seek out their largest carrots and offer them with ceremony to their future brides. Afterwards the size and splendour of these prodigies are examined by the entire village amidst laughter and rude gestures to decide which youth has produced the winner.

CICORIA DI RADICE • root chicory

a form of *Cichorium intybus* • family ASTERACEAE (formerly COMPOSITAE)
xicoira (C) • radíkia (G)

A winter vegetable which is the root of the cultivated form of wild chicory (p 194). Commonly called *radicchio amaro* (bitter root) in markets, it has a decidedly acrid taste; one eats it with pleasure. There is something in the prevalence of pork products in the Italian winter which demands a compensatory bitterness in its accompaniments.

CONTORNO DI RADICCHIO AMARO (boiled root chicory). This is prepared in the simplest way. The long creamy-white roots are scraped, cut into little finger lengths and immersed in acidulated water to prevent discolouration. Boiled till tender, then served with olive oil and lemon juice to accompany grilled pork.

BARBA DI PRETE · SCORZONERA
salsify   scorzonera

Tragopogon porrifolius	*Scorzonera hispanica*
barba de frare (C) · skoulí (G)	escorçonera (C) · starída (G)

Salsify, which in its wild form is purple goat's beard (p 188), the spindly-leaved apparition of early March, belongs as does root chicory and scorzonera to the daisy and dandelion family. When cultivated, its insignificant rootlets attached to a central tap-root explain its name – the priest's beard. Its bladelike, glaucous leaves contain a milky fluid which is beneficial to the liver. When the plant is young, the central leaves can be chopped and eaten as a salad.

Scorzonera, of Spanish origin, takes its name from the Catalan *escorço*, meaning viper, for whose bite the wild plant was once regarded as a cure. It resembles salsify, only its root is black, so is called black salsify.

PREPARING SALSIFY OR SCORZONERA. Pare the skin, putting the roots in acidulated water. Cook and serve in the same way as root chicory, above. Or blanch for 15 minutes in salted boiling water, drain, pass under the cold tap, dry, shake in fine flour and fry in hot oil. (This applies equally to root chicory.) Serve with lemon juice, a delicacy, with pork.

CICORIA 'CATALOGNA'

a form of *Cichorium intybus*

This plant, cultivated for its tall, luscious, dandelion-like leaves, is in abundant supply in northern Italy in winter. It comes to market severed at the root.

PREPARATION. Soak for an hour or so in water, then cut into hand lengths and throw into a large pan of boiling, slightly salted, water. Drained after 15 minutes, it is either served cold, dressed with oil and lemon juice as a salad, or accompanies pan-grilled pork cutlets; in the latter case it is tossed in the frying pan in the fat and juices of the pork, then dressed with lemon juice.

CICORIA 'ASPARAGO' • 'asparagus chicory'

another form of *Cichorium intybus*

The Apulian winter vegetable par excellence, cultivated for its asparagus-type shoots: it has the same outer dandelion-like leaves, but the heart within contains a fistful of these shoots.

PREPARATION. When young, it is cut at the base of the shoots, well washed and served raw with bulbous fennel, at the end of a meal. Or, to cook it, tear off the outer leaves, break off the swollen shoots, wash them and throw them into a pan in which 2 cloves of peeled garlic and 2 hot chilli peppers (preserved in oil, p 317) are briskly cooking in olive oil. Toss them in the oil, add a little salt and, say, half a glass of water, put on the lid and turn down the heat. After 10 minutes the shoots are tender, the water has evaporated, and the delicious vegetable is ready to serve in its aromatic juice. We are in Magna Graecia, and this very much resembles Greek practice in vegetable cookery.

THE ROMAN WAY (*puntini, puntarelle*: salad of asparagus chicory). Break off the points at their base, trim them, then make four neat cuts down each hollow stem and put them in water. After a while the stems will curl outwards in eight curls. Drain, shake dry and dress with oil and vinegar. Very pretty, this salad is only made with fresh young green shoots.

IN AN APULIAN SALAD. The smallest side-shoots are often included in a salad of curly endive and scarole, both stemming from *Cichorium endivia* (p 173). In late February one can add at the last minute to these salads the first blue flowers of borage.

RAPA • rape

Brassica rapa • family BRASSICACEAE (formerly CRUCIFERAE)

This plant is an instance of the effect of the sun's inclination on vegetable growth. In northern Europe it is grown extensively and fed to cattle. In the far south it is one of spring's most welcome greenstuffs. Sown broadcast in autumn in a cultivated patch, it bridges the gap in February/March between winter's asparagus chicory, spinach, fennel and the advent of the native artichoke. The plant produces a central flower head which, cut before the stem develops, induces other flower-heads (*cime di rapa*) to appear in the same way as winter broccoli. The season is short, you pick the new growth every other day; turn your back on it and the rape patch bursts into brilliant yellow flower. The relative delicacy of rape is the result of this rapid growth.

TO COOK. Wash the flowerheads, still green, trim off any leaves and stems which are coarse, and immerse in water. Cover the bottom of a pan with olive oil, heat it and put in some peeled garlic and one or two chilli peppers. Remove the garlic when it begins to brown, throw in the wet heads, add salt and toss the rape in the oil. Add a wineglass of water and put on the lid. Turn down the heat. By the time the water has evaporated, the rape is cooked. Broccoli are cooked in the same way.

WITH PASTA. See the recipe for *Orecchiette con la rucola* (p 105). You can prepare this dish in the same way with rape or dwarf broccoli heads.

CIPOLLA • onion

Allium cepa • family LILIACEAE
ceba (C) • kremíthi (G)

CALÇOTS, a new light cast on the Spanish onion: the Catalan word, meaning onion shoots, comes from *calçar*, to put on one's shoes, boots, stockings. So this means that the onion shoots are earthed up, like celery, cardoons, fennel.

In order to produce these shoots, small onion sets of the large, sweet, white variety are planted in January and allowed to grow till June/July when they have reached a certain size. They are pulled and dried off in bunches in the shade of a fig tree, then stored in a dry place. In September they begin to sprout and are planted out in a trench like celery. During the autumn they produce as many as seven or eight green sprouts, which are earthed up as they develop. By January each sprout attains the size of a gigantic leek.

LA CALÇOTADA • the onion shoot feast

This is a pre-spring festival in the neighbourhood of Valls, held in the open air under the almond trees in flower, and sometimes in the snow. Originally it was a family affair but now draws crowds of people. It starts with the onion shoots, carefully grilled on mattress-sized grills, and proceeds with roast chickens, mutton cutlets, and sausages (*llonganissa de Valls*) and a great deal of wine drunk from the *porró*.

The pulled shoots are trimmed of their roots and the green tops are carefully cut to equal size. The leek-like alliums are set close on the grill over a fire of vine cuttings and roasted on all sides. The shoots are then extracted from the burnt exterior and eaten with a sauce called *Salvitxada*. To make this sauce, first grill a whole head of garlic in the ashes of the wood fire, then assemble (quantities per person):

60 g (2 oz) grilled almonds · 2 grilled cloves of garlic and 1 ungrilled
a pinch of paprika · a little chopped parsley and mint · salt
1 grilled tomato, skinned · vinegar if you like · olive oil

Pound the above in a mortar, beginning with the almonds, and finally lubricate with a little olive oil; the sauce should not be thick.

These onion shoots are a great resource in early spring in the Salento – they are ready just when last year's garlic sprouts. And I am not exaggerating their size. They are eaten raw with bread, as a mid-morning *merenda*, by those who rise at dawn – reviving. They serve as a substitute for onions to flavour *la salsa* – both parts, the white and the green, being chopped – and are used in the same way to flavour haricot beans. Their dialect name, *sprunzale* or *spunzale*, means marriage, inspired perhaps by the fact that these shoots grow closely together, in pairs.

CIPOLLE ARROSTITE · roasted onions

In Mantua and Verona, bitterly cold in winter, the market people keep themselves alive with charcoal braziers, and at the same time are roasting on them the large purple winter onions, complete with skins, in a big perforated tin. You take them home, peel and eat them with salt and olive oil. They are often sold in vegetable shops, having been roasted in a nearby bread oven, after the bread has been baked. You can roast them yourself in a moderate oven; they take about 50 minutes.

AGLIO · garlic

Allium sativum · family LILIACEAE
all (C) · skórdo (G)

Beatrice d'Este, writing from a hunting lodge in the Ticino, to her sister Isabella in Mantua, in 1491: 'And I must tell you that I have had a whole field of garlic planted for your benefit, so that when you come we may be able to have plenty of your favourite dishes.'*

* I owe this to Julia Cartwright, citing 'A. Luzio and R. Renier, *Delle Relazioni di Isabella d'Este Gonzaga con Ludovico e Beatrice Sforza*, Archivio Storico Lombardo, xvii'.

People wonder when garlic is peeled or not peeled in cooking. The answer is peel it to pound it, to chop it, to fry it, but don't peel it when braising, just give it a slight bash with the pestle or your fist – unpeeled, there is little risk of it burning. (Once it has sprouted, it is better to plant it than to cook it.)

The garlic normally cultivated in Italy is Bianco comune, which has the best keeping qualities.

See *aïoli, allioli* (p 119-20); *ail-y-oli* and *purée d'ail* (p 35). The Catalan *allioli* is at its best made with garlic freshly pulled in June before it has been dried; it rapidly emulsifies.

It is no use being seduced by the 'giant' or 'elephant' garlic, which is one of the cultivated forms of *Allium ampeloprasum*. This species is the wild ancestor of the cultivated leek, and in some forms is referred to as 'wild leek'; the 'giant garlic' has a huge bulb though in colour and leaf form it is like a gigantic leek. Its taste is different from and milder than garlic. It is popular in Germany and the United States, perhaps because it is easier to peel, but it is not a substitute for real garlic.

Those who dislike the bulb can be consoled by reading Horace's Epode III; Virgil's friend had a delicate stomach. They could also reflect on the salutary effects of garlic, long recognised by doctors.

SPINACI spinach		BARBABIETOLA spinach beet
Spinacia oleracea espinacs (C) spanáki (G)	family CHENOPODIACEAE	*Beta vulgaris* var *esculenta* bleda (C) pantzarófilla (G)

Spinach appears in Italian markets in its first youth as the plant entire with bright green shiny little leaves and a rosy blush where the leaves join the severed root. Spinach beet, more massive, is sometimes sold as the plant entire, and sometimes as a bunch of lustrous green leaves, their thick white stems bound together.

Both are habitually served as an accompaniment to meat. They appear as a side dish with veal, with boiling sausages (see *zampone, cotechino*, p 230) or with smoked sausages, split and grilled.

Italians, so preoccupied with their health and digestion, regard the salubrious spinach and spinach beet as a natural way to these ends. Both plants are chopped and added to soups a few minutes before they are ready to serve, and both are used in the stuffing of *tortellini* with nutmeg and fresh ricotta – delicacies to be particularly enjoyed in little *trattorie* round Siena. In this case they are pressed until absolutely dry, then chopped and pounded. Spinach forms the green element in *lasagne verde*. It can be incorporated, chopped and simmered in butter, in a *frittata*, or in a Catalan omelette (*truita*).

PREPARED IN THE SIMPLEST WAY. Wash, tear apart and throw wet into a pan with a minimum of boiling water for 5 minutes; then drain and firmly press between two plates. The leaves are then ready to be chopped on a board and cooked for a few minutes in butter, veal broth, or cream, seasoned with a pinch of salt and a grate of nutmeg. Sometimes a small finely sliced onion or shallot is first browned in the butter before putting in the chopped spinach.

The leaves of *barbabietola*, spinach beet, are treated in the same way, but need more pressing. The stems, with the fibrous element removed, are cooked separately, stewed in oil or butter, as they take longer. See also goose-foots, these plants when wild (p 198).

ESPINACS AMB PANSES I PINYONS
spinach with raisins and pine kernels

This Catalan dish is similar to Artusi's 'Spinach for lean days as practised in Romagna', except that it contains pine kernels (*pinyons*) as well as raisins (*panses*). If making it with spinach beet, be sure to remove the stems and ribs of the leaves. The dish is served at the beginning of a meal, cooked at the last moment, 5 or 6 minutes only.

1 kg (2¼ lb) spinach or spinach beet
a handful of Malaga raisins and the same of pine kernels
4 tablespoons olive oil · salt

Wash the spinach well, then put it dripping into a large pan, cook on a moderate heat with a little salt for a few minutes until it has rendered its liquor. Drain well.

Put the olive oil into a frying pan or, better, a *paella*, heat it and throw in the raisins, which swell in 2 minutes; add the pine kernels, which will brown in a moment; then add the spinach and the salt. Turn it about with a wooden fork for a few moments, then serve at once.

CAVOLFIORE · cauliflower

Brassica oleracea var *botrytis* · family BRASSICACEAE
col-i-flor (C) · kounoupíthi (G)

Of the many varieties, the Violetto di Sicilia is the most exquisite, presenting a deep violet or deep green 'head'. This cauliflower is less substantial than the white varieties and is steamed, or boiled at speed, then dressed while hot with olive oil and a few drops of wine vinegar.

CAVOLFIORE COLLA SALSA VIRGILIANA
cauliflower with Virgil's sauce

The cauliflowers for this should be tight-packed with spiral inflorescences, of the cultivar called Palla di neve (snowball).

Cut the florets and plunge them for a few minutes in salted boiling water. They must remain whole and crisp. Strain them, put them in a china dish and dress with a sauce composed of 4 or 5 cloves of garlic, peeled and crushed with a little salt in the mortar, to which you add a thread of oil as for mayonnaise, stirring in one direction, then add 2 tablespoons of grated dry breadcrumbs, a few drops of wine vinegar and some chopped parsley. This sauce is even more piquant if you pound a filleted anchovy in the mortar first, and add some capers.

ZUCCA INVERNALE • winter pumpkin

Cucurbita maxima, C moschata • family CUCURBITACEAE
carbassa (C) • kokkinokolokýthia (G)

The first species is called *zucca comune*; it is large, long and smooth with a golden exterior. *C moschata* is gnarled on the outside. Both are sweet, either can be used.

ZUCCA INVERNALE 'IN INSALATA' • pumpkin salad

Something Virgilian remains in this Apulian dish.

Peel, seed and dice half a winter pumpkin. Use the other half for pumpkin soup (p 75) or pumpkin preserve (p 308).

Boil the golden cubes in slightly salted water in a pan, then strain. Put them in an earthenware dish, and make a dressing of garlic, olive oil and white wine vinegar with some chopped leaves of mint. Sprinkle the cubes with fresh grated crumbs, then pour on the dressing, which will be absorbed. Serve cold.

RADICCHIO ROSSO, CICORIA DI TREVISO, ROSSO DI VERONA

red salad variety of *Cichoria endivia* • family ASTERACEAE

One of the best winter salads, both for colour and taste, especially if combined with corn salad (*valerianella*). Dress with olive oil and vinegar.

BATATA • sweet potato

Ipomoea batatas • family CONVOLVULACEAE
batata (C) • glikopatáta (G)

Sweet potatoes, originally introduced from Spain and the Canary Islands, were in common use in England long before the so-called Virginia potato.

On Naxos they were a staple form of winter food, roasted in the ashes of a wood fire or in the bread oven as it cooled. In places where poverty restricts the purchase of sugar, they are prized, as is the winter pumpkin, both being rich in sugar.

One can of course bake them like parsnips in the oven, or take a hint from Parkinson and, having baked them, reduce them to a purée and serve with beef marrow and powdered cinnamon. In Falstaff's time they were roasted, then steeped in sack (which derives from *vin seck*, dry wine, i e dry sherry, imported also from Spain) and sugar.

CAVOLO • cabbage

Brassica oleracea • family BRASSICACEAE
col (C) • láhano (G)

Cavolo verza (variety *sabauda*), a little cabbage soprano, sounds a tender note in the winter repertoire. Slice it raw on a *mandoline* and serve as a salad with an oil and vinegar dressing.

TO COOK. Slice very fine with a truffle slicer and simmer in a little olive oil in a pan with a finely sliced onion. Add a teaspoon of seeds of dill, and a little salt. Keep the lid on. Ready in 10 minutes.

FOR MAKING *DOLMÁDES*. In late winter the *verza* becomes more substantial and can be used instead of vine leaves for this purpose. The leaves have to be carefully separated, and blanched for 4 or 5 minutes in rapidly boiling water, before making the little packets of well-flavoured rice. The colour is more brilliant than when the rather pale, but more resistant cabbage called *cappuccio* is used.

CAVOLO 'TESTA DI NEGRO' STUFATO • stewed red cabbage

a large firm red cabbage of port wine colour • a good shredder
2 large Spanish onions • 3 cooking apples
1 tablespoon pure pork fat • salt and ground pepper
1 heaped tablespoon of brown sugar • a pinch of mace or nutmeg

4 ground allspice · a strip of orange zest
1 dessertspoon of goose fat
1 glass of red wine · 1 dessertspoon of wine vinegar

Cut the cabbage in four, cutting out and discarding the thick white stem, and shred it finely. Slice the onions; peel and cut up the apples.

Melt the pork fat slowly in an enamelled iron casserole, put in some onion, then some cabbage and some of the apple. Sprinkle with salt, sugar, and all the other seasonings and repeat the sequence. When the receptacle is full, add the goose fat, wine and vinegar, put on the lid and simmer slowly, from time to time turning the whole mass with a wooden spoon. Cooked slowly, no water is required, and the colour is retained, a perfect foil for the goose and equally good with pheasant (p 245).

YOUNG VEGETABLES: COOKING *À LA GRECQUE*

While English travellers in the 18th century cultivated their passion for Greek ruins and their romantic sensibilities, Frenchmen extended the repertoire of culinary practice by direct observation in the course of travel. This is why cooking *à la grecque* is a perfectly familiar part of classic French cooking. But I must say that it is, as you would expect, a refined version of what the Greeks actually do and applies only to very young vegetables, for instance: cauliflower florets, celery hearts, broccoli, young artichokes, bulbous fennel, mushrooms and fungi, small 'pickling' onions, cucumbers and young leeks.

Make a court-bouillon of the following:

3 parts water to 1 part of olive oil with lemon juice
salt · a dozen coriander seeds · a few whole peppercorns
a bouquet garni composed of parsley, thyme, fennel fronds,
celery tops, coriander leaves, a bayleaf

Boil the liquor for 5 minutes to extract these flavours, then throw in the selected vegetable, neatly trimmed to a uniform size. Cook rapidly till tender without a lid; the water will be absorbed and will also evaporate, leaving a delicious oil and vegetable 'essence' which is strained over the vegetable as a sauce (the bouquet garni having first been removed). Add some very finely chopped parsley or coriander leaves and serve to start off the meal.

When leeks and broccoli are cooked *à la grecque*, the lemon is omitted in the cooking, as it discolours them. So squeeze half a lemon over the dish just before serving. See page 110 for leeks *à la grecque* served by Irving Davis with *fagioli borlotti* and *ventresca di tonno* as a first course.

BIETOLA DA ORTO • spring beetroot

Beta vulgaris var *esculenta* • family CHENOPODIACEAE
bleda d'hortalissa (C) • kokinogoúli (G)

Spring is the time to acquire a bunch or two of little round beetroots.

Boil them in salted water for 20 minutes, slip off their skins, and serve whole, dressed with olive oil, pepper and a thread of wine vinegar. They taste like fruit. Colour: magenta, when grown in Tuscany.

In Apulia a variety quite unknown further up 'the boot' is cultivated; it is a glorious pink and of a much finer texture. Prepared as above, but flavoured with the chopped leaves of *sedano* (green celery) and served with goat's cheese, in the Sculptor's opinion 'a heavenly marriage'. Its dark green leaves stained with red are cooked like spinach.

CARCIOFO • globe artichoke

Cynara cardunculus var *scolymus* • family ASTERACEAE
carxofa (C) • anginára (G)

This giant thistle, native of southern Europe, with silvery grey-green leaves, resembling the acanthus leaf in shape, grows at its best where the flower spike comes quickly to maturity; hence its cultivation in vast fields in the Bay of Paestum, the Bay of Naples, Sicily and the plain of Bari. Artichokes are very heavy feeders and, if grown near other plants, at once inhibit them. Natives of limestone, they dislike frost and normally flower below the frost line.

There are two main varieties: those with a pointed head and prickly leaves, Spinosa Sardo, and those with a rounded head and no prickles, Romanesco. See their use in a *frittata* (p 91), cooked *à la grecque* (p 169), preserved in oil (p 317) and fried (p 171). Here I shall only say that of the many ways the simplest are often the best:

CARCIOFI VICENTINI • Vicenza artichokes

Use small spring artichokes with succulent stems in early youth. Peel back the outer leaves, cut off about a third of the calyx at the top, and cut off the stems – pare the tender part of these and cut into small pieces. Open out the artichokes a little, gently. Wipe them with the cut halves of a lemon; this prevents discolouration.

Fit them into an enamelled pan, bottoms down, putting the stems in the gaps. Add water, but not so as to cover, then pour some olive oil into each of the slightly opened artichokes. Add salt, pepper, some coriander seeds, some leaves of mint, bring to the boil with the lid on, and cook vigorously for 20 minutes. The liquid will be partly absorbed and will partly evaporate.

Serve hot or cold, dressed with olive oil, wine vinegar, and a little of their liquor.

The reason that artichokes are always served to begin a meal is that their flowers and those of the allied cardoon contain a milky substance which, dried, was used to coagulate milk in cheese-making. As with the fig, this has a peculiar effect on the taste of wine.

CARCIOFI FRITTI CON PARMIGIANO GRATTUGIATO
fried artichokes with grated parmesan

A simple way of dealing with more mature artichokes, which I learned from a Lucanian gastronome, Francesco Radino. Peel back the outer leaves of 8 artichokes, cut off the tops and divide each artichoke into four even pieces (halve, then quarter) and nip out the choke. Put some olive oil in a heavy pan and fry the slices, but not too fast, adding salt and 100 g (3½ oz) of parmesan sprinkled over them. They gradually become crisp and brown. Drain and serve with lemon slices.

CARCIOFI COLLE FAVE • artichokes with broad beans

Young artichokes go well with broad beans. In this case you slice them into eight segments and simmer them for a few moments in olive oil in an earthenware pot. Add salt and the podded broad beans, and some leaves of mint. Cook, covered, for 10 minutes. No liquor is required, as the broad beans make their own. Shake the pot from time to time.

CARCIOFI CON RISO • artichokes with rice

Peel back the outer leaves of 6 artichokes, leave an inch or so of stem, quarter them and remove the choke. Fry in olive oil in a shallow pan with 2 peeled cloves of garlic. When slightly brown, add a cupful of rice (*superfino arborio*), cook for 3 minutes, stirring, then add 3 cups of hot chicken stock, a little at a time. Rinse a dozen capers and put them in; also, if you have them, some freshly podded green chickpeas. Cook, uncovered, till the liquor is absorbed, then add chopped coriander leaves or parsley. Turn out into an earthenware dish and cover with several layers of cloth. In 10 minutes it is ready to eat, with or without hard-boiled eggs, a spring dish for lunch.

ADDING ARTICHOKES TO BRAISED CHICKEN. Trim and cut into eight sections 4 or 5 artichokes, removing the choke if any and including a few cm of pared stem. Immerse in acidulated water. Rinse and dry, then fry (unfloured) in olive oil till brown, adding the juice of a lemon in the last few minutes. These morsels, strained of their oil, are added to a braised chicken in the last 10 minutes of cooking; they will absorb the juices of the bird.

A FINAL NOTE. An explanation of the particular delicacy of the Salentine snail called *municedda*, little monk (*attuppatedda* in Sicilian), is that they feed on the delicate new leaves of artichokes before vanishing underground for their summer 'sleep'. (See Snails, p 152.)

SCARIOLA · escarole   ENDIVIA · curly endive

Cichorium endivia var *latifolium*   *C endivia* var *crispum*

INSALATA DI ENDIVIA E SCARIOLA: a spring salad. The crisp *scariola* has a salubrious bitter taste; its heart is blanched. The *endivia* is tousle-headed, fine-leaved, also blanched, and normally called 'curly endive' – the familiar winter salad. Both are of the family ASTERACEAE.

Place the well-washed and carefully separated and shaken leaves of these salads in a large wooden bowl. Add 2 desalted anchovies cut into small pieces; a dozen capers, rinsed; a small white onion, bulb and stem, chopped; some tiny shoots of *cicoria 'asparago'* (p 162); and a freshly pulled bulb of fennel, sliced into fine pieces. Dress with a vinaigrette and toss the salad, then add a few leaves of newly sprouted mint.

LUPPOLO · hop

Humulus lupulus · family CANNABACEAE
llúpol (C) · lykískos (G)

SALAD OF HOP SHOOTS. These shoots, picked about 7.5 cm (3″) long, blanched for a few moments in boiling water, then dressed with oil and vinegar, are delicious; poor man's asparagus. Picking time is April. The shoots can also be used in a *frittata* (p 91).

FAVA · broad bean

Vicia faba · family FABACEAE
fava (C) · koukí (G)

Broad beans, being native to Apulia (as they are to Catalonia, Sicily and Greece), this simple culinary advice comes from the origins.

For the consumption of raw broad beans, see Fasting on Naxos (p 61); and for raw beans eaten in Tuscany see page 251. The best cheeses to eat with raw broad beans are the Greek *féta*, salty, and the Sardinian *marzotica*, a kind of ricotta made from ewe's milk, well drained, dried and conserved with salt (made in March, as its name implies).

FAVE FRESCHE (fresh broad beans). When in April broad beans become just too large to eat raw, but are tender, the outer skin being green, they are thrown into hot oil in an earthenware pot (*la pignata*) in which a sliced *sprunzala* (onion shoot) is already simmering and are cooked for a brief time with a little salt and a sprig or two of mint. A delicacy.

FAVE FRESCHE IN STUFA • broad beans stewed

When the beans are larger (older), husk them and pinch off their outer skins, no longer green but creamy white. Slice up a sweet white onion, put the slices in an earthenware pot (or enamelled pan) in a little olive oil, and, before they begin to brown, put in some strips neatly cut from a slice of *prosciutto crudo* (not paper thin), or, failing that, *pancetta* (salt belly of pork), both fat and lean, and brown them. Add the washed beans, salt and pepper, and some chopped mint or coriander leaves or fronds of dill. If the beans seem to be drying before they are tender, add a very little chicken stock. (A fresh green chilli pepper, seeded, is sometimes sliced and simmered in the oil with the sliced onion.)

FAVES GUISADES • Catalan broad beans stewed

The Catalan way is different. The beans are 'sweated' in an earthenware *olla* (no oil, no water) on a very low heat, slightly salted. Aromatics are prepared in a separate pan: a sliced onion, a sliced garlic clove, a bouquet of fresh parsley, thyme, rosemary and origano – all simmered in pure pork fat for a few minutes, then transferred to the *olla*, which is shaken from time to time to prevent the beans from sticking and to distribute the aromatics. The bouquet is removed and the beans are served with various sausages, *botifarra negra* (a blood sausage, p 232) and *bull blanc*, a white pork sausage, separately cooked.

PISELLI • peas

Pisum sativum • family FABACEAE
pèsols (C) • bizélli (G)

In Apulia peas ripen after broad beans, though both have been planted together, from late October to December. The native pea is small, and abundant; the plant growing in open ground needs no support. Their season is short, the month of May, as the May sun quickly dries them. During this month they provide the daily fare; it is impossible to tire of peas and beans when growing them oneself. It is often the broad bean for lunch and a vast dish of peas for supper. But the first peas are eaten raw with bread and salt and a glass of wine before supper.

TO COOK THEM. Pour some olive oil in the bottom of an earthenware pot, or a *pignata* if you have one. Put in the washed peas 'wet' (i e rapidly drained), add salt, a sliced new onion, and some leaves of mint. Cover and cook gently on a low heat. They will make their own liquor. Shake or stir occasionally. In 10 minutes they are ready to serve, on their own or used as a dressing for pasta (spaghetti, *orecchiette*, *laganelle*, etc). Often one or two hot chilli peppers go into the pot with the sliced onion.

ZUCCHINI · baby marrows, courgettes

Cucurbita pepo varieties · family CUCURBITACEAE
carbassons (C) · kolokithákia (G)

Infant zucchini can be boiled in salted water with a little olive oil for a few minutes; then, brilliant green, they are drained, sliced while hot, and dressed with oil and vinegar. They have a curious taste of seafood.

IF YOU GROW YOUR OWN. Pick them at early morning very young with some of their orange flowers, slice them slantwise across and cook in olive oil with a sliced sweet white onion, salt, and mint or basil, with the lid on. This takes 10 minutes.

TO DEEP-FRY. Slice them lengthways ½ cm (¼″) thick, salt the slices and leave them to exude their liquor for an hour. Rinse, dry, and shake the slices in a clean cloth with flour. Precipitate them into very hot oil, in which they take only a few minutes to cook. Drain on paper.

A SALENTINE WAY. In the Salento, where these *cucuzze* are grown by every agriculturist, little breads are made called *cuccuzzare* in which segments of zucchini and hot green peppers, lightly fried, are worked with olive oil into the dough (a variation of the *puccia*, which normally contains black olives).

FIORI DI ZUCCHINI FRITTI (flowers of courgettes fried in batter). Make a batter (*la pastella*, see p 200) and immerse the flowers in it for an hour. Heat some olive oil (or sunflower seed oil) in a deep-frying pan and, when it begins to smoke, put in the flowers a few at a time. The batter will quickly brown – whisk them out, drain, and eat at once.

ZUCCHINI AL FORNO · courgettes in the oven

3 or 4 small courgettes · salt
1 kilo (2¼ lb) plum tomatoes · salt · origano
2 fresh eggs · a little flour · olive oil
a mozzarella · 2 hard-boiled eggs
pangrattato (fine oven-dried crumbs) · grated parmesan

Slice the courgettes lengthwise ½ cm (¼″) thick, sprinkle them with salt and leave them on a plate to disgorge their liquor, with another plate on top; after an hour rinse and dry.

Make the tomato sauce by simmering the tomatoes for half an hour, seasoned with salt and origano, in the minimum of water, then pass through a sieve; the sauce is not dense.

Beat up the fresh eggs, dip the courgette slices in the egg, then in flour, and fry lightly in hot oil, to brown them.

Oil an earthenware casserole, put a layer of courgettes on the bottom, season, add a few thin slices of mozzarella and a little of the sauce, cover the layer with more courgette slices, season, add sliced hard-boiled egg, some mozzarella and some sauce, and repeat until all is used up.

Cover the top with fine oven-dried crumbs and grated parmesan, and pour over it a thread of olive oil. Bake in a moderate oven for half an hour.

Aubergines can be prepared in the same way.

PEPERONE DOLCE	PEPERONE AMARO
sweet pepper	chilli pepper

Capsicum annuum	*C frutescens*
family SOLANACEAE	
pebrot (C)	pebre coent, bitxo (C)
piperiá (G)	kokkinopípero (G)

August and September is the time when red, yellow and green 'sweet' peppers are at their best, large and firm. Chilli peppers, *peperoncini amari*, fruit in July and August, but these usually remain green until well into September, when they finally turn a fiery red. In hot weather they are a definite stimulus to appetite.

A Carrarese friend insisted that Italians are so busy worrying about their digestions that they have given up *la peperonata*. But this is as improbable as the Greek contention that watercress is an aphrodisiac.

Versions of the dish called *la peperonata* appear wherever sweet and hot peppers are grown – in Italy, Greece, Spain, Turkey, Hungary, Romania, Morocco, Israel etc. It is served cold.

LA PEPERONATA

3 large red and 3 yellow peppers
1 large sweet white onion
½ kilo (1 lb 2 oz) plum tomatoes
olive oil
thyme and origano
salt
1 glass of red wine

1 green chilli pepper
2 cloves of garlic
parsley
basil leaves

Cut the red and yellow peppers in half and remove core and seeds. Slice the onion. Pour boiling water over the tomatoes, peel, seed and chop them. Cover the bottom of a solid pan with olive oil, set it on a low flame and put in the onion, peppers and tomatoes. Sprinkle with the herbs and a little salt and put on the lid. Simmer for a few minutes to allow the vegetables to produce some juice, then pour in the wine. Simmer slowly for 20 minutes, making sure at the end that the peppers don't stick.

Roast the chilli pepper on the grill or over a flame, peel and seed it, then pound it in a little mortar with the garlic and chopped parsley and torn basil leaves. Liberate with a little oil and pour into the pan. Simmer for a few more minutes, turn out onto a white china dish and peel off the very fine skins of the peppers – it is these skins which are not digestible.

PEPERONCINI AMARI · hot green chilli peppers

When the sun enters the Lion these fruits are crisp and green. Picked at early morning, they are washed, then thrown entire into a pan in which some olive oil is heating, almost smoking hot. This produces a hissing sound and the immediate collapse of the hot little peppers. Turn down the heat, add salt, 2 or 3 crushed tomatoes and a leaf or two of mint, and shake to prevent sticking.

This is eaten cold with thick hunks of bread and draughts of strong red Apulian wine. A Salentine joke is to offer this dish to strangers. For those working in the fields it is a distinct restorative at 9.30 a.m., work having started at dawn.

What would Tuscans think of this dish? They spoke of our 'emigration' to Apulia as a 'descent into Africa'. Tradition has it that the Turks who raided the coasts of this region for centuries introduced the chilli pepper, which they hoped would be the inhabitants' undoing. Instead they became a fundament of Apulian cooking. These peppers, once turned red, are preserved *sott'olio* (p 317) and also in vinegar, *sott'aceto*; are used in *la salsa secca amara* (p 322); and are dried on strings, then grilled over the fire to produce a domestic form of cayenne pepper.

MELANZANA · aubergine, eggplant

Solanum melongena · family SOLANACEAE
albergínia (C) · melintzána (G)

Aubergines; the French name, which we also use, derives from the Catalan *albergínies*. Dr Grewe says that these fruits were introduced to Europe by the Arabs, but their consumption was limited for centuries to the Iberian peninsula, Sicily, southern Italy and Greece. This information is underpinned by the presence of four recipes for *albergínies* in the 14th century manuscript *Sent Soví*, three in Robert de Nola's *Libre del Coch* and one in the Neapolitan manuscript called 'Marignani'. (In connection with this name, it may be of interest to know that the Salentine dialect word for aubergine is *marangiana*.)

Those interested in the history of gastronomy and in this exotic plant, which we sometimes grow, should consult Elizabeth David's article 'Mad, Bad, Despised and Dangerous' in *PPC* 9. For a mind-bending account of the evolution of aubergines (originally called *badhinjan*) in Islamic cookery, see Charles Perry's 'Buran: 1100 Years in the Life of a Dish' in the *Journal of Gastronomy*. (For these articles, see Bibliography).

That wonderfully disgruntled traveller, Tobias Smollett, writing in 1764, naturally found this fruit insipid – but esteemed by the Jews of Leghorn (Livorno). 'Much eaten,' he wrote, 'in Spain and the Levant as well as by the Moors in Barbary.' (*Travels through France and Italy*)

MELINTZÁNES • aubergines cooked in an Athenian way

The economy of means in Greek cooking is to be emulated. Observed in an Athenian tavern: the chef takes a large shallow pan and covers it with olive oil. He slices a number of aubergines in half lengthwise, lays them unpeeled in the bottom of the pan, sprinkles them with olive oil and salt. On this foundation he puts a layer of sliced onions, the white variety, sweet in taste, and on top of them a layer of peeled and roughly chopped tomatoes, and a little more salt.

He then pours on a little water, a glass of wine and a tablespoon of wine vinegar. The pan is covered and put on a hot fire. When it begins to steam, he reduces the heat and leaves the aubergines to simmer until they are soft, the onions tender and the tomatoes pulpy, the liquor having practically evaporated or been absorbed.

He ignored, I noticed, the common practice of first getting the fruit to disgorge their liquor, by applying salt to the cut surface and pressing under a weighted plate for an hour, before rinsing and drying them; but this is recommended when frying them in slices.

MELINTZANOSALÁTA • aubergine salad

This delicious Greek dish is served chilled in summer; it can be made in the cool of the early morning.

Make a vine-twig fire out of doors and, when it flares up, put a number of young shiny aubergines on a grill directly on the flames. Keep the fire going fiercely and, when the undersides blacken, turn them over. In 10 or 15 minutes they will be pulpy (they collapse) and completely black.

Empty the aubergines of their pulp by cutting them in half, and remove some of the seeds if they are too numerous. Then, in a basin or large mortar, pound 2 or 3 cloves of peeled garlic, put in and pound the pulp, adding the juice of 2 or 3 lemons which will blanch the preparation, and salt.

Beat in 2 raw egg yolks, then pour in a thread of olive oil. Aim at the consistency of cream. Add some capers, rinsed of their liquor, and some freshly chopped parsley or basil leaves. Serve for supper out of doors with hard-boiled eggs, black olives and good bread.

MELANZANE RIEMPITE • stuffed aubergines

Take 4 fine shining fruits and boil them in plenty of water for about 20 minutes. Drain and pass them under the cold tap, then cut in two lengthwise, carefully detaching the stalk. Scrape out the pulp, which should be fairly soft, without damaging the skins. Chop it up and mix with 2 tablespoons of dry crumbs of rye bread (first soaked in milk, then squeezed), some chopped garlic, a tablespoon of parmesan, a few capers, salt, pepper, a chopped hard-boiled egg and some leaves of mint. Beat up 2 raw eggs and mix into the pulp, then stuff the aubergines.

An Apulian summer dish, these stuffed aubergines are often put into the bread oven in an oiled *tiella* (baking tin), with a little tomato sauce and some grated *pecorino* – a very digestible way, but are often fried.

As the vegetable lady Clorinda says, aubergines certainly are indigestible, especially when conserved in vinegar. Experience shows that grilling them whole or in slices on an ardent fire expels the poison; so does preliminary boiling, as above, and salting the slices.

CETRIOLO	•	MELONE
cucumber		sweet melon

Cucumis sativus	family	*Cucumis melo*
cogombre (C)	CUCURBITACEAE	meló (C) • pepóni (G)

Speaking of poison, cucumber contains an indigestible element, which also can be expelled by preliminary salting. In Apulia, the warty cucumber is more often grown, a cultivar of *Cucumis sativus*, rather than its relation – the long smooth variety: warty cucumbers for salad purposes, dwarf warty cucumbers for conserving in vinegar.

But the cucumber scene is complicated by the fact that another 'cucumber', short, oval, dark-skinned, hairy, plays a double role. In July when young it serves as cucumber, needs no preliminary salting, is crisp and refreshing; but, when one or two specimens are left on the plant, they swell into delightful round green melons which, cut in late September, can be stored indoors and keep till Christmas. In dialect it is *cucummarazzu* or *milune*, but more often *minne di monaca*, 'nun's tits'. These are the ones we grow.

At the 'cucumber' stage they appear at table, washed but whole, and are eaten peeled or unpeeled; or they are partially peeled, cut into chunks, dressed with a little salt, oil, vinegar. The mature fruit, very delicate in taste, is served with *prosciutto crudo* to start a festive meal in autumn or winter.

There are some other kinds of cucumber-melons, first masquerading as oddly shaped cucumbers and eaten as such, later declaring themselves as green or golden ovoid melons. These also keep till Christmas but are not so good as the 'nun's tits'; add a touch of ginger or lemon.

ÓKRA, BÁMMIA (G) • okra

Hibiscus esculentus • family MALVACEAE

On Naxos, okra ripened in September and we were always glad to find an 'offering' suspended on the doorhandle of the desert lorry, a bag of okra. This is how they are cooked in Apollona.

ÓKRA KE PATÁTES • okra and potatoes

1 kg (2¼ lb) okra	2 or 3 tomatoes, peeled and
3 or 4 potatoes	chopped
1 onion	a wineglass of Naxian amber
2 tablespoons of olive oil	wine
salt and pepper	a few crushed fennel seeds

Trim the okra by paring off the little caps, and cut the tips. Cut the peeled potatoes into substantial slices. Slice the onion and put everything in the pan with some olive oil on a good heat.

After a few minutes reduce the heat and barely simmer. They will be cooked by the time most of the liquid has evaporated. Add a little olive oil and some chopped parsley or coriander leaves. Served hot or cold.

They can also be cooked, the fruit prepared as above, in olive oil, on their own, and simmered with mint leaves, and a little salt.

When not in their first youth, i e no longer brilliant green, and more than 5 cm (2″) long, it is best to top and tail them, season with salt, pour a little oil over them and leave to marinate for a day; this removes a certain viscosity in older fruits. Then rinse them and cook as above.

POMODORO • tomato

Lycopersicon esculentum • family SOLANACEAE
tomàquet (C) • domáta (G)

The first mention in the Old World of the *mala aurea* or *poma amoris* (Latin, meaning golden apple, love apple) occurs in a herbal of 1554 by Pierandrea Mattioli; he said that the Italians ate this fruit with oil, salt and pepper, as they still do.

See pages 319, 322 and 324 for types of tomato cultivated in southern Italy.

AMANIDA • Catalan tomato salad

Salad tomatoes in Greece and Catalonia seem to be of a different race, larger, firmer, tasting like fruit. They are always used green, with only the faintest tinge of pink, in salads. Crisp in texture, they are perfumed and sweet.

At Vendrell lunch began every day (this is universal summer Catalan practice) with these fruits cut in half across, scored with the point of a knife on the exposed surfaces, some slices of peeled garlic inserted, then sprinkled with salt and *orenga*, wild marjoram. Some very fine slices of raw sweet white onion were laid on top of each half, and sometimes one or two desalted anchovy fillets. Always prepared at the last moment for the sake of freshness. Everyone helped themselves to olive oil from the *setrill*, a little glass bottle with a fine spout.

ESCALIVADA • a vegetable braise

Eating out of doors in Catalonia is a commonplace in the delightful sense of an age-old habit. Every peasant took a carpet-covered picnic basket with him to the fields, his lunch protected from the heat and dust in the same way as his cart was lined with finely woven straw matting and rich oriental carpeting.

The country is so wild and so exposed that on any expedition inland one leaves behind the thought of finding an inn and gets into the way of taking along a wire grill, some little fishes, vegetables, oil, salt and a *porró* of wine and a loaf of bread.

This is a very pleasant way of spending the heat of the day. Even in the most deserted landscapes one often finds on sighting the ideally situated oak or cork tree, beside a narrow stream confined by boulders, that the position is already occupied. In the mountains Llanos de Urgell we suddenly confronted a cassocked priest sitting on a stone beside the ashes of a recently made fire. On our approach, he rose and with a ceremonious gesture indicated that the shady place which had been his was now freely ours. It is difficult to forget a courtesy extended in a stony desert punctuated with cistus and sages, the silence broken only by the wing flash of golden orioles, hoopoes, swallows, dragonflies.

3 aubergines	olive oil
2 long green (mild) peppers	garlic
2 long red (moderately hot)	thyme
peppers	rosemary
4 large tomatoes	winter savory
4 large Spanish onions	salt

Make a fire of dried maquis and, when it dies down, sprinkle it with the herbs and put the vegetables directly on the glowing embers. Turn them about from time to time until all the skins are black. The tomatoes cook the quickest, the peppers and aubergines take 20 minutes, and the onions take an hour.

Take them off the fire, remove the charred skins, and wash your hands in the stream. Cut them up into strips, put them straight onto slabs of bread. Sprinkle with olive oil, chopped garlic and salt.

Escalivada means a braise in its original sense, that is, cooking on glowing embers. This is prehistoric cooking before the invention of earthenware. It refers to the method, not to the vegetables, because the method dates back at least 8000 years (first earthenware pots in Europe) and probably to the beginning of fire; while the vegetables employed here are of recent introduction. (The onion is said to have been introduced from Egypt by Alexander the Great around 330 BC; the aubergine, for which see page 178, was a gift from the Arabs in early mediaeval times; the tomato arrived in the 16th century, on the heels of the conquest of Mexico, and so did the peppers, coming from both America and India.)

Before these vegetables appeared on the scene, there were bulbs and roots that may have served. Learning from the Elder Pliny (Book XXI under Bulbs) that the bulbs of the sea squill, *Urginea maritima* and the tuber-like root clusters of asphodel were cooked in this way in Roman times, I made an experiment with a bulb of the sea squill, which outwardly resembles a giant onion in form. The taste was extraordinarily bitter and explains why the roasted bulb was pounded with figs in Pliny's time.

Castelpoggio

WHEN we came to the high-up village, high up above Carrara, it was like winter but it was April, not a tree out, and sometimes it was mist and rain like Wales. The Sculptor had been given the use of a ruined villa – confiscated by the Comune from a noted fascist – and here, under a partially covered balcony of the roofless villa, the first marble sculptures were made. As most of the men in the village were quarry-men or marble-workers, the presence of a sculptor did not seem strange.

We lodged with La Dirce, a widow, in the top of her house. The marble table in the kitchen was cold, the marble floor was cold, we had to light a fire at night. It was a mystery to us what to do about wood. Wood was everywhere. It was being chopped in the fist-sized piazza under the naked plane trees outside our window. It was being cut on every chestnut hillside, trussed and faggotted and trotted in on muleback. It was being carted morning, noon and night on women's heads, faggots proudly sailing through the village. In Dirce's backyard the bundles were stacked as high as the roof.

Every inch of the surrounding wooded hillsides belonged to particular peasants. Some evenings, out among the Spanish chestnuts, we made a firewood bundle and on the way back stuffed a donkey-bag full of fircones. Passing through the village at dusk, we were eyed with a touch of incredulity . . . so they've been for wood, have they? . . . and a touch of scorn . . . funny sort of *signori* to be carrying their own firewood. The mother of a marble worker Ermano, used to intercept us and ask: 'Why don't you make a proper-sized faggot and carry it like everyone else on your head?' We were, so to speak, in a cleft stick.

Dirce, seeing us arriving with our trophy, was delighted that we had the foraging instinct. Foraging was her way of life. If she heard of a tree cut but still hanging over some ravine far off, off she went to get it. On the way she cut the pathside grass with a little billhook for the rabbits and stuffed it in a bag. If the new shoots of old man's beard gleamed coppery by the wayside, she cropped them rapidly, as good as wood sorrel in soup.

Going for a forage with Dirce was keeping an eye needled on opportunity; it was bearing in mind the specific needs of calf, hens, rabbits, the kitchen cauldron and her son Alfredo, who came back up from Carrara at night. It also involved a kind of eager childish delight in the sudden spring-time warmth, the breeze on the mountainside, the freedom of leaving the village.

When the sack was full, the tree chopped, the work done but for bearing it home, we left the plunder and the billhook on the pathside and walked on into the pine, larch and cypress plantation which densely clothed a once eroded mountainside. Dirce sniffed the air with pleasure; every tree had its own scent, she said. We sat down in the short grass and started cracking pine-nuts on a rock. They had dropped out of the over-ripe cones of the stone pine. Going back, she twisted her head-kerchief into a little crown, set it on her head, knelt down and straddled the enormous sack onto it, then somehow managed to stand up.

Her life was spent in leaving the village in four different directions: to the vineyard on the far hill; to the chestnut grove past the disused red marble quarry on the piece of bare mountain, all rocks, wild thyme and rabbit grass, once prospected for likely marble; past the Madonnina's starred blue shrine, down to the little fields where earth hard as terracotta had to be hack-hoed and manured to raise the haricot beans; up the steep goat path above the village which lead to the hay meadows. The whole of the mountainsides round Castelpoggio were parcelled out in this manner.

Vipers and snakes here are *le biscie*, the word hissed out. Dirce would have you believe that the chestnut woods were rattling with serpents, as the sky is rocked by the devil when a storm breaks. Her eyes glittered at the devil's works and flickered at the thought of serpents. We were always supposed to go into the woods with ankle-high boots. Once we saw a long black and gold snake draped round a tree stump. Sometimes there was a rustle in the dry chestnut leaves, too slow to be mistaken for a lizard, and probably a slow worm. But when you stepped on something in the leafed-up groves, it was usually last year's chestnut spines.

Below the village the chestnut woods descend into deep ravines for two thousand feet. They are threaded with winding mule paths which lead down to shaded streams, past waterfalls, rockroses and plumes of erica, to a remote village, Casano. Another way led down a wooded ridge to onion-domed Ortonova, perched on a little hill overlooking the plain and the Magra. Distances were telescoped by steepness and it was not until one had embarked on the labyrinthine paths in the deep woods that one began to gauge them.

The Castelpoggians were very conservative on the subject of flowers. Flowers were the rose, carnation, geranium and just possibly marguerites; and lilies and chrysanthemums, of course, the flowers which are set against the marble 'chests of drawers' in the cemetery perched on a hill above the village. The drawer-like tombs are placed one above the other against the cemetery walls. The ceramic photographs of the departed – tight-lipped peasant women, grandfathers in high-crowned quarrymen's hats – are fixed in keyhole position on the drawer-face. Dirce said these tombs are fine, they keep the rain off the dead. Saints and angels in whitest marble and plastic flowers are all about the place; on Saint's Days, the 'flowers' are those mentioned above. There is a high entrance gate to this necropolis through which the fireflies in late May flicker at night; their apparition marks the moment for planting the haricot beans.

Field flowers don't count. They cost nothing, they have no names, unless they are mauve and are called *viola* or star-shaped and called *stelle*. Only those flowers which the cattle won't eat are named, asphodel, spurges, and wolf's weed which is *Aristolochia* (pitcher plant). Flowers are not named, I realized, because in essence they are hay to a mountain peasant. They are unseen because no one goes into the mountain pastures until it is time to cut it.

We often wandered after work into these alpine meadows, where now began the wonderful procession of the limestone flowers.

The asphodels, starting in glades, dells, margins of the chestnut woods, later swirled down the mountain slopes. The river of deep green leaves wound like a snake and began to burst into starry flowers. The white green-striped *Allium triquetrum* flowered in the woods and on the upper shelves of Monte Faito.

The powdery white plumes of tree erica faded away and May began with an explosion of maritime broom. The little fields were a dense mass of flowers, it was purple *Orchis*, *Ophrys* and *Serapias* time, there was a peculiar yellow 'parrot' flower, perhaps a nettle; drifts of vermilion clover, many vetches, campanulas, marguerites just starting, forget-me-nots, the magenta cranesbill, stonecrops and saxifrages in the rocky parts, many kinds of spurge, and giant plantains that looked as if their flowers were trying to imitate the explosions of the asphodels. There were lady's bedstraw, marestails in the boggy parts, brilliant blue anchusas and pink and yellow columbines and stars of Bethlehem; the white bladder campion and the ragged pink one, deep blue larkspurs and the litmus flowers of the borage tribe.

On the steep slope behind La Pizza high up and nearly on a level with the glittering Campoceccina quarries beyond, there were still wood anemones, traces of cyclamen, primulas including the mealy-faced auricula, *Primula suaveolens*, and the mountain cowslip and many violets. The early spring flowers lingered on, the green and foetid hellebores, primroses and cowslips, where the sun failed to strike them.

On these slopes which offer a marvellous view of the distant wall of mountains of the Garfagnagna, still crowned with snow, were to be found, on a groundwork of dwarf broom and heather, many orchises, leaves of hellebore as large as paeony's, green spurges with coral centres, the yellow spurge which smells of honey, exquisite Solomon's seal, wild fennel, and the sinister dragon arum growing in the cleft of a stream. Later on this slope I found in summer besides wild Canterbury bells, the deep orange *Bombifolium* lily and the alpine gentian, and another gentian, less intensely blue, of a more shrubby kind.

Coming back down the mountain to Castelpoggio which, compact and shapely, crowned its precipitous hill, overlooking the far off glittering sea, we walked through a meadow deep in white clover and white chamomile, descending to other meadows, the grass a foot high and dense with flowers. This is the hay, which, cut and dried, then piled in beehive stacks secured on a central pole, is fed to the cows and yearling calves imprisoned in the village in their dark stalls.

Edible Weeds

EDWARDIAN Englishmen laughed at French governesses for picking wild chervil, dandelions and sorrel in spring for salads, for cutting nettle-heads for soup. The governesses ridiculed the Englishmen for their addiction to stewed rhubarb. Each person, through instinct, habit or prejudice, likes to pursue his or her own way to health.

I became interested in weeds on Naxos: everyone in Apollona, but more especially women and children, wandered about in February and March, before the spring declared itself, in search of weeds, picked before their flower-heads appeared. They called them by the portmanteau name *radíkia*, meaning plants with beneficial roots and leaves, but also specifically dandelions.

Many of these weeds belonged to the daisy and dandelion family. The most beneficent in this group are dandelions, *Taraxacum officinale*, and wild chicory, *Cichorium intybus*, but it includes yellow and purple goat's beard, the latter being wild salsify; wild endive, *Cichorium endivia*; hawkweed, hawksbeard and hawkbit; a daisy, *Bellis silvestris*, larger than the common one; the ox-eye daisy or marguerite; various kinds of sowthistle and a plant called *Urospermum picroides* resembling them (*picroides* meaning bitter, *picrá* in Greek). The more bitter the weeds, the better, as far as the Naxians were concerned. Milk thistles were also gathered, as was the blessed thistle. The field marigold, *Calendula arvensis*, was gathered whole when it first appeared, as was the corn marigold, *Chrysanthemum segetum*, and little plants of chamomile.

Their baskets also contained four umbelliferous plants – wild carrot, wild parsnip, wild fennel and wild chervil – and several crucifers – wild mustard, *Sinapis alba*, and allied white rocket, *Diplotaxis erucoides*, growing in cultivated fields, and also yellow rocket, *Eruca sativa*, growing in the wild. In the collection several mints appeared, particularly pennyroyal, *Menta pulegium*, as well as wild thymes and mountain savory, *Satureja montana*.

Most of these plants were gathered by cutting a section of the root, thus preserving the plant entire. Washed at the fountain, they were boiled and served with oil and lemon juice, the lemons picked from neighbouring groves. During the Lenten fast they were eaten in quantity like vegetable *spaghettini*, but without the olive oil.

Filling my water jar at the spring, I had a daily opportunity to examine these weeds and ask advice, and began to gather them myself, but at first always offering them for inspection. At the time I was reading the landscape and its flora with as much attention as one gives to an absorbing book.

Mediterranean people value 'bitterness' in weeds, as once did all European peoples. On Naxos, on a restricted winter diet, everyone suffered from appalling pains in the liver region, deriving not only from monotonous diet but also from impure water and the terrible north wind. The Sculptor and I soon discovered the benefits conferred by weeds.

*   *   *   *   *

Chi vo far 'na bona zena	Who wants to eat a good supper
i magn'un erb' d'tut la mena	should eat a weed of every kind

This old Carrarese saying puts the matter in a nutshell, diversity being as important in weeds as it is in human beings.

I had my first weed lesson in Castelpoggio with Dirce. She used to pounce on a great variety of mountain plants, pull them out with a

penknife, and thus abstract the crown of leaves with a piece of root. She stuffed them in a cloth and thrust them into the foraging sack. She called them all *radici* or *radicchi*, meaning roots.

These plants were much the same as those gathered by the Apollonians from the carrot and daisy families. They also included several kinds of sorrel; lady's smock, *Cardamine pratensis*; primrose, *Primula vulgaris*; foxglove but (NB) only the yellow kind; mountain cowslip; mountain orache, *Atriplex hortensis*; plantain and dock. Dirce also snatched at new shoots of wild clematis, wild hop, wild vine and wild asparagus.

At home she washed them all under the tap which she kept permanently running in the kitchen, as if it were the village fountain – piped water being a recent event. She boiled a cauldron of water on the fire, fuelled with Spanish chestnut faggots, boiled the weeds, drained them and ate them with olive oil and a few drops of wine vinegar, and hard-boiled eggs. She often shouted up the stairs with an offering of a dish of weeds, gladly accepted, both bitter and delicious.

Dirce said that during the war people ate the tuberous roots of mountain asphodel and the bulbs of the sea squill, *Urginea maritima*, belonging to the lily family. (For the method of cooking them, see *Escalavida*, p 182.) Speaking of bulbs, I mention here a cousin of the grape hyacinth. This is the tassel hyacinth, *Muscari comosum*, whose little bulbs are prised from the hard red earth in Apulia in March, called *pampasciune* in dialect and *cipollotto col fiocco* in Italian, a very welcome salad (p 202). The Naxians treat the corms of *Crocus cancellatus*, a pale lilac autumn-flowering crocus, in much the same way. (This should not be confused with the autumn crocus, *Colchicum autumnalis*, which is poisonous.)

At La Barozza I had a profitable weed lesson from a little girl of seven called Eugenia, who had an amazing weed vocabulary culled from the vineyard which her father worked. As she picked each plant, she said: 'This is for cooking' or 'This is for salad' (her plant categories).

The Tuscan vineyard weeds divide into two kinds, those that are boiled, *radici, radicchi*, which include most of the weeds already mentioned, plus wild leeks and wild garlic; corn poppy; wild clary, *Salvia sclarea*; comfrey, *Symphytum officinale*; young plants of borage; rampion, *Campanula rapunculoides*, which is a small campanula with fleshy white roots; sweet violet, *Viola odorata*; a white bulbous-flowered campion, *Silene inflata*; and alexanders, a celery-like plant, *Smyrnium olusatrum*.

Much of the medicinal value of these plants lies in the root, which is why they are picked with a stub of root; but only a stub, so that the plant is not destroyed but grows again.

The salad herbs, the other kind, include the flowers of borage, tasting of cucumber; rocket, *Eruca sativa* (which is also cultivated in gardens), and white wall rocket, *Diplotaxis erucoides*, and another little rocket, *Bunias erucago*, all three sharing the name *rucola* and all tasting of mustard. The leaves of the bladder campion when they first appear are also used as salad. So are the leaves and white roots of wild radish. Burnet is another salad plant, as are the small fresh leaves of centaury, hawkbits and hawkweeds, all with a bluish tinge. Fronds of wild fennel are picked for salad, and so is the buck's horn plantain, picked in its first youth; also wild lettuce, *Lactuca viminea* and *L scariola*, and corn salad, *valerianella* in Italian. All these vineyard plants are painstakingly washed and scrutinized for fading leaves, before being incorporated into a delicious mixed salad, dressed with olive oil and wine vinegar.

The time to pick them is when they are crisp after a touch of frost. Once the flower-head appears the taste is lost, but in wet periods in May there is another crop. The leaves of this vineyard salad are small, various, perfumed and crisp. All these plants grow on the vertical slopes which separate the vine terraces, and in late May their flowers, scythed with the grass, become the fragrant hay fed to the cow whose main function is to manure the vines.

In Italy one is always coming across a portmanteau word which describes a wide variety of things. *Radicchio* and *radice*, like the Greek *radíki*, are portmanteau words for anything with a succulent root, edible leaves and bitter taste, and the plants they refer to provide a balm for the liver. *Erbe* and *erbucce* are all the delicate wild salad plants.

Knowledge of these and other plants was for centuries our common European heritage. The English, once familiar with these weeds and their specific virtues, as described in early herbals, are now showing a revived interest in this heritage.

The first treatise on medicinal plants was written by a Greek doctor, Cratevas, in the 1st century BC. This illuminated codex existed in Byzantium (Constantinople) until the 17th century and served as a model for subsequent treatises, but was then lost. Because of this, Dioscorides' *De Materia Medica*, written in the 1st century AD, has come to be regarded as the original study of plants. Christian monks, both Greek Orthodox and Roman Catholic, pursued these studies, raised the wild plants in their walled gardens, dried their roots and leaves, pounded them to powder, and produced unguents and specifics for many ills.

The monks' gardens or *herbularii* contained beds in which were separately grown rosemary, mint, sage, lilies, iris, rue, gladiolus, roses, fenugreek, fennel, cumin etc. For an account of these gardens, see the work by Abatangelo cited in the Bibliography.

What is significant is the survival of this 'knowledge' in seasonal culinary practices, among Greeks, Italians, Catalans, in a tradition unsupported by literacy. The 'knowledge' is handed down, chiefly from mother to child, while stooping to gather the plants. (Fallow deer behave in the same way, the mother showing the fawn which plants to eat.)

The question now is – without Greek village ladies, Etruscan Dirce, and little girls like Eugenia, how are people to begin to recognize and identify plants? The answer is, I suppose, to consult good books on the subject, although this will be a slower and more uncertain method than those described above. One book to consult is Roger Phillips' *Wild Food*. In it you will find a warning. The subject – edible weeds – has aroused an interest just when its pursuit is threatened by the use of pesticides and weed-killers. One has now to acquire an acute awareness in any locality of the use of chemicals. In the Salento the user of these commodities hangs up a bottle or tin from a tree at the entrance to his terrain as a warning sign.

But there is another problem: in Britain, for example, certain wild plants are 'protected', and one must know which they are. Ignorance of the law can lead to heavy penalties.

So, quite apart from the ability to discern the edible plants, and awareness of their seasonal apparition, exact knowledge on two counts is required – the Law and the application of pesticides.

It is unfortunate that many modern plant books, relying on colour photographs, ignore the nature of the roots of plants, often vital to the identification of edible weeds by amateurs. The entire plant is to be considered, not just its visible parts.

Nor are botanists particularly interested in edible properties of plants today, with a very lively exception in Geoffrey Grigson (*The Englishman's Flora*). His considered opinion of particular edible English weeds, even when prepared by a Queen of Cooks, is not always encouraging.

For a useful stimulus, read the pioneering pages on 'Wild Edible Plants' in Loudon's great *Encyclopaedia of Gardening*. He did not illustrate the weeds, but there is a complementary resource, showing entire plants as they appeared in old herbals: the book by the botanist Richard G. Hatton listed in the Bibliography.

Cooking and Eating Weeds

The essence of a 'dish of weeds', whether cooked or served as a salad, lies in employing a variety of different plants. There are exceptions, of course. For instance, the poppy plants are sometimes cooked alone, as are wild asparagus, and the corms of the tassel hyacinth and *Crocus cancellatus*; and the Greeks cook the leaves and shoots of mallow, *Malva rotundifolia*, in spring to pacify the stomach and relieve it of winter ills. But the general approach, and the best one, is essentially that of Dirce at Castelpoggio (p 189). It is very similar to that of the goat in the hedge, who nibbles at a plant here and a plant there. The goat knows what will do it good. We can no longer say this about man and woman. So we have to fall back on botanical studies. Paul Schauenberg's *Guide des Plantes Médicinales* analyses the active principles of each plant and is well illustrated. A work of this kind is invaluable in indicating the method of drying plants and the preparation of infusions, and how the plants are used to mitigate common ills. But the real importance of weeds is that they help you to maintain good health.

CICORIA SELVATICA or RADICCHIO (I)
wild chicory (succory)

Cichorium intybus · family ASTERACEAE (formerly COMPOSITAE)
xicoira (C) · radíkia (G) · cicora, cicuredda (Sal)

The ways of cooking weeds are simple; the trouble is in cleaning them. Gathering the chicory with a stub of root in autumn or in spring, you scrape the root stubs with a knife, pick off old or yellowing leaves, and, plant by plant, throw them into a crock of rainwater. Change the water at least twice. Leave them in water till next day.

THE SIMPLE WAY. Drain and rinse again the prepared chicory, and throw it into a cauldron of slightly salted boiling water. Cook for 20 minutes and strain. Serve hot with oil and lemon juice, the purest way. Or dress with olive oil and grated *pecorino sardo*.

ANOTHER WAY. Clean and cook as above, strain and throw the chicory wet into a pan containing a little hot olive oil (or pure pork fat) with two cloves of peeled garlic and one hot chilli pepper. Toss them in the oil or pork fat and serve, adding a few drops of wine vinegar.

FOR FEAST DAYS. In the Salento in autumn, chicory is served with collar of pork. The pork, rather fat, is boiled with bayleaves, then cut into robust chunks and put into the pan to render some fat. When slightly browned, the pork is set on a heated dish and the *cicuredda*, already boiled, is tossed in the fat and served on a separate dish with slices of lemon.

ANOTHER WAY. A more refined dish emerges if you cut a slice of *pancetta* (salt belly of pork, fat and lean) into neat small strips, brown them in a pan, then add the boiled chicory and toss it for a few minutes in the fat, then add a few drops of wine vinegar.

These simple preparations apply to many weeds, when not destined for salad.

See Vegetable Heritage (p 160-2) for the cultivated vegetables which derive from this invaluable wild plant.

RADICCHIELLE • dandelions

Taraxacum officinale • family ASTERACEAE (formerly COMPOSITAE)
queixals de vella, xicoies (C) • radíkia (G)

Dandelions, though never cultivated, were brought to market in England in the 19th century, just as weeds are brought to market round the Mediterranean today. 'When lettuce and endive are scarce, the dandelion might be dug up from the roadside and pasture in winter and forced in pots like succory.' (Loudon, *Encyclopaedia of Gardening*) Succory is a portmanteau name which may apply to *Cichorium intybus* and to other plants (*Picris* spp) with a certain bitterness; these were formerly cultivated and 'forced' for salads ('forced' means blanched by earthing up). They are among the many plants with dandelion-like leaves, all sheltering under the *radicchiella* umbrella, all edible.

INSALATA DI RADICCHIELLA • dandelion salad

Gather young dandelions by cutting a stub of milky root together with its head of leaves, or take the plant whole when small. Wash under the tap, pare the root, leave in water for one hour, then drain, shake dry, and serve with a vinaigrette dressing, or add to a well dressed beetroot salad.

Visitors to Girona in Catalonia should enquire in autumn after a pheasant or a duck prepared with dandelions (*El faisà o l'ànec amb queixals de vella*). In the Pyrenees at high altitudes the variety *alpinum* is equally edible.

RADÍKIA ME RÍZI TIS KYRÍAS AGÁPIS dandelion and chicory cooked in Kyría Agápi's way

In Kavála, Macedonia, now a megalopolis, culinary traditions carry on: grandmothers and great-aunts go on cooking in the age-old way. Here I should mention that weed-gatherers have never been known to measure or weigh.

After thoroughly washing the gathered dandelions and chicory, changing the water several times, Kyría Agápi chops them finely on a board, pours olive oil into a pan, puts in the chopped plants, adds a little water, salt. When they have cooked for a few minutes, she throws in a handful of long-grained rice and some pine kernels, and continues to cook until the rice is tender and the liquid is completely absorbed.

If the pine kernels are lacking, this dish can be served with a grated piquant cheese. The Sculptor, in spring, often has this for lunch. Weeds promote energy.

CONSOLIDA • comfrey

Symphytum officinale • family BORAGINACEAE
consolda (C)

Having transplanted a wild form of comfrey from the neighbouring ravine into the garden and having imported Russian comfrey, I sometimes include their leaves in a dish of weeds.

RECIPE. Picking a handful of comfrey in spring when it reappears, a handful of wild beet, some young leaves of borage, growing wild, and some shoots of fennel, I wash them well, tear them apart and throw them wet into a pan containing hot olive oil. Turning them about in the pan, their liquor first exudes and then evaporates. After a few minutes the dish is ready to serve with grated *pecorino*. Oddly enough, one can do a hard day's work on this, when eaten with good bread.

ACETOSELLA
wood sorrel   field sorrel

Oxalis acetosella	*Rumex acetosella, R scutatus*
family OXALIDACEAE	family POLYGONACEAE
agrella (C) • xiníthra (G)	agrella (C) • xinolápathon (G)

Two plants with a single Italian name.

Wood sorrel, a small trefoil: this 'of all Sorrell sauces is the best,' wrote Gerard. These fragile leaves and stems were those originally used by the French in their *Julienne* soup, according to Kettner. Wood sorrel is less acid than field sorrel. It appears in the soup as little 'threads', these being the stalks, the trefoil leaves having dissolved. They are the origin of the fact that a *Julienne* soup should contain little vegetable slithers finely cut and hence of the phrase *en julienne*. Gerard's sauce was sorrel 'stamped' (pounded) raw to which was added sugar and vinegar, a sauce for roast meat. In his day a polished brass cannon ball was sometimes used as pestle.

Field sorrel is well worth growing in the garden when woods and fields are far away. In the Salento three kinds of field sorrel, all forms of *R scutatus*, grow among the stones piled on the margins of the fields; one picks them in November at the same time as field agarics, in autumn and again in spring.

USES of both include, besides sorrel soup (p 74):

¶ as a sauce, chopped and melted in butter over a gentle heat, stirring, for fish;

¶ as a stuffing for fish, chopped and mixed with breadcrumbs, egg yolks and butter;

¶ as a last minute addition to a wild spinach soup, just before passing it through the *mouli*;

¶ simmered in butter and used as a dressing for steamed potatoes.

FINOCCHIO SELVATICO • wild fennel

Foeniculum vulgare • family APIACEAE (formerly UMBELLIFERAE)
fonoll (C) • finucchiara (Sal) • márathon (G)

In March, or sooner in limestone districts, the succulent shoots of fennel are sought out at the base of the plant and cut off with their little plume of fronds emerging from a sheath.

Boiled till tender and eaten with olive oil and lemon juice. Or boiled for a few minutes, dried, tossed in fine flour and fried in hot oil. Much used in preparing fish soups.

See page 328 for what to do with its seeds and flowers.

BIETOLE SELVATICHE · wild beets

Beta spp • family CHENOPODIACEAE
bledes (C) • seviche (Sal) • vlíta (G)

Sea beet, wild beet and wild spinach beet all fall into the category of goose-foots, as do Good King Henry and orache, mentioned below.

Coming to the ruin, Masseria Spigolizzi, standing on a low hill in sight of the Ionian Sea, I was quick to notice the clumps of wild beet growing around it, and quick to use them.

As all these beets look much alike in form, colour, a rich dark green, and leaf texture, and resemble their cultivated forms, there is less need to sort out their names, and no doubt about their uses which are identical with those of spinach and spinach beet. Good King Henry, *Chenopodium bonus-henricus*, a close relation of the wild beets with similar culinary uses, is perhaps more familiar to British and American cooks. For other American chenopods, see the book cited under Fernald and Kinsey in the Bibliography. Orache, *Atriplex hortensis*, is another close relation.

USES. You use them in soups, as a vegetable, in purées flavoured with nutmeg, or as a stuffing (with or without *ricotta*) for ravioli. And you take the greatest care, after cooking them in the very minimum of boiling water, to drain them and then press out the excess moisture between two plates. If you detach the central rib from the large leaves, they can be cooked in hot oil without more ado, to accompany grilled meats. See also the Catalan dish *Espinacs amb panses i pinyons* (p 166).

CHENOPODIO, FARINELLO BIANCO · fat hen

Chenopodium album · family CHENOPODIACEAE
quenòpode (C) · vromóchorto (G)

Fat hen, the well known annual, has bluish green leaves with a silvery sheen, and does not resemble the wild beets. Its much smaller leaves can be used in salads or simply cooked in butter; they taste a little of broccoli.

I was astonished to find that in the Salento people call this plant *la saponara* and use it to clean their hands after working in the fields, rather than eating it. It is often found in cultivated ground next door to deadly nightshade. The shape of their leaves is similar, but those of the nightshade are dark green; so study both plants before gathering fat hen.

SALICORNIA marsh samphire, glasswort	SALICORNIA rock samphire	SALSOLA saltwort
Salicornia europea CHENOPODIACEAE salicorn (C) almyrídes (G)	*Crithmum maritimum* APIACEAE fonoll marí (C) krítamo (G)	*Salsola kali* CHENOPODIACEAE salicorn (C)

These three plants are similar in use, so I treat them together. They are collectively known as *les salicornes* in French, and have their uses further north, into which I do not enter here.

Glasswort, a peculiar fleshy plant, grows in company with its friend saltwort in salt marshes near the sea. They both make a rather bracing salad, with or without some drops of wine vinegar, to consume with an aperitif; picked in June when the tender new growth appears, from a marsh behind the beach, after bathing. In this marsh also grows the flexible reed, *Juncus effusus*, which is gathered to make the little woven baskets (*fiscelle* in Salentine dialect) used to drain fresh sheep's cheeses.

Immerse the shoots in water for a while, shake dry and serve with a glass of wine. Crisp and salty. They can be conserved in white wine vinegar and consumed with an aperitif but, I find, lose both in freshness and in colour.

Samphire, *Crithmum maritimum*, is called *fenucchiu* or *critimu* in the Salento; it grows abundantly on the rocks, a beautiful succulent whose fleshy leaves are tender in early summer – later it develops prickly points and superb umbelliferous flowers. I include some sprigs of rock samphire and their incipient flowers in this seaside salad, but regard them as diversions rather than as stand-bys.

In Catalonia samphire is very much appreciated. Conserved in white wine vinegar, it is used in salads in winter; with thyme, mountain savory, and origano it is used in preserving olives; and when salted anchovies are prepared in oil, it is added as an aromatic.

elderberry · SAMBUCO   ACACIA · false acacia

Sambucus nigra, CAPRIFOLIACEAE	*Robinia pseudacacia*, FABACEAE
saüc (C)	acàcia (C)
sammucu, zammucu (Sal)	akakía (G)

FRITTELLE DI FIORI DI SAMBUCA (elderflower fritters). Make a light batter (*pastella*) to do justice to the delicate flowers of elderberry or those of false acacia. Mix 100 g (3½ oz) flour with a tablespoon of oil, 1 egg yolk, a tablespoon of *grappa*, a pinch of salt and enough water, mixing a little at a time, to make a not too liquid batter, beat it, then leave to stand for a few hours. Before use, beat and incorporate the white of the egg. Dip the flowers in boiling water for an instant, shake them dry and immerse in the batter. Deep fry in hot oil.

Zucchini flowers can be cooked in the same way (p 175), but without first dipping them in boiling water.

ASPARAGO SELVATICO · wild asparagus

Asparagus acutifolius · family LILIACEAE
espàrrecs del bosc (C) · ágrio sparángi (G)
sparacina (Sal)

In southern Italy the end of March is the moment to gather the shoots of this prickly-spined climbing plant which springs out of dry walls in deserted places and ramps about the limestone maquis.

Since 'I love all wastes and solitary places,' I am wandering about picking asparagus in the wide landscape, when I should be hoeing. There is snow in the wind, the wild pear trees are crowned with white flowers, the asphodels stand out like candelabra lit with stars, the bee orchid is underfoot, and rosemary is again covered with blue flowers. A food gatherer sees in a far field men and women laboriously planting out early tomatoes, the tomato race having already begun.

Wild asparagus grows in wildernesses round Rome, in limestone maquis and all over the foothills of the Pyrenees, where it is brought to market in Girona and Figueres. The long shoots are only tender at the tip, so you break off 8 cm, allowing the plant to develop side shoots.

RECIPE. Bind up the bunch with bast and put it into salted fast-boiling water for 5 minutes. The colour changes from bronze to brilliant green. Drain and serve with olive oil. If you add lemon juice it spoils the colour. A delicacy.

ANOTHER WAY. Cut in equal pieces, fry in oil (or butter) for a few moments, then add 3 beaten eggs, season, stir the contents of the pan, fold it over, and you have a Catalan omelette, generically called *truita* (p 93). Or use as the basis of a *frittata* (p 91).

The first shoots of *luppolo*, (hop, *Lupulus humulus*) can be used for either of these preparations. The purple shoots of *asparago di roveto* (bramble, *Rubus fruticosus*), of *salsapariglia* (smilax, *Smilax aspera*) and those of *clematide* (wild clematis, *Clematis flammula*) when they first appear, can also be treated in this way, but their taste cannot compare with that of the wild asparagus, being 'peppery'.

OROBANCHE · broom rape

Orobanche crenata · family OROBANCHACEAE
orobanque (C) · orobáxi (G)
spurchia (Sal)

This curiosity, a parasitic plant which grows on the roots of beans and peas, makes a refreshing salad. Examine the broad beans in March. The plants that are drooping are already victims of the parasite. You dig them out, trying not to disturb the bean plant itself.

Selecting the youngest *orobanche*, which are pale like French asparagus, you wash them carefully, leave them to soak, then carefully pare the slightly swollen base. Then boil them, leave for a time in the cooking water, drain and lay on a dish. Pour over them a dressing of white wine vinegar, olive oil, chopped mint and capers. Add two tablespoons of fresh crumbs which absorb this dressing. Quite good, but no compensation for the loss of beans or peas.

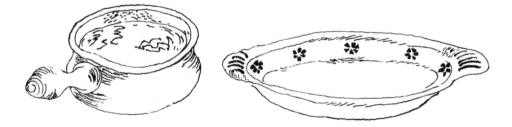

CIPOLLOTTO COL FIOCCO · tassel hyacinth

Muscari comosum · family LILIACEAE
kremmydoúla (G) · pampasciune, lampascione, vampagiolo (Sal)

Cousin of the grape hyacinth, this delightful plant has a 'mad' flower with purple 'tassel' and a delicious edible bulb; it grows wild on limestone, but is so much appreciated in early spring that it is also cultivated. The wild bulbs are smaller and more excellent. They are dug out of the earth when three straggly leaves first appear.

RECIPE. Wash the bulbs, then boil them. When tender, say after 20 minutes, drain and remove the rough outer skins while warm. The peeled object slightly resembles a very small peeled onion, only it is tinged with faintest green and purple. Cut them in half (or not), sprinkle with salt, pour over them a little olive oil and wine vinegar. Serve cold as an *antipasto*; they are delicious.

    The corms of *Crocus cancellatus* on Naxos were prepared in the same way, dug up in autumn.

CRESCIONE D'ACQUA · watercress

Nasturtium officinale · family BRASSICACEAE
créixens (C) · kárdamon (G)

We were laughed at in Apollona when we returned in winter from a wild walk along the cliffs with a great bunch of watercress, found flourishing in the cleft of a freshwater stream. The village Greeks regard it as an aphrodisiac; we ate it gladly as a salad.

LA PORCELLINA • purslane

Portulaca oleracea • family PORTULACACEAE
verdolaga (C) • mbrucacchia (Sal) • andrákli, glistrítha (G)

Native of Mexico, perhaps imported accidentally with the Indian fig, this little succulent appears spontaneously in late summer in cultivated ground in Greece, southern Italy and Spain. Fleshy-leaved, emerald green, this plant makes an excellent addition to a tomato salad, when picked before its small yellow flowers appear. It was grown as a pot-herb in England in Victorian times, a kitchen garden annual, but was already mentioned by Gerard in 1597, as was the then 'fabulous' Indian fig, which he showed, drawn from hearsay, as an arboreal cathedral!

ANGELICA • angelica

Angelica archangelica & *A sylvestris* • family APIACEAE
angèlica (C) • zavirna (Sal)

Both these angelicas grow wild near abandoned ruins and damp places. In February the Salentines go feverishly in search of them. This is the moment when the incipient flower-heads are still enclosed in their sheaths right up against the greenish-purple stem. You cut these sheaths with a knife.

ZAVIRNE FRITTE. Boil the sheaths for a few minutes, leave them in water for an hour, drain and dry. Dip in beaten egg and then in flour. Fry in hot oil. Aromatic and faintly sweet.

ZAVIRNE ABBRUSTOLITE. Set the sheaths on a grill over a hot braise, and after a few minutes turn them over. Slice them across, making two or three cuts, and serve with a dressing of olive oil and a few drops of wine vinegar, and a pinch of salt. With a glass of wine before a meal, agreeable to the palate. *Abbrustolito* (singular) means lightly roasted.

AS SALAD. Boil some salted water, and throw into the pan an equal number of sheaths of angelica, dwarf garden-grown broccoli heads and the points removed from the head of a cluster of *cicoria asparago* (p 162). Boil fast for 4 or 5 minutes, drain and dress with olive oil and a little wine vinegar. Eaten hot or cold, this dish is pleasant in both taste and colour, a vivid green.

LA PAPARINA (Sal) · field poppy

Papaver rhoeas · family PAPAVERACEAE
rosella, quiquiriquic (C) · paparoúna (G)
paparinu, paparinula (Sal)

This poppy, in the Salento, though glorious in flower, is a pest, invading cultivated ground, especially where broad beans, peas, chickpeas are grown. It is easy to gather, while hoeing, before the flower heads appear. Pull the plants out with a twist of the wrist, pick them over, pinch off most of the root, and throw them into a vat of rain-water. Drain, change the water, and leave them to soak for a few hours.

RECIPE. Drain the poppy plants again, then plunge them into a large pan of boiling salted water. When tender (10 minutes) strain, pressing them in the colander with a wooden pestle. Simmer them in hot oil with garlic and a chilli pepper (conserved in oil). Pound them a little in the pan, then add a handful of rinsed black olives. Like all weeds, they greatly reduce in volume while cooking. Serve with a piquant cheese, grated.

At Gallipoli poppy plants are sometimes cooked with rape, cabbage and dock, to which black olives are subsequently added.

These poppies have another use. When pigs are being raised, the plants are fed to them in early spring. In an unusually rainy season, they grow too luscious and have been known to have an exaggerated soporific effect on the pig. This plant is the source of the 'non-somniferic' poppy seeds much used in Greece when baking bread, as are the seeds of *P somniferum*; neither contains opium.

Fungi and Michelangelo

VERY marble sculptor finds his way to Caprese di Michelangelo – the mountain eyrie behind San Sepolcro where, in the last Tuscan outpost on the border of Le Marche, Michelangelo was born: a pilgrimage inevitably offering a disappointment – he is confronted by plaster effigies in the castle museum – and unexpected rewards in the only inn, which, perched over a deep abyss, overlooks a blue haze of mountain ranges.

Arriving on this crag one day in autumn, the welcome we received decided us to stay. Installing a typewriter on the terrace to type a draft of one of the Sculptor's poetic works, I was able to enjoy the view and observe through a hatch everything that was going on in the adjoining kitchen, from which delicious scents of herbs and fungi were drifting. Paradise regained: the woman who asked us if we would mind having three different fungi dishes for supper had the sweetness and civility for which Tuscany was once so famous.

She served *Polenta colla salsa di funghi* to start with; made with a refined maize flour, almost white, and with a less solid consistency than the Venetian polenta but cooked in the same way (p 226). This was poured into deep soup plates and covered with a delicate sauce made of the pared stalks of *porcini* (*Boletus edulis*) chopped very fine and simmered in olive oil with finely chopped onion, garlic, parsley and powdered rosemary, then lubricated with a little tomato purée and clear veal stock, and finally reduced by rapid boiling.

Next came the caps of the *porcini*, which had been sliced, lightly floured, deep-fried and served immediately with grilled pork chops flavoured with mountain sage. Finally, large orange milk caps (*Lactarius deliciosus*) appeared which had been seasoned, oiled and roasted on a plaque in the hot oven.

Next day this lovely cook took me on a fungi expedition and, when we finally tore ourselves away from the inn, we had not only the completed poetic draft but a large jar of *porcini sott'olio* which she had made (p 317).

FRITTO MISTO DI FUNGHI, CERVELLA, ZUCCHINI E CARCIOFI
fungi, brains, little marrows, artichokes, deep-fried

Old-fashioned restaurants like Sabatini and Da Camillo in Florence reveal a kind of genius in these delicate frying operations. But if you happen to arrive early you will have to wait until the usual clientele appear – the cooks and *camerieri* will be feasting in the kitchen while the huge cauldron of oil is heating.

The young boletus caps are sliced across, passed rapidly under the cold tap, then dried and shaken in fine flour in a cloth. The zucchini are cut into sticks, and the hearts of artichokes are quartered, then treated as above. The calves' brains are blanched in acidulated boiling water for a moment, quenched in cold water, the delicate membranes are removed, then the brains are sliced, dried and floured.

They are plunged into the cauldron of smoking oil and in a few moments, when golden brown, are removed with a perforated ladle and drained on absorbent paper, then served with lemon slices. A great delicacy.

But one must go into the precipitous chestnut woods to search out the habitat of these magnificent fungi.

In the mountains of the Lunigiana behind Pontevecchio and Fivizzano – that lost mysterious region where the Bronze Age warrior *statue-stele* were found (see the work by Anati cited in the Bibliography) – we once made our way to a hamlet which at first sight seemed to have been deserted.

We entered the place as one might enter a church-yard, it was so haunted by the spirit of departed lives. Every ramshackle habitation was shuttered, the stone cobbles of the paths were rank with grass, the church roof had caved in; it was invaded by the stillness of the surrounding mountains. Turning a corner I came upon an open doorway and the stooping form of a very old peasant carrying a large curved and blackened frying-pan in which were a heap of fungi.

I greeted her and asked how she was going to cook them. 'In the usual way,' she replied reprovingly. She invited me into the kitchen, a space so bare it reminded me of Naxian rooms. All it contained was a small table, two broken chairs and a black cast-iron stove with pipe in the centre of the room, a pile of sawn-up chestnut wood beside it. She began to slice up the boletus heads.

FUNGHI TRIPPATI • boleti cooked like tripe

She sliced them fine like tripe, simmered them in oil with garlic, mountain savory, thyme, parsley, seasoned them with salt and black pepper, added a spoonful or two of tomato sauce she had bottled and a little stock from boiling the carcase of a scraggy hen. This was simmered and reduced. When fairly dense, some grated *pecorino* was added – her lunch, eaten with some slices of rough bread.

SOME OTHER BOLETUS SPECIES

The best place to study fungi is in your own particular environment. In the Salentine *macchia* we find a variety of boleti, including *Boletus edulis*: some of them have a 'lurid' aspect, notably *B luridus*, *B erythropus* and *B cyanescens*, which all turn blue when touched. This alarming colour vanishes in cooking, when they assume a reassuring yellow colour. Some people think this colour change is ominous. It isn't. They also believe that a boletus which has been nibbled by small animals must be innocuous to man. This is not the case. I recently saw the nibbled white cap of *B satanas*, a fungus highly suspect. Get to know it.

Two other edible boleti of dramatic appearance are *B appendiculatus* and *B regius* found in pine woods and among kermes oaks on calcareous soil.

The great thing with all boleti is to cut specimens in their first youth when both cap and tubes are firm and the swollen stem is not yet attacked by insects.

TO COOK THEM. These are then cleaned, wiped and sliced. Heat some olive oil in an earthenware pot or enamelled pan. Fry the fungi, adding salt and pepper, on a good heat, turning them with a wooden spoon until they're golden brown and crisp, then drain on kitchen paper. Pour off the oil (which can be used again), replace the fungi in the pot or pan, add a good piece of butter and some freshly chopped parsley and garlic, and reheat. Serve very hot.

If I have a certain reputation in the wilderness for 'knowing about fungi', it is not just the result of years of study but owing to the possession of an invaluable reference work: *Les Champignons comestibles et vénéneux* by A. Maublanc (see Bibliography). This work, meticulous and scientific, is embellished by colour plates made from water-colour drawings by two artists, Mlle J. Boully and M Porchet, which are of more assistance in identification than colour photographs with their less accurate colouring. Every fungus is shown in its entirety, accompanied by (very important) its cross-section and a magnified portrait of its spores.

The following recipes, French and Italian, demonstrate the essential simplicity in cooking fungi. The next chapter examines this absorbing subject from the Catalan point of view.

ORONGE, COCON, JAUNE D'OEUF, AMANITE DES CESARS (F)

Amanita caesarea
reig, ou de reig (C)
ovolo buono, fongo ovo, bolé (I)

Two famous French mycologists, L. Quélet and F. Bataille, in their *Flora monographique des amanites et des lépiotes*, give the following recipe for this imperial fungus:

> *Épluchez vos oronges, sans les faire bouillir.* [Perhaps in 1902 when this work appeared people were still trying to 'make sure' by plunging these marvels in boiling water. 'Épluchez' in this case means 'carefully scrape away any debris, sever the stalk from the orange cap and with a stainless steel knife cut both into even slices'.] *Faites fondre un morceau de beurre frais dans une poêle. Préparez un hachis d'herbes fines, persil, ciboulette* [chives] *avec un petit bol de crème douce. Mettez le tout dans la poêle, ajoutez sel et poivre. Laissez cuire cinq minutes, ensuite servez.*

Nothing simpler: it can be applied to *mousserons vrais* (*Calocybe gambosa*, St George's mushroom, p 213) and to field mushrooms. *Amanita ovoidea*, the fungus similar in aspect and stature to *A caesarea*, but white and floury to the touch, can also be cooked in this way.

It is ironic that the most dangerous mushrooms (the fatal *Amanita phalloides*, and *A verna*) belong to the same genus which includes four of the most excellent non-toxic fungi, the two mentioned above and *A rubescens* and *A spissa*. The Curator of the Haslemere Educational Museum has underlined the absolute necessity of correct botanical identification before embarking on any culinary adventures with fungi.

He recommends for this study Roger Phillips' *Mushrooms and Other Fungi of Great Britain and Europe*, 1981.

In case you wonder how a museum in Haslemere suddenly appears in a book written so far from Surrey, I should perhaps explain that I began to study fungi long ago in a pine wood near Rogate, Sussex, and not so far from this museum, which in autumn displayed edible fungi to the general view.

My studies, undertaken at weekends with a biologist from the Ministry of Agriculture, consisted of gathering specimens of every fungus, edible or not, in the adjoining pine woods and among the Spanish chestnuts and silver birch crowning a hill. They amounted to more than 200 species. With the help of John Ramsbottom's book (see Bibliography), we sorted out the edible species and cooked each separately, to decide which were worth eating; we finally had a list of about 30 species which were not only edible but also delicious.

Since Ramsbottom's book appeared in 1953, I asked the Curator of the Haslemere Museum what book was now the current bible.

CHANTERELLE, GIROLE, GIRANDOLE, JAUNOTTE, CRÊTE DE COQ (F)

Cantharellus cibarius
rossinyol, agerola (C) · galetto, gallinaccio, capo gallo (I)

Chanterelles cannot be confounded with any poisonous fungi, are innocuous and have their own woodland fragrance. You look for them in silver birch and Spanish chestnut woods in early autumn.

This recipe comes from *Les Secrets de la Cuisine Comtoise* by Pierre Dupin, 1927, a book given to me by Irving Davis. It had been presented to him with the '*cordial hommage*' of a Franc-Comtois.

CHANTERELLES À LA FRANC-COMTOISE

Freshly gathered, you clean them as best you can without washing them, leaving them whole but paring the tip of the stem. Put them in an earthenware or enamelled pan on a very low heat with the lid on. Almost at once they will render some of their liquor in which they continue to cook until this evaporates, care being taken not to let them stick. At this point add a good piece of fresh butter, salt and pepper. Cook till tender, a few minutes. At the moment of serving pour some fresh cream into the pan, stir vigorously and pour the contents onto a dish.

The initial cooking in their own juice is significant, a way of tenderizing a mushroom inclined to be tough.

MUCCHIAREDDI (Sal)

Lactarius torminosus	*L volemus*
lactaire toisonné (F)	lactaire orangé (F)
agarico torminoso (I)	peveraccio giallo (I)
cabra (C)	lleterola (C)

Varieties of *Lactarius* are to be found in the Salentine *macchia* which are locally highly prized but appear in Italian fungi magazines as 'toxic' or 'emetic'. As we eat them every evening in autumn, I can only say: the experts are sometimes mistaken. Nevertheless they must be cooked, either on live wood braise or in an earthenware pot, and not in a metal pan. Nor should they be set on a metal grill. I use a resilient little Tuscan pot for them, and for other small late-autumn fungi – *Tricholoma*, *Ramaria* and *Cortinarius* species.

The largest specimens are set for a few minutes on live braise, then skilfully turned over and subsequently snatched from the fire; they will have shrunk a little. Dusting off the ash, they are turned about in a sauce (*salsa endiavolades*) already prepared in the mortar, consisting of 2 pounded chilli peppers (conserved under oil for winter), 2 cloves of garlic, fresh leaves of rosemary, cut and pounded, salt, and olive oil. (This wholesome method, undoubtedly ancient, can be applied to the parasol mushroom, *Macrolepiota procera* – the hot braise quickly reduces the water content of this large mushroom; and also to related agarics. See also page 214 under Rovelló.)

The smaller specimens, cooked in earthenware, make an excellent sauce for pasta (see *Fettuccine colla salsa di funghi*, p 99). The system is of the simplest. Pour some olive oil into the little pot, add the fungi sliced, a little salt, and some fresh rosemary very finely cut, 2 cloves of peeled garlic and a hot chilli pepper. Simmer on a low heat and, when the fungi have rendered some liquor, stir in a spoonful of *salsa secca* (p 321) or tomato concentrate. Add a very little chicken stock to dissolve the tomato paste, and a little red wine if you like. When the sauce has achieved consistency, pour it onto the cooked pasta in individual plates.

Assaulting the Language Barrier

THE study of fungi has been pursued with scientific dedication by the French, the Catalans, Italians, Anglo-Saxons, Russians, Scandinavians. In the early 1930s, the then Director of the Institute of Catalan Studies, the famous naturalist Dr Font i Quer, began to catalogue the untold species of fungi and their varieties appearing in the mountains and plains of Catalonia. Altogether, 627 species were identified and described. He was then joined by enthusiastic mycologists – English, French and American – who, embarking on a 'Five Year Mycological Plan', in a few seasons brought the list up to 1458 species (see Bibliography, under Font i Quer). Of these, at most 200 species were known, named, used by country people.

To trim this vast subject down to size: Mercè Sala and Ramon Pascual have contributed an interesting paper to *Congrés Català de la Cuina 1981-2* – its title 'La Micologia a Catalunya'. The object of this Congress was the organisation of a series of local culinary festivities in order to study, divulgate and restore the great tradition of Catalan cuisine which has suffered through years of inflation, political turmoil, the invasion of mass tourism, the changed rhythm due to industrialisation, to the point when a completely new interest of a large section of the population in real food emerged together with a claim for enlightenment.

In the report that followed, different aspects of Catalan cooking were examined and recipes collected during the gastronomic gatherings from farmers' wives, fishermen, mountain people and restaurateurs. It is as if Catalans are saying: 'Culture is based on sound culinary traditions.' The coupling of enlightenment and festivity is an example of truly democratic inspiration. 'Man is nostalgia and a search for communion,' said Octavio Paz.

To return to the fungi: a better acquaintance with these mysterious apparitions is encouraged annually by an exhibition in the palace, Palau de la Virreina in Barcelona, on the third Sunday in October, fungi being brought from all parts of Catalonia for popular inspection.

Out of the vast range of fungi, Mercè Sala and Ramon Pascual list 45 of the most well-known, nine of which are denoted as excellent

(*** in the list which follows). Not surprisingly, several of the species treated in the preceding chapter reappear.

I give the Catalan name, the English one (if it exists), the scientific name, and where possible the French and Italian. They are the common names; but I do not wish to obscure the fact that fungi have many dialect names, some of which I mention.

In the category of 'excellent':

*** OU DE REIG

Amanita caesarea

It appears in late summer in cork woods, among Spanish chestnuts and in oak woods. This fungus takes pride of place, as it did in ancient Greece and Rome. When still an 'egg', this is sliced and served uncooked, dressed with a thread of olive oil, lemon juice, salt and pepper. (In Italy round Alba, where the white truffle, *Tuber magnatum*, is found, this *ovolo buono* is served as above but with a white truffle, equally finely sliced – a counsel of perfection.) Once cap and stem have developed, the caps are grilled, fried, or cooked with other species of the same category of excellence in the oven.

See page 208 for names in other languages and a French recipe.

*** SIURENY or SURENY · cep

Boletus edulis
cèpe de Bordeaux (F) · porcino, brisa (I)

This boletus is the undisputed best (though *B aureus* runs it close) of the large group of fungi to which it belongs, all easily recognizable by the presence of spongy tubes instead of gills under their caps. Excellent cooked when freshly gathered, and ideally suited to conserving: sliced and dried; dried and powdered; conserved in oil (see p 317); conserved in vinegar. See 'Fungi and Michelangelo' for ways of cooking them, and consult the chapter on Fungi in *Plats du Jour* by the author and P. Boyd, where a number of regional French recipes are to be found.

*** RABASSOLA or MURGOLA · morel

Morchella vulgaris
morille (F) · spugnola (I)

Both this and *M rotunda* appear in March and June in vineyards and woods rich in humus. Morels are specially suited for stuffing and slow cooking in earthenware in the oven. They can be dried and are also reduced to a powder after drying, for flavouring dishes of game.

*** MOIXERNÓ, BOLET DE SANT JORDI
St George's mushroom

Calocybe gambosa (= *Tricholoma georgii*)
mousseron vrai, mousseron de la St-Georges (F)
prugnolo, spinarolo (I)

It appears in the mountains in April in grassy places, in rings, a fungus of substance, prepared in as many ways as agarics, though of more delicate taste, and similarly dried.

*** TÒFONA NEGRA • black truffle

Tuber melanosporum
truffe de Périgord (F)
tartufo nero, tartufo di Norcia (I)

The gastronomic treasure of December and January, its evanescent perfume can be preserved for a while in *vi ranci* (or cognac); but most people would be unable to resist employing it instantly, even if only in the simplest ways:
(1) sliced extremely fine, dressed with olive oil, lemon juice, salt and pepper;
(2) sliced and added to an omelette a few moments before it sets – heat releases the perfume which must then immediately be 'contained' by folding the omelette at once;
(3) to perfume a risotto, finely sliced and used to crown the dish one moment before serving.

*** PUAGRA VERDA • green russula

Russula virescens
russule verdoyante, palombette, blavet, verdet, cul vert (F)
colombina verde (I)

The best of the russulas appears in summer, autumn, winter in beech woods, among Spanish chestnuts and in hazel-nut plantations. The Catalans cook its caps together with *Amanita caesarea* and *Hygrophorus agathosmus* (p 214), thus combining the fragrance of these three delicacies, dressed with olive oil, chopped parsley, garlic, topped with grated cheese and lightly *gratiné* in the oven.

*** CAMA-SEC • fairy ring mushroom

Marasmius oreades
faux mousseron (F) • gambasecco (I)

The specific name *oreades* means mountain nymph. Found in summer/autumn growing in rings, this small and abundant fungus develops its flavour when dried, and is thus used in winter soups and stews, for instance in a Catalan dish of pig's trotters and carrots slowly cooked in the oven in earthenware.

*** ROVELLÓ

Lactarius sanguifluus
lactaire sanguin (F) • lattario sanguigno (I)

This species is very close to *L deliciosus* (p 215), but its milk is red rather than orange and the cap is less zoned. It is found in pine woods from August to November. *Rovelló* means 'rust' but also 'yolk of egg', referring to the brilliant orange colour of this fungus. Like the Salentines the Catalans are addicted to a number of species of orange *Lactarius* growing in the cistus maquis. These fungi have a symbiotic relationship with the roots of cistus. The collective Salentine name for them is *mucchiareddi*. These cistus mushrooms (*L torminosus* with a cluster of close relations, some smoother and paler) have a certain acridity, for which reason in fungi books they are regarded with suspicion, even by north Italians.

   These are the autumn treasures sought after by many; they appear after the first autumn rains in periods of scirocco. Cooked on a glowing braise and eaten with a piquant sauce (*salsa endiavolades*), they are particularly delicious (see p 210 for this and other ways of cooking them). They are conserved in oil (see *funghi sott'olio*, p 317), using the youngest specimens.

*** LLENEGA

Hygrophorus agathosmus

'Excellence' has been conferred on this autumn species, rather than on the more robust *H marzuolus*, regarded as a delicacy by the French and Swiss and brought to market in spring. All the *Hygrophorus* species are rather viscous, but of pleasant taste. None of them are poisonous, which is consoling. The two here mentioned can be conserved under oil (p 317), in vinegar and in brine. Cooked with *Amanita caesarea* and *Russula virescens*.

This ends the 'excellent' species of fungi, which I think the authors have chosen not only for gastronomic merit but also with regard to safety, these nine species being difficult to confuse with toxic fungi.

Sala and Pascual's lesser categories are 'very good' (**), 'good' (*) and 'regular' and 'acceptable', of which a selection is given below.

** PINETELL or ROVELLÓ • orange (or saffron) milk-cap

Lactarius deliciosus
lactaire délicieux, barigoule, briqueté, polonais (F)
lepacendro buono, fungo dal pin (I)

They justly relegate this species, to the 'very good' category, despite its name *deliciosus*, which Linnaeus is thought to have given it in error, confusing it with the less well-known but truly 'excellent' *L sanguifluus*. Particularly when it is oiled, dressed with garlic, salt and parsley and cooked on an oiled plaque in the oven, it is very good. It can also be preserved in oil (see p 317), in vinegar, and in small earthenware pots between layers of sea salt, in the proportion 15%, i e 15 grams of sea salt to 100 grams fungi.

** ROSSINYOL (or AGEROLA)

Cantharellus cibarius

A fungus growing among Spanish chestnuts and birches, known to many. See page 209 for its names in other languages and how to cook it. It is suitable for conserving in oil or in vinegar, and is also salted.

* TÒFONA BLANCA • summer truffle

Tuber aestivum
truffe d'été, truffe de la St Jean (F) • tartufo d'estate (I)

Receives only a moderate rating, unlike the wonderfully perfumed white truffle of Alba, *T magnatum*. Once well brushed and wiped, its aroma can be trapped for a time in *vi ranci* or cognac, in a small glass jar with hermetic closing. Treat in the same way as the black truffle (p 213), or slice finely into perfectly fresh scrambled eggs.

* BOLET DE TINTA • shaggy ink-cap

Coprinus comatus
coprin chevelu, goutte d'encre, escumelle (F)
agarico chiomato (I)

Good, as many people know, when cooked in butter in its first youth; it cannot be conserved. This advice applies also to *Amanita vaginata*, in Catalan called *pentinella* and *candela*.

Of the agarics, two are rated 'good'. These are *BOLA DE NEU ANISADA (snowball with a taste of anis), *Agaricus silvicola*, the wood mushroom; and *CAMPEROL, *A campestris*, the field mushroom known to all. The latter can be conserved in salt or put under vinegar. Another agaric, BOLA DE NEU (snowball), *A arvensis*, the horse mushroom, is only deemed 'regular', although in France it is esteemed under various names: *boule de neige, champignon des bruyères, rosé, pâturon blanc*, etc.

*MOIXERNÓ BLANC, *Clitopilus prunulus*, the miller, is also 'good', though Maublanc rates it much higher, 'très délicat'. It is *langue de carpe, meunier* or *mousseron* in French, *prugnolo, grumato grigio* or *lievitato* in Italian.

Among the 45 species listed (I have omitted some of the less familiar ones), only one receives the mildly grudging description 'acceptable'. It has in cultivated form an agreeable flavour but lacks substance. This is ORELLANA, the oyster mushroom, *Pleurotus ostreatus*, now widely raised in commerce, and in Italian *gelone*.

Sala and Pascual do not mention *Hygrophorus poetarum*, fungus of the poets, growing in the mountains, sometimes in association with beech trees, a delicious mushroom occasionally found on calcareous soil under very old fig-trees, where it attains a size of 20 cm across the cap; white touched with rose, it can sometimes be detected from a passing car. This fungus, when you can find it, certainly comes into the category of 'excellence', grilled in sections, and then dressed with olive oil and pounded garlic.

Catalan Fungi Dishes

Whereas Josep Pla (*El què hem menjat*, see Bibliography) is an enthusiast, as I am, for grilling fungi on live braise and eating them with a piquant sauce, Mercè Sala proposes a tantalising list of fungi dishes which must excite both interest and appetite in many less 'neolithic' cooks.

She has collected these dishes from old Catalan domestic recipes; from recent Catalan cookery books and republications of 19th century works (see Bibliography, Part II) others from good friends, personally explained; and some which she has created herself. The list of these dishes below is somewhat reduced so as not to bemuse the reader.

In her contribution to the interesting paper which she and Ramon Pascual wrote (see the earlier part of this chapter) she did in fact offer to supply anyone interested with recipes. When I asked her if this applied also to myself, as a foreigner, she kindly sent me Pascual's latest book *El Libro de las Setas*, which includes a collection of recipes provided by herself, in Spanish. This was ironic, because the language which I had been studying was Catalan, to which I am particularly drawn, perhaps because of its underlying anarchic spirit.

The language barrier deprives many people of the precious experience of Catalan *micòfags* (fungi enthusiasts), and of many delightful dishes. What we now await is a work by Ramon Pascual and Mercè Sala translated into English.

FUNGI TO START A MEAL

Sopa de fredolics: a soup made with *Tricholoma terreum*, the grey agaric, a delicate mushroom with a delicate taste which grows in clumps in the cistus maquis.

Gratinat de macedonia de bolets: different varieties of fungi sliced and seasoned with olive oil and mountain herbs, cooked *au gratin*.

Rabassoles farcides: morels stuffed with parsley, shallots and butter slowly cooked in the oven.

Xampignons farcits de gambes i calamars: agarics stuffed with shrimps and baby squid.

Guisats de patates i murgoles seques: a stew of potatoes and dried morels. The fungi are soaked in warm water to restore them; this water, now perfumed, is used with a little olive oil, garlic and parsley, to cook them slowly in earthenware.

Pomes farcides de rovellons o llenegues: apples cored and stuffed with sliced milk-caps (*Lactarius sanguifluus*, p 214, or *L deliciosus*, p 215) or with wax-caps (*Hygrophorus agathosmus*, p 214) cooked with butter in the oven.

Reig, puagres i llenegues a la llauna: Amanita caesarea, Russula virescens and
   Hygrophorus agathosmus cooked in an oiled earthenware dish with
   herbs and garlic, sprinkled with fine crumbs and oil, in the oven.

FUNGI AS ACCOMPANIMENT

Truites de rossinyols frescos: Catalan omelettes with chanterelles. The
   fungi are first cooked in the omelette pan in oil or butter, and then
   the lightly beaten eggs (already flavoured with salt and parsley) are
   poured into the pan, stirred for a moment and folded.
Conill i rovellons en 'papillote': small joints of rabbit seasoned with salt
   and paprika pepper, sprinkled with oil, then wrapped in foil with an
   orange milk-cap (salted) in each packet, placed in an earthenware
   dish and cooked in a hot oven for half an hour.
Rostit de vedella amb rossinyols: loin of veal roasted with chanterelles.
Botifarres amb mongetes i rovellons al forn: black blood sausages cooked in
   the oven with haricot beans (previously cooked) and orange milk-
   caps.
Canelons de xampinyons i pernil dolç: cannelloni, squares of pasta previously
   blanched, then stuffed with agarics, chopped ham, herbs and garlic,
   rolled and cooked in an oven dish in a thin tomato and onion sauce.
Carlets amb porc senglar: a dish of *Hygrophorus russula* (a substantial
   purplish mushroom growing in woods of white pine, mid-autumn
   and mid-winter) with wild boar.
Estofat de siurenys i vedella: a stew of *Boletus edulis* and veal.

Perhaps this is sufficient to stir the imagination and inspire a visit to
Catalonia in autumn, the province of Girona being the most favourable
destination with regard to fungus research: a fungi paradise.

Two Kinds of Spirit

A book about food can be as fatiguing as sitting through a six course dinner, so I propose to intrude a digression – offered like a glass of *marc* or *eau de vie* to brace the protagonists.

Many people think of anarchism as a symptom of social breakdown, they confuse it with anarchy. The distinction becomes apparent in Kropotkin's memoirs. Anarchism – which admits both individualism and human brotherhood – is a positive force. And anyone who has spent time in Carrara recognizes it as a way of life.

The handling of gigantic blocks of marble presents impossible tasks. The tasks are tackled by a group of men under a *capo* – foreman. But in the moment of danger the man who recognizes it is granted complete authority. This is a safety device. Danger fosters personal responsibility, solidarity among equals and improvised methods of dealing with it.

Amidst heated discussion, means of moving marble are devised on the spot. With inadequate tools – a couple of iron bars, perhaps – by sudden compression of the thorax, harsh grunting sounds are produced which concentrate the timing and direction of the common effort. (This technique was used by Catalan fishermen similarly engaged on the 'impossible task' of launching their ponderous fishing boats on the flat beach at Calafell.)

The strong anarchic spirit of the Carraresi has to do not just with danger but with their origins – as they admit without rancour – as forced labour working the quarries in Roman times. The surrounding mountain villages were slave settlements originally. Hence their insistence on their individual freedom.

Going to work had always been voluntary among the *lizzatori*, the bunch of men who until the mid 1960s were charged with bringing down the marble from the mountain crests on wooden sledges (*lizza* being the sledge), plunging down the steep morraines at daily risk of life and limb.

If any of them didn't feel like climbing the mountain one day, he stayed in bed. At the Ponte della Bugia – the bridge of lies – there were always a few freelances at hand at 3 in the morning ready to stand in when the teams met up and especially to avoid the number 13, before the two teams of seven men tramped off up the mountain carrying their gear.

For centuries the output of the quarries depended on the skill of these men, who, if they went on strike, were able to disorganize the whole production. The quarryowners have since eliminated this threat by

building zig-zag roads up the morraines and getting the blocks down in lorries carrying 30 tons. When this blow fell, the *lizzatori*, epitomizing personal liberty and courage, found it difficult to adapt to less adventurous work. Attuned to danger they also shared their free time together and lived it up – witness the evening we spent with a band of them celebrating a two-day strike in the Piazza Alberica.

They came pouring into the bar with their 'idol', a beautiful youth with a fine tenor voice. He started by singing some nostalgic romances, participation being limited at first to the refrains. When the vociferations of his companions began to drown the sound of the guitar, he struck up the agitated rhythms of the *stornello*. Successive men began to improvise a string of personal and provocative stanzas within the framework of the falling cadences, contriving to combine a heroic build-up of the target with a neat ironic take-down.

The contestants took up two rival themes of a more abstract kind and strove to outdo each other in singing the virtues of work and idleness, the consolations of love and death. The *stornello* form is the mediaeval forerunner of Grand Opera, a vocal drama accompanied by dramatic gestures, whose essence is verbal improvisation within a definite musical framework. But it has its roots in something far far older, as can be seen from Virgil's *Eclogues* – The Singing Match between Corydon and Thyrsis: 'So the pair set to, singing alternately against each other.'

Several hours and many *fiaschi* later, trials of voice gave way to another contest: *il braccio di ferro*, the 'iron arm', with elbows set in saucers and lighted candles set to singe the arm which wasn't made of iron. The leader of the marble men was about evenly matched with a muscle-bound Israeli sculptor and a very young and powerful black. The shock effect of this unpremeditated party on the polite precincts of Piazza Alberica whose shutters closed at 9.30 p.m. lasted several years.

* * * * *

A shoemaker in Carrara kept an open door for anyone who wished to consult his library of anarchist writings – Cafiero and Malatesta – while he carried on mending a pyramid of shoes in a dilapidated little workshop. This man had practised what others preach. Inheriting as a young man an estate in Castelnuovo di Magra, he gave the land to the people who were working it, and went away to work in Germany, so as not to embarrass them in their possession of it. Years later it was the best worked land in that part of Versilia.

* * * * *

An anarchist who often climbed up the muletrack to La Barozza always placed a copy of *Umanità* on the kitchen table before saying Hullo. This was the man, taunted by the blackshirt fascist *'mani morti'* (dead hands) for queuing with his famished companions at the entrance of the Opera House during the war, who replied: *Credete voi che siamo soltanto affamati per il pane e la minestra? Siamo anche affamati per l'Arte!* (Do you imagine that we are only famished for bread and broth? We are also famished for Art!)

It was he who maintained that *la lirica* was the perfect example of democracy – everyone being united in inspired participation. Carrara had always been the operatic 'try-out' for the Parma opera. In our day the anarchist bar was providentially situated in the same building as the opera house, and the moment the orchestra tuned up, they walked through a door from their bar into their box!

The soloists and the orchestra came across the mountains from Parma, the chorus for decades had been supplied by the *cavatori* who could still sing their way accurately through 'Norma' and 'Nabucco'.

In 1864 when Dickens visited the town (*Pictures from Italy*) he found in the beautiful little theatre, newly built, 'the chorus made up of labourers in the marble quarries, who are self taught and sing by ear'. This custom died out in the last war, but in the brief opera season, every male Carrarese was to be found there, and some of the older members of the audience had to be restrained from joining in.

* * * * *

One of the staunchest partisans in the war kept the German occupiers pinned to their chairs in a bar as he trained on them a machine gun, while singing the marvellous song of his own composition: *Già lo sguardo del la mia parte della terra* . . . That man is a legend and those who remembered him were still discussing the manner in which the song was to be sung and vying with each other in singing it.

*   *   *   *   *

The Carraresi are anti-church – they follow the coffin of a comrade on foot as far as the door of the *duomo*, but will not step inside. But wherever *Già lo sguardo* is sung, it rings like a profession of faith.

Thank God! This has nothing to do with food, nor has the following incident.

One day in autumn our neighbour at La Barozza, Uncle Nello, a retired quarryman who cared for the vine and its fruits, declared that we were going to make *grappa*. As such projects tend to be one of conviviality's pleasant dreams – like roasting a whole lamb in March – we gave it little thought. The dumping of the pressed grapeskins at the wine harvest was the result of the prohibition on distilling, and we had not set eyes on anything remotely like a retort lying about.

Uncle Nello, deceived by a poor wine harvest, was determined on combative action. An hour was fixed for the use of our chimney piece. The time came and no one appeared. There had been a difficulty in locating the receptacle, which when found in the cowshed, was extremely rusty. Looking at our tapless kitchen, it was hard to imagine how *grappa* could be made without cold water to condense the alcohol.

One sleeting November evening Uncle Nello staggered in carrying a large cast-iron cylinder from which he had removed some rust. We offered it up to the chimney hook to see if room were left to make the fire below. When this was proved, he fetched a *bigoncio* – a wooden tub 1 metre high in which the grapes are harvested and later fermented, after crushing. We installed it by the hearth and began to set up the *grappa* 'apparatus'.

This consisted of the gas cylinder, converted by an ingenious son-in-law who had sawn off the neck and given it a strong screw thread, manipulated by a gigantic hand-made spanner. In place of the gas-lead was a small-gauge hollow copper tube, *la serpentina*, which issued from the cylinder, its spiral being accommodated in the adjacent wine tub and emerging from it through a conveniently sited bung-hole. The correct angle had to be found for the copper tubing, contrived by raising the tub on a couple of bricks. We had to plug the bung-hole with tufts of flax so that it wouldn't leak all over the kitchen. We had to temper the wine tub by filling it with icy water from the rain cistern to minimize the leaking.

The *bombola* was filled with wine-lees and forcefully screwed up with the giant spanner. We then just managed to suspend it from the chimney hook. We made a fire underneath and at that point Uncle Nello announced he was going off to supper, leaving me to do the mopping up. 'Call me' he said, 'when it starts to flow, and don't put too much wood on the fire, *grappa* must come slowly. It's hardly likely to explode . . .'

I was left alone. The spectacle of the monster suspended in the chimney, the fire licking round it, filled me with a certain dread. The likelihood of the heated wine lees making enough steam to pass through the needle-eye of the copper serpent and, cooled by the water in the tub, to issue forth in the form of *grappa* seemed remote. Contrary to scientific propriety, the only thing that was actually happening was that the cistern water was heating. I hastily wrapped some soaked rags round the hot copper tubes and set a jug on the floor at the outlet. Suddenly there was a hissing sound and a few drops of ash grey liquor spluttered into the jug. I rushed out of the house calling for Uncle Nello.

The next hours were amicably spent – the Sculptor having at the crucial moment staggered up the hill from work – to the tune of a faint trickle of *grappa* which was now clear, at the rate of a small wineglass about every quarter of an hour. We kept on tasting it. Uncle Nello was entranced by the proceedings. When two evenings had passed in this way, there were two litre bottles of *grappa* into each of which we put a sprig of rue. The colour was the shade of palest straw. One bottle was fantastically powerful, the other only moderately so – the hard won fruits of anarchism.

La Polenta

ACCIAMO la gran' polenta! Indeed, polenta ideally is cooked on a grand scale in a large beaten-copper cauldron hung over a fire of incandescent olive wood, as it still is in the farmhouses in the Veneto. In fact, polenta is nothing in its own right except a substantial form of nourishment like porridge. Its gastronomic associations are due to the delicious things served with it: roast quails, stewed hare, braised pheasants, snails. Presented on a polenta board or in a large white porcelain tureen; it reappears at the second course, accompanying, this time, a selection of soft cheeses, *gorgonzola dolce*, *stracchino*, ricotta, *pecorino dolce*.

A companion to improbable things – for instance grilled in slices and served with *lavarelli* (Lake Garda fish, p 125), with grilled sardines, with salt cod (deep-fried in batter) – it is an excellent thing in winter, an admirable poultice. There is, moreover, something in the hard limestone water of the Veneto which makes cooking it a pleasure.

Made one day to serve hot, what is left is sliced and fried in hot oil till golden (*polenta fritta*), or brushed with oil and grilled (*polenta ai ferri*), to eat next day. If chopped salame, parmesan cheese, butter and egg yolks are added to the polenta once it is stiff, and, when it has cooled, the beaten egg whites are folded in, and the preparation put into an oiled oven dish, what emerges after 45 minutes in a hot oven is a *torta di polenta*.

De-salted fillets of anchovy cooked with it and some finely chopped leaves of fresh rosemary improve the taste: use 4 anchovy fillets to ½ kilo (1 lb 2 oz) of polenta flour. Milk or stock can be used instead of water to cook it in. What is certain is that it is greatly improved by the addition of grated parmesan stirred in, once off the fire, and acquires a sheen when butter is added.

The idea of polenta, planted firmly in the north Italian imagination, is the antithesis of modern aspirations. It therefore intrudes on modern life like a vague emotional regret.

The Carraresi, industrialists by origin, were ever intent on forsaking old ways for more ostentatious delights, for example replacing their marble kitchen tables with plastic, their marble sinks with stainless steel. But they still attached a powerful nostalgic feeling to what they would have liked to appear to have discarded. Polenta, synonymous with poverty, their common past, had to be held at arm's length.

If one met a man for the first time in company in some trattoria where polenta figured on the menu, nothing could prevent him from telling you how it is made, accompanied by dramatic gestures. But just as his grandmother, his mother and his wife had preserved him from washing dishes all his life, so these ladies had certainly prevented him from interfering in the making of polenta. And there he was, emphasizing the fact that, as a foreigner, you never could have made nor ever would be able to make it yourself.

LA POLENTA

The most important thing is a capacious heavy pan, ideally tinned copper. Fill it three quarters full with water (3 litres: 110 fl oz) for ½ kilo (1 lb 2 oz) of polenta flour. Bring it to the boil, boil vigorously. Let the flour, fairly coarse, deep yellow, fall from your right hand in a fine rain, stirring with a wooden spoon with your left hand (unless you are left-handed). Stop pouring when it is getting really thick. Add salt and a dessertspoon of olive oil. Stirring hard, let it plop and splutter for 10 minutes, then lower the heat and cook slowly, stirring a good deal of the time, for say 30 minutes, by which time it becomes more or less solid (i e adheres to the wooden spoon when held aloft). Pour it onto a board to the thickness of say 5 cm (2″) or more and serve with any one of the things already mentioned, or with smoked sausages, split and grilled, or slices of grilled *zampone* or *cotechino*.

Savina Roggero in *I Segreti dei Frati Cucinieri* has described several variations in the preparation of polenta in certain monasteries. This book would be of interest to travellers (many monasteries offer hospitality) and vegetarians (Fast-Day dishes are described), as well as to those interested in nourishment associated with a certain parsimony.

But returning to Carrara, I cannot abstain from describing the marble-workers' favourite dish, a culinary example of 'piling Pelion on Ossa', which in their dialect is known as *polenton*.

POLENTA INCATENATA • polenta in 'chains'

Make a haricot bean soup (p 63) of some consistency, boil vigorously, then stirring, pour in one or two handfuls of polenta flour. Stop pouring when it is solid. Serve in deep soup plates with virgin oil.

Reflections in a Winter Landscape

INTER in Italy. A dense mist spreads across the endless plains through which meander the river Po and its many tributaries. Dykes, canals, flanked by tenuous lines of poplars, and huge farms emerge from the gloom; a Flemish landscape but for the contortions of the leafless vines, raising their skeleton forms in an extended perspective.

Far-spaced villages appear, their arcaded barns clustered round huge crenellated castles built of brick, which disappear in the time it takes to read the word Gonzaga or Borgoforte on a signpost. As we proceed in a north-easterly direction across these cultivated wastes, the mist thickens. Every tree is clothed in white rime, and every plumed grass on the roadside is a wand of crystal. The vines are encased in the terrible embrace of the hoar frost.

If there is anyone walking on the deserted road, it is a man wound in the folds of a black felt mediaeval cloak. In this frozen void one realizes the significance of the horse – portrayed by Mantegna with the same vital attention as his master in the Sala degli Sposi in the Gonzagas' palace at Mantua. In the 1490s a man was nothing without his equestrian companion; today he is the shadow of a man without his Fiat.

Mantua rises above its encircling waters, from whose sullen surface wraithlike vapours rise. The city is built as a bastion against extremes of cold and the rigours of summer heat – a reminder of which lingers in the faded ochres, cinnamon browns, burnt orange and ox blood of the stuccoed house facades. It has the aloofness of hard-won wealth wrested from a fertile but inclement countryside.

Far from the 'mainstream of events' it is still a place where one can confront the imagination and pretensions of another age. Here is a crucible in which genius was given power to make its imprint in structures of rose-red brick. The mathemetial genius of Alberti and his passion for Roman spatial volumes resulted in a sense of urban splendour which pervades the city, as nowhere else but Rome. Inspired by Alberti, Mantegna built himself a house in which a perfect square encloses a perfect circle, the circle being the courtyard – a 'conceptual' project realised very much at the expense of the rooms within.

The princely life of the Mantuans has been obliterated by time, malaria and the Austrian occupation, leaving only its shell. Oblivious of this, farmers from the countryside come into town and are found imbibing a dense bean soup at ten in the morning in the *trattorie* underneath the arcades of the Palazzo della Ragione which towers over the market place.

The shops are stuffed with gigantic hams; every kind of smoked and fresh sausage; *coppa*, smoked loin of pork in the form of a large sausage closely bound with string; *bondiola*, a smoked boiling sausage round in shape; *musetti con lingua*, made from pig's snout and tongue; *lardo*, salted pig's fat cut from its rump; *capelli dei preti* also called *triangoli*, small triangles of stitched pork skin stuffed with sausage meat, then smoked, for boiling; and nuggets of smoked pork strung together to be flung into the soup.

In agricultural areas where communications are spasmodic, the pig figures as the winter saviour of mankind. Its products can be kept at hand without deterioration, and, if not of domestic manufacture, can be acquired on weekly trips to town.

The fact that pork is indigestible gives a greater significance here to game in autumn. It also throws vegetables into relief, the green leafy ones, spinach, spinach beet, *cicoria 'Catalogna'* (p 161); the astringent artichoke and cardoon; and most particularly, those root vegetables whose virtue lies in a certain bitterness – root chicory, salsify, scorzonera, and black radishes. All are ritually prepared to offset the ill effects of the delicious products of the pig. One can cultivate a better acquaintance with these roots by growing them.

In this centre of pork confections, it is worth recalling that the first European to publish a work on diet in relation to health, Platina, not only studied in Mantua, but was in the service of Cardinal Francesco Gonzaga, portrayed in Mantegna's frescoes. His book, *Opusculum de obsoniis ac honesta voluptate*, was printed in 1475 in Venice, reprinted in Florence and Venice, and in the 16th century translated and published in France. Platina (Bartolomeo Sacchi) is not to be confused with Bartolomeo Scappi, who published the first Italian cookery book, *Il Cuoco Secreto di Papa Pio Quinto*, in 1570, a work which I once studied, a copy printed in Latin having been unearthed by a friend uncatalogued among a pile of manuscripts in the British Museum Library!

Pork brings the whole question of fasting into focus. For thousands of years, the way of life was entirely subject to the seasons and eating habits derived from the sporadic and providential nature of supply. The excessive consumption of the products of the pig in winter naturally led to digestive troubles. The days of abstention (Wednesday and

Friday) imposed by religious authority was initially required for physical wellbeing. The church must have inherited the basic rules for the good life discovered long before, and the weekly fasts took on their religious aspect. But all this has gone by the board, among Catholics.

The month of fasting during Advent and the six weeks Lenten fast, still kept by island Greeks on Naxos, survived in all its rigour partly because, as we experienced, the supply of food at both these times had in fact dried up. The deficiencies of diet that this implied, in the case of the Greeks, was partially remedied by the consumption of *taramá* and *halvá*, and formerly in the case of Italians, Catalans and particularly Provençal French by the importation of Norwegian, Icelandic and Labrador salt cod. The value attached to salt cod (*stoccafísso* and *baccalà*) is only comprehensible in this connection – concentrated nourishment.

If we congratulate ourselves on having escaped both the grip of necessity and the decrees of the church, we eventually find ourselves face to face with a far less poetic necessity in the form of a diet sheet.

But to return to the pig. The pig has always been a prophetic animal; it can 'see the wind'. The first person to whom Odysseus revealed himself, when he came back to Ithaca, was his swineherd. The men who tended the swine of Irish kings were poets. As I have pointed out, a leg of *prosciutto crudo* can be a real inspiration to a cook.

Some Products of the Pig

COTECHINI, ZAMPONI, BONDIOLE, CAPELLI DEI PRETI
smoked boiling sausages

N O mystery attaches to cooking these sausages. They take longer to cook, however, than one might think.

The *cotechino*, of some size, priced by weight, is simply pricked with the point of a carving fork in two places to prevent its explosion in the pan, is wrapped in a clean linen cloth, secured at both ends, put into an enamelled-iron casserole, and covered with cold water, which is brought to the boil and simmered with the lid on for at least 1½ hours. Any juice which this object exudes is retained in the cloth and poured over it in the serving dish. (The liquor, skimmed of its fat when cold, is used for cooking haricot beans.) Serve the *cotechino* hot with *pommes à l'huile* (p 88), or polenta (p 226) or *passato di patate* (p 89), and with spinach or a root vegetable.

The *zampone*, minced pork stuffed into the hide of a pig's trotter and seasoned with pistachio nuts and whole peppercorns, takes longer. Pierce it twice between the toes, leave it to soak overnight, then wrap it in a cloth and simmer for at least 3 hours on a very low heat. The very pure white pork fat released from these sausages can also be used next day for a *soffritto* of aromatic vegetables and herbs as the point of departure for a soup employing the liquor. This stock sets into a jelly when cold and is excellent as the basis of a lentil, split-pea or chickpea soup.

The *capelli dei preti*, priests' hats, although small, take quite a long time to cook, say 1¼ hours, and the round *bondiole*, larger, rather longer. Once you have turned off the heat, leave all these sausages for ¼ hour before unwrapping them. What remains can be sliced and grilled the next day.

For a brief but informative survey of Italian sausages, fresh or dried, see Tom Stobart's *The Cook's Encyclopaedia* under 'Salsiccia'.

LOMBATA DI MAIALE ALLA TOSCANA • Tuscan loin of pork

Ask the butcher to bone a loin of pork, removing ribs and chine bone, and leaving at most a ½ cm of fat, ready to be rolled and secured into a neat round shape with string.

Pound 2 cloves of garlic in a mortar with a little sea salt, some thyme and 6 juniper berries. Add a little olive oil, squeeze some lemon juice over it, anoint the inside of the loin, then roll up and secure.

Rub salt over the thin outer coating of fat, pour over it some olive oil, then roast on a grid over an earthenware dish in a hot oven for the first 20 minutes, then moderating the temperature for a further hour, assuming the loin to weigh about 1½ kilos (3¼ lb). Untie the string before serving in its dish. Red cabbage (p 168) goes well with this.

PANCETTA, PRESALATA • salted rolled belly of pork in sausage form

The pig's belly, fat streaked with pink meat, lightly cured with salt, seasoned with ground black pepper, rolled, sometimes slightly smoked, is often used finely chopped as the initial element in a *soffritto* of chopped aromatics and herbs to flavour haricot beans, pulses, *risotti*, or a sauce for *past'asciutta*; and in braising veal, beef and game. It can also be sliced and fried with wild chicory (p 194).

LARDO • the fat from the pig's rump preserved

The fat rump of the pig, cut into sections leaving the skin intact, preserved in dry sea salt, is a culinary winter standby in northern Italy. A particularly excellent version of this was the *lardo di Bergiola*, a village above Carrara, where blocks of *lardo* were conserved in dry salt in marble basins with dried mountain herbs.

Without these basins, but with the pig, its rump fat is perfectly simple to preserve. Cut it into pieces about 5 cm (2″) square and 4 cm (1½″) deep, rub it with coarse sea salt, sprinkle it with dried thyme and savory, add a few bayleaves, and put it into a glazed earthenware pot between layers of salt, packed in well. Cover with more salt and put on the lid. Brush off the salt before use. You can eat it, sliced, on bread.

This *lardo* remains as sweet and fresh as the day you put it in, and serves as the point of departure, diced and melted in a frying pan, for a *soffritto* of aromatics when preparing rustic bean soups, braising meat and game, or by itself, well-browned in small dice in a *frittata*. The pig's skin can be preserved in the same way, to be used as the foundation of a braise. In northern Italy it is available in all pork butchers' shops. In the south you make your own on the morning after the pig is killed.

The lard of lesser substance and more delicate taste from the pig's innards is slowly melted down, then whipped and flavoured with finely chopped parsley. This *lardo strutto* is often used as above but also, without the parsley, for yeast cakes and pastry.

MAIALE SULLA BRACE • grilled pork

When grilling pork chops don't forget that juniper berries or coriander seeds or those of fennel are good accomplices. Pound the selected seeds in the mortar with or without a hot grilled and seeded pepper, add salt and a clove of garlic, pound to a paste, moisten with olive oil, and apply to the meat a few hours before grilling. Cook on a slow braise, not a fierce one.

LA BOTIFARRA • the Catalan sausage

This takes many forms. With the help of Nèstor Luján (lecture on 'Pork Cookery' delivered at Solsona, 1981), I indicate a few of these sausages, for investigation by travellers.

La botifarra blanca crua in which raw lean meat predominates. It can be eaten raw or cooked: an ingredient of *Escudella i carn d'olla* (p 269); cooked in earthenware with haricot beans in the oven; fried to accompany broad beans, etc.

La botifarra negra is made, like the French *boudin noir*, with pig's blood and includes not only nodules of pork fat but also lean meat. Accompanies haricot beans and broad beans; included in the *escudella*.

Els bulls de bisbe, o de bisbot, are made with lean pork, the pig's blood and black pepper.

El bull blanc is another version of the above. Both accompany broad beans in spring.

La botifarra d'ou made in the Empordà with eggs, a feature of Carnival.

Another kind of *botifarra* is made with pig's blood and eggs, in coastal regions, for instance in Pineda. A sausage at Pla d'Urgell is made of pounded fat meat from the collar, with salt, pepper, eggs and grated breadcrumbs.

La botifarra dolça is made with sausage meat, very little salt, a lot of sugar and zest of lemon, a delicacy.

LLENGUES DE PORC AMB SALSA DE MAGRANA
pigs' tongues with pomegranate sauce

2 pigs' tongues	½ kg (1 lb 2 oz) potatoes
1 large pomegranate	200 g (7 oz) pure pork fat
1 onion	a ladle of veal broth
a glass of *vi ranci* (or use dry sherry)	olive oil

Put the tongues in boiling water for a few minutes, then peel while hot, scraping them with a small knife. Apply some sea salt and leave them to imbibe this for a few hours. Then rinse them.

Cook the tongues in pork fat in a casserole (or a *greixonera*, the earthenware dish used for frying) until they begin to brown. Add the finely chopped onion and, as it begins to colour, the pomegranate seeds. Cook, stirring, for a minute, then pour in the *vi ranci* and veal broth. Cook, covered, very slowly until the tongues are tender (1 hour).

Prepare the potatoes by slicing them very thin and fry them in a little olive oil in a *paella* (or frying-pan); sprinkle them with salt and cover the pan.

To serve: cut the pigs' tongues in neat slices, place them in the centre of an oval dish, cover with pomegranate sauce and place the potatoes at either end.

LLOMILLO ARREBOSSAT
fillet of pork fried in breadcrumbs

pork fillet · 1 egg · dry breadcrumbs
salt · pepper · olive oil

Cut the fillet into 1½ cm slices, beat up the egg on a plate with salt and pepper; flatten the slices with a wooden mallet and dip them first in egg and then breadcrumbs. Fry in hot oil and drain on brown paper.

This Catalan dish is served with haricot beans, which are cooked in the usual way, drained, and thrown into the hot oil to brown a little, for 5 minutes or so. In autumn it is often accompanied by *rovellons* (p 214, the orange milk cap mushroom), roasted on the braise.

The Naxian Pig

This usually unique domestic animal was raised on pigswill, and kitchen detritus, tomatoes, squashy figs and apples, in a small enclosure of piled-up stones close to the habitation, and was ceremoniously killed in late autumn at the age of one year by its owner, who was to be seen studiously passing a smooth stick through yards of gut and washing the entrails on the beach.

Everything that was not immediately roasted on the fire (principally the pig's innards and its ribs), or made into sausages, or boiled (the head) or bartered (a shoulder or a leg) was immediately preserved by cutting into small pieces of modest size, and rubbing them copiously with sea salt collected from the rocks. They were then stored in layers of dry sea salt, strewn with mountain thyme, winter savory, and bayleaves, in earthenware crocks. (These pigs, by the way, were astonishingly small.)

This furnished two distinct products for winter consumption: fragrant blocks of lard, sometimes with a thin streak of pink meat from the pig's rump, and smaller nuggets of pig fat with meat attached, cut from the belly and the ribs, which were preserved separately but in precisely the same way.

The blocks of lard were removed a piece at a time, scraped of their salt, and served sliced on home-baked rye bread in winter for breakfast or supper. The 'nuggets', scraped of their salt, which remained in dry and crystalline condition, were flung into the frying-pan and quickly browned for production on festive occasions, speared with a fork from the communal dish. This was eaten with hunks of bread, washed down with Dionysian wine drawn directly from great barrels into large melon-shaped glass decanters.

The pig's lard, particularly fragrant and appetizing, played a vital part in our restricted winter diet; it was a specific against Boreas, the north wind, and was the main item in a system of barter initiated by the old lady Erýnni (see Fasting on Naxos).

what to do with a pig's head

One day in Apollona a pig's head in its terrible entirety was set before us to celebrate the termination of a fast. The pig's head had been boiled for a long time with some lemon slices, peppercorns and bayleaves, and its pale featureless liquor was served first as broth.

There was no question of carving this object; our host attacked it at random with his knife, first gouging out the eyes. As this description might appear to slight Apollonian hospitality, I hasten to add that the feast proceeded with a delicious dish of boiled weeds served with tiny lamb cutlets, followed by a wonderful fresh goat's cheese, the first cheese of spring, offered by a shepherd to our friend as reparation for some damage caused by his goats.

Ask the butcher to cleave the head in two, then each half in two again, and partially detach the ears. Wash and remove any little splinters, wipe and singe if necessary over a flame. Soak in cold water for a few hours.

Put the pieces into a large marmite, cover with either still cider or cold water, put in 2 bayleaves, a slice or two of lemon, a thread of wine vinegar and a few crushed allspice or juniper berries. Bring to the boil; skim, simmer for 1½ hours to 2 hours. But, when it has cooked for 20 minutes, remove the brains, white and easily recognizable, with a spoon, then detach their membranes. Leave them to cool. They provide the basis for the sauce.

When tender, leave to cool in its liquor, then remove whatever flesh is to be found with a sharp knife. This occurs mainly on the cheeks. (The fatty parts should be rendered down in a dish at the bottom of the oven.)

For the sauce, crush 2 large garlic cloves with some sea salt in a mortar, add some capers, pound again, put in the brains, pound smooth, then pour in olive oil drop by drop. A perfectly smooth sauce will be obtained. Add some finely chopped parsley or coriander fronds and the juice of half a lemon. Garnish the meat with hard-boiled eggs sliced in two and little gherkins.

a swineherd's hospitality

The swineherd Eumaeus led Odysseus – changed by Athene beyond recognition – to his hut, piled up some brushwood and covering it with the shaggy skin of a wild goat, made him welcome: 'for strangers and beggars all come in Zeus's name,' he said. Before long 'the swineherd broke off, hitched up his tunic and his belt, and went out into the sties where the young porkers were penned in batches. He selected two, carried them in, and slaughtered them both. Next he singed them, chopped them up and skewered the meat. When he had roasted it all, he served it up piping hot on the spits, set it in front of Odysseus and sprinkled it with white barley meal. He then mixed some mellow wine in a bowl of olive wood, took a seat facing his guest, and invited him to eat.' The same evening when the other herdsman got back, a five year old hog was slaughtered in his honour, Eumaeus honouring Odysseus with the 'tusker's long chine'.

Furred and Feathered
Holocausts

With its fast-rushing river, picturesque old bridge, great castle, waving
cypresses, and prospect so delightful and so cheerful! Pleasant Verona!

Pictures from Italy, Charles Dickens

N winter Verona's fast-rushing river freezes over; in winter it is
all the more delightful. Lying between the foothills of the Alps
and the great plains of the river Po, it attracts all good things –
mountain butter, a great variety of cheeses, Garda salmon trout
and *lavarelli* (p 125), Venetian *calamari*, eels and mullet; black
truffles of Norcia, white truffles from Alba, fat poultry, game, the
products of the pig; the best of Italian wines besides its own Valpolicella
and nearby Lugana, Lazize, and Bardolino (*chiarorosso*) and the dark
slightly sparkling Lambrusco di Sorbara, near Modena.

By mid-February it displays new peas and small zucchini. Its food
shops are arranged with an order inspired by artistry; food is served with
a civility unparalleled. In summer this gastronomic centre might go
unnoticed, so rich it is in other wonders. Praise is lavished on Bologna
as the gourmet's paradise. Her crown of laurels has been wrested in a
contest between equals – Verona, Mantua, Parma are her peers.

Even when the hunting season closed, the shop in Via Mazzini, a few
steps from Piazza Bra, displayed a spectacle of game that might have
inspired a Victorian lithograph. (The morphology of animals and
birds was a Victorian passion – see 19th century editions of Oliver
Goldsmith's *Animated Nature*.) On the right of the entrance hung a golden
cerf, and in a row along the wall inside, the grey hide carcases of
antelopes. Half a dozen hares and as many rabbits, russet-furred, made
a proscenium frieze, while clusters of hen pheasants, wood pigeon,
partridges and quails, hung by the head, formed on either side swags
of feathered game composed on the same principle as Mantegna's
swags of fruit. Wild duck, called *marzaiole* (*Anas querquedula*), with their
blue-flashed wings fanned out, were suspended against the shop frame
vertically, with some glorious cock pheasants as a brilliant tailpiece.
Inside the shop were quails dressed with sprigs of rosemary and sage,
freshly made turkey sausages, and guinea fowl shorn of their speckled

plumage, all but the tail feathers. It seemed as if the law had been suspended here in the name of gastronomic well-being. The law proclaimed that Italian game can only be sold during the hunting season – August 21 to January 1 at the time; the truth was different. It turned out that everything had been imported; the cerf was Swiss, the antelope from Kenya. The pheasants were of Polish or English origin, these last beyond compare in the opinion of the *padrone*. The partridges came from San Vincente di Alcántara in Spain, *perdici rojas*, with coral-coloured beaks and legs. The hares were Czechoslovakian. The only creatures shot on Venetian soil were the wild duck, which, being regarded as *cibi in transito* (food in transit) rather than indigenous, were exempt from the restriction.

The same principle of importation applied mysteriously to bread – apparently to do with wine production: Apulian wines were imported to fortify Valpolicella and Bardolino, lacking in alcohol, and enormous loaves of Apulian bread weighing several kilos arrived by train for sale in grocers' shops and *sementi*, which deal in comestible seeds.

Working at Garda, an hour away, one winter, we went to Verona ostensibly to buy Apulian bread – a weekly excuse to visit Pisanello's *St George and the Princess*, then temporarily housed in a building close to Sant' Anastasia, and the Venetian paintings in the Castel Vecchio. The passion for animals so evident in Pisanello's paintings thus found an echo in Via Mazzini; he lovingly delineated their bones which form with human ones a ghostly mosaic underneath the dragon's tail in the almost ruined section of the fresco.

St George, the equestrian knight, was particularly loved by the Venetians, people who valued above everything the horse, and who, in the old days, were quick to translate passion into action. He remains, in spite of the Vatican, the embodiment of a principle close to English hearts, and to the Catalans, the Greeks and the Dalmatians whose patron saint he has long been. The Veneto is the place to ponder his significance: not only in San Giorgio degli Schiavoni in Venice where Carpaccio painted his exploits for the Dalmatian community, but in San Zeno in Verona where he was depicted by an unknown painter in a beautiful 13th century fresco. The wonder of this active saint must have dawned on the Venetians during their dominion over Dalmatia, Corfu, the Peloponnese and the Cyclades, lasting four centuries, and only brought to an end in Byron's time, by the Turks.

The Castel Vecchio houses the 'orchard' painters; here the Christ child clutches a bunch of grapes, a gleaming pear, a bullfinch – the bird who feasts on the buds of the plum tree. The Madonna is set against a swag of fruit – grapes, pears, nectarines, peaches, cherries – on which two finches perch (Crivelli), or fat quails brush against her skirt (early Pisanello).

The *mostarda di frutta veneziana*, a syrupy preserve invented in this orchard country, the Veneto, where quinces, figs, apricots, pears and cherries march with the vine, concentrates in the depth of winter the glowing colours of ripe fruits; colours painted by Crivelli, Buonsignori, Tura and Carpaccio and found to one's delight again by staring into casks of syrup on the counters of Verona's *salumerie*.

These delicious piquant preserves, prepared with fermented grape juice (*mosto*) and flavoured with mustard oil, exist in several varieties. The one which contains whole fruits, figs, plums, cherries, pears is the *mostarda di Cremona*; the golden purée of apples and quinces punctuated with red cherries is the *mostarda vicentina*; and the one that consists of segmented fruits is the *mostarda mantovana*. I have not been carried away by the Venetian orchard painters to describe this *mostarda di frutta* without reason. It is used in association with game, with pickled tongue, with chicken, goose and turkey, and indeed with the *bollito* (p 274), that mediaeval dish of boiled meats which is one of the best things in northern Italy, especially in Milan, to eat in winter.

Wild Boar, Fox, Hare, Pheasant, Partridge, Pigeon

RIVING through Provence late one November, we saw hanging outside a butcher's shop in Vidauban three wild boars, suspended from their hind-legs, their huge snouts jutting forward with ivory crescent tusks. These shaggy beasts, as dark as Cerberus, were the only presences in the deserted street.

The boar is sacred to the horned moon goddess; she is the patron of poets and metalworkers. The thought of the wild boars, their immense size, the mountain wilderness from which they came, haunted us for a long time.

The best boar, however, that we encountered was in a back street tavern in Volterra, to which we had been directed by a reassuringly portly gentleman after visiting the Etruscan museum. In this museum the Boar Hunt is portrayed as an emblem of death on funerary urns, with other themes: the Wheel of Fortune, the Combat outside the House of Death, the Flower of Immortality, the Chariot, the Embarcation.

CINGHIALE ARROSTO • braised wild boar

To return to the tavern: *arrosto* means roast, but it is often employed to indicate a braise. First eat your wild boar, and then hasten into the kitchen, if you dare, to enquire how it has been prepared. This is what I gathered from Giovanna Benedetta, the skilful cook:

Hang the boar for 7 or 8 days. The meat employed is taken from the haunch and saddle with a bare centimetre of coating fat. Reckon with nearly ½ kilo (1 lb 2 oz) per person; its volume shrinks in cooking. Wash the meat in cold water first thing in the morning, then sprinkle it with good wine vinegar.

Two hours before the meal, cut it into substantial pieces, at least 3″ (7½ cm) cubed, then wipe them with a cloth. Put some olive oil in a cast-iron pot and then chop very fine *tutti gli odori*, that is every aromatic herb and vegetable you can lay hand on (onion, garlic, green celery, carrot, parsley, sage, thyme, savory, rosemary, bayleaves and crushed juniper berries).

Simmer this *soffritto* in the oil and, before it begins to brown, increase the heat and put in the pieces of boar. Brown on all sides. Then add a glass of Chianti, reduce this a little, and put in a few peeled and crushed tomatoes; the liquor with which the boar is to cook is scant. Cover hermetically, i e seal with a flour and water paste, and cook as you would a *daube* for at least 2 hours, in the oven.

Remove the boar's meat from the pot onto a heated white porcelain dish and strain over it the juice and aromatics, without pressing, through a fine sieve, to obtain a very fragrant but scarce sauce. Serve with no accompaniment, so as to appreciate the unique taste of the fabulous dark meat, and follow it with a green salad.

LA VOLPE • fox

Here are the recommendations given to me by an old anarchist in Carrara for cooking a fox:

'A male fox shot in January or February. Skin it, and keep the carcase in running water for 3 days, or, otherwise, hang it up outside in the frost.

'Clean it and cut it up into joints like a rabbit, then put it in a lidded pot with some olive oil on a slow fire. In this way a certain amount of liquor will be released. Continue to simmer until this liquor is reabsorbed; the process abolishes a certain acridity in the taste of fox.

'Now it is ready to prepare *alla cacciatora* – that is, pour a little more oil into the pot, add 3 unpeeled cloves of garlic, slightly crushed, raise the heat and brown the pieces, sprinkling them with mountain herbs (thyme, savory, fronds of fennel). Add a little salt.

'When the joints are thoroughly browned, say in 10 minutes, add a glass of red wine, a few peeled and crushed tomatoes and a glass of good stock. Put on the lid and cook until the liquor has practically evaporated.'

Exactly the same method can be applied to badger, *il tasso*, though it takes longer to cook. I met a number of people around Carrara not at all averse to cooking a fox. The 'preliminaries' are vital, since they remove the rather bitter 'foxy' taste, and can be equally applied to goat.

LEPRE CON AMORE • *civet de lièvre*

As there is no better way of cooking this noble animal, it would be folly to describe any other preparation such as *lepre in agrodolce*.

The Mantuan poulterer who sold me a male hare weighing 3½ kilos (8 lb) on a freezing January afternoon said it had been killed 5 days before, that it would be easy to skin – you just make a couple of slits in the hind-legs and peel it off (undress it) but give it time to thaw out first. It had been concealed in the freezer to escape the fine for being out of season.

It was a beautiful creature. We left it hanging to thaw out overnight

in a fairly warm room, putting a plate underneath to catch the blood. There was no question of roasting the saddle, because there wasn't an oven. The absence of alternatives is often a great relief in cooking. You use what you've got, you do what you can.

A *civet de lièvre* is not a *civet* but a hare stewed in red wine, if the hare's blood is not incorporated. On this occasion it was.

The things to hand were a large new glazed earthenware beanpot; Bardolino wine, that village being only a few kilometres away down the lake; herbs (bayleaves, thyme, savory, rosemary); juniper berries; sea salt and peppercorns; a lump of sugar; pork fat from boiling a Veronese *cotechino*; onions, carrots, parsley and garlic; some red wine vinegar; olive oil; a little brandy to be added to the blood; flour and butter.

The hare was not at all easy to skin. It was a struggle performed out of doors in the snow, the hare suspended by its back legs from an iron pergola. It was then jointed, and the head, thorax and heart were put in a basin of cold water and then into a marmite for soup.

The back jointed in three, the forelegs and the massive hindlegs might have been marinaded in olive oil, herbs and wine vinegar, but this is only necessary when there is a lapse of time between jointing and cooking the animal, or if it is old. In this case the hare was splendid and we were in a hurry. The skinning began at 3 p m and we wanted to eat at 8. Some time was spent carefully detaching the two membranes which encase the animal's limbs and back, with a very sharp pointed knife. Thyme, savory, rosemary were pounded in a mortar with juniper berries and black peppercorns to a powder. The joints were pasted with this; it has a tenderizing effect. The clarified pork fat was heated and the large pieces of meat browned with 4 or 5 unpeeled cloves of garlic in a large frying-pan, then dusted with flour and quickly browned again.

Meanwhile 2 onions and some carrots cut in slices were sweated in the beanpot in olive oil, and after about 20 minutes the browned meat was transferred onto this *fonds de braise*. A litre (36 fl oz) of Bardolino was heated in the open pan and quickly poured into the pot. A thread of wine vinegar was added, two bayleaves, salt and a lump of sugar to counteract the acidity of the wine. Left on the lowest possible flame, the pot was left to simmer.

What happened to the liver? Reboul says that the finely chopped liver incorporated with the blood in the sauce ruins its texture because of its granular consistency. So, taking his advice, we simmered it separately in pork fat for a few minutes, and added it, cut into its four lobes, to the pot at the last minute.

After two hours I tasted the simmering liquor; it hadn't enough bite, neither did it seem as if it would achieve in another hour the qualities of an unctuous sauce. I pounded 3 more large cloves of garlic with some chopped parsley to a paste, for adding later. As for the texture of the sauce, the solution was the last minute addition of *beurre manié* (a walnut of butter kneaded with a lesser volume of flour in the fingers, used in fragments). Everybody, by now titillated by the marvellous scent of the hare, was beginning to champ with impatience.

The garlic and parsley impasto, liberated from the mortar with some of the hare's liquor, was added to the pot. A superb green olive oil (Garda) was poured into the frying pan and heated; architectural slabs of polenta, cooked the day before, were fried in it till crisp and golden. The tender joints of hare were extricated and kept hot in a covered pan; their sauce was poured through a strainer into another pan to eliminate the aromatics, and set on the heat. When this was just bubbling, the blood (and the brandy which had been added to it) were poured in, stirring, and the little fragments of floury butter were dropped in, more stirring. The four quarters of the hare's liver were added, the meat put back for a few moments and it was ready to serve in a deep white salt-glazed dish chosen to set off the wonderfully dark sauce, with the golden polenta on a separate platter.

A great deal of Bardolino was consumed with this royal dish. A salad of black radish, raw, sliced to a hair's breadth and dressed with olive oil and parsley, followed.

Someone may quibble over the addition of the *beurre manié*. When the beast is large and requires a litre of wine to immerse it, it would take more flour in the initial browning than one would care to use to thicken it, involving also the danger of burning the flour. The sauce in a *civet* must be copious – as copious as the sauce for a *coq au vin* cooked at Beaujolais, and with a similar consistency, not thick, not thin; one must have an idea of this consistency in order to be able to bring it about.

What remained of the hare and its sauce was served the next day as an admirable dressing for *tagliatelle* (*Tagliatelle al sugo di lepre*).

HOW TO COOK BIRDS WITHOUT AN OVEN

You braise them. This originally meant cooking in the braise, that is in glowing embers; a neolithic and gypsy practice embracing the roasting of small birds, hedgehogs, rabbit, squirrels, enclosed in a coating of damp clay, slapped directly on the feathers, prickles, fur, which later conveniently 'came away' with the clay, hardened in the fire, when fractured on removal.

A perhaps over-refined version of this method is practised in country *trattorie* round Florence; a chicken, plucked and wrapped with herbs in oiled paper is coated with clay, then cooked in a charcoal braise and dramatically shattered to delight the diner.

This primitive method was replaced by domed earthenware pots set in the glowing ashes. The first earthenware cooking-pots in Europe were found in Thessaly, in use 8,000 years ago (see Hourmouziades). In Roman times both bronze, silver and earthenware pots were used for cooking: photographs of surviving examples from Pompeii and Roman sites in Britain are in *The Roman Cookery Book*.

Tinned copper vessels appeared much later; they are mentioned in the 14th century *Sent Soví*. In the early 19th century cast-iron pots of oval form (*cocottes-en-fonte*) made their appearance with concave lids on which were laid live coals, as previously occurred with copper vessels, thus effecting the all round cooking of the bird or beast – cooking between two fires, *fra due fuochi*. (But in Italy in well-to-do households copper utensils prevailed until Mussolini decreed their melting-down in the last war.) This way of cooking between two fires leads to barding or larding the bird's breast (or upper surface of a piece of venison, or back of a hare, or leg of lamb) to prevent the meat from drying out from above.

The aromatics or *fonds de braise* employed in browning the larded or barded object in a little olive oil, butter or pure lard were and still are: diced *lardo* or *prosciutto crudo*, or a piece of salted pork-skin (*couenne de porc*) or salt pork, in which, once browned, onions, carrots (sliced) and unpeeled garlic are sweated. The pork element is essential, giving an unctuous quality to the sauce. After browning the creature on all sides, its flavour is improved by a small quantity of cognac, *Armagnac, Savignac, marc, eau de vie* or *grappa* which, set alight and poured over the bird, is quickly reduced, then followed by a glass of good wine, heated, some *jus de viande*, melted, or reduced stock, to complete the cooking in the steam released as the liquor evaporates. The lid, hermetically sealed with a flour and water paste, has a few live lumps of charcoal put on it and the pot is set in the hearth on a glowing braise.

The use of wood, charcoal and cooking in the hearth having

practically vanished except in rural situations, cooking *fra due fuochi* is a rarity. The method of braising has consequently been modified. You now have to rotate and baste the bird, using a suitable cast-iron pot or tinned copper lidded *cocotte* or pan, but following the principles outlined above. The vital thing is that the vessel should only just contain the bird – or there would be an over-hasty evaporation of the liquor; and should not be sealed, since basting is required, but covered with a weighted well-fitting lid. The fact is that roasting has also changed its nature; oven-roasting is a travesty of roasting in its traditional sense, which was on a rotating spit before a glowing fire.

Spending a winter – to mitigate the rigours of Carrara – in the Veneto where every kind of game was to be had, in a cottage without an oven, I had recourse to braising. The results could not have been entirely due to the quality of the game and poultry – to say more might be to extinguish interest with envy.

FAGIANO ARROSTO • braised pheasant

a plump bird • 5 cloves of garlic • a handful of pine kernels
a sprig of thyme • salt • a thin slice of *lardo*
4 or 5 tablespoons of olive oil • a dessertspoon of *grappa stravecchia*
a *cavalliera* (¼ litre, 9 fl oz) of red wine • ground black pepper

Supposing the pheasant to be well hung and already plucked, cleaned and trussed (in many Italian poulterers only the first assumption holds good), put a peeled garlic clove inside the bird, with the pine kernels, and bard its breast, having first sprinkled it with thyme and salt.

Pour the olive oil into a suitable pot on a moderate heat, add the 4 remaining garlic cloves, unpeeled and slightly crushed, and brown the bird turning it about and spooning the hot oil over it all the time.

Heat the *grappa* in a silver spoon, set it alight and pour it over the bird. Then pour in the heated wine, add some black pepper, set it on a moderate heat and secure the lid. After 7 minutes turn down the heat to avoid an over-rapid evaporation of the liquor. Every ¼ hour rotate the bird and spoon over it the liquor, then quickly replace lid and weight.

It will take about 1¼ hours to cook. During the last ¼ hour pay particular attention, because at a certain moment the oil, the wine and the juices of the bird combine to form practically a glaze which, if further reduced, will burn. At this point, spoon the sauce over the pheasant to which it will adhere, and set it on a heated dish.

You can make a dish of polenta while it is cooking, or a purée of lentils (p 69) and a salad of curly endive and *radicchio rosso* (p 167).

PERNICE ALLA VICENTINA
partridge in the manner of Vicenza

A way of roasting, then braising a partridge for a short time with the addition of some *mostarda di frutta vicentina*, made with apples, quinces and cherries.

2 partridges · slices of fat from loin of pork (or of *lardo*)
2 sprigs rosemary · 2 garlic cloves
a large russet apple · sea salt · freshly ground black pepper
a glass of red wine (or a little butter) if needed
2 tablespoons of *mostarda di frutta vicentina*

Wrap the birds in slices of pork fat or *lardo* and roast them on a grid on a dish in a moderate oven for 1¼ hours, with a sprig of rosemary and a peeled garlic clove tucked inside each bird. For the last ¼ hour remove the barding to brown them.

Take them out of the oven dish and transfer the rendered fat and juices of the birds to a heavy pan with lid. Heat it on top of the stove, adding the russet apple, peeled, cored and sliced, and simmer while you divide the partridges lengthwise along the breast with a sharp knife.

Put the pieces into the pan and cook gently with the lid on while the apple slices disintegrate. Add the salt, some ground pepper and the garlic cloves, crushed, from inside the birds. Spoon the juices over the partridge joints and, if the apple looks like sticking, lubricate with a glass of red wine, or add a little butter.

After 15 minutes add the *mostarda di frutta*. Simmer for another 10 minutes, by which time the partridge pieces will be tender and the sauce of the right consistency. Put them on a hot dish, coat them with sauce, and serve without accompaniments.

PERDIU AMB COL • partridge with cabbage rolls

This Catalan recipe seems to take a long time, but don't be put off. Divulged to Irving Davis by Senyora Solé of the restaurant Pi at Vendrell – who was a mistress in the art of slow cooking. Partridges should not roast too quickly, it toughens them. One cannot make a *sofregit* in less than half an hour; this one will only have its true flavour if prepared in the fat and juices of the roast. This sauce then slowly impregnates the birds, and only then are the cabbage rolls put in for the last 15 minutes.

2 plump partridges
salt
150 g (just over 5 oz) pork fat

for the sofregit:
3 cloves of garlic
½ a large onion
2 large tomatoes

for the picada:
a handful of pine kernels
chopped parsley

for the cabbage rolls:
1 green cabbage
1 egg
2 dessertspoons of flour
a glass of water
olive oil in which to fry them

Rub the partridges with salt and coat them with pig's lard. Roast them whole in a moderate oven for 1½ hours on a grid over an earthenware dish, basting them from time to time. Take them out and cut into halves along the breast.

Prepare the *sofregit* by adding a little more lard to the fat and juices in the earthenware dish, chop the garlic and onion very finely, and gently brown them in this dish on top of the stove. Add the peeled tomatoes, crush them and simmer slowly for half an hour.

Pound the pine kernels, parsley and a little salt to a fine paste in a mortar, then add it to the sauce. When it has acquired consistency put in the partridge pieces, cover the dish and set in a slow oven.

Carefully separate the leaves of the cabbage from the stalk using a sharp knife, discard any that are not perfect, and blanch the leaves in rapidly boiling water for nearly 10 minutes. Quickly drain, run under a cold tap, drain again. Take each leaf separately and roll it up into a little packet, two for each person. Make a light batter by beating up the egg, flour and water in a bowl. Dip the cabbage rolls in this and fry them in very hot oil. Drain on kitchen paper.

Put these rolls in the dish with the partridges and simmer for a further 15 minutes in the sauce. A classic Catalan dish.

PERNICI CON PASSIONE

Three little partridges with red beaks and coral feet flown from San Vincente de Alcántara in Spain and hung for a week by the Veronese *pollaiolo* in Via Mazzini, induced a confederate to dash out in the snow and come back with a bottle of Vecchia Romagna.

the 3 birds · 3 sprigs of thyme · 4 garlic cloves · salt
4 tablespoons of *extra vergine* olive oil
a scarce handful of dried *porcini* (p 212)
100 g (3½ oz) pure pork fat · a tablespoon of Vecchia Romagna
¼ litre (9 fl oz) of Valpolicella · a dessertspoon of goose fat
2 sprigs of lemon-scented thyme
300 g (10½ oz) of little pickling onions
a tablespoon of oil (or butter) · salt · a pinch of sugar

We plucked the birds, emptied their crops, removed their entrails and severed their necks and coral feet; stuffed sprigs of thyme inside them with a garlic clove and salt and applied some salt outside; then trussed them, laid them in a deep dish and anointed them with a little olive oil. We soaked the fungi in a little tepid water.

The birds were browned in a copper frying pan in pure pork fat, to which goose fat was added. The fat was then poured off into the braising pan and the birds were flared in the heated Vecchia Romagna before they too were transferred to this pan. Three unpeeled garlic cloves and two sprigs of lemon-scented thyme were put in, the heated Valpolicella was added, the lid put on and weighted, and the pan set on a low heat to cook at a lively bubble, the contents being basted from time to time. After 40 minutes the fungi were strained, and put in with the birds, with very little of their liquor.

The little onions were blanched in boiling water for 10 minutes, skinned and put into a small pan with oil, salt and a pinch of sugar. Shaken now and then on a low flame, in 20 minutes they were golden.

When the partridges were almost ready the onions were put in but not their oil, and after 1¼ hours all told the partridges were set on a dish with the glazed onions, the fungi-impregnated sauce being poured over them, and served with *passato di patate* (p 89).

There were three partridges and three people – the best partridges these people had ever eaten. According to the game man in Verona, the hare, the partridge and the turtle dove are the only game which cannot be raised by human agency. This is wild food, respectfully treated; one abandons knife and fork and eats it with the fingers.

PICCIONE SELVATICO • wood pigeon

1 pigeon per person • 1 slice of *pancetta* (p 231) for each
sprigs of rosemary, or juniper berries • olive oil
½ kilo (1 lb 2 oz) young carrots • 2 wine glasses of red wine
for the sauce: 3 or 4 cloves of garlic • 50 g (1½ oz) pine kernels
a small bunch of parsley • olive oil • 1 teaspoon of wine vinegar

The wood pigeon shot in Italy are more tender than English birds; this naturally reduces the cooking time. What takes time is plucking them. This done, decapitate them, sever their legs, empty them, truss them and tie a slice of *pancetta* on the breasts of each. Put some sprigs of rosemary inside, or a few crushed juniper berries.

Sauté the birds gently in olive oil on all sides, browning them slightly; this takes about 10 minutes. Do this in an iron pan, add the carrots, scraped but left whole, and turn them about to absorb the oil, on a low heat. Lubricate with the red wine, avoiding the birds, raise the heat a little, put on the lid and cook for 30 to 40 minutes, basting from time to time and turning them once or twice.

While they are cooking, pound the cloves of garlic, pine kernels and freshly chopped parsley, dilute with good olive oil, add a few drops of wine vinegar and serve this as a piquant sauce. By the time the pigeons are cooked the carrots will have absorbed practically all the liquor.

The turtle dove, *la tortora*, can be cooked in the same way. If you have an open wood fire with a chimney hook and an iron cauldron, a very good way of cooking these birds is as above, but over a lively fire of apple boughs. In this case you will need to use more wine, total immersion, because the initial heat of the fire will produce far greater evaporation. The pigeon will take rather longer to cook.

Feasting

For de la bella caiba
fugge lo lusignolo

Out from the fine cage
flies the nightingale

ND then they went on to Harddlech, and they sat them down and began to regale them with meat and drink; and even as they began to eat and drink there came three birds and began to sing them a certain song, and of all the songs they had ever heard each one was unlovely compared with that. And far must they look out over the deep, yet was it as clear to them as if they were close to them; and at that feasting they were seven years.'

These birds were the immortal birds of Rhiannon.

The passage comes from 'Branwen daughter of Llyr', one of the Four Branches of the *Mabinogion*. It belongs to the episode of the Wondrous Head, and marries feasting with poetry for all time. It is close in spirit to the antique Mediterranean world of which we have perceived the shadow. A feasting is marvellously evoked. We do not see the materials of the feast, we do not hear the birds, we only know all songs were unlovely compared with that and that it lasted seven years. This underlines the transition from common transient time to timelessness of which real feasts are the instrument; their essence also involves the intrusion of the unpredictable. And this is why I am not going to describe feasting; I shall name some feasts.

The feast that began with the May Day bean feast at La Barozza was a feast of a company of friends and relations of the vine grower, a friendship that had long been cemented by successive wine harvests. It started a whole week of feasting – there were excuses enough, May Day being, that year, immediately followed by the Feast of the Ascension. The wonderful month of May flowered in matchless *stornelli*. The vineyard was full of flowers, nightingales, cuckoos, four-leaved clovers, laughter and the scent of acacia flowers drifting from nearby woods.

The company only reached the imperishable heights of song through perfect familiarity with celebration, of which this week in May was the apogee; the wine had also reached perfection just as the vines were sprouting. Kilos of raw broad beans brought from the market at Sarzana in a sack were consumed, and quantities of *tordelli* and grilled chickens, at a long trestle table on the terrace.

The euphoria created by this festivity and the succession of workless days conspired to prolong it. One evening Uncle Nello sitting on an upturned cask on the paving that divided the *cantina* from the precipitous vineyards, from where the remaining few could see the sun setting beyond the mouth of the far off river Magra, exclaimed: 'I want to live a hundred years! And if I die, I wish that those present die with me – I cannot bear to leave this delightful company.' Etruscan feelings of an old quarryman, delivered in dialect.

*   *   *   *   *

There was the feast I never heard the end of, in a half-finished building down the hill which had for the time become a wine bar exhibiting a bayleaf *frasca* – equivalent of the English hollybush. A rabbit, long discussed in many other bars, was the focus of the feast, lovingly prepared by the wife of the owner of the phantom structure. The protagonists were members of an inspired and raffish society called the 'Lovers of the Precious Nectar'. Their president was an infinitely tall marble carver who was not only a brilliant improviser of words and music, but knew every note of Bellini, Donizetti, Verdi, Puccini by heart. On this occasion, their number, which was five, was extended by temporary membership to a select band of friends.

To reassure any anxious male chauvinists, I should say here that the celebrations of the Carraresi totally excluded female company on principle and in practice. The spouses of the working population despised revelry – to them it only manifested itself as a conspiracy against bread-winning.

It was my extraordinary privilege, but not on this occasion, to be accepted by this lyrical company of men, in which the Sculptor was the guitarist. (As 'audience' I acted as a kind of 'sounding board'.) The rabbit feast began, after work, in the late afternoon. A monstrous demijohn was placed upon the table. The presiding genius issued a challenge: 'None shall rise till this is finished!' It culminated around midnight with the solemn strains of '*Va pensiero*', chorus from *Nabucco*, sung with an intensity that not only brought tears to some eyes, but is normally only associated with La Scala.

*   *   *   *   *

I recall the summer banquet under the glistening leaves of a towering Spanish chestnut in the mountains above Carrara overlooking Fosdinovo and the Lunigiana, where a lovely Israeli singer bewitched the countryside; a band of hunters, slung with cartridge belts and guns, crept silently out of the groves and advancing, formed a mesmeric circle round the singer. This feast ended in a wrestling match in the back of the lorry between a Michelangelesque Israeli sculptor and a fierce little Mexican, as we hurtled down the mountain to Carrara at dusk.

*   *   *   *   *

The wedding feast of Angelos's son Mítsos took place in the high-up village of Komiáki above Apollona on Naxos. This was distinguished by the size of the cauldrons of macaroni cooked out-of-doors, which recalled the cauldrons of old, accompanying the seven goats well-spitted and roasted on open fires, and by the luminous green-gold wine, 17° in strength. Angelos, the patriarch, treated us like honoured guests in the Homeric way, as if, as strangers, we were conferring a dignity on the occasion. It ended with the bride and groom treading an endless dance, the grape-treading Naxian dance: timelessness intrudes again.

*   *   *   *   *

I shan't forget once wandering on foot through the Veneto and reaching, on a summer mid-day, a ruined castle in a stretch of uncultivated land, a kind of heath. Out of an upper window a marvellous baritone voice was singing, a troubadour in a waste land. When this voice stopped singing I made my way round to the other side of the castle and discovered a wedding feast in full swing at long tables, laden, in the ruined courtyard.

*   *   *   *   *

There was the feast in the house of the vine grower in the Priorat, the mountain fastness behind Reus in Catalonia. This ended with a neolithic cake of pressed dried figs flavoured with aniseed and bayleaves, and with it a hundred year old wine. Fenosa played Sor on the guitar.

*   *   *   *   *

And the feast of the Three Fishermen of Calafell, recorded by Irving Davis, a garlic feast, if ever there was one, in the old palace at Vendrell. We celebrated Fenosa's hundredth birthday in anticipation; the Sculptor, in a fantastic disguise, became the magician who bridged by mime the linguistic shortcomings of the company.

*   *   *   *   *

When it is real it is usually improvised: this applies to the words (but not the cadences) of the Tuscan *stornello*, to the fooling and the dressing up at the bean feast, the outbursts of wit, the mad capers, the horseplay; it also applies to arriving at the true pitch in singing, by which I mean the song sung this time for all time.

Whether the feast lasts for seven years or whether it lasts for a week or a night, and whether we have forgotten the abundance and nature of the fare and the colour of the wine, and whether the faces of the company are as clear as they then were, or are blurred, we still feel we have taken part in an unique event. In fact a feast beginning with an ample supply of drinks and victuals generously offered, is always destined for an unknown goal, one which is inspired and revealed by the imaginative gifts of the participants.

And if one has no such gifts? In good company there is a place for you: a disposition for amusement, a healthy appetite, an attentive ear, a capacity for laughter, each is fuel for celebration's fire.

If you think I exaggerate, by assembling a handful of memories (seven; which are by no means all), let us also recall the other face of feasting epitomized by Aeneas' landing in the Strophades – the Turning Islands – when, the feast of raided cattle and goats having been prepared, and seats of turf cut and set beside the shore, the meal of Aeneas and his companions was ruthlessly pillaged by the Harpies. This feast ended in a useless war against the dreadful birds and the prophecy by one of them, Celeano, that Aeneas would never be granted the city he was seeking to found, until he had starved.

Quail, Rabbit, Guinea Fowl, Goose, Turkey, Chicken

TALIANS fancy themselves as hunters. In Carrara there were 15,000 men with gun permits and about six small birds. You couldn't walk through the vineyards in autumn without meeting a gun pointed in your direction, and lead pellets rattled against the shutters. So where do all these quails come from? Once they were caught in nets as they flew in from Africa, were fattened on maize, and brought to market. Now they are raised.

QUAGLIE • quails

You need two for each person. Ideally each little bird should be sprigged with clary (*Salvia sclarea*), oiled and wrapped in a vine or figleaf, or in a thin slice of *lardo*, threaded on a spit and roasted over a wood or charcoal fire.

But they can be pan-grilled, in which case leave in the heart, liver and gizzard, put inside each a peeled garlic clove and some myrtle berries, rub them with ground black pepper and anoint them with oil.

Heat a heavy iron pan and when it is really hot, put in the oiled birds, well-seizing them on all sides; it takes about 20 minutes. You may need to add a little more oil. This is aiming at a grilling result without a grill. Serve with polenta (p 226) or a purée of dried broad beans (p 71).

GUATLLES AMB PANSES I PINYONS
quails with raisins and pine kernels

2 quails for 2 people (Catalan quails being larger)
a dessertspoon of pine kernels and
a dessertspoon of seedless raisins (soaked for 2 hours) • butter
1 tablespoon of dry sherry • 1 tablespoon of olive oil • salt • pepper

Rub the quails with sea salt and pepper, put them in a roasting dish, pour oil over the birds. Set the dish high up in an already hot oven. In 10 to 12 minutes they should be golden.

Drain and dry the pine kernels and raisins and cook them in a pan in butter for a few minutes until they colour. Transfer the roasted quails to the pan, heat the sherry in a silver spoon, set it alight and pour over the dish.

CONIGLIO ALLA TOSCANA • Tuscan fried rabbit

On Tuscan hillsides where the rustic life and the vine coincide, rabbits prosper and multiply in wooden cages raised off the ground. They are fed on the succulent grasses and bitter herbs growing on the steep slopes between the vines. Such rabbits are delicacies in spring with very tender white flesh. They are despatched and skinned on the eve of a feast day. Sunday lunch starts with enormous plates of *past'asciutta* and proceeds with rabbit.

The rabbit is neatly jointed, dusted with flour and deep-fried in a deep heavy aluminium pan, drained on brown paper and served crisp and golden on the outside, tender and white within, with a salad of vineyard herbs, dressed with olive oil and wine vinegar made on the spot after the vintage. This association of the animal and what it has fed on – often thought to be the inspiration of the connoisseur – is in fact the outcome of an instinctive feeling for those things which are by nature allies, by vine-growers who are natural gourmets, and of the two things being readily to hand.

This rustic lunch is brought to a conclusion with a cake flavoured with vanilla and *anice* (aniseed liqueur), called *pane d'angelo* (see angel bread, p 293). It is served with the 'best' wine of the year made of selected muscat grapes mixed with some of the best of the bunches of red, which are crushed by hand, not pressed, and the resulting juice fermented in a glass demijohn; called *le lagrime*, the 'tears' of the grape. This wine is golden in colour, powerful and rather sweet. In Tuscany it is thought, but erroneously, that only 'sweet' wines appeal to women!

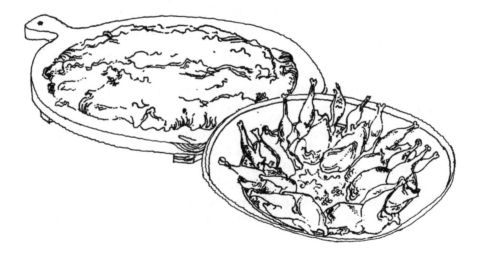

CONILL AMB PRUNES I PINYONS
rabbit with prunes and pine kernels

1 rabbit neatly jointed	12 splendid prunes
6 tablespoons of olive oil	a handful of pine kernels
1 large onion	2 or 3 slices of lemon
salt and pepper	*for the picada:*
2 large ripe peeled tomatoes	12 peeled almonds
thyme	a garlic clove
1 bayleaf	a few peppercorns
a glass of red wine	salt

Cover the bottom of a large pan with oil and fry the rabbit joints, browning them. Hash the onion very fine. Remove the browned rabbit joints and simmer the onion in the same oil; add salt, pepper and the crushed tomatoes and cook on a very low heat for ½ an hour.

Put the rabbit back in the pan, add thyme, the bayleaf, and cook in this for 1½ hours, either on top of the stove, covered, or in earthenware in the oven. After 1 hour lubricate with the glass of red wine.

While the rabbit joints are cooking, chop the almonds and pound them to a paste with a little salt, in the mortar, with the garlic and peppercorns. This *picada* is added to the dish ¼ of an hour before it is ready.

Soak the prunes unstoned for an hour, then simmer them barely covered with water in a little pan with lemon slices, for half an hour with the pine kernels added at half time. Drain and add to the rabbit's sauce a few minutes before serving, the *picada* having already been put in.

This dish has a beautiful dark colour. Prepared by Senyora Solé in the restaurant Pi at Vendrell, perfectly delicious, it was confided in the above details to Irving Davis.

CONILL AMB ALLIOLI • rabbit with garlic sauce

Rabbits have a tendency to dryness. The remedy discerned by Catalans is to grill them and serve with a powerful garlic sauce (*allioli*, p 120).

Split a young rabbit down the spine and joint it into neat pieces for grilling, dividing the legs in two, far the largest portions. (Use the ribcage and any doubtful trimmings, including the head, for soup.) Marinade the joints in olive oil with thyme and rosemary for an hour.

Make a good fire and grill the pieces, inserted into a double grill, fast at first, then more slowly, anointing the meat now and then with a branch of thyme dipped in the marinade. Serve the sauce in the mortar. You will not complain.

FARAONA ALLA MIA MANIERA • guinea fowl my way

Guinea fowl, rather delicate birds, delicate in flavour, somewhere between a chicken and a pheasant, with speckled plumage and snake-skin legs (the origin of birds is reptilian), are as common in Italian poulterers as they were in Victorian England. But they are not often interesting served in *trattorie*. I propose the following anarchic method: carry it out before protesting.

Make an infusion of the juice of 2 lemons, a dessertspoon of sugar, plenty of ground black pepper, the zest of 1 lemon and a small wineglass of water, by boiling it up for a few minutes. Take it off the fire, add 3 liqueur glasses of *grappa stravecchia* and if you are anticipating a cold – I am writing this in winter – drink some of it hot. Leave what remains to infuse.

1 guinea fowl weighing just over a kilo (2¼ lb)
a small handful of pine kernels
4 unpeeled garlic cloves, slightly crushed
a sprig of rosemary • salt
5 tablespoons of olive oil • a tumbler of Bardolino or Valpolicella
what is left of the grog

Take your guinea fowl, lay it on a stout board, chop off its head, sever the neck and the reptilian feet, and make a tiny anal incision. Draw out the intestines, liver, gizzard, heart, then empty the crop. Dip the feet in boiling water, skin them and use for stock. Put some pine kernels inside the bird, a garlic clove and the sprig of rosemary. Tie the legs neatly against the carcase, tie in the wings, apply some salt.

Heat the oil and brown the object in a frying pan with the remaining crushed garlic cloves. Transfer to a heavy, lidded pot which just contains the bird. Rinse out the frying pan with the tumbler of red wine, heating it, and pour it into the pot. Heat and add what is left of the grog. Proceed with the cooking on top of the stove on an asbestos or wire mat in a careful manner, basting from time to time and between whiles weighting down the lid, for 30 to 40 minutes. Serve with a purée of lentils (p 69).

OCA • goose

A counsel of perfection: the best prelude to goose is a platter of oysters.

One cannot do enough for a goose in the way of inducing it to render its fat, both for the sake of the taste of the meat, and for the uses to which this marvellous fat can be put.

Anything that detracts from the taste of the goose is to be avoided, which is why, after experiment, one refrains from stuffing it with anything except prunes (soaked for an hour, unstoned), apples (peeled, cored and cut in four) and pine kernels when one can afford them. This is the Catalan festive stuffing for goose and chicken. Stuffing a goose with apples is another instance of dressing a bird with what it feeds on.

Supposing the bird weighs no more than 6 or 7 kilos (11½ to 13½ lb), stuff it with a dozen prunes, 3 large cooking apples, a handful of pine kernels and a clove of peeled garlic, slightly crushed.

Put the goose on a board and prick it lightly all over with a carving fork, without penetrating the meat, and specially in the fatty parts, sides and underside. Rub it all over with sea salt, and some thyme and rosemary pounded to a powder.

Heat several tablespoons of olive oil in a pan, put the goose on a dish, nose down, and pour the very hot oil over it so that the skin sizzles. If you fail to pour it all over the first time, reheat the oil and repeat.

Take your largest earthenware or fireproof porcelain dish, set a grid on it, wrap up the goose in buttered foil, using it double, but leaving the underside free for the fat to seep out. Set it on the grid in the dish, put it in a fairly hot oven to start with, and lower the temperature when the fat begins to drip. A goose must cook slowly.

After the first hour, open the oven door and ladle some of the fat out of the dish, to obtain very pure fat. At the same time, lift the foil and baste the bird. Do this at intervals, several times. The goose will cook in about 3½ to 4 hours. Remove the foil during the last ½ hour and baste to brown it.

Oca is Italian as well as Catalan for goose. In the Veneto, the accompaniments to roast goose are red cabbage (p 168), polenta and *mostarda di frutta* (p 239). An alternative to polenta are potatoes cooked in the oven. One really wants as much goose and as little of anything else as possible.

The goose's liver has doubtless disappeared, *sauté* in oil or butter, then pounded with salt and garlic in the mortar with some chopped parsley and a little butter, and pasted on rye bread – the cook's *merenda* while attending on the goose.

The carcase of the goose makes a wonderful soup.

SOME USES FOR THE GOOSE FAT. First of all in a *cassoulet*, but anyway in a dish of haricot beans. Added, a spoonful, to a split-pea soup, or stirred into a dish of lentils. Instead of olive oil or pork fat in making a *soffritto* of aromatics as the basis of a winter soup of cabbage, beans or chickpeas. On bread, with salt and pepper. On hot toast. On your chest, rubbed in in winter. On leather boots if they squeak. On your hands if they are chapped.

PETTO DI TACCHINO CON VINO DI ORVIETO SECCO
breast of turkey with dry Orvieto wine

The symbiosis which exists between fungi and tree root can also crop up in ordinary life: I am thinking of that butcher in Garda-sul-Lago with his maize-fattened chickens and young turkeys, who had to be dragged from La Candida's bar to unhand the poultry. The plump breasts of his birds reminded one of Edwardian mono-bosoms. The situation he was obliged to leave was dominoes in cheerful company well heated by a terracotta stove. His poultry shop was cold and it was snowing.

Acquire half a breast of turkey, to include the wing, weighing about 1 kilo (2¼ lb).

This is braised entire in a mixture of olive oil and butter in a heavy pan, that is: browned with 2 slightly crushed unpeeled cloves of garlic and a sprig of thyme, then flared with Vecchia Romagna. Pour into the pan a glass of Orvieto secco and cook, tightly covered, on a fairly low heat on an asbestos mat to spread it for, say, 40 minutes, basting occasionally. At half time add a handful of rinsed capers, or some juvenile mushrooms already simmered in butter. Serve with a salad of *radicchio rosso* (p 167) and *passato di patate* (p 89).

POLLASTRE AMB SAMFAINA • braised chicken *en ratatouille*

a tender chicken • olive oil • salt • 4 or 5 onions
½ kg (1 lb 2 oz) of tomatoes • 2 green peppers • 1 aubergine per head

Cook in a cast-iron pan some finely chopped onions with sufficient oil, and when golden add 2 peeled tomatoes, and salt. Cut up the chicken into 4 sections and put these in the pan once the *sofregit* has reduced. Simmer them for about an hour in this sauce, basting and turning occasionally.

Separately fry in oil in a *paella* 2 or 3 onions finely chopped, and when they are transparent put in the peppers, cored, seeded and sliced. Cook slowly till tender, then add the remaining peeled tomatoes. Season.

Cut the aubergines into slices and fry them in a separate pan. Drain the slices on kitchen paper and add them to the onions and peppers.

Remove the chicken pieces for a moment from the cast-iron pan, transfer the *ratatouille* into it, and replace the chicken pieces. Simmer very slowly for half an hour with the lid on.

POLLO FRITTO COLLA SALSA DI NOCI
fried chicken in walnut sauce

When walnuts are first in season, shell and peel a dozen and chop them as finely as you can with 2 cloves of peeled garlic and a handful of parsley and basil leaves. Add salt and dilute with a little olive oil in a bowl.

Cut a young chicken in eight pieces and fry them in oil and butter until brown, turning them about, then drain on brown paper. In another pan toss them in the walnut sauce, so that the sauce adheres to the pieces of chicken, then serve at once.

When walnuts are not to be had, fried chicken is good with sorrel sauce, in this case served separately. It is made by simmering a good handful of sorrel leaves, roughly chopped, in butter, stirring. In a few moments it achieves the consistency of a sauce.

A POULTRY MARINADE

Chicken improves in flavour if you cut it up as soon as you bring it home. Put the joints in an earthenware pot, sprinkle them with olive oil, thyme, ground pepper, add garlic, a bayleaf, a piece of lemon zest. Cover, keep in a cool place, and turn the pieces occasionally. This procedure, older than the refrigerator, prevents the bird deteriorating. It applies also to rabbit, quail, little legs of lamb already fractured by the butcher.

Vinegar is not added to this poultry marinade. When you come to fry the pieces, you wipe them, heat a little butter in an iron or copper pan, brown them, and only then add the strained oil from the marinade.

ALLA CACCIATORA • cooking the hunter's way

It is perhaps time to resurrect the original concept of cooking *alla cacciatora*. What did these hunters actually do? Don't tell me they took a frying pan out hunting.

This is Wolfe Aylward's view: 'I think that they shot the bird or rabbit, grilled it as best they could over an open fire with lots of herbs, probably sacrificed a little *prosciutto grasso* from a *panino* stuck in their back pocket or at the bottom of the game bag, to lightly bard it. They then tipped a minute quantity of wine over it at intervals – this they undoubtedly had in a flask slung from the waist – so that the meat didn't dry out before it had finished cooking.'

And here is the method transferred to the kitchen of a mountain peasant woman in a *trattoria* high up above Castelnuovo di Magra at Marciano; the chicken and rabbits here were raised on the spot.

POLLO ALLA CACCIATORA CON OLIVE NERE chicken, the hunter's way, with black olives

The chicken, tender and weighing about 1 kilo (2¼ lb), is jointed, then chopped into pieces of the same size – on the small side. These are fried in a heavy pan in olive oil in which 3 crushed but unpeeled cloves of garlic and 2 sprigs of fresh rosemary and some leaves of mountain sage (*Salvia sclarea*) have first been simmered.

When the pieces are golden, 2 peeled tomatoes are crushed in the pan, salt and a glass of white wine are added, and in this very scarce sauce the chicken cooks more slowly, covered, until most of the liquor is absorbed and the pieces are tender (10 minutes for frying, and 15 minutes once the wine is put in). During the last few minutes a dozen luscious black olives, unstoned, are put into the pan.

Served on a white oval dish with the olives and the scarce sauce, which is passed through a strainer, or should be, to eliminate the aromatics. In fact, in the Osteria da Rizieri, both the rosemary and the thyme, indeed also the garlic, put in an appearance in the dish.

While preparing this, the *padrona* brought a plate of mountain *coppa* and *mortadella* into the vine arbour, *coppa* being smoked loin of pork in sausage form, the colour of port wine, and *mortadella* a coarsely ground farmhouse pork sausage, slightly smoked and flavoured with whole peppercorns. The meal finished with *pecorino* cheese made in the vicinity, a fresh ewe's cheese served with summer pears (p 44).

L o o k i n g   f o r   a   W o r k   P l a c e

T HE wind plays over Apulia. It plays on every stone that is raised, until it is worn to filigree; the castle erodes in the same way as the rock on which it stands. There is a feeling of being marooned in an older kind of time; the peninsula is like an island 'full of noises' that brings invisible Ariels and Calibans to mind.

The castle farms look like great ships from afar, riding a waste of stones or riding at anchor among the vines. Approach them and the castle becomes a shepherd's byre in a ruined Renaissance watch tower. The towers were built five hundred years ago in the reign of Carlo Quinto in expectation of the pirates. Nothing in Apulia has endured longer than this expectation.

White villages built like honeycombs on the crest of hills turn blind walls to the wind. Stone huts (*pagghiari*) built among the olive groves admit no aperture except a doorway: little structures, erected with precision, stone by stone, in beehive form. The face of Apulia vanishes behind the legendary olive trees, as a little boat disappears behind the crests of waves. Muffled, the voice of Apulia, as the wind trifles with olive fronds. Silent the stare of the Apulians as they perceive the pirate in the gait of every stranger.

In the silence, gazing from the watch tower, one can feel the earth slowly swinging as the mast of a ship sinks below the far horizon of the Ionian – what is far being as clearly delineated as what is near.

The wind visits the castle farms, searching out the crevices in their square towers, singing through the windowless windows. It would be tapping at unlatched doors, if these had not long since been burned in winter by shepherds huddling beside their voracious hearths. A magpie taking a lift from the wind, alights on a tower and drops a seed of a fig which in no time at all will be the roof's undoing. There is little activity in these deserted structures except the works of nature undoing the works of man. Looking down from the tower, an army of Indian figs has already broken through the crumbling dry-walling of the courtyard and rooted itself like a barbarian encampment at the door.

Two people are wandering about looking for a workplace.

A thousand crickets flash their scarlet and cobalt wings as they dart about the aromatic scrub which surrounds the castle. The wind carries the pungent scents of sage, rosemary, thyme, myrtle, cistus and the acrid smell of lentisk. Larger crickets blunder about opening transparent wings. The barbed seeds of minute leguminous plants leap into trouser turn-ups and settle; here and there, as if snatched from a Persian miniature, are tiny scented narcissi, fragile starlike crocuses and little cyclamen, and being October, the ground is littered with the huge bulbs of the sea squill bearing their succulent crowns of virid lily leaves. Near the castle in the eroded rockface lies the fossilized imprint of pearly palmer's shells, reminding one that, ten million years ago, Apulia was submerged. Patches of orange lichen burn on these rocks and patches of red umber earth between the rocks develop overtones of purple in a sudden storm of rain. Colours are gauged against the prevailing tone of pale calcareous stone and ashen sun-dried grasses. The sky shows whiskers of white cloud and near at hand is an expanse of satureja, its white flowers trembling at the visitation of countless swallowtail butterflies.

During these wanderings, now fifteen years ago, no measures had been taken to provide for strangers. Instead of bewailing their fate, they fell into the habit of filling a *fiasco* with good wine in any village where olive fields had given place to vines, in *Vini* or *Alimentari* concealed behind a rusty chain curtain in the mainstreet. They filled their water jar, earthenware or zinc, of Attic shape, at the village pump; stocked up in morning markets with muscat grapes, almonds, fresh *caciocavallo*, *scamozza*, mozzarella, or *cacio affumicato* (smoked) or *manteca*, a globelike cheese whose central core is butter (*mantega* = butter in Catalan) and a mound of rustic bread. Settled under an olive tree or in the shade of a *pagghiaru*, October here being as hot as August in Tuscany, they picked some leaves of *rucola* to season the cheese and were free to contemplate the opaque blue dome of the Apulian sky.

In a climate where rain clouds only began to assemble at the end of October, there was no need to experiment with accommodation, one slept out in the *terra libera* of the sand-dunes, where, as the sun sank into the Ionian, it was possible to witness the full moon's rise – a huge orange disk looming out of a violet haze – in the diametrically opposite direction to the setting sun .

The Work Place Found

But do you think it is wrong to pour boiling water onto a wasps' nest, I asked, there's one near the threshing floor. The Sculptor didn't seem to be listening. Tilting the bentwood chair, he was examining the ceiling. Where the white wall of the cow-byre met the white arch of the roof vault, an excrescence had appeared just above the invisible rectangle, which, each night was lit up by the intermittent beam of the lighthouse 15 kilometres away at Santa Maria di Leuca, like a vacant television screen.

Just imagine, I said, I mean try to imagine a bachelor in Apulia. Even the *idraulico* – a rather grandiloquent name for a plumber hardly out of the chrysalis – doesn't turn up to work without the moral support and physical presence of his fiancée, the girl's sister, and to make up the weight, their widowed mother. Rather hard on the grandmother, don't you think? he muttered.

I let the grandmother pass and in the gathering dark looked about: the young man had directed a boy of eight with a man-sized pickaxe, helped by a grizzled septuagenarian, to penetrate the walls, freshly plastered and five feet thick, through which he was to pass in the name of hygiene some iron pipe. At least they're not plastic, I thought. The floor was littered with enormous boulders, encrusted with earth and terracotta-coloured rubble, resulting from the fresh disembowelling of the structure – an area of devastation newly routed and 'levelled' by eye, by a wall-eyed man with a compressor.

The specialist referred to as *il tubista*, dressed in tight cotton pants, was bare from the waist up but for a carefully arranged coiffure and a fine gold chain with a little medallion round his neck, St Anthony one supposed, the patron of things lost and forgotten, which had not prevented him from neglecting to provide for the eventual discharge of the water he was contriving to introduce into our future kitchen from a large cistern across the road.

But take Luigi, I said, where would a plasterer be without the presence and approbation of his mother, his wife, his wife's sister, his two terrible little boys, and that apple of his eye Ornella, not to mention his aunt? An adventure of this kind, far from the confines of the village, requires witnesses, he replied, expelling a thin smoke-screen of *trinciato forte*, (shag), and I didn't ask you to make coffee for all of them. No, you just said: Go out and talk to them. The mama is deaf, speaks only in dialect, she didn't understand a word I said. The wife was shouting at the boys, who for lack of a dog's tail were mauling the vine shoots. The wife's sister – a beauty with the dark neat head of a little serpent – who had left school at fourteen in order to make her trousseau and fill her marriage chest immediately began asking me about English wedding customs, while Luigi's mother scrutinized the ungarnished third finger of both my hands and pursed her lips a little. (The chest seems like a direct heritage from the ladies on the terracotta plaques, cast in bas-relief, of Magna Graecia, who are carefully putting their exquisite linen into key-patterned marriage chests with lion's paw feet, in the Museum at Taranto.)

It's natural curiosity, he said. And a conversation of that kind is less stereotyped than the usual one: How lonely you must feel here! Aren't you frightened of vipers? You need a gun, a dog, against nocturnal intruders . . .

I know, said I, but it does worry me rather to think what happens to a girl who spends the next seven years making her trousseau and dreaming of being a princess for a day in a pearl-encrusted tiara, if the chap at the last moment doesn't come up to scratch. All those embroidered table-cloths, those lace-trimmed monogrammed sheets, the crocheted centrepieces, the doylies, the drawn-thread work – and even when she does get officially engaged, he dashes off to Switzerland to earn enough to furnish the *salotto* – the parlour showpiece.

You have plenty to worry about, without getting worked up about that, he said, as he gazed at the vault where the hornet was enlarging the freshly made and extremely neat hexagons of its nest.

Of course I am wondering why making a trousseau never once entered my head. And, as I asked you before, do you think it is wrong to pour boiling water onto a wasps' nest in an old boot?

I don't know why we need all these pipes, he said, it is far more satisfactory shitting under a figtree.

Calf, Cow, Ox, Horse and Buffalo

I N the far south of Italy – Calabria, Basilicata, Apulia – where I first ventured with Irving Davis twenty five years ago, meat was rarely displayed, the butcher's shop (*macelleria*) being identified by a pair of ox horns, which were also mounted on the roofs of isolated farms, to keep off the evil eye. The carcases were kept in large cold-storage cabinets: one entered an empty cell through a bead curtain to see nothing but a notice on the weighing machine saying 'credit is not extended to-day' and a bunch of tripe, an ox hoof or an oxtail, hanging from a hook. This was for reasons of hygiene, and has since changed with the installation of refrigerated display cabinets. But, until a few years ago, the purchase of meat was restricted to feast days – Sundays and Saint's days. Now it is ostentatiously acquired on any day as solid proof of well-being.

In the old days, magnificent herds of tawny oxen roamed the waste lands with a herdsman and his little wolf dogs; these herds have vanished. The delicious fresh *mozzarelle* sold daily in *alimentari*, once derived from them, are now made industrially from the milk of confined cows. But in the plains of Paestum in Campania, the original *mozzarelle* are still being made from the milk of Indian cow-buffaloes, and also in the Maremma and in the Pontine marshes.

On Naxos we did not see a joint of beef for a year on end. Oxen were rare and cows precious. White with splendid horns, they had sensationally lean flanks. They were kept in stalls and not only had to produce milk but were harnessed to the plough even when in calf.

In the country round Carrara the cows were kept in stalls at the top of the vineyards. Their food was brought to them by women toiling up hill with mounds of sweet hay freshly sickled in early summer, secured by sacking and balanced on the head. Later, the second crop was dried and stacked for winter in beehive shaped structures mounted on central poles on the hill-tops. Women's devotional exercises extended to supplying the rabbits with greenstuff and the chickens with maize, the latter freely ranging until the grapes began to ripen. The yearling calves were bought by butchers who tramped over the hillsides striking hard bargains.

Where these beasts have the chance to graze, for instance in the high uplands above the Tiber, in the Tuscan mountains behind San Sepolcro, in the uplands of the Abruzzi, the beef is excellent and furnishes superb steaks grilled on open fires.

In Catalonia the climate does not permit the raising of beef, which is why the Catalan *escudella i carn d'olla* has always been made with veal. Like its French counterpart, the *pot-au-feu*, this consists on the one hand of the *escudella*, the broth (and the bowl it is served in), and on the other of the *carn d'olla*, boiled meat with vegetables. Macaroni is cooked in this broth, which results from cooking veal, pork (including the pig's feet, ears, tail) and half a chicken, to which are added chickpeas, potatoes, dumplings, haricot beans, root vegetables and *botifarres* (black blood and white pork sausages) and cabbage, all cooked in the same earthenware pot or *olla*. This nourishing dish, until a generation ago, was eaten by rich and poor alike nearly every day in winter.

Not without reason Josep Pla has said that there has always been 'a certain monotony' in Catalan cooking. One might say, but ironically, that this monotony has been 'relieved' by the political and economic convulsions of recent years. The consequences of inflation and of the demographic 'explosion' alone have put this traditional sustenance well out of reach, and what now replaces it in no way competes in taste or nourishment. But I do not wish to depress the reader by examining the effects of industrialisation. The fact is the Sculptor prefers wild food to hormone-injected veal and beef. Perhaps this comes from living in the wild, living with marble, living with stone. In Carrara game abounded, as also in the Veneto (p 237). In Apulia where flocks of sheep still safely graze, and pigs are locally reared, or one rears the pig oneself, one is, as it were, on firmer ground.

I am not alone in my conviction that one should eat less meat. By chance I have just opened, while writing this, the *Metamorphoses* of Ovid, to find in Book XV Pythagoras's address to the inhabitants of Crotone, which city was located just across the Ionian; its promontory can be clearly perceived on certain days in winter from Spigolizzi's roof. This address is the most moving conjuration in favour of vegetarianism ever written. All the same I have to admit that from time to time I have a certain hankering for beef!

INVOLTINI • veal, stuffed and rolled

Sometimes called *imbottiti* (stuffed or quilted), sometimes *uccellini* (little birds), these particular *involtini* are the ones made in rustic *trattorie* in the mountains above Lucca.

2 thin slices of veal per
    person
100 g (3½ oz) of *pancetta*
    (rolled salt belly of pork)
oil or butter
1 bulb of fennel, or wild
    fennel, shoot and frond

single-leaved parsley
a garlic clove
a few capers
salt and black pepper
white wine
chicken broth
toothpicks

Slice the *pancetta* into strips and brown them in oil or butter. Trim, then beat with a wooden mallet the thin slices of veal on a board. Chop up finely the fennel (or wild fennel) with some single-leaved parsley, the garlic and the capers. Put a little of this preparation on each slice, add salt and ground black pepper, then roll up neatly, fixing each one with a wooden toothpick inserted lengthwise. Simmer, turning them about, in the oil or butter in which the *pancetta* has browned, until they colour (10 minutes), then add a small glass of white wine and a very little reduced chicken stock, and cover. Simmer for 15 minutes, set them on a dish and eliminate the *pancetta* by straining the scarce sauce through a sieve, over the little rolls.

CARN ESTOFADA AMB PRUNES I PATATES
Catalan veal stew with prunes and potatoes

Anyone whose notion of the prune is connected with infant hygiene might be taken aback by its association with meat dishes in Catalan cookery. In fact, its character changes completely when used in this way, and it has a different texture in consequence of being soaked for no more than 1 hour (sometimes in wine) and cooked for a short time.

1 kg (2¼ lb) of lean veal
a large onion
3 cloves of garlic
2 large tomatoes
a liqueur glass of Spanish brandy
½ a teaspoon of paprika
50 g of bitter chocolate,
    broken

a pinch of ground cinnamon
a bouquet garni (thyme, bay,
    parsley)
a large glass of white wine
1½ glasses of water
12 fine prunes
2 small potatoes per person, peeled
    and cut into cubes
olive oil

Soak the prunes for 1 hour. Heat some olive oil in a pan, cut the veal into substantial pieces and brown rapidly on a hot flame. Transfer the meat to an earthenware pot. Slice the onion and brown it in the same oil, with the unpeeled garlic cloves. Peel the tomatoes, first dipping them in boiling water for a few moments, crush them in the pan and add the wine and brandy.

Reduce the liquor over a slow fire by at least half, simmering for 20 minutes, then add the paprika, the bitter chocolate and the pinch of cinnamon. (The chocolate is used rather than flour to give consistency to the sauce; its taste vanishes.) Put in the bouquet.

Now stir the sauce, diluting it with the water, cook it for a few minutes, then pour it over the meat in the earthenware pot. It should only just cover the meat. Simmer, covered, on top of the stove on a very low heat on an asbestos or wire mat (or cook in a moderate oven, closely covered) for 2 hours, then remove the herb bouquet.

Meanwhile cook the prunes for ½ an hour in very little water and drain them. Fry the potato cubes in hot oil; they should be golden.

The *estofada* is served in an oval dish, preferably white to show off its rich dark colour, with the fried potatoes at one end and the prunes at the other.

BRACCIUOLINO DI VITELLO • shoulder of veal, rolled

An economical way of cooking veal, excellent hot or cold. The bones which are removed (ask the butcher to do this) provide the basis of a stock for *Pasta in brodo* (p 104), also called *Minestra in brodo* in the north.

a shoulder of veal, boned	a sprig of fresh rosemary
olive oil	1 bayleaf
the juice of 2 lemons	origano (wild marjoram)
salt	a garlic clove

Lay the meat out on a board, put a leaf of rosemary and origano here and there, crush the garlic and paste the meat with it. Add a few drops of olive oil. Roll it up into a good shape and tie it with string.

Heat some olive oil in a cast-iron pot or copper pan, put in the meat and brown on all sides (20 minutes) on top of the stove. Add the juice of 2 lemons, put on the lid and cook on a tripod in the hearth over a slow braise, or in a moderate oven for 1½ hours, basting from time to time.

If you serve this cold, put the joint on a dish, remove the string, and strain the juices in the pot slowly over the meat; it sets into a glaze.

CAP I POTA · calf's head and knuckle of veal

The Catalan approach to the relatively inexpensive extremities.

½ kg (1 lb 2 oz) each of calf's head and knuckle of veal
1 lemon · 2 bayleaves · 2 parsley stalks · 2 peppercorns
1 large onion, finely chopped · 2 peeled tomatoes · olive oil
1 dessertspoon of paprika · 1 wineglass of dry white wine
½ kg (1 lb 2 oz) potatoes, peeled and cut into rounds
for the picada: 4 almonds, 2 cloves of garlic and salt

Wash and soak the head for a few hours, then put it in the pan with the knuckle, just cover with water, add salt and slowly bring to the boil. Skim, then simmer slowly with slices of lemon, the bayleaves, peppercorns and parsley stalks for 1½ hours. When tender, strain off the broth, and cut the meat into small pieces.

In the meantime brown the chopped onion in a heavy pan in olive oil, then add the tomatoes, crushing them. Sprinkle with the paprika and pour on the wine. Reduce to the consistency of a fairly liquid sauce; this takes about 20 minutes.

Put in the pieces of meat and the potatoes, and add just enough strained broth to cover. Cook with the lid on for ½ an hour. Just before serving add the *picada*, having pounded the almonds, garlic, salt in the mortar, and having diluted this with a little of the sauce from the pot; then pour the contents of the mortar back in. The potatoes will have absorbed most of the sauce.

FEGATO ALLA MIA MANIERA · liver

The difference between calves' liver and liver of other animals is a matter of flavour, texture, tenderness and price. In Carrara the source of liver was more often a mare, a pig, an ox, and even a mule (I wondered). The butcher sliced it into mean slices. (Inadvisable to try and identify it or to fry it.)

½ kg (1 lb 2 oz) of liver · black pepper · olive oil
thyme · savory · chopped parsley · garlic · salt
a dessertspoon of Dijon mustard · a large wineglass of red wine

Put the liver on a board, remove the valvelike parts, cut into narrow strips and sprinkle them with pepper.

Put these strips with a little olive oil in a heavy pan, sprinkle with the herbs and gently simmer. Add the chopped parsley, sliced garlic and salt, but only when you have turned the strips of liver. Mix the mustard with the juices released in the pan. Then pour in the red wine and raise the heat a little to hasten evaporation and the resulting cohesion into a sauce. The time taken: not more than 8 minutes. Serve on its own with a dish of *patates vídues* (p 87) to follow.

LINGUE DI VITELLO IN SALSA DI CILIEGIE MARASCHE
calves' tongues with morello cherry sauce

This recipe derives from growing morello cherries in the garden.

2 calves' tongues each weighing
    about ½ kilo (1 lb 2 oz)
sea salt
aromatics:
½ an onion
a carrot
a piece of celery
6 juniper berries

for the sauce:
3 or 4 tablespoons of morello
    cherry jam
a wine glass of six-year-old
    red wine
40 g (1½ oz) butter
a wine glass of reduced broth

Rub the tongues with sea salt and put them in an earthenware crock for 24 hours packed with a little sea salt above and below.

Next day: rinse the tongues and put them in a pan, cover with water, bring to the boil and simmer with the aromatics for 1½ hours, covered, on a low heat. Leave to cool in the broth.

Take them out of the pan, peel and trim them, then replace them to keep hot in the liquor which you have quickly heated and reduced.

If you have made the morello cherry jam (p 308) or have managed to buy some (Romanian, German or Bulgarian) prepare the sauce:

Put the butter in a pan large enough to take the tongues, add several spoonfuls of morello jam, melt it stirring on a low heat with the butter, then add a wineglass of red wine and very little of the hot broth, passed through a strainer. Put the tongues into the sauce, still on a low heat, to absorb the colour and the flavour; after a few minutes turn them over and simmer for another few minutes.

Set the tongues on a white flat dish and pour the scarce sauce complete with cherries over them. To carve: slice them horizontally, in thin slices. Very simple and delicious.

In spite of my lack of enthusiasm for veal (*vitello*) and older veal (*vitellone*, you can hardly call it beef), and may anyone Italian reading this forgive me, I must include the Milanese *bollito misto* and the Venetian *lingua salmistrata*, both recipes belonging to ancient tradition, medieval memory and peasant origins, dishes which throw a beam of light on eating habits which persist in the face of the most blatant modernity in the harsh winter climate of northern Italy.

IL BOLLITO MISTO • Milanese boiled meats

One of the splendours of Lombard and Piedmont cooking – boiled meats served with an astonishing variety of piquant accompaniments. To get the idea of it one must go to a Milanese restaurant frequented by thickset energetic business men in the neighbourhood of La Scala. (The study of the clientele of any eating place is often a better indication of what will issue from the kitchen than a perusal of the menu.)

But failing this, before embarking on its preparation, one should acquire some vision of Milan – even at second hand. No better portrait nor more amusing exists than the one by Andrea Giovene in *The Book of Giuliano Sansevero*, the chapter called 'The Monkeys'. The other person imaginatively connected with that city is Stendhal who once declared that by dint of being happy at La Scala, he had become a kind of connoisseur – of music. It is the intensity underlying the experience of happiness – or its contrary in Andrea Giovene's case – which is the prerequisite of knowing about anything.

This is how to prepare what the Sculptor insists, paradoxically, was his most memorable meal, perfectly cooked and presented by Chiarella Zucchi. She says: 'For 6 or 8 people you need 2 kilos [4½ lb] lean beef, a medium sized ox tongue, a free-range chicken and a *zampone* or *cotechino* [p 230].'

Contrary to general belief, each of these items is cooked in a separate pot, immersed in cold water, brought to the boil, the beef, the tongue and chicken broths being scrupulously skimmed until absolutely clear; the *zampone* or *cotechino* is wrapped in the usual way in a fine cloth. To each pot are then added a little salt, a carrot, a bayleaf, a stick of celery and an onion, unskinned. The beef, tongue and *zampone* should simmer for 3 hours, the chicken for 1½ hours (the same time for the *cotechino* if used). When the tongue is ready it is carefully skinned, the little bones and mucilage at the root are removed, also some of the fat; it is then put back in the pot to keep hot.

There are two main ways of serving the *bollito misto*:
1. The boiled meats are carved in slices, placed in a tureen or heat-resistant glass bowl with the broth from the beef and the chicken (only these, passed through a strainer lined with cloth to eliminate any fat), and served piping hot with the following accompaniments: *salsa verde* (p 120) in a sauce-boat or bowl; *giardiniera*, mixed cut vegetables in wine vinegar from Italian delicatessens; gherkins conserved in vinegar; *carciofini sott'olio* (p 317); *mostarda di frutta* (p 239). These arranged on a circular, compartmented hors d'oeuvre dish present a very delightful spectacle.

2. The boiled meats are presented on a large oval dish, steaming hot, and carved at table while the chicken and beef broths are combined and served first. This is *la stracciatella*, made thus: break 3 eggs into a bowl, add a pinch of salt and 3 dessertspoons of grated parmesan. Bring the combined broths rapidly to the boil and, when boiling fast, pour the beaten egg mixture, a little at a time, into the pot, whipping with an egg whisk. Continue to whisk while the soup boils for 4 or 5 minutes, and serve. *La stracciatella* is a positive form of 'curdled egg'; if the operation is successful the soup contains a mass of little 'threads'. Chiarella chose this way. The fresh ox tongue is often replaced by *lingua salmistrata*, pickled tongue.

LINGUA SALMISTRATA • pickled ox tongue

One of the sights in winter in the Veneto – pickled tongues, magnificent, in butchers' shops. Here is the Venetian principle of pickling them, producing not only a fine colour but an agreeable flavour. (Calves' feet, a calf's head or a piece of belly of pork can conveniently be put into the pickle at the same time.)

THE PICKLE. Dissolve 1½ kilos (3 lb 6 oz) of sea salt in 5 litres (180 fl oz) of water with 150 g (5 oz) saltpetre (from a chemist). Add 300 g (11 oz) brown molasses, boil for a few minutes, then add a branch of thyme, a twig of rosemary, 2 or 3 leaves of sage, 3 or 4 bayleaves, a dozen juniper berries and a dozen peppercorns, all confined in a muslin bag, and leave till cold. This takes some hours.

Pour the liquor over the ox tongue in a glazed earthenware crock (or stoneware crock should you have one), put a clean board over the meat and weight it with a large pebble or non-porous stone to keep the tongue immersed. Leave for a week in the pickle. (In the depth of winter it can stay longer.)

TO COOK IT. Take it out and immerse in tepid water for a few hours to remove some of the salt. Then put it in a large marmite with plenty of cold water to cover. Bring to the boil, skim off the scum as it rises, then simmer slowly – 25 minutes for every ½ kilo (1 lb 2 oz) and ½ an hour besides – with the lid on. It takes longer than a fresh tongue because the saltpetre has the effect of slightly toughening the meat. Throw away the cooking water. The scarlet tongue, peeled and trimmed of its little bones and excess fat, is served hot with a *passato di patate* (p 89), leaf spinach and *salsa verde* (p 120) and *mostarda di frutta* (p 239).

CARNI EQUINE • horse meat

An English lady arrives at Spigolizzi all smiles and delighted with the Salento. After one or two glasses of wine she suddenly becomes pensive: 'I was shocked to find so many horse-butchers!' A French, a Belgian woman would not have felt indignant. The Gauls, the Belgic tribes, the Greeks, the Messapians, horse lovers all, did not have this taboo on horse meat. Nor do today's Salentines. Indeed, the horse meat butchers are, by far, more highly skilled than other butchers.

There are two favourite and economical ways of using this meat:

1. In the form of *polpette*. Prepare these with twice-minced meat in the way described in the recipe for *Pasta al forno* (p 102), but making them twice as big, i e walnut-sized, and fry them. Then simmer them in a thin tomato sauce flavoured with basil, in earthenware on the stove on a low heat. Serve hot with potatoes, or cold as an *antipasto* with *carciofini sott'olio* (p 317) and black olives. This is traditional food to be found in Salentine *osterie*, and has much in common with the *keftéthes* of Crete.

2. The other traditional dish is *pezzetti*: pieces of lean meat simmered with water, oil, aromatics and hot peppers, to which, when tender, is added a liberal amount of tomato sauce. The resulting liquid is used to flavour a dish of pasta, with the meat served at the same time on a separate plate.

This approach is all too similar to the Naxians' way of preparing goat. I give here a more sophisticated way of making *pezzetti* elaborated by our friend Vincenzo Verardi:

Ask the butcher for a kilo (2¼ lb) of horse meat cut from the rump. Take it home and cut it into substantial blocks, as for a *daube*. You will need a particularly sharp knife. Cutting it up yourself gives you a good idea of the nature of the meat.

Put the pieces in an earthenware dish and add to it: a sliced onion, 2 sliced carrots; green celery chopped, leaf and stem; some pounded juniper (or myrtle) berries, some fennel seeds; 2 hot chilli peppers; 3 or 4 tomatoes; 2 or 3 sliced cloves of garlic, salt, a little olive oil and a dessertspoon of red wine vinegar. Leave to marinate, turning the meat once or twice.

Next day take the meat from the marinade, wipe the pieces and brown them in olive oil in a frying pan. Add 3 or 4 peeled and seeded tomatoes, the marinade and a glass of dry white wine.

Transfer to an earthenware (or cast-iron) casserole and simmer, covered, on a very low heat for 3 hours, making sure that the meat does not dry out; if it does, add a little stock. The meat must be tender but not 'frayed'. Set it on a dish and pass the scarce sauce through a sieve over it. Serve with *passato di patate* (p 89).

Here I record a delicacy, with no other name than *carne secca* (dried meat), made in the Veneto by horse butchers, which in appearance is similar to *rillettes*, i e a mass of fibres, but unlike them in that it has a dry consistency. The horse meat, after salting, is dried in the sun. Once dried, it is cut into equal chunks, which are then pounded to shreds in a heavy mortar. You eat these shreds with wine as an aperitif; they have an excellent taste.

In Antwerp, the Sculptor's birthplace, horse meat is smoked, sliced very fine and eaten with or without sliced ham; this is called *gerookt vleesch* in Flemish.

In London's Soho a lady called Rose nourished a great many students daily during the war on horse meat steaks. I daresay she fried the *pommes frites* that accompanied them in pure horse fat. She was French of course.

In buying horse meat we can repose in the thought that horses have not been submitted to hormone injections. In the Salento they are imported at Gallipoli from Hungary.

P r o s p e r o ' s   F e a s t

THERE is one feast I feel impelled to describe.

It is seldom that perfect hosts have the heart, the imagination to be also the perfect guests. Don Andrea Giovene and the lady Adeline arrived one summer afternoon at Spigolizzi, bearing in hand and covered with a cloth an enormous baking tin containing a *crostata*, a rustic cake baked in Ugento that morning, made with golden yeast pastry into which a good many eggs and some vanilla sugar had vanished, crowned with dense pear jam (*la perata,*. p 306) and pastry cross-hatching. So gladly we sat down at the table under the vine to do it justice, with a delicious bottle of Ugentine muscat wine they had brought with them.

This visit heralded an invitation to lunch in two days' time. Precisely at 12.30 we were to find them on the outskirts of Ugento, a city older than Rome, but twice razed to the ground by the Saracens. The house where they were improbably staying belonged to the daughter of the tobacconist in the piazza whose husband manned the petrol pump. We could not imagine what form this feast would take; lunching out in Apulian villages is quite a risk.

We found Don Andrea dreaming in a deck chair on a small area of paving in front of a newly built concrete villa, its windows closed against the mid-day by metal roller blinds called 'saracens'. Waiting for us, he said he had been imagining what it would be like to be the owner of this villa, and in doing so, had succeeded in finding a genuine sense of satisfaction and achievement. In performing this imaginative feat, quite considerable for one whose past is intertwined with palaces, he had bridged the chasm which divides the old concept of peasant life from the concrete aspirations of their sons and daughters. As our neighbour said only the other day with a touch of irony: 'Now we are all *signori*.'

The villa was separated from others of its kind by a little garden of apple, peach and orange trees among which a few rows of dark-leaved summer chicory were growing, and round the corner we came upon Donna Adeline, a dish of roast red peppers in her hand, which, she lamented, though cooked in the local bread oven, had not been divested of their outer skins, nor seeded. So I sat down with her on a concrete parapet to do this, while Don Andrea and the Sculptor sauntered up the dusty August road to see how the feast was shaping. We followed at our leisure with the dish in hand, covered with a napkin.

Entered from the main street, what appeared to be a wine bar contained a beautiful little star-vaulted cell behind, which in days gone by had been a *trattoria*. It was now perfectly white and empty but for a few cobwebs and a trestle table and chairs set in one corner, from where one had a reassuring view through an open door of a small kitchen in whose ample hearth already a splendid olive wood fire was glowing. In Apulia the hidden things are the things that matter: cool vaulted rooms, the secret gardens behind high walls betrayed by the delirious scent of lemon flowers, the deep ravines.

Lunch began in the conventional summer southern way with spaghetti in a deep red tomato sauce, served with grated *pecorino*. 'It is right' said Don Andrea, 'for the first course to be eaten in silence. This vaulted room reminds me of the rule of silence during meals in the Convent of the Lily when I was at school.' The next dish provoked a torrent of opinions – scorpion fish, to my delight, their rosy forms bathed in a rosy *sughetto* in which were traces of green celery and wafts of garlic. Donna Adeline proclaimed that the scorpion's head was the best part of the fish, and was shocked when I said 'Yes, I appreciate the cheek'. 'The cheek is nothing to the rest of the head' she protested, as, tearing it apart with fork and fingers, she vigorously sucked the fragments. The Sculptor chivalrously passed his head across the table, Don Andrea firmly remarking that the only civilized way of eating fish was with a fork in one hand and a hunk of bread in the other.

Meanwhile the barman's wife was anxiously hovering about the table praying that everything was as it should be; and he was bending over the hearth and before long materialized an exquisitely bronzed offering of month-old lamb, cut from the fragile bones, perfumed with olive oil, thyme, rosemary, some drops of lemon juice, and expertly wound and impaled onto long hardwood spits. The roast peppers were served with this, an inspiration perhaps of Donna Adeline, and now dressed with black pepper, olive oil and garlic.

Perfection thus attained, to our amazement a dish of grilled red mullets followed, fished that morning, as were the *scorfani*, off San Giovanni, the one-time Messapian port of Ugento, now submerged.

Then came a salad containing leaves of *rucola*, cultivated rocket, rather piquant, with a lovely fresh goat's cheese from Gemini. Then a green melon, called *melone* or, in dialect, '*minne di monaca*', nun's tits, refreshing; and then came wisps of almond cakes which may have been called '*sospiri*', sighs, reflecting other sighs of profound satisfaction. Don Andrea, a Prospero conjuring wonders from the void, was perfectly light-hearted. He had enchanted the normally gloomy hearts of an Ugentine Caliban and his Rita. 'Ri-ta' he called in his voice pitched rather high, rolling the *r* through the doorway into the kitchen. Rita darted back into the cell, her cheeks flushing. We drank the golden muscat wine, Ugentine, to start with, and a dark red wine with the lamb and mullets. Four villages, besides the sea, had been ransacked at his bidding.

Should I have made an error in recalling, this could be corrected. I can imagine the feast described in detail in some huge book, beautifully bound for him by Donna Adeline, and filled with extracts from his journal, written in a superb calligraphic hand and decorated with drawings and jewelled letters.

But I *have* forgotten something. There was a fifth guest: the young director of the Ugento Museum, but he was speechless. A bell must have rung. We were lunching with a genius. I now realise that Don Andrea and Gertrude Stein have one thing in common. They both have written somebody else's autobiography. And there is nothing to prevent anyone from getting to know him through *The Book of Giuliano Sansevero*.

Lamb and Kid

ARROSTO D'AGNELLO ALL'ARETINA
lamb on the spit in the manner of Arezzo

A way of roasting a leg or quarter of young lamb adopted to remove any trace of the stall adhering to it. A normal leg of baby lamb is sufficient for two people. Killed when a month old, or two months at most, they are skinned immediately and hung for 24 hours before proceeding: Rub the little leg with salt and ground black pepper and pour over it a tablespoon of red wine vinegar and rather more olive oil. Prick the leg here and there on the surface with the point of the knife and leave to marinate for a few hours in an earthenware dish, turning it once or twice.

Wipe it and stick one or two sprigs of rosemary into the meat and a clove or two of peeled garlic into the pocket next the exposed bone. Thread it on a spit and, using the rosemary sprig, anoint the leg with the marinade as it roasts, while turning it over a glowing braise. When the juice begins to drip, try and catch some of it in a pan. It cooks in about 25 minutes.

The most excellent sauce for roast lamb is *la moutarde provençale*. Cook 4 whole heads of garlic in the ashes of the fire, then peel and pound them. Bone, wipe, then pound 4 salted anchovies, which have been soaked, into this garlic paste. Use the juices retrieved from roasting the leg of lamb and pour the essence of the meat into this preparation in the mortar, stirring.

COSCIOTTO D'AGNELLO ALLA CACCIATORA
leg of young lamb cooked in the hunter's way

Ask the butcher to chop a leg of young lamb weighing about a kilo (2¼ lb) into 3 cm (just over 1″) pieces, then marinate them in olive oil and the juice of a lemon.

If you have a wood fire going, put the pieces in the double grill and grill them first, before finishing them in the frying pan as described below. If not, brown them in the frying pan in olive oil with 2 crushed garlic cloves (unpeeled), and 2 sprigs of fresh rosemary. Sprinkle them with salt, ground pepper and powdered savory (*Satureja montana*). Brown on all sides, turning them with a wooden fork. Pour a glass of red wine into the pan and add 2 crushed peeled plum tomatoes. Simmer until the scarce sauce has practically evaporated and the meat is tender. Serve with artichokes cooked with broad beans (p 171) or with garden peas.

See page 83 for a more substantial leg of lamb cooked by Fenosa on a clockwork spit.

HAEDUS SIVE AGNUS CRUDUS • 'kid or lamb raw'

The simplest recipe in Apicius (see *The Roman Cookery Book*) has an unfortunate, indeed misleading title, but it is almost unique in that it is not what my father called 'a messed up dish'. I quote: 'Rub with oil and pepper, sprinkle outside generously with pure salt mixed with coriander seed. Put in the oven, roast, and serve.' The coriander seeds should be previously pounded.

The Roman oven had the same 'beehive' form as Apulian ovens then and now. Lambs, more usually jointed, sometimes 'quartered', are anointed much in the same way (though rosemary replaces coriander seed), and are placed in a capacious baking tin of heavy aluminium (*teglia, tiella*) and roasted at the same time as the bread, at Easter. This oven, *furnus* (Latin), *furnu, furnieddu* (Salentine dialect), *foúrnos* (Greek) is in the form of a stone hut attached to the *pagghiaru* or *llama*, rustic summer dwellings. The 'floor' of the oven, at waist level, is paved with *chianchi*, calcareous stone, and the corbelled dome is now lined with fire-resistant bricks. The oven is lit with big bundles of olive twigs, from the biennial pruning. A first fire is lit the night before bread making, and a larger one at early morning, while the loaves are rising. The glowing ashes are then raked to one side and as many as 50 one-kilo loaves are put in. In summer when the heat hardens bread very quickly,

little curled loaves of barley or wheat flour called *frise*, *frisedde*, are baked instead, then halved while hot by drawing each one through a looped wire hanging on the wall, and baked again. This is the summer evening stand-by: the stone-hard bread is soaked in cistern water for a moment, then shaken and anointed with olive oil and crushed tomatoes and garlic. Very satisfying.

GNUMMARIEDDI
young lamb's pluck and gut cooked on the spit

I mentioned the Naxian version *splína ke kokorétsi katsikíou* (in La Merenda, p 50) without perhaps giving it its due. Skill is required in its preparation, confirmed by this quotation from Kevin Andrews' *Flight of Ikaros*:

> For fifteen years his father had made his living hiring himself out to restaurants as a specialist in roasting a delicacy called *kokorétsi*, entrails wrapped round and round a spit.

Clean the pluck from a month-old lamb: spleen (*milza*), heart (*cuore*), liver (*fegato*), lungs (*polmone*) and slice them neatly on a board.

Open the gut, rub it well with salt, then wash in tepid acidulated water. Sprinkle with flour and wash again. Rinse several times, then dry the gut. Cut it into 8″ lengths (20 cm) and lay the strips on a board. Lay across each strip a slice of spleen, heart, liver, lungs, with some fresh parsley or coriander leaves. Then wind the gut round to make a 'faggot', each of equal size, and secure each packet with a thread. Oil the faggots and sprinkle with a few drops of lemon juice. Thread on metal or hardwood spits with a bayleaf between, and roast them slowly, turning them round over a lively wood braise.

Gnummarieddi can also be grilled on a wire grill over an incandescent olive wood fire (on a single grill you will have to turn them by hand) but they can if necessary be cooked on a grid over an oven dish high up in a fairly hot oven.

This is a prized Salentine dish, also made with calf's pluck (*coratella di vitello*), but not so good; these *gnummarieddi* are normally prepared by butchers in spring, on lamb slaughter day, and sold the morning they are made.

SPEZZATINO D'AGNELLO • Roman lamb

The consolation of the Sculptor, having an exhibition in Rome, was the eating places around the Piazza Navona, which today are severely diminished. In little *trattorie* something entertaining was always going on, and one evening he became a member of a merry and spontaneously

formed *società di cani affamati*; the other famished dogs were three very vocal medical students.

Spezzatino derives from *spezzare*, to break; in this case small pieces are chopped from the shoulder of lamb, the meat with the bone attached. Slithers of garlic are inserted between meat and bone, with a leaf or two of rosemary.

Prepare a *soffritto* consisting of chopped carrot, green celery, chopped leaf and stalk, and a sprig of sage and sprigs of parsley, finely chopped and all simmered in hot oil in a pan; the pieces of lamb are then fried in this *soffritto*. Once browned, a glass of wine is poured into the pan and 2 or 3 crushed peeled tomatoes, salt and pepper are added. This is simmered for about a quarter of an hour with the pan covered, by which time the meat is tender and the sauce scarce. You cannot call this a lamb stew although the dictionary does.

Served with new peas in March in a *trattoria* where the waiters were old indeed. One of them was sitting down in a striped apron in front of a heap of dried rosemary, stripping the branches of their leaves and flowers and stuffing them into glass jars. I have already said that rosemary has its best effect when fresh. Dried rosemary is most liberally scattered in Roman dishes! As for the sage, *Salvia sclarea* and the three-lobed variety *S triloba*, plants originating in the wild in Italy and Greece, both are more delicate in flavour than the common garden sage, *S officinalis*.

BOÚTI ARNIOÚ STIFÁDO • braised leg of kid

Something must be done to goat before cooking it; this applies also to kid. Put it on a dish, rub it with salt, pepper and pounded thyme and fennel seeds. Anoint it with wine vinegar and oil, but be parsimonious, cover it with a muslin cloth, and leave it in a safe place for a few hours (on Naxos, a basket hanging from the roof beam). The leg, removed from its aerial retreat, was then put into the black pot with olive oil, a chopped onion, a carrot, and coriander leaves likewise chopped, and seized on all sides, turning it, to brown it. The scarce marinade was poured from the dish into the pot, a glass of golden Naxian wine was added and a bayleaf, and the lid put firmly on. It was then left to simmer on the outdoor fire, for 40 minutes, and turned occasionally. If it looked like drying out, a few crushed tomatoes were added. The recipe applies equally to leg of goat, only it takes longer to cook.

SUPPER WITH THE SHEPHERDS

At seven it was beginning to get dark. Not a sign of the goat man. The moon was still behind the mountain. We lit a lamp under the vine for a sign.

Suddenly out of the dark Apostólyi appeared with two shadowy companions. We started on the supper: olives, bread and wine. Apostólyi countered our bread with better wife-made bread drawn from his shirt. The moon peered over the mountain and splashed the sea with silver.

I produced a pan of sizzled goat and proffered forks: the goat was eaten with the fingers. Kid cutlets sprinkled with mountain thyme, they vanished in a moment. Then okra and potatoes, Apollonian dish, cooked with tomatoes, oil and wine (p 181). Then tomatoes in a salad with garlic and basil. The wine from Koronós was not considered good, it had no kick. The gourmets passed this judgement, then drank it with abandon. I brought out the fresh goat's cheese they had made for us in our habitation two days before. They wouldn't touch it. They'd made it for us. We must eat it and go on eating it tomorrow. Manólyi materialized another kind of cheese, we had to taste it.

By this time the fire of the shepherds' hunger was barely smouldering. Their faces glowed. They began a reminiscence of the dishes, scoring each item. The talk had been mostly toasts and gastronomic grunts, compliments mixed with lost forks and laughter. Last came a huge earthenware dish piled with rose red grapes. While these were eaten Angelos appeared, grey as a ghost. He was carrying a wicker bottle. It contained the last of his good wine. He sat down with us on the dark terrace, too tired to drink and yawning. He had been carting gravel on top of days of wedding frummel (the Sculptor's word for fuss, *fassaría* on Naxos) – four festive sleepless nights.

The Sculptor proposed we drink a loving cup of the good wine. Manólyi said 'No, not after grapes'. His brother said 'No', a final No with gesture. 'You don't drink wine after grapes. They make a peculiar mixture in the stomach.' 'Sometimes it doesn't matter being ill,' the Sculptor said, raising his glass: 'I drink your health.' Apostólyi, gleaming, then seized the cup and poured its contents down his open throat. A shepherd lives by inspiration. The others weakened. The cup went round. The wine tasted like centuries old Madeira.

Apostólyi owned the mountain above Apollona on the southern limit of the bay, which ended in a headland. He spent his life chasing a herd of goats and long-tailed sheep across the mountain at speed; we used to see him flying across the thistly scrub. He was a part of the mountain, one saw this in his dancing. The Naxian dance employs exactly the same steps as are used in treading the grapes, which is not extraordinary looking back on Dionysus' presence there. When Apostólyi performed this dance at the *panigýri* in summer he transformed it – using the sweeping movements of the eagle as it drops from a great height, the hissing sounds and coiling movements of a serpent, and the caprioles of the mountain goats, his daily companions.

Pasticceria and the Apulian Baroque

ARÊME maintained that *pâtisserie* was a branch of architecture. He illustrated this statement with a marvellous set of apparently edible constructions engraved with a delicate precision in his *L'Art de la Cuisine Française au 19ᵐᵉ Siècle*. 'The fine arts are five in number, to wit: painting, sculpture, poetry, music, architecture – whose main branch is confectionery.'

Years ago in the Salentine capital, Lecce, architecture first struck me as a highly elaborate branch of *pâtisserie*. But I have since come to think of this remote region – now our home – as a kingdom under the moon's dominion, and its baroque architecture as an adorable instance of lunatic inspiration.

I can't help wondering whether what finally determined us to settle in this 'moon-scarred' wilderness was not a domestic altercation filling the narrow street down which we happened to be walking, which reached its climax with a wooden spoon flung from an open window. I picked up the spoon. I am using it still.

Lecce is peculiarly sited on calcareous terrain whose easily quarried surface stone has the plastic qualities of gingerbread. Like gingerbread, it hardens with exposure and assumes with time the colour of burnt gold.

The city within the walls calls to mind the Bourbon Kings of Naples, who once a year ordered the construction of castle edifices made of stout edible materials – gigantic hams, cheeses, enormous *mortadelle*, and the fore and hind quarters of deer and Indian buffalo, in order then to gloat at the spectacle of the starving Neapolitans – admitted at the moment of completion – vociferously and violently vying with each other, to the accompaniment of martial music and gunpowder explosions, in their destruction. These fanciful structures, which I used to pore over in the library of Irving Davis, can still be contemplated in the wonderful *fête* books in the Print Room in the British Museum.

In outward appearance the Leccesi are as solidly materialistic as the Milanesi and even better shod. Their city is likewise in eruption, its baroque core encircled by a chaos of apartment blocks and maze of motorways. However one responds to the late 16th century Spanish and Catalan influenced city – baroque being here of Elizabethan and

Jacobean date, whence its exuberance – and to its latterday conurbations, there is no doubt about the supreme talents of the Leccesi as pastrycooks.

We put this remarkable fact immediately to the proof by entering the Caffe Alvino in Piazza Oronzo, in front of whose art nouveau mirrors the more well-to-do inhabitants were already installed at 10 in the morning, gorging themselves on magnificent cakes: conch shells of crumbling cinnamon-flavoured *pâte feuilletée* with a ricotta filling, whose delicious freshness was enriched by a sweet chestnut purée and pralinated almonds; éclairs light as air, containing a dense chestnut syrup, the exterior reinforced with a delicate carapace of curled bitter chocolate. This was in October; other seasons bring other things – pine kernels, strawberries, quince, and *pasta mandorlata*.

IL PESCE DI NATALE • the Christmas Fish

The Almond has this connection with the Virgin, that it has long been considered to bear fruit without previous fecundation. This ancient belief, still held by Salentine peasants, is mentioned in a discussion of the *XXIème Arcane majeur du Tarot de Marseille* – the card representing the World, in which the central figure is enclosed in an almond-shaped vesica of laurel leaves. (See Veyrier in the Bibliography.)

So, in relation to the Christmas fishes made of *pasta di mandorla* at Lecce one sees in their point of departure, in the shape of the nut, the *vesica piscis* – also called *la mandorla* (almond), the divine nimbus, the aura of sanctity, the cosmic egg. The ritually made fishes celebrate the birth of Christ in conjunction with the era of Pisces.

The nuns of a convent at Lecce are famed for these confections, but live permanently withdrawn from the world, so I am not able to give their recipe in all its simplicity, in all its refinement. But the basis of these sublime creations is as follows.

A quantity of almonds are shelled (let us say ½ a kilo – 1 lb 2 oz – when shelled, of sweet almonds, but including 3 or 4 bitter ones). Covered for a moment in boiling water, they are rapidly peeled. Laid on a linen cloth, they are set to dry in the sun for 2 days. The shining white almonds are then pounded, a few at a time, in a stoneware or marble mortar to a very fine powder with a marble pestle.

Originally one supposes the ground almonds were amalgamated with honey to achieve a firm but plastic consistency capable then of being pressed into lightly oiled traditional fish-moulds made of pearwood, copper, zinc, tin and plaster of Paris, patterned with carp-like scales. Nowadays a quantity of caster sugar (see footnote on next page) equal to that of the almonds is used, but it is incorporated in an original way: in a copper pan the sugar is melted by stirring over a very low heat, using a minimum of hot water to bring this about without burning, the almond flour is sifted in, stirring vigorously and continuously the while, and the pan is taken off the fire only when the mixture coheres and comes away from the bottom and the sides. It is then left to cool in a bowl until it is lukewarm.

When filling the oiled mould, a depression is made in the centre of the fish into which some pear conserve (*la perata*) is carefully spooned, then covered with more paste. *La perata* has the aspect of dark amber, both the fruit and its syrup being transparent and glazed. (See p 306.)

When the fish is turned out, a coffee bean is pressed into its eye socket. As coffee was only imported in the 17th century, arriving in Venice in 1615 from Moka,* and the fish stem from time immemorial – as do the almond cakes called *divino amore* at Gallipoli – one wonders what constituted the eye before that, a raisin perhaps.

Some adepts lay on top of the pear preserve a narrow layer of *pan di Spagna*, a refined sponge cake, impregnated with rum, surely a Bourbon intrusion at the time when Lecce formed part of the Kingdom of Naples.

The significance of the pear preserve dawned on me one afternoon when a Leccese friend, Laura Rossi, sitting under the fig-tree, complained of the price of pears at Lecce, their conserve being, she emphasized, *obbligatorio* (obligatory) in the making of the Christmas fish. This word *obbligatorio* – more often used with reference to religious duties than to culinary procedure – stuck in my mind. And then I remembered that some Greek Orthodox friends had brought an Easter offering of delightful aspect – a shallow wicker basket containing haricot beans wreathed round with acacia flowers and leaves and on it a little crown of newly sprouting thorny wild pear. In the Greek Orthodox Church the wild pear is Christ's thorn, His Crown.

Sometimes in spring a neighbour appears at Spigolizzi to graft onto the wild pear trees, that grow spontaneously on the calcareous hillside, the shoots of a cultivar which produce the small honey-sweet pears for *la perata*. Thus another aspect of the Christmas fish is revealed: the destiny of the Christ child, concealed in the stomach of a fish.

Holy lambs are made of *pasta mandorlata* for Easter, in the same way, their heads of painted plaster, with red and gold paper flags. It is said that one cannot enter into the World of Symbols without cultivating a certain receptivity: the Leccesi who are devoted both to truth and to *friandises* act on this advice literally when confronted with the delectable *pesce di Natale*.

* For the fruits of recent research on coffee, sugar, and other foodstuffs in both hemispheres, see the Proceedings of the *Oxford Symposium Documents* in the Bibliography.

A Few Sweets

HERE are a few sweets, some of which also employ almonds, or pine kernels, excellent with a glass of wine. They are of course 'light years' away from the feast-day fishes and lambs of Lecce and the inspired creations of the Caffè Alvino, the new proprietor of which has seen fit to exchange the original art nouveau décor for dull wood panelling; this somehow has affected the cakes.

CASTAGNACCIO • a chestnut flour flan

In Castelpoggio, the mountain village in the Apuanian Alps where we worked one spring and summer, Spanish chestnuts and the white flour (*farina dolce*) they produce when ground provided for centuries a basic diet. Polenta was made of chestnut flour and *castagnaccio*, a kind of rustic *torta* which has the consistency of a pudding and the aspect of a shallow cake. It used to be made in round shallow copper and brass pans, which were set in the ashes of the fire. In the last war, chestnuts, fungi and weeds were the only form of nourishment, unless the Castelpoggians undertook dangerous expeditions across the mountains, on foot, to Parma, a four day tramp often under fire, to barter their chestnut flour and salt for cheese and oil. Some people went on making this cake, baking it in the village bread oven, others preferred to forget it.

Sift 250 g (8½ oz) of chestnut flour through a flour sieve into a mixing bowl and mix it to a thick paste with cold water, being careful to remove every little lump. Add more water, stirring, a little salt, some pine kernels, a few stoned Malaga raisins, and some fennel seeds.

Stir vigorously with a wooden spoon until the paste is of a consistency that can be poured from the bowl into a round flat baking tin, which has been generously oiled. Pour it to the thickness of about 2 cm (a little less than 1"). The oil will rise and cover the surface. Bake for about 30 minutes in a moderate oven. The surface should acquire a chocolate brown crust. If you make it too thick there will be rifts in the crust. The inside is a pinkish brown and moist. Turn it out of the tin, cut into triangular sections and eat it hot with a slice of ricotta. But, as an old lady said to me, 'we often eat it without'.

Castagnaccio is sold in winter in the Piazza delle Erbe in Verona from a stall also selling winter pears, *frittelle* (fritters) and huge hot doughnuts cooked on the spot in boiling oil.

PANE D'ANGELO • angel bread

In spite of its name, *pane d'angelo* is the ordinary home-made Castel-poggian cake, a cake a child can make.

½ kg (1 lb 2 oz) plain flour • 3 eggs
400 g (14 oz) of sugar flavoured with a vanilla pod
100 g (3½ oz) butter (or a coffee-cup of olive oil)
a lemon • a little yeast diluted in a glass of warm milk
a brandy glass of *anice*, aniseed liqueur • a handful of pine kernels

Cream the sugar and butter (or oil) beating with a wooden spoon in a china basin, then lightly work in the eggs. Sift in the flour and mix lightly. Add the grated rind of the lemon. Pour in the yeast when it is frothing. Add the *anice*. The mixture should be light and creamy.

Oil a baking tin with sides about 8 cm (3″) high, pour in the mixture and sprinkle its surface with pine kernels. Bake in a moderate oven; the crust should be lightly brown, the cake risen and the texture light. This is Dirce's recipe; one got the *anice* by the glass from the bar across the street, and baked the cake in the baker's oven up a little alley.

PANELLETS • little Catalan almond cakes

1 kg (2¼ lb) shelled almonds • 900 g (2 lb) sugar
100 g (3½ oz) vanilla sugar • 2 or 3 potatoes • a glass of *anís*
a glass of Spanish brandy • 120 g (¼ lb) grated coconut
a little orange or lemon essence • a handful of pine kernels
a few extra almonds • pestle and mortar

Pour boiling water onto the almonds and peel them. Spread them on a cloth and dry them in the sun. Then reduce them to a powder, a few at a time. Boil the potatoes in their skins, then peel and mash them. Mix with the almond flour, then add the sugar and vanilla sugar. Divide the mixture into two parts. To one part add the grated coconut and the *anís* liqueur. To the other, add a small glass of Spanish brandy and a little orange or lemon essence.

Form the first part into little domed cakes, and stick one or two split almonds on top. Continue with the second part; this time the little domes are crowned with pine kernels.

Place some of these little cakes on a flat oiled plaque and put them high up in a hot oven for a few minutes, so that they brown. Take them out and replace them with the rest. When cold pack in airtight tins. These little rocks are dipped in wine.

LA COCA DE LLARDONS • *la tourte aux lardons* (a lard cake)

Coca is the generic Catalan word for flan which can be either sweet or savoury. It is sometimes made with spinach, haricot beans and *botifarra blanca*, a white pork sausage. The Neapolitans have a rather similar yeast cake containing *lardoni* and pieces of chopped smoked ham sausage or salame called *casatielo* (*tielo* or *tiella* being the tin in which it is cooked). At Easter this dish is transformed into a festive offering by pressing into it, before baking, four eggs in their shells.

The fat used is cut from a *jambon cru*, called *pernil* in Catalan or *jamón serrano* in Spanish (and is sometimes used when rancid). It is cut into little dice and fried to reduce the fat content.

1 lb (450 g) of fat (see above) diced and fried	baker's yeast
3 eggs	a glass of milk boiled with a stick of vanilla
a cup of sugar	a few drops of *anís*
a pinch of cinnamon	¼ lb (110 g) pine kernels
the grated rind of a lemon	a soupspoon of oil
a glass of sherry	1 lb (450 g) plain flour

Beat the eggs, amalgamate the sugar, beating to a cream, put in cinnamon and the grated lemon rind. Incorporate the lardons and then the sherry.

Sift the flour into this mixture. Dissolve the yeast in a little of the milk. When it froths pour it into the dough, stirring, add the rest of the milk and the drops of *anís*, and the pine kernels, still stirring, then cover with a cloth and leave for an hour in a warm place. Pour a little oil into a round baking pan and spread the dough in it, then cook in a moderate oven for 45 minutes.

AMARETTI • little almond cakes

300 g (10½ oz) caster sugar
180 g (6½ oz) sweet almonds • 20 g (¾ oz) bitter almonds
2 egg whites • pine kernels • lemon zest

Blanch the almonds in the usual way, then peel and dry them in the sun or in the oven. Pound them very finely in a mortar, adding one white of egg poured in a little at a time, while continuing to pound.

This done, mix half the sugar with the almond flour, working it with one hand. Put the mixture in a basin and, continuing to manipulate it by hand, add half the remaining egg white, the grated lemon and then the rest of the sugar and finally what is left of the egg white. Work it to a consistent paste, then roll out and divide, say, into 30 pieces.

Wetting your hands, take each piece, form it into a little ball the size of a walnut, then flatten each out to the height of 1 cm and lightly press a few pine kernels into each. Take an iron oven plaque, smear it with a little butter, then dust it with flour and caster sugar. Arrange the *amaretti*, leaving room for them to spread, and sprinkle each with fine sugar. Cook in a moderate oven for about 20 minutes; they should turn golden brown.

CREMA CREMADA • Catalan *crème brûlée*

4 egg yolks	half a stick of cinnamon
4 tablespoons of granulated sugar	the rind of a fresh lemon
2 tablespoons of plain flour	a little caster sugar
1 litre of milk	a poker (or salamander)

Beat up the egg yolks in a bowl with the sugar. Mix the flour with a little of the milk to a paste, in a basin. Infuse the cinnamon stick and grated lemon rind in the rest of the milk, just bringing it to the boil, then letting it cool.

Strain the perfumed milk onto the flour and milk paste, stirring, then add this gradually to the egg yolks and sugar. Transfer to an enamelled pan and heat it cautiously, stirring the while; when it comes to the boil, pour out the thickened *crème* onto a flat fireproof porcelain dish and leave until the next day.

When you come to serve it, sprinkle it with caster sugar and gently burn the surface with a red hot poker or salamander if you have one.

GINGERBREAD

I mention gingerbread here not only because of its association with the Leccese baroque, but because there is a sculptural pleasure in making it. Take down your gingerbread moulds, wash them and dry them, then later sprinkle them with fine flour, otherwise the paste will stick when you come to take the imprint.

Put in a pan and stir till melted: a large cup of black treacle; 60g (2 oz) of butter; 100 g (3½ oz) brown sugar; 1 large breakfast cup of boiling water.

Sift into this sticky mass 2½ cups of plain flour, 1 teaspoon of powdered ginger, ½ teaspoon of powdered cinnamon and ½ teaspoon of bicarbonate of soda, dissolved in a little boiling water, adding a pinch of salt.

Knead with a wooden spoon until smooth and very stiff to work. Add more flour if it doesn't seem stiff enough. Knead it well and roll out to 1 cm (¼″) thickness on a floured board. Press the dough into the mould. To take a proper imprint the paste must be very stiff. (Sprinkle with more flour and work again, if you are in doubt.) Set the mould upright and carefully ease out the paste. Put it on a buttered oven plaque and bake in a slow oven; you can tell by the smell when it is cooked. Take it out, ease the gingerbread onto a wire tray and leave it to cool, when it will harden. (Look out! If the oven is too hot, the pattern will vanish.)

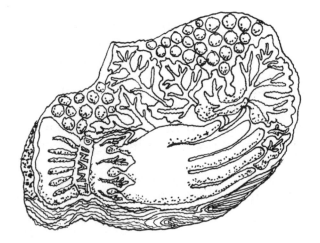

SALSA • Eivissenques Christmas Pudding

This is a survival of *menjar blanc*, mentioned in connection with the 14th century manuscript *Sent Soví* (p 32), whose ingredients have been noticeably reduced with the passage of the centuries, but which is nevertheless interesting. The recipe was given to Irving Davis by Senyor Joan Ribas of Cala Saladas and I quote it in full:

'1½ lb [675 g] of almonds, skinned (by soaking for a few minutes in
hot water), dried and reduced to a fine powder in a mortar
3 pints [38 fl oz] of hot water • 4 eggs • 2 sticks of cinnamon
(or 2 large spoonfuls of powdered cinnamon)
10 large spoonfuls of white sugar • a spoonful of salt
4 spoonfuls of olive oil • a small spoonful of powdered saffron
2 or 3 dry biscuits pounded

'Heat the water. Put the pounded almonds in the centre of a bowl, break four eggs into it and mix with the almond flour. Add sugar. Put this mixture in the saucepan and with a wooden spoon mix well with hot water. Bring to the boil. Add the salt, the cinnamon and the pounded biscuits. After this mixture has cooked for an hour add the powdered saffron and the oil and cook for at least two hours.

'This is the *Eivissenques* Christmas Pudding eaten only at Christmas. Like an English Christmas Pudding it can be prepared in advance. This is a very ancient dish probably brought to *Eivissa* (the Catalan name of the island of Ibiza) by the Phoenicians. I feel that the sugar has replaced what was originally honey. Pounding the almonds is not an easy operation in the absence of a special mill for the purpose. Otherwise use a pestle and mortar adding the almonds a little at a time. An old lady of *Eivissa* to whom I showed this recipe told me it is better to put chicken stock than water! This pudding is served by ladling out into separate bowls.'

The 'old lady' was of course right, harking back to its origins.

An Apulian Bachelor

And when other means fail, we are found to prevail,
When a Peacock or Pheasant is sent as a present.

Aristophanes, The Birds

EPPI Marra – an old fox. Personally I prefer an old fox, a dark horse, a crocodile to the man who slaps his chest while insisting that 'we're all brothers'. Then there's his avarice. He used to rent out his threshing floor so that his chickens could peck at other people's barley. And, of course, a colossal saving, he never married. 'My brother died and I had to look after his kids,' he says with a trace of a simper.

A natural comic, he has the cockiness of youth, the vanity of an old maid and the acquisitiveness of a character in Dickens. You can't help thinking he long ago received the benevolent attentions of the priests, though not perhaps on account of his looks.

There is something Edwardian about Marra. He instinctively combines style with frugality, and insists a good deal on credentials hanging on the wall – twin portraits of King Victor Emmanuele and his Queen – 'a real lady' – in the *salotto* which remains exactly as it was created by his parents in 1900, survives as a commentary on the deterioration of all subsequent *salotti* and contains the elegant understatements of the bentwood era. Pictures of three Popes cling to the looking glass and out of a drawer tumbles a chef d'oeuvre of the local photographer – Marra aged 39 in a stiff collar with his 'soul mate', a sailor boy, each imprisoned in a palpitating red heart.

In the old part of the village you reach his habitation by passing through an archway which pierces the ground floor of a palace. It leads directly into a little courtyard where a vine of immense age has stretched its serpent coils to form a pergola at a great height. Marra's house consists of a series of gothic-vaulted rooms opening into each other and out behind onto a walled orange and lemon garden, neatly dug, in which patches of artichokes, basil, chicory and pumpkins, zinnias and peppers are cultivated in proximity to water vats. On the paved terrace flanking the house another pergola of vines, grown high, lends shade in summer to a stone basin for washing up.

Entering his house, you step into what could claim to be a 'morning room' should memory of such a room have not yet faded, like Edwardian chintz. Here on the round table the incomparable finger of taste has stuffed a bunch of full-blown hundred-petalled roses. The walls are taken up by a wine cupboard, a gouache painting of his 'country seat', portraits of grapes with Victorian girls, and calendars with Lambretta girls. Taste with pursed lips one moment, forgets itself the next; rooted in parsimony, its celebrations are impulsive. Taste is an active principle, is not for sale, cannot be acquired. Perhaps such notions, like the morning room, have all but vanished.

We hasten into the kitchen to slake a thirst acquired by exposure to the mid-day. Marra invites us to sit down at the oil-cloth covered table; chattering in his high-pitched voice, he brings out a bottle, a dish of olives, a loaf, while we gaze with satisfaction at the bachelor's installa-tion; a gothic-vaulted cell, white, on whose walls a large wire sieve, two sticks of stockfish, baskets of pears and peppers, a huge jar of freshly pickled capers on a shelf, stand out like emblems. A raised hearth contains an iron gallows for suspending copper cauldrons over the fire in winter. Beside the hearth a little stove perches on a shelf, and on the wall behind hang pots, pans, ladles. An old brown *credenza* (cupboard) leans against the whitewashed wall and through a long window appears a slice of azure sky and oranges hanging among dark boughs.

The conversation inevitably turns to the acquisition of some piece of land and the attendant difficulties, measures and foxiness required to get it, interspersed with references to how able, cunning, devious and up to it our host is, and how well-loved, well-known, appreciated, pious, important he is and has been; but carrying with it a small refrain in a minor but high-pitched key — how alone, helpless, pitiable is the condition of a bachelor whose well-being has been pledged for the benefit of his nephews and great-nephews.

At this moment, when all the stops are out, there appears as if from nowhere an elderly crone bearing in hand some platters. This genius has apparently passed through a secret door which communicates directly with the house next door, whose owner is Marra's friend and this his servant. She greets us cordially and soon returns with some plates, stuffed aubergines, fried *polpette*, which she thrusts before us, while examining my ring and asking 'Is it gold?'

We set to, while Marra continues to declaim — that he only eats to keep us company, that really he has no need to eat at all, and would gladly serve all this superfluous food to the pig. All the same, he repairs to the *credenza* and urges on us some little fishes floured and fried, then marinated in breadcrumbs, capers and vinegar to round off the meal (*Pupiddi a scapece*, page 124), then rushes off into the *salotto* and returns clutching some rumpled photographs of a Pop evening to which he has lent his elderly presence in company with a youthful '*compère*' caught bending over a microphone.

In due course we wander out into the sunlight, our host following us out: 'And when are you going to give me a little carving? I really must have a little *ricordo* [souvenir] in marble!'

Marra pursues his labours on an old bicycle pedalling to his dispersed properties – a house surrounded by oleanders and vines near the sea, a spacious *terreno* on the plain full of vines and ancient olive trees, a walled garden in the village and other bits of earth besides. 'I'm just a *contadino*,' he moans, 'a poor unfortunate', but the impish smile, the giggle belie the words. Whenever anyone else speaks about him, they always rub thumb and forefinger together, hand language for 'he's got the cash'. But Marra is certain that everyone owes him something; he wakes up in the night with a sensation of being robbed.

I am not going to discuss the way the fox always gets the best grapes. The principle is well known, attachment to those in power and services rendered to people in the right places. In this way you can alter the course of a projected road to skirt, not traverse, your property; you can fend off a denunciation and spin it back onto the person who made it; you make sure you are tipped off, should the *carabinieri* be tempted to inspect your outhouses in wartime.

The first two situations are dealt with by knowing exactly when and to whom a very large fish, a *cernia imperiale* (p 117) for preference, wrapped in the aromatic leaves of the maquis, should be delivered on a bicycle, never mind the distance, in the first case to the surveyor, and in the second to a judge the day before the case is heard. The third is met by passing a leg of fresh pork to the policeman who comes to tip you off, having been led on other occasions to expect a trifle of this sort.

*   *   *   *   *

One is often confronted with the 'shocking' figures relating to illiteracy in southern Italy. Literacy, which is thought to broaden the mind, in Apulia leads directly to a seat in a lawyer's office, where the possibilities of extortion are legitimized. Illiteracy can thus be seen as a handicap. But what newspapers don't recognize is that a person who has devoted no time to reading has had far more time to study behaviour. Thus northerners will look askance at what in their eyes is bribery and corruption; they ever fail to perceive the hilarity, the Goldoniesque atmosphere in which such deeds are perpetrated and recalled.

Language, for lack of writing it down, has retained forms and expressions proper to Goldoni's time and so have facial expressions, pure *commedia dell'arte* with which they are delivered. And as, off the stage as well as on it, the foxy character steals the lines, I am not writing about an Apulian of virtuous intent. The fact that Marra is capable of boasting of the distribution of imperial fishes and solid legs of pork – 'for half a century my heart has been a-flutter'! – indicates not an incredible naivety but a knowledge of men and an insatiable craving to outwit them.

There is little doubt that meannesses can accumulate in seventy odd years to the point where fellow citizens actively look forward to the day when it is your turn to be hauled to the cemetery, and some have been heard to say that they at least will abstain from following the coffin, which is quite a thing in a village where death is held in reverence and where several hundred people turn out to meet it, with or without a band.

*   *   *   *   *

One feast day, San Giuseppe, we called in, bearing the offering attaching to a visit in bottle form. The door was open and to our ritual cry '*Permesso!*' a feeble voice from an inner room replied '*Avanti!*' The old boy was lying practically 'laid out' in bed with a nightcap on his head. A precipitation of blood to the brain had put him in a condition, the doctor said, of being any moment's candidate for the next world.

From where he lay on a bed of painted tin, thinly inlaid with mother-of-pearl, he could catch a glimpse – through the open doorway of the bentwood *salotto*, which gave onto the entrance courtyard, the archway, and narrow main street – of the procession, which he said, was due to start at any moment, if we liked to hasten out for a closer view. The Virgin in person was being borne along, dipping her head to avoid the electric cables drooping across the street, accompanied by child communicants in long white dresses and orange blossom crowns, followed by the female population in gauzy wisps of headgear, carrying lighted tapers and muttering Hail Marys, which did not prevent them from darting their eyes in our direction. The plangent notes of the brass band bringing up the rear had not failed to have their effect on Beppi Marra who, when we returned, lifted his hands, cast his eyes to Heaven and in despairing tones said: 'I already see the funeral crowns approaching!'

These wreaths which stand higher than a man, of palm, of laurel, studded with lilies and carnations, are affixed to sensational effect to the house where death has struck; funeral crowns, the very word *corona* pronouncing a finality which the word 'wreath' tries to avoid.

*   *   *   *   *

When some time later we called again, the door was ominously locked. But on enquiring next door, we found that he insisted, on his first day out, on visiting his garden up the street. We made our way down a narrow alley, come to a wooden door in a high wall, and stepping in, saw Beppi Marra tottering about in a kind of trance, grasping here at a bunch of grapes, and there pulling up some onions and parsley sprigs, his voice quavering, his gait unsteady, but a certain undaunted resolution in his eye suggested that he was grappling onto victory and his earthly possessions. Exhausted but triumphant, 'I had to see my garden,' he declared. He handed us a bunch of grapes to celebrate what might turn out to be an indefinite reprieve.

Nevertheless, the movement of conscience we had discerned when he was prostrate showed itself again one day when, on entering our kitchen where the Sculptor had lately painted in earth colours a moon fool on the limewashed vault, he looked up, stepped back nimbly with a cry of horror, then in a loud voice with a perceptible crack in it cried: 'The Devil himself!' and darted backwards out of the door. I had the same feeling then as when, in the last act of *Don Giovanni*, Leporello confronts the Commendatore.

Preserves

. . . singing in chorus as directed
on orders which of course presume
that thievish mouths cannot consume
their masters' berries undetected
so long as they're employed in song . . .

Pushkin, *Eugene Onegin*

LATE in life Madame Oda Slobodskaya – the supreme exponent of Tatyana's role – gave a lecture at the Guildhall School of Music on *Eugene Onegin*. She began by outlining the characters in Tchaikovsky's opera and then proceeded to describe the scenes with the help of extracts on tape operated by two technicians.

In the first act a chorus of raspberry pickers intrude upon the stage. Madame Slobodskaya was describing the idyllic atmosphere of the Russian summer, of the old Russian country life. The tape recorder boys were all set up to produce their excerpt of the raspberry pickers' chorus.

Then, seized by the nostalgic memories of far off days: 'Ah!' she exclaimed, 'the wonderful smell of raspberries on summer evenings in Russia!' The technicians fiddled with their instruments. 'Of course they make it quite differently here, the raspberry jam, much too thick . . .', she went on, relegating pectin to the lower depths, and then, with fine contempt for 'gelling': 'In Russia it is syrupy, you can *taste* the fruit!'

She turned to the recording team who were really keyed up by now; one felt the audience quicken to their plight. Surely they must switch on now. 'Take 10 lb of raspberries,' she sang out, 'I'll tell you how it's done if you like.'

'Take 10 lb of raspberries and 10 lb of sugar. Boil up the sugar into a thick syrup in a preserving pan. Pour in the raspberries and boil fast for 10 minutes. When the jam has cooled put it into glass jars. This is the only way to make such jam, to preserve the wonderful perfume of the fruit.'

The audience, mostly 20 year old music students, were completely stunned by this culinary revelation that hit the concert hall with the triumphant impact of an unexpected high C. The two technicians sitting behind her on the platform were paralysed by this deviation

from the programme – genuine improvisations are always shocking. 'Now let us hear that chorus,' she commanded, with a little gesture of impatience, turning towards them.

She might have added that if you live in a damp climate or beside the sea: 'Don't forget the advice of Princess Tscherbackaya in *Anna Karenina* – before closing, put a round of paper on top of the jam, bathe it with rum, and it won't develop mould'.

If Russian raspberry pickers are felt as an intrusion in the Mediterranean scene, I can only say that the spirit of Apulia often seems like an echo of the Russia of Tolstoy and Turgeniev, and that the singer's approach to jam making is the essential one – enthusiasm.

VIN COTTO D'UVA • grape preserve

Here is the possibility of a sugarless preserve. Take 5 kilos (11 lb 2 oz) of ripe rosy grapes, detach them from their stems, wash them and put the fruit in a large pan with a glass of water. Cook slowly till soft with the lid on, say 20 minutes (I do this in a cauldron). Pass the contents of the pan twice through the tomato sauce machine, eliminating pips and skins. You are left with a bowl of dense purple purée. Put this in a preserving pan over a very low heat with some minutely chopped lemon zest and 2 fresh bayleaves. Stir with a wooden spoon frequently, taking care that the purée, which reduces very gradually, doesn't catch; when it becomes extremely dense and a rich dark brown in colour, pour into glass jars and cover when cold. A very rustic preserve.

It is however, infinitely better both in taste and colour (purple) if you add 300 g (10½ oz) of sugar per kilo (2¼ lb) of fruit to the purée before reducing it. It improves with keeping.

LA PERATA • pear conserve

The pears used are small, sweet with a rosy blush, they do not keep. There are two ways of proceeding.

First method, the slow way in which ripe pears are used and no sugar (regarded as a triumph of economy). Peel and core the pears and cut them up; put them in a pan, barely covering with water. Bring to the boil, simmer until the fruit is soft, and continue to cook, stirring often, until you have a much reduced dense dark brown mass. Pour into glass jars and secure the lids when cold.

Second method, the better way: Using 300 g (10½ oz) of sugar per kilo of fruit (cored and cut in equal segments but not peeled); some shreds of lemon zest, the juice of 2 lemons, 3 or 4 fresh bayleaves, and water barely to cover the fruit.

Simmer till the fruit turns slightly pink, then let it cool a little. Add the sugar and boil up rapidly. Before long the fruit becomes transparent, the colour amber; keep stirring, then put in 3 or 4 sprigs of basil. Pour into glass jars when the syrup is very dense and close when cold. Should you use more sugar there is a danger that the jam may crystallize; these little pears have a very high sugar content. This is the conserve used for the *pesce di Natale* (p 290).

MARMELLATA DI FICHI • Donna Adeline's fig jam

'Pick in the early morning some small butter-yellow figs, the ones that ripen at the end of August, often growing in the wild, having insignificant seeds. Choose only those figs that show a little bead of nectar at the opening, then sit down in the shade and carefully peel them, putting the peeled fruits unbroken in an earthenware pot.

'Pour over them an equal quantity of sugar, cover, and leave to make some syrup in a cool place until the next day. Put figs and syrupy sugar in a preserving pan and cook on a lively heat, stirring with a wooden spoon. Add some dried fennel seeds, 2 bayleaves, the zest of lemon cut into tiny strips, and its juice. Skim the froth and after 10 minutes or so the figs should be transparent and still whole, the syrup a wonderful dark amber colour. Put in preserving jars and only close when cold.'

This is nectar. As figs vary with the season, it sometimes takes longer to achieve the perfect density. These figs can be served as a sweet in winter in little glasses. The syrup has the taste of honey. Small black figs, semi-wild, locally called *fichi di Morciano*, can be used as well.

FICHI MANDORLATI • dried figs stuffed with almonds

In Campania and Apulia in late August and early September, figs are dried on shallow trays of split-bamboo on the roof, the figs being split in half with a knife but without entirely severing them. This takes a week or so; you keep on turning the figs.

Put together some almonds, blanched, peeled and lightly roasted in the oven; some dry fennel seeds, a stick of cinnamon bark, the zest of a lemon cut into minute pieces on a board. Select the best figs, whose colour has 'blanched' in drying, and stuff each with one roast almond, a few fennel seeds, some fragments of cinnamon bark and two minute pieces of lemon zest, then press the two halves of the fig firmly together and stack them one against the other on an enamel tray. This is quite time-taking. When the tray is filled, more fennel seeds are sprinkled over the figs, and it is then put in the outdoor bread oven when the heat has died down after bread making, until the baked figs are a rich dark brown colour and are hard and firm.

Put, while still hot, into glazed earthenware lidded pots, firmly packed, with dried bayleaves interspersed; they taste like neolithic Christmas Pudding. In Campania, packed in little baskets, they are sold in vegetable shops. In Apulia everyone makes their own, dried figs being a fundament of winter diet.

MIRTILLI CONSERVATI • to preserve bilberries

Bilberries (*Vaccinium myrtillus*) appear in July in Carrara, having been picked clean by the sons of shepherds, who go up to the heights in summer with their flocks to graze on high mountain pastures. They live up there in wattle huts, making delicious ricotta cheese brought down daily to market. Bilberries and ricotta, an amicable alliance: sprinkle the berries first with sugar and lemon juice, and eat with the ricotta.

To conserve for winter: fill as many clean preserving jars as you can with ripe fruit, packing them in well. Filter half a cup of sugar into each jar and stand them low in the oven at a very low temperatures to heat slowly. Have some fruit in an extra jar for filling up, they shrink a little while heating. Boil a large kettle of water.

When the jars are thoroughly hot (¾ hour), remove them one by one from the oven, holding the bottle with a cloth. Fill up with fruit as necessary then pour boiling water to the top and immediately secure the lid. They need no cooking when you come to eat them in winter.

MARMELLATA DI CILIEGIE MARASCHE • morello cherry jam

One of the best jams, but it is not always easy to get it to set. So pick the fruit when it is dark red and use an equal weight of sugar for every kilo of fruit.

Put the sugar in a large pan on a very low flame to heat while you remove the stones from the cherries with a pointed knife. They at once emit a little juice which you pour into the preserving pan to start the sugar melting, while you turn it about with a wooden spoon to prevent it burning. This avoids using water to melt the sugar and facilitates the setting. In due course with much stirring you bring the syrup to the boil. When it clears put in the cherries and increase the heat. Put the stones in a muslin bag, crush them with a hammer, tie the bag up and put it in the pan. Skim the jam. The boiling must be violent and short-lived to preserve the texture and flavour of the fruit. Ten minutes. Setting point is reached when a drop remains on the spoon when raised. By this time the fruit is transparent. Whip out the bag of stones. Turn off the heat and pour the jam into heated jars. The flavour improves with keeping, if you can resist eating it at once. (See page 273, *Lingue di vitello in salsa di ciliegie marasche.*)

MARMELLATA DI ZUCCA INVERNALE • pumpkin preserve

1 kg (2¼ lb) of winter pumpkin (p 167), peeled and
sliced into segments and neatly cubed • 750 g (1 lb 10 oz) of sugar
¾ litre (27 fl oz) of water • a sliced lemon
2 tablespoons of *mostarda di Cremona* syrup and
2 or 3 of its chopped fruits (p 239)

Make a thin syrup with the sugar and water and the lemon slices, boiling it up in a shallow pan to the point where a drop will adhere to a wooden spoon. Only then throw in the pumpkin cubes. After ¼ hour of vigorous boiling add the *mostarda* and a few of its chopped fruits (plum, fig, pear, peach, cherry). Boil for a few more minutes. Put into small jars when cool and cover when cold.

The point of the shallow pan is to allow for maximum evaporation aiming at a preserve which consists of almost transparent orange pumpkin cubes in syrup. The *mostarda di Cremona* contains mustard oil which is just what the pumpkin needs to give it a little bite. If unobtainable, one can used preserved ginger, chopped with some of its syrup.

KYDÓNI GLIKÓ • Kyría Erýnni's quince jam

There are probably no finer quinces than those growing on Naxos, very large, with a delicate perfume, a luminous-green gold in colour, and not covered with the usual down.

Kyría Erýnni gave me a basket of these quinces one autumn day and installed herself in our dwelling to 'supervise' the making of the conserve. This is what she made me do.

Wipe and weigh the fruit and acquire an equal amount of sugar. (I had to dash to the village.) Peel, core and cut into equal segments a precise ¾ cm thick (say ¼″), putting the cut fruit into acidulated water (add lemon juice) or it discolours, and using a stainless steel knife. Leave overnight in an earthenware pot.

Next day put the quinces into a large preserving pan with the acidulated water. Put the pan on the fire and bring to the boil, from time to time dipping a sprig of basil into the water, sprinkling with it any pieces of quince not totally immersed. Simmer the fruit very gently until it is tender and has turned a rosy pink. Turn off the heat and wait 10 minutes. Then pour the sugar over the fruit and juice and bring to the boil as fast as possible. In the course of boiling up, the quinces begin to turn a deep rose red. After 10 minutes or so the fruit is transparent and the syrup at setting point. This conserve has a perfect colour, flavour and consistency. Put in a few sprigs of basil in the last few minutes. Store in glass pots.

Although living now in the land of *la cotognata* (p 342) where we immediately planted quince trees, I stick to this recipe of the old Naxian lady, but should add that Apulian quinces, being more 'woody', take longer in boiling up.

KARITHÓ GLIKÓ • green walnut preserve

One day we went up to a mountain village from Apollona in search of food and found the owner of a little *kapheneíon* up to her wrists in walnut juice. She was making a preserve of green walnuts, the green husks sapid, juicy – the nutshell unformed inside. Before finishing the work she put some dark walnuts in syrup of last year's making on little plates for us to taste and served it with glasses of water and thimblefuls of *rakí* (Greek *marc*).

Here is her recipe: 'Put 100 green walnuts in a large glazed earthenware crock with cold water, and keep them there for a week, changing the water 2 or 3 times.

'Drain them and delicately pare off the fine outer skins. These stain your hands and the walnuts begin to turn black.

'First boil the pared walnuts in a thin syrup sufficient to cover them, made in the proportion of ½ kilo (1 lb 2 oz) of sugar to ½ litre of water (18 fl oz), until they are soft but unbroken.

'Meanwhile prepare a dense syrup using 1 kilo (2¼ lb) of sugar per ½ litre (18 fl oz) of water. Boil until the syrup adheres to a wooden spoon when raised. Strain the walnuts from the first syrup, immerse them in the dense syrup, put in a vanilla pod and add the juice of ½ a lemon. Boil until the syrup once again adheres to the wooden spoon. When cool put into glass jars and seal when cold.'

This delicacy, another Greek restorative, is well worth the trouble it takes.

STAPHÍLI GLIKÓ • grapes in syrup

This preserve, on Naxos, is made with large firm grapes called *rosakí*, sweet rosy grapes ripening at the end of August. It is served in summer at any time of day on a saucer with a spoon, accompanied by draughts of mountain water, a sovereign remedy against heat and exhaustion (see p 49).

Weigh the fruit. Peel the grapes and take out the pips with a needle or wooden toothpick, without breaking them – a daunting operation, it's worth it.

For 1 kilo of grapes use 1 kilo of sugar (2¼ lb), a vanilla pod and a lemon. Put the peeled grapes in a muslin bag and hang it over a bowl to drain for 4 hours. Then in a large preserving pan boil up a syrup with the sugar, the juice that has dripped into the bowl and a tumbler of water, until it sets, i e a drop adheres to the spoon when raised. Put in the grapes, a vanilla pod and the lemon juice. Boil rapidly, skimming off the froth.

When the syrup is set again, say in 10 minutes, remove from the fire and leave to cool, then pour into a china basin and cover with a clean damp cloth. This induces the grapes to imbibe the syrup and swell up. Remove the vanilla pod. Have some clean jars ready, pour into them the grapes and their syrup and close hermetically.

Large golden muscat grapes can be used instead, especially when they have a sunburnt 'bronzed' look; they don't have many pips.

LA PERSICATA • wild peach jam

In the south *il persico*, the peach tree (*Prunus persica*) grows wild; it never seems to ripen its fruits, at best they remain a golden green. This is the stock on which early-ripening peaches are grafted, but as cultivated peaches need watering, and water is what we lack, we remain with the wild one. In October, when its fruits are large, plentiful and still unripe, I gather them to make a delicious green jam.

Use 800 g (nearly 2 lb) of sugar for each kilo (2¼ lb) of green peaches. You have to peel them and stone them by cutting inwards in equal segments. Simmer the fruit barely covered with water, with two bayleaves, for 10 minutes, let it cool a little, then pour on the sugar.

Add some minute strips of zest cut from a fresh lemon or citron (untreated with dephynyl). Boil up rapidly. When the fruit is transparent and the syrup adheres to the spoon held aloft, pour it into heated preserving jars and seal when cool. Unripe apricots can be cooked in the same way, but being smaller, you cut them in half.

The bay-tree, *Laurus nobilis*, here grows wild, and in preserves the freshly picked leaves are used, not the dried. The citron, *Citrus medica*, large and more knobbly than the lemon, has an even more perfumed zest.

MARMELLATA DI PESCHE • preserve of ripe peaches

If one is making a preserve of large blushing ripe peaches in July there is no preliminary cooking of the segmented fruit. Pour boiling water over them, they then peel easily. In this case use 700 g (just over 1½ lb) of sugar per kilo (2¼ lb) of peaches. Squeeze 2 or 3 lemons over the sugar and peach slices in the pan and cook on a low heat while stirring. The sugar quickly melts and raising the heat you go on stirring, marvelling at the changing colour of the fruit reminding one of Modigliani's paintings. In 10 minutes or so, the jam is an intense gold, the fruit transparent. Put in 2 sprigs of basil. Make sure that the syrup really is at setting point or this *marmellata* will not keep.

The Olive Field

LIKE the pains of child-birth, one quickly forgets the olive-picking pains. In childbirth you are on your own, while in the olive field the ordeal is endured in good company. What you need ideally is short thighs and a long back. Adopting a martial attitude – like the bronze Zeus discovered at Ugento, now in the Taranto Museum – but bending from the hips and keeping the head permanently down, with an extraordinary rapidity you pick up the olives with both hands, the endless olives. The women are on the ground, the men are in the trees.

Already we have made in late October a kind of dancing floor or dish round every tree, removing weeds, raking off the stones, flattening the earth with a stiff broom, and raising it at the perimeter.

As there are only forty trees, one day in November we and our companions, four or five men, with luck, and two of their wives, set off to strip them, carrying sacks, nets, buckets, a *merenda* and a flask of wine, over the steep rough limestone, down to where the olives grow.

Starting with the largest trees which are farthest down, everyone begins to clear the ground of already fallen olives. Then the men spread out a fine plastic net and climb into the tree. Using a little rake in one hand and picking off the more recalcitrant olives with the other, in a shower of olives, leaves, twigs, they denude the tree. Meanwhile we women, or I, if I'm alone, clear the ground of olives under the next tree. Then darting back, the freshly fallen olives have to be quickly cleaned of leaves, twigs, branches, and the olives poured into a sack.

The men meanwhile rush into the next tree. This goes on with a brief pause at mid-day, often in bad weather, for three or four days, and sometimes longer. In a 'good' year when the olives are legion, everybody some of the time is grovelling under the trees, but women never climb into them. Female manual dexterity complements masculine agility; the effort is in common.

At night the sacks weighing 50 kilos or more are slung onto the broadest shoulders and the steep climb back up the rocks begins. The sacks are emptied on the studio floor, the olives would ferment if they were enclosed, and still one has to pick out more leaves, twigs, stems whose tannin content would impair the quality of the oil. When every olive is gathered they are taken to a village oil press (*frantoio*), in sacks or containers.

In taking part, new standards of agility and dexterity dawn on one, and also an extraordinary vision of the good humour and patience with which this time-out-of-mind harvesting is done. Because the work is endless, there is a strange feeling of timelessness among the trees. When you are most exhausted you suddenly find that your fingers have acquired eyes and are gathering olives on their own. The phenomenon of the second, third, fourth wind appears. Your mind is free to listen to a bird's song or to the ceaseless conversation in the trees.

As the day goes on, everybody recalls events of long ago – olive picking dissolves the sense of 'now': what is recalled is often comic, but more often has to do with youth, hardship, and long tramps barefoot carrying home a rope-tied faggot gleaned from the maquis, on an empty stomach, after a hard day's work with the mattock in the fields. A chasm divides the present – in which everybody is struggling and perhaps achieving to be 'well off' – from the far off days of misery to which, however, a definite nostalgia clings.

The pretensions of the present and the uncertainty in which they are enveloped have given this harsh springtime a kind of glow. What is missing, now that everyone has their own house, ground, means of locomotion and cultivator (often achieved by years of work in Switzerland), their pensions and hospital treatment, is the feeling of companionship, of hardship shared, which was the one thing they could boast of long ago. This feeling in the olive field is for a few days revived.

It would be absurd for me to embark on an account of the cultivation of the olive and the oil-making procedure. Or answer the question: what is the best oil? The oil made from the olives you pick in company with friends, then pressed by a friend in the village oil press, would be my answer. Many books have been written on this subject. But once the olive trees are yours, you learn not from books but from

your neighbours.

In Apulia the cultivation of the olive has always gone hand in hand with the vine. Planted together, the olive trees come into their own forty years later when the vines are in decline. It would be odd indeed to make your own oil without also making your own wine. For this an apprenticeship, not scholarship is required, which the Sculptor served during the years we spent in the vineyards above Carrara.

Everyone agrees that the magnificent wine he makes is better than the neighbours'. There are many reasons for this, one is that nothing is put in it, medicaments I mean. An artist who has taken risks all his life accepts the risk of his wine 'going off' and only takes the more care of his barrels. The agriculturalist spoils his wine by 'making sure'.

from the Sculptor: A WORD ABOUT WINE

We weren't in Catalonia during the grape harvest, but the wines we were offered in the Priorat, renowned since the Middle Ages, were grown on an extensive scale. The wines we now make in Apulia, like those we drank and used for cooking on Naxos and in Tuscany, are grown on a small-holding scale and almost exclusively for the grower's use. Some growers hire a room opening on the village street and announce the sale of the wine they drink themselves by hanging a bushel of bayleaves above the door.

This is the most direct way of getting a demijohn of unadulterated wine; having nevertheless taken the trouble beforehand to discuss its trustworthiness in the piazza.

The surplus grapes of the vineyards in our neighbourhood have in recent years been booked some months ahead by individual buyers who want to make sure of *un vino sincero*; 'sincere' being understood as not watered down nor chemically preserved from turning into vinegar.

This is why the grower's temporary *cantina* must not be confused with the permanent wine bars marked *Vini*, the origins and nature of whose supplies are usually dubious enough to turn the card-playing patrons into beer drinkers.

These bars also serve a sweet Sicilian wine referred to as *passita*, ostensibly made of grapes which have been spread out in the sun before fermentation – *uva passa* are raisins. Although it has an attractive pale amber colour, it would be a great mistake to imagine one has come across something anywhere near the unresinated 'golden nectar' of Naxos. The Pugliesi suspect this *passita* because the taste is immediately engaging; for it is in the first sip, they say, that the chemist baits the merchant's hook.

Appreciation of the local wines comes gradually, while drinking, and by accepting their peculiarities. '*Bisogna farsi la bocca*' is the rule. The mouth must adjust, and on the whole it does this best while eating. (Naxian quarrymen professed to eat only to honour the wine.) One is in fact asked to get over the shock of their uncontrolled diversity, which fluctuates not only with the weather during the year and on the day of the harvest, but according to the wine-maker's hunches. These can affect the amount of pressure applied in the crushing, the length of the fermentation, whether the 'must' needed coddling, whether it was aerated and how often, the conditions in the cellar, the state of the barrels, when the wine was decanted, if at all, and so forth. The result is that one encounters both wonders and horrors such as are never met with in bottled wine.

Traditionally Apulian wine was kept in glazed earthenware jars three or four feet high, then decanted into glass demijohns, whence it was carried straight to the table by the jugful. The current year's vintage is still preferred and the cellar usually contains just enough to reach the next *vendemmia*. The bottling of wine for one's own consumption is something of an innovation, among enthusiasts only.

Grapes ripened in the Salento give the wine the strength to withstand the kind of rough treatment which no Tuscan wine could possibly survive. A Tuscan wine apprenticeship is therefore to be recommended precisely because the relative instability of these lighter wines gives one a clearer idea of the essential care involved. One learns the rudiments while helping with the work. Any gaps in one's understanding are later filled in during lengthy tasting occasions in the cellar, mainly through passionate argument and amusing stories.

Apulian wine by contrast practically looks after itself: providing one doesn't exact more than the grape gives willingly, and that one treats the barrels like the best of friends.

*   *   *   *   *

One wine-grower, on drinking the wine made by a neighbour: 'Yes. That's quite something. [pause] Why, it's almost as good as mine!'

The distinction of the wine receiving such praise is that it was made with good health and conviviality in mind, rather than sales. Its production is not maximized and consequently its preservation and its amiability need no deceit. For adulteration always came in the train of overmuch acumen. Praise like the above (the highest!) goes to the *vino sincero*.

A Few Conserves

OLIVE CONSERVATE • olives conserved

HE black olives conserved in the south are not those from which the oil is made, which have large stones from which the oil largely derives. They are a slightly larger more fleshy kind with small stones, called *l'osciolo*. These are harvested in late autumn, glistening and blue-black, stripped from the trees so as not to bruise them.

They are washed and then soaked in glazed earthenware vats for 40 days in water that is changed every 2 days. This removes their bitterness. They are then drained and placed in large terracotta jars, glazed inside, with 2 handfuls of sea salt for 3 kilos of olives, alternating the salt with the fruits while filling the jar, and then covering with water. The olives remain hard, black, shiny, and imbibe some of the salt. They keep perfectly for 2 years.

In the Salento many people put fennel seeds, bayleaves and slices of lemon with the olives, which then begin to taste like Christmas pudding. But my opinion, after trying both ways, is that what one really wants to conserve is the taste of the olives.

During the 40 days, while changing the water, one discards any fruit that is imperfect. The water is changed by tilting the vat and pouring the water through a special terracotta sieve. The vat stands under the outdoor tap. All this is work, of course; the encouraging thought is that provision for the year is being made.

These black olives are used in making delightful little breads called *púccie*. They are added to braised pork and chicken, sometimes to weeds (*la paparina*, p 204). Basically, they are the workman's *merenda*, eaten with a glass of wine.

PEPERONI SOTT'OLIO • sweet peppers conserved in oil

You need 2 kilos (4½ lb) of firm red sweet peppers (*Capsicum annuum*). Make a good fire out of doors, let it subside a little, and roast the peppers over the glowing ashes. When the skin is blackened and the fruits are soft, remove their skins and extract the cores and seeds. Wipe them with a damp cloth.

Have ready a screw-top jar large enough to lay in the whole peppers, put in a bayleaf, a few peppercorns, 2 peeled cloves of garlic, add salt, and when the jar is full cover with olive oil and screw on the top.

PEPERONCINI SOTT'OLIO • hot chilli peppers conserved in oil

In early autumn acquire the very smallest kind of chilli pepper, sold in a multitude on a single plant (variety of *Capsicum frutescens*), which, already ripe, have turned from green to red. They can be pointed or round fruits. Cut the little peppers from the stems, on a board, and then cut off each green cap to expose the seeds. Put them in a bowl with a handful of sea salt, for 24 hours, shaking them in the salt now and then. Imbibing the salt, they shrink a little. Drain, dry in a cloth, and pack close in glass jars. Add a bayleaf. Cover with oil and close.

The very hot seeds of the chilli peppers gradually impregnate the oil which can be used with or without 1 or 2 hot peppers to enliven many a winter dish.

FUNGHI SOTT'OLIO • fungi conserved in oil

This way of preserving very young *porcini* (*Boletus edulis*) comes from Fivizzano in the Lunigiana behind La Spezia, a famous fungi region. It can be successfully applied to very young field agarics (gills still pink), to baby chanterelles (*Cantharellus cibarius*) and to orange milk mushrooms (*Lactarius deliciosus, L sanguifluus*, etc, see pp 215, 214).

So, using fungi freshly gathered in an immature state, remove the base of the stems, but otherwise leave them whole. Clean them well, put them in an earthenware or enamel pan and just cover, half and half, with white wine vinegar and water, adding 2 peeled garlic cloves. Bring to the boil and cook for 8 minutes, at most, then drain them. Dry on a cloth, then leave them overnight in a warm place on another dry cloth.

Next day: put them into clean glass jars with 2 bayleaves, the garlic cloves, some fragments of cinnamon bark and the heads of 2 cloves.

Cover with olive oil and close with an airtight lid.

Leave for at least six weeks to allow the oil time to overcome their impregnation with vinegar. Serve as an hors d'oeuvre.

CARCIOFINI SOTT'OLIO • little artichoke hearts in oil

The same procedure can be applied to immature artichokes. These, trimmed of their outer leaves, and their points sliced off (they are too young to have a choke), and including 2½ cm (1 in) of stem, are halved or quartered and precipitated into vinegar and water to which is added the juice of several lemons to blanch them, and then cooked as for *funghi sott'olio*. After cooking, they are drained, dried and put into glass jars with a few coriander seeds; they don't need to dry overnight. Slip in 2 fresh bayleaves. Cover with oil and close.

At the end of the artichoke season the smallest flower heads appear, and are sold at a lower price. You buy a bundle of 40 heads, and sit down to pick off the leaves, reducing them to a trimmed heart, because by this time the leaves are tough. The chokes have to be carefully removed by swivelling a round-headed stainless steel knife into the heart. They take a few minutes longer to cook. Drain and dry them, then put them in jars with a fresh bayleaf in each, cover with oil and close.

With regard to this bundle of artichokes, acquired for conserving, it is interesting that in 1499 a fit gift made to Lodovico Sforza, Duke of Milan, by a Genoese nobleman, Giovanni Adorno, consisted of 40 artichokes and a bunch of magnificent roses. This reveals the rarity of these vegetable fruits at the turn of the 15th century, and perhaps the area – round Genoa – in which they were first cultivated in northern Italy. (See Cartwright in the bibliography.)

LA SALSA • bottled tomato sauce

The sauce that many Apulian householders prepare for winter is made on a large scale, involving the whole family and at least a hundred kilos of Leccesi tomatoes grown for this purpose, but often far more.

In the first weeks of July the ripening tomatoes are picked at dawn with their short stems, then laid out in a covered space to ripen further (in a garage, spare room, or wine-making place, *il palmento*). During this time bottles, elegant old liqueur bottles or mineral water bottles, are assembled, washed, laid upside down to drain in the hottest sun. Cauldrons are scoured, glazed earthenware vats are washed and turned upside down, firewood (olive) is prepared, corks or metal caps lined up, the tomato machine examined, herbs gathered, packets of sea salt acquired.

One day at 6 in the morning, the operation begins. While the man of the house prepares the outdoor fires and sets the iron tripods, the women, crouching over a deep scarlet sea of tomatoes on the floor, at speed remove the stalks and carry basins of fruit to the now filled vat, pouring them in, then lightly squeezing the tomatoes under water to release some of the seeds and some of their acid, and rapidly fill the cauldrons. Into each cauldron half a purple onion is sliced up, some sprigs of thyme and rosemary are added and a handful of salt, together with a cup of water. The man then bears the cauldrons away and sets them on the fires, putting on their lids. While the contents of the cauldrons cook, every domestic vessel is being filled with more slightly crushed tomatoes, taken from the water vat. The cauldrons are stirred from time to time and, once they come to the boil, cook (10 minutes) till the contents acquire a deeper colour and are soft.

Near the fire is a large tin bath with over it a beautiful circular rush mat, a kind of sieve. The man, protecting his hands with rags, pours the contents of the first cauldron onto the rush mat. The juice runs through and a dense tomato mush remains. The mush is carefully poured into another earthenware crock, placed on a table, to which the tomato separating machine has been affixed, under a tree. By now, it is 8 o'clock and already hot.

Someone starts putting the tomatoes into the top of the machine with a cup and someone else winds the handle and prods. The seeds and skins spill out onto a plate on one side, and the sauce pours into an earthenware vessel on the other. Meanwhile ever new cauldrons are being boiled up.

Some of the liquor of the last cauldron can be added if the sauce is too thick. The aim is to get a sauce which is very dense, but not so dense that once in the bottle it will refuse to come out. By this time everyone is covered with tomato juice and their hands which have been yellow turn black, the effect of the acid.

In the end there is a huge vat of dense sauce on the one hand, and a mountain of skins and seeds on the other. The seeds released into the water vat are removed with a fine sieve and dried in the sun against next year's planting, when they will be sown on heat in February covered with plastic sheets.

The sauce now has to be measured; this is done by transferring it by litre measure from one vat to another. Supposing the outcome of this operation is 60 litres of sauce, a measured quantity of salicylic acid is going to be added: 1 gram for each litre of sauce, plus 2 grams for every 10 litres – total 72 grams of salicylic acid.

Two or three handfuls of sea salt are added to the sauce and stirred in; it is then transported indoors to an aerated room and covered. At dusk the salicylic acid, precisely calculated, is poured in, the stirring repeated, and the sauce left to rest overnight, then stirred at dawn.

BOTTLING THE SAUCE. Using a funnel and some kind of jug, you fill each bottle leaving a little space at the top, the space being filled afterwards with a sprig of basil and a covering of olive oil. But first you have to 'bump' the bottles to get the air bubbles out. You then with a clean white rag clean the inside neck of each bottle, and line them up on a table, insert the leaf of basil, fill up with olive oil, and put in the corks. After two or three days you drive them in, and now have more than enough tomato sauce for winter, which is good, because you can give some of it away.

There are two other ways of making *la salsa*: (1) *sotto la manta*, under the cloak; (2) sterilising the freshly bottled sauce, by packing the bottles in straw and fitting them into a gigantic petrol bin, and boiling again. I have described the method we always use imparted by our neighbour Teresa because it is good. Without her help and instructions we might never have got down to it. Once the operation is mastered it is possible at the same time to prepare some *pomodori pelati*, a conserve of plum tomatoes, and *la salsa secca*, probably the most healthy conserve in existence.

LA SALSA SECCA • a rustic concentrate

The tomato concentrate *par excellence* is most simply made on the same day as *la salsa*, by abstracting a quantity of freshly passed tomato sauce before its transfer by litre measure to the second vat, as described on the preceding page.

At this point you line up as many plates as you can find, say 30, and rob the vat, using a breakfast cup – a cup of sauce goes into each plate. A little salt is sprinkled on the surface, and the plates are transported onto the parapet of the roof. Please note: the paste only dries with the help of the north wind, and if the *scirocco* is blowing it is of no use.

In any case, one has to keep on stirring the paste, with a wooden spoon, and later, with a knife, one pares off the little fragments that dry at the edge of each plate. If it is extremely hot (38-40°C) and a good wind is blowing, by nightfall the paste will have so reduced that you can combine the contents of two plates and use the vacant ones to cover the others for the night. Next day: scrape away at these plates, working the dried bits into the thickening paste. You do this 4 or 5 times a day. By nightfall the contents of the 15 plates can be reduced to 7, covering them again and taking down the spare plates to wash them. On the third day, by stirring and scraping, the paste may have dried sufficiently to be amalgamated onto one large dish, which you cover. Next day: critical inspection, the mass should be convincingly dry and of a deep red colour. If in doubt, continue to work it from time to time until midday. Then take it down, cover with a cloth, let it rest.

Next day you massage this lump of rich red concentrate with the best olive oil until it shines. Then oil some litre or ½ litre jars lavishly inside, rolling the oil around, stuff in the paste and cover with 2½ cm (1″) of oil.

This is used in winter in preparing legumes; is spread on a bread; enriches the bottled tomato sauce for pasta and in cooking *pezzetti*; is added to a poultry braise; i e is employed in a thousand ways.

LA SALSA SECCA AMARA • hot tomato concentrate

For every 8 litres of freshly passed sauce, use 2 kg (4½ lb) of sweet red peppers and 3 or 4 hot chilli peppers. Cook separately in a minimum of water with basil leaves, peeled garlic cloves, a bayleaf, sliced onion; simmer till soft on a very low heat. Pass through a sieve and dry the result on a plate on the roof. Combine this fire-eater's mixture with *la salsa secca* on the last day on the roof, and carry on as above. Spread on bread, it requires a good deal of Spigolizzi wine to accompany it.

POMODORI PELATI • conserve of plum tomatoes

On tomato sauce making day I take advantage of the Sculptor's patience as fire-maker and cauldron lifter to make some jars of *pomodori pelati*; the varieties used are San Marzano and San Marzano lampadina, the so-called plum tomatoes, which fruits have been picked at the same time as the Leccesi tomatoes and have ripened to darkest red along with them on the floor of *casa ospiti*, the guest room.

These magnificent fruits are immersed for a few moments in boiling water, are peeled while hot, and emptied of some seeds and liquor, keeping them whole, by gently squeezing. They are at once put into clean 1 litre preserving jars with sliced onion, a sprig of basil, thyme, a bayleaf, some peeled garlic and green chilli peppers. A little salt is added. No water. Far more of the *pelati* go into a litre jar than you would expect; we certainly never weigh them. The jars are then closed with new rubber rings, and are securely tied down by the Sculptor.

The two fires are still going, all other operations have ceased. The jars are placed in clean cauldrons on a floor of wheatstraw with more straw pressed between them (newspaper could equally well be used), then covered with cold water, the lids put on, and the cauldrons put on the fires. Two or three branches of olive wood are added to encourage the fires, and we leave them to cook, making sure that they boil; then, after they have bubbled steadily for 45 minutes, we take them off the fires.

By this time we are sitting under the figtree at the well-cleaned table enjoying a well-earned *merenda*, having already washed receptacles, machinery, measures, vats; if you don't do this immediately the crushed tomatoes dry onto everything.

The jars are taken out much later when they are cool. They are useful in winter as a dressing for pasta. First pour off their liquor, acid again, and heat the *pelati* in olive oil; they taste like fresh tomatoes.

POMODORI SOTT'OLIO CON ACCIUGHE E CAPPERI
dried tomatoes stuffed with anchovies and capers

I mention this Apulian preserve for interest's sake, I doubt that anyone could dry the tomatoes in a less ardent sun. In this case, ripe round 'salad' tomatoes, of the cultivar San Marzano, are gathered at the summer solstice; they form low bushes planted in open ground along with the Leccesi and Pelati varieties.

Taking a split bamboo rack (*canizzu*), a sharp knife and some sea salt and the tomatoes onto the roof, one sits down to split the fruit across, so that they open in two without coming apart. They are put on the rack, the surfaces sprinkled with sea salt. Attending on them every day and adding a little salt if necessary, when the tomatoes begin to shrivel, you turn them over. After a week they will have lost all water content, are light as air (sometimes blow away) and shrivelled; they can be considered 'dried'.

Prepare a small quantity of salt anchovies (soaked, boned, cleaned, rinsed, dried) and divide them into little pieces. Rinse and dry some conserved capers, and find the jar of dried fennel seeds.

Place a piece of anchovy in each dried tomato with 3 or 4 fennel seeds and 2 capers, then press the two sides firmly together. Have ready some little lidded jars and pack in the tomatoes, pressing them again, one by one, until the jar is filled. Put in a bayleaf, fill up with olive oil and cover with a cork or stopper. Eat them with a glass of wine in winter.

POMODORI APPESI • fresh tomatoes conserved for winter

Still another kind of tomato called *da serbo* (for keeping), a real winter standby. These are usually small. The plant is picked entire, before the tomatoes are ripe; they are green, yellow, and red, and grow in 'clusters'. The clusters are cut off with some stem, and assembled into bunches, by laying the individual clusters on a double line of string, which is then gathered up, tied, and suspended by a firm loop and hung in a sheltered place from a series of nails, a very satisfactory sight in autumn. They are used in winter, crushed on bread, but also in soups, in oven dishes, in fact in any way fresh tomatoes are used in cooking. These cultivars are '*a fiaschetto*' and '*a mazzetti*'.

All the tomatoes mentioned are grown without watering, a miracle in the permanent summer drought. Where, for commercial purposes, the plants are sprayed with water, this has a disastrous effect on both their taste and texture, which is not compensated by their larger size.

A Parting Salvo

ERMAN de Vries, the Dutch artist, in his remarkable catalogue entitled *Natural Relations I – Die Marokkanische Sammlung*, 1984, dedicates this work 'To the Memory of What is Forgotten'.

The Sculptor refers to the introduction as a 'cenotaph to lost knowledge'. It is about the relation between people and plants. It begins by quoting from an account of the Chenchu Indians of central India and the Kalahari bushmen today; then looks back into the European Middle Ages, specially with regard to German and Polish peoples' relations to plants (edible weeds), where I was not surprised to find the weeds gathered in Tuscany, in the Salento, on Naxos and in Catalonia flowering again under their German and Latin names.

For so many years I have had the good fortune to experience the human-plant relation as a precious and everyday fact – quite apart from its relevance to the cooking pot. I know that people living in cities have been robbed of this vital contact and understanding of growing things. Deprived of the life-giving relation to plants people may, quite unconsciously perhaps, try to make up for it by inhaling their essence.

This thought came to me again while examining De Vries's catalogue of the collection of dried plants he had made in Morocco and exhibited in dried form in the Galerie Mueller-Roth in Stuttgart. It contains a great deal of information about hallucinogenic plants, those used as cures for human ills, as food, and as aphrodisiacs. It has a splendid bibliography. But it was a profound shock to find that fennel, hitherto regarded as a 'sacred' plant (p 159), today serves another purpose: its seeds ground to a powder are used in Sicilian ports to distract police dogs from nosing out forbidden weeds. Does the City bear the blame? Won't it have to be transformed?

> On all sides the eye is as it were bewitched with the sight of delicate gardens, as well within the City as neere the same. The gardens without the walls are so rarely delightful, as I should think the Hesperides were not to be compared with them; they are adorned with statues, laberinthes, fountains, vines, myrtle, palmes, citron, lemon, orange and cedar trees with lawrels, mulberies, roses, rosemary, and all kinds of fruits and flowers, so

as they seem an earthly Paradise. The fields are no less fruitfull,
bringing forth abundantly all things for the use of man.

This is not an illspelt description of a hallucination but an account of
Naples by Fynes Moryson in *An Itinerary*, 1617. Man has now three
hundred and sixty nine years later, betrayed nature, and nowhere more
so than in Naples. How fortunate it is that his 'fruits and flowers' are
growing still – witness the next and final chapter.

Can we be living in a fool's paradise? When people come to Spigolizzi
in summer they are often heard to exclaim: '*Qui c'è un vero paradiso*' and
they sometimes receive the Sculptor's reply: '*Ma l'inferno purtròppo è
tanto più comodo!*' (Here is a real paradise. But Hell is so much more
convenient!).

While writing this book I noticed the typing paper getting thinner and
our needs more modest. In summer young people come to test their
aspirations against a way of life which is the outcome of working in
marble, working in stone, and working in metal. Not an easy one, it
starts at sunrise in summer and in winter, with no electricity, hot water
or telephone, no libraries to hand, no postman and no dustman. It is
absorbing work – our own and agricultural. There are good neighbours
by day, they vanish into distant villages at night. Magnificent works in
marble are planted in the landscape; wilderness is at the door and an
immense horizon. There are sunsets and sunrise, lamplight, moonlight
and starlight, an olive wood fire in winter and 180 degrees of Ionian Sea
to be discerned from the roof.

   In Apulia any 'alternative' life runs against the social current.
Stigmatized as 'old fashioned', it is more often accounted as 'living in
misery'. Living well, referred to as *stare bene*, is now conceived in terms
of income.

   In the Salento the newly-wedded are bent on the symbolic attributes
of the modernistic but wholly unpractical installation promoted as the
'cucina americana'. Ironically, in order to own this kitchen, people are
prepared to speed up the ripening of a crop and boost its weight by
every means known to science, however deleterious that may be to the
intrinsic value of the foodstuff. The kitchen of which I speak is perfectly
maintained as a showpiece; cooking takes place in some little corner
down the passage on a humble stove, so as not to impair the brilliance
of stainless steel nor dull the lustre of polished granite surfaces.

   The recipes in this book belong to an era of food grown for its own
sake, not for profit. This era has vanished. If cooking and eating were
all I had had in mind when writing them down, the pleasure they
might afford would be largely nostalgic.

Predictions are sometimes made about the future development of two kinds of food: the one producing costly organically grown cereals and vegetables; the other offering a more 'accessible' diet of industrially reconstituted protein. This prospect places the ingredients I use firmly among the most outrageous luxuries.

Famine! Only Marie Antoinette could have written a cookery book while ignoring the famished. I have lived long enough among unsubsidized vine-growers and agriculturalists to realise that we shall have fired a shot in the war against want when food is grown to be eaten, and not mainly to be 'handled'. In Apulia surpluses don't need to be 'demountainized': in an exceptionally good year, the farmer at once ploughs in the crop whose price has fallen well below the grower's cost of raising it.

I do not envy the economist or politician who tries to sort this out. In the meantime I am interested in growing food for its own sake and in appetite. The health-giving and prophylactic virtues of a meal depend on the zest with which it has been imagined, cooked and eaten. It seemed to me appropriate to show something of the life that generates this indispensible element at a time when undernourishment bedevils even the highest income groups.

Abstinence, enjoyment, celebration, all have nature's approval; if you practise the first, you maintain what is priceless – enjoyment, and its crown, celebration.

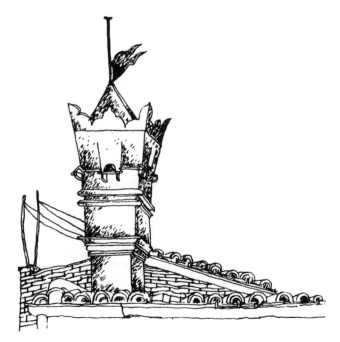

Some Flower Buds, Seeds, Fronds, Pods, Nuts, Fruits

BORAGO · borage

Borago officinalis (family BORAGINACEAE)
borratja (C) · boràntsa (G)

THE azure flowers of borage, tasting of cucumber before cucumbers are ripe, are a delight in spring salads. The young plants are included in a dish of weeds in March (p 196). In the neighbourhood of Lleida in Catalonia borage is served as a vegetable and the young leaves in salad.

The plant leaps from the field into the garden, although originally, some say, it was a garden plant which became naturalized in the wild. When borage over-procreates in the garden, you chop it up with a *zappa* and use it as a mulch like comfrey.

FINOCCHIO SELVATICO · wild fennel

Foeniculum officinale (family APIACEAE)
fonoll (C) · màrathon (G)

The incipient flowers of wild fennel appear in late August and September, and are gathered and steeped in white wine vinegar. Used to flavour capers, likewise conserved, and in winter salads.

The fragrant seeds are gathered in autumn. The umbels bearing them are hung up to dry, then stripped of the seeds which are conserved in airtight glass jars. Used for flavouring soups, fish broths; also in baking bread and *taralli*, which are hard biscuits in the form of a ring, served with wine, found south of Naples in varying forms – the best are brushed with oil before going into the oven. These sometimes contain, instead of fennel seeds, hot peppers, and are then *taralli con peperoncini*, to be found in bakeries and *alimentari*.

The fronds and sheaths of fennel have been frequently mentioned in this book. In Catalonia, they are used in soups, with fish (*llobaro amb fonoll*, sea bass with fennel), in cooking snails, with pork and wild boar, and the seeds are used in pâtisserie. In Greece and Italy the fronds often appear in a dish of weeds. A magnificent Tuscan salame, *la finocchiona*, is flavoured with fennel seeds.

ANETO · dill

Anethum graveolens (family APIACEAE)
anet (C) · ánitho (G)

Dill, both wild and cultivated, has even finer cut fronds than wild fennel and has similar uses both for its fronds and seeds. These seeds are used in pickling gherkins (dwarf cucumbers) and are particularly good as flavouring when cooking cabbage or potatoes. Use the fresh green fronds to stuff a fish, in a risotto, with *Pasta al forno* (p 102), and in tomato salads, a revelation.

CORIANDOLO · coriander

Coriandrum sativum (family APIACEAE)
celiandre, coriandre (C) · koríandron (G)

Coriander, which I have often mentioned, has a delicious fragrance in its fragile leaves and perfumed seed. This seed has the merit of germinating even when five years old. An annual; sow it at the end of April. Both leaves and seeds are used in Greek cooking, but especially in Cyprus; likewise a favourite herb of the ancient Romans. In Catalonia today it is hardly used, although the seeds are an ingredient of *bunyols* (delicious doughnuts) in the region of Empordà; in medieval times it was much used for its fronds, both fresh and dried, and seeds (see *Saliandre* in *Sent Soví* and *Seliandrat* in de Nola).

SEDANO · celery (the herb)

Apium graveolens (family APIACEAE)
api (C) · sélino (G)

This plant, already mentioned on page 31 in connection with the Italian *soffritto*, is widely grown as a herb, unblanched and therefore green. It has more finely serrated leaves and is much smaller than cultivated celery. It also has a more pungent taste. To be grown from seed.

In Sicily, the plant, growing wild, gave its name to Selinunte.

PREZZEMOLO · parsley

Petroselinum sativum (family APIACEAE)
julivert (C) · maïdanós (G)

Although all parsleys belong to the same species, the smooth, single-leaved variety grown in Catalonia, Italy and Greece is closer to the ancestral plant (the *Carum petroselinum* of the old herbals) and the most aromatic. Single-leaved varieties supplied by Italian seedsmen are Comune – the most pungent – and the far larger Gigante di Napoli, both dark in colour. Grown in a pot, this giant develops into a stately plant, a delight to the eye. For the curled variety they have Nano ricciutto, a bright green curly dwarf.

CAPPERO · caper

Capparis spinosa (family CAPPARIDACEAE)
tàpera (C) · kápari (G)

This trailing perennial shrub, native in the Mediterranean, frequents the rocks by the sea, ruins, and ancient walls. The sight of this bush trailing its bluish leaves from a high wall announces the south, but they already begin north of Lucca and are established in the bastion walls of the Campo Santo at Pisa.

USING SALTED CAPERS. The flowers picked in tight bud in May are rolled in pounded sea salt to preserve them, and sold thus 'loose' in village groceries in Tuscany and the Veneto. Take them home, rinse them of their salt, and steep in white wine vinegar, adding if you can find them some scarcely formed flowers of wild fennel.

USING FRESH CAPERS. These appear in early June in the markets at Cagliari in Sardinia, and in Apulia, brilliant green and 'graded'; the smallest are the best. Buying them fresh, pick off the stems, steep them in sea salt for a day or two (a handful of salt for ½ kg / 1 lb 2 oz of capers), shaking them occasionally; thus they imbibe some salt and shrink a little. Rinse them in a colander, pack into glass jars, add some immature flowers of fennel, fill up with white wine vinegar, and close.

BASILICO · basil

Ocimum basilicum (family LAMIACEAE)
alfàbrega (C) · vasilikós (G) · misiricoi (Sal)

The most fragrant herb of all. I have mentioned (p 33), the variety used for *pesto*, Grande di Genova, in Liguria grown in open ground.

The most perfumed basil is *O minimum*, a small-leaved species grown in pots, tins, old crocks, in the sun and called Nano verde, 'green dwarf', by Italian seedsmen; in Catalonia *alfàbrega de fulla menuda*.

Even in the south, basil is sown in late April, for fear of frost, but one can keep it going right into late autumn, in pots.

TIMO · winter (mountain) savory, and summer savory

Satureja montana and *S hortensis* (family LAMIACEAE)
sajolida (C) · throúmbi (G)

While every cook is familiar with many kinds of thyme, they are sometimes perplexed by winter and summer savory, which are both referred to in southern Italy as *timo*, and in the Salentine dialect as *tumu*, and in the 'Greek' villages as *trumba*.

Winter or mountain savory is white-flowered and has small thyme-like leaves, more grey than green; a woody shrub that grows in clumps on the verges of the *macchia* on calcareous soil and serves all the uses of wild thyme. This is the *sajolida* of the Catalans, equally widespread in the foothills which are covered with the same aromatic plants as in the south Italian *macchia*. Winter savory is used in grilling meat and fish, in braises, and in conserving olives; dried in autumn, when it flowers, it provides an excellent infusion or *tisane*.

The far less important summer savory is an annual, appearing in the same calcareous situations and, being more delicate, sometimes replacing the winter one when preparing a fish court-bouillon or roasting fish.

Both savories serve to flavour fungi when these are roasted, and are used with fresh rosemary in grilling or roasting lamb.

Timo, cistus, lentisk, Jerusalem sage, myrtle, wild olive and rosemary are the aromatic plants used to swill out the wine barrels before use. These plants, leaf and stem, are boiled up in water in a cauldron, to which after 15 minutes wine is added. The strained liquid is poured hot into the barrels, which are then rolled about. The flowering shoots of *timo*, the winter kind, are bunched and used to keep the fruit fly from entering the barrels while fermenting in the *cantina*.

TIMO · thyme

Thymus vulgaris	(family	*T serpyllum*
farigola (C) · thmári (G)	LAMIACEAE)	serpol (C) · thiósmo (G)

T vulgaris is the one employed in the Catalan thyme soup, *Sopa de farigola* (p 77); in Provençal this wild thyme is *la farigoule*. No need to insist on its virtues in cooking fish, meat, sauces.

T serpyllum, growing in more mountainous situations, is the creeping thyme more used in infusions, having an even better perfume. Use it when cooking a hare, following the precept of cooking animals with the things on which they have fed.

SANTOREGGIA • maritime thyme

Thymus (formerly *Coridothymus*) *capitatus* (family LAMIACEAE)

This, the strongest of all thymes, has already been mentioned (p 77) in connection with restoratives, and makes a most excellent infusion. Regularly taken in this form it combats winter ills.

It grows in maritime situations in the mountains and also on the shore in the Mediterranean. It has tiny spiky leaves, produces a dense mass of purple flowers, and is of shrubby growth. To be gathered in June when in full flower. Used for roasts and grills as well as *daubes*.

Awkwardly enough, it is just another *timo* (or *tumu*) in the Salento.

ORIGANO • wild marjoram (in the USA, oregano)

Origanum vulgare (family LAMIACEAE)
orenga (C) • rígani, oríganon (the *agrioriganos* of Dioscorides) (G)

This is the origano used in infusions. Of relatively dwarf habit, especially perfumed, peppery, growing on mountainsides. Good for tomato salads, tomato sauces, stews, zucchini, aubergines, pizzas, etc. An interesting thing about *origano* is that its flavour is communicated by stewing rather than in frying. You therefore seldom find it included in a *soffritto* or *sofregit*, i e fried in oil.

The American name oregano comes from the Spanish *orégano*, a corruption of the Latin *origanum*, better preserved in Italian and also as the English word origanum.

MAGGIORANA • sweet marjoram

Origanum marjorana, Marjorana hortensis (family LAMIACEAE)
marduix (C) • taken to be the *sampsuchon* or *amaracon* of Dioscorides

From the above nomenclature you can see there is some difficulty in distinguishing these fragrant herbs and, if I have done so correctly, it will be thanks to Geoffrey Grigson's *The Englishman's Flora*. Both *origano* and *maggiorana* have been employed in cooking for a very long time. A picture from an Italian illuminated manuscript shows in the late 14th century a lady watering an ornamental garden pot containing plants of 'maiorana', and underneath is written: 'confortat cerebrum et omnia viscera' (comforts the head and all internal organs).

Garden marjoram is apparently African in origin. Dried in shade, then stripped, it is also taken in infusions; a tonic for a tired stomach.

MENTA · mint

Mentha viridis (family LAMIACEAE)
menta (C) · diósmos (G)

Some wild mints: *M sativa, l'herba sana* (C); *M arvensis*, corn mint, *menta selvatica* (I); *M piperita*, peppermint, *peperina* (I); *M spicata*, spearmint; *M aquatica*, water mint; *M pulegium*, pennyroyal, *poliol* (C), *menta romana* (I).

M piperita, the mint much cultivated in gardens, is a cross between *M spicata* and *M aquatica* according to Grigson.

I have already mentioned a sprig or two of wild mint, usually corn mint or pennyroyal, boiled in a dish of weeds (p 188). Both plants (leaves and flower spikes) can be used in infusions, fresh or dried; see also the infusion of fresh mint leaves (p 77).

In Apulia the leaves of garden mint are used with a variety of vegetables prepared *'in insalata'* (p 167) and in cooking broad beans and peas.

SALVIA · sage

Salvia officinalis (family LAMIACEAE)
sàlvia (C) · faskomiliá (G)

I have referred to the restorative properties of sage (p 50). If you soak 90 g (3 oz) of sage leaves in 1 litre (36 fl oz) of sherry for 9 days, then drain the liquor, let it rest for a day, and decant it into a bottle through a paper filter, you have an excellent disinfectant mouthwash of Catalan extraction. (See also p 34, for *S triloba*.)

ROSMARINO · rosemary

Rosmarinus officinalis (family LAMIACEAE)
romaní (C) · dendrolívanon (G)

There are two plants much used in cooking – rosemary and bay – which I am convinced are better used fresh than dried. Both are more perfumed growing in the wild.

TO PRESERVE. Pick rosemary when it is in flower, which happens at least three or four times a year in the Salento, cut it very fine with scissors and immediately put it in a glass jar, covering it with olive oil. Both the oil and the cut-up leaves and flowers can then be used to flavour a *soffritto* (p 31), their taste unimpaired. Remember to replenish the jar next time you meet a bush of rosemary.

MALVA • mallow (family MALVACEAE)

| *Malva rotundifolia* (common or round-leaved mallow) | *M sylvestris* (dwarf mallow) | *Althaea officinalis* (marsh mallow) | *Lavatera arborea* (tree mallow) |

The leaves, flowers and seeds of these beautiful plants – all *malví* (C) and *molócha* (G) – are a balm to the stomach on account of the mucilage or viscous vegetable substance they release on contact with water.

Here I must confess that, having boiled the young leaves of the tree mallow – which has naturalized in our garden – to combat a momentary malaise, the resulting viscosity was such that it inspired me to use it as a foot-bath instead. This proves refreshing.

The leaves of the dwarf mallow, a plant growing by the wayside, and those of the round-leaved mallow are the ones to use for pacifying the stomach; boil them like spinach in a minimum of water.

The beautiful flowers of the mallows are gathered in spring, dried well in sun, and used for infusions, with a few of their smallest leaves and seeds. This is not only stomachic but good for bronchial conditions.

Okra, delicious vegetable (see p 181), belongs to the same family and shares this viscosity.

LAURO • bay laurel

Laurus nobilis (family LAURACEAE)
llorer (C) • dáfni (G)

A shrubby evergreen which finally becomes a tree; it has wonderfully fragrant leaves. In the Salento it grows wild in the shelter of ravines. It was by transplanting one of these into the garden that the conviction dawned that it should be used fresh not dried. This applies particularly in the making of conserves (see Conserves, p 316), but also in poaching fish, in a tomato sauce, and in a *civet de lièvre* (p 241).

The black berries of the bay laurel were often used in ancient Roman cooking, pounded with other fragrant bitter seeds and herbs. This is the tree into which Daphne was transformed when pursued by Apollo.

ZAFFERANO • saffron

Crocus sativus (family IRIDACEAE)
safrà (C) • krókos (G)

The Phoenicians brought saffron to Spain, where it was to become an essential ingredient in certain rice dishes and broths; to Provence, where it later on flavoured and coloured the *bouillabaisse*; and to England, via the Cornish tin trade, where it naturalized.

The orange stigmas, three per flower, of this wild crocus have become the most expensive spice in the world. I mention it because it is a characteristic of the Catalan *paella* (p 84), to which it gives a marvellous colour, and because its cultivation, though diminishing, is carried on in the neighbourhood of Tarragona and in the Balearic Islands.

The chief centre of cultivation in Italy is in Piana di Navelli near Aquila, where it has been grown since the mid 15th century; its commerce initially was handled by Teutonic merchants who settled in Aquila. At that time its price by weight was higher than silver; now it is equal to that of truffles. An essential ingredient of the Milanese risotto.

Zafferano was originally used in the 'conserve' of little fishes at Santa Maria di Leuca called *Pupiddi a scapece* (p 124), sold on Saints' days. Now it has become a blatant yellow through the use of turmeric (the powdered rhizome of *Curcuma longa* and a popular spice in Asia).

VANIGLIA · vanilla

Vanilla planifolia (family ORCHIDACEAE)
vainilla (C) · vaníllia (G)

A species of tropical orchid originating in the forests of South America and introduced into Spain in the 16th century; the Spaniards had noticed its immature pods being used by the Aztecs to flavour a chocolate beverage. It then entered into many forms of Catalan *pastisseria* where milk was employed. Boiled in milk, it communicates its special flavour, is then removed, dried, and can be used again and again. A pod, placed in a jar of sugar and tightly closed, will flavour it.

CANELLA · cinnamon

Cinnamomum zeylanicum (family LAURACEAE)
canyella (C) · kanélla (G)

Cinnamon arrives in the kitchen in the form of 'sticks', which are rolled segments of the bark of the tree. This spice was highly prized in mediaeval cooking, English, French, Italian, Catalan, Castilian. It was used in association with broths, game, roasts, and in *pâtisserie*. Still used in certain sweets, such as *Crema cremada* (p 295); and indispensable in stuffing figs (*Fichi mandorlati*, p 307).

NOCE MOSCATA • nutmeg

Myristica fragrans (family MYRISTICACEAE)
nou moscada (C) • moskokárido (G)

The nutmeg tree produces two spices: the nutmeg being the kernel inside the nut of the fleshy apricot-like fruit, and mace the coral-like membrane that covers the nut, scarlet when fresh and golden when dried. Grated nutmeg in very small amounts is used with potatoes (see *Passato di patate* and *Torta di patate*, both on p 89), in cooking spinach, and when filling ravioli with spinach and ricotta or ground meats. It is one of the aromatics (with black pepper, cinnamon, juniper berries, savory, rosemary, bay) which, pounded, are used in conserving pork. Much used, with cinnamon and ginger, as a flavouring in mediaeval cooking, and thus found in creations with a long tradition such as the *panforte* of Siena.

MANDORLO (the tree), MANDORLA (the fruit) almond

Prunus dulcis (formerly *Amygdalus communis*) (family ROSACEAE)
ametlla (C) • amígdalo (G)

Sweet almonds are produced by this tree in some of its forms; the bitter (and some intermediate) ones by others. Both kinds grow in the wastes of Catalonia, in Naxian valleys, and all over southern Italy, as well as being cultivated on a grand scale in the great plain of Bari and in Sicily. They flower in January, in the worst of winter.

Almonds are widely grown in impoverished soil on Mediterranean hillsides. Grilled and salted, they provide something to eat at any time of day; pounded with garlic and parsley in the Catalan *picada*; pounded and stuffed with herbs and breadcrumbs into the stomach of a fish; used in a fantastic array of confectionery and cakes; and pounded in quantity with the aid of an almond mill, to make the almond milk called *orxata d'ametlles* in Catalan, *latte di mandorle* in Italian – a refreshing summer drink.

Almonds appear in all Salentine villages on Saints' days on stalls in the piazza, usually roasted in their shells in the oven, together with hazelnuts from the uplands of the Abruzzi. See *la picada* (p 32), *Menjar blanc* (p 32), the Ibizenkan Christmas pudding (p 297), *romesco* (p 121), *panellets* (p 293), *amaretti* (p 295) and *Il Pesce di Natale*, (p 290).

NESPOLA · loquat, Japanese medlar

Eriobotrya japonica (family ROSACEAE)
nespra (C) · moúsmoula (G)

The loquat became established in Mediterranean areas in the early 19th century but had already arrived from Japan in England in 1778. In Tuscany it is often planted on the margin of a vineyard to give its dense shade. Flowering in late October and November, the fruits develop during winter, and are the first fruits with kernels to appear in April and May. They are peculiar little apricot-coloured fruits, growing in clusters, with a large brown nut inside. In northern Italy a rather penitential fruit, sharp and acid; sweet-sour and refreshing further south. Peel it, pop it in, spit out the stone.

PRUGNA, SUSINA · plum

Prunus domestica and *P damascena* (family ROSACEAE)
pruna (C) · damáskino (G) · brunu, prunu, prinedda, tamascina (Sal)

Domestic plums appear to have their origins far back in prehistory as a cross between sloes, *P spinosa*, and cherry plums, *P cerasifera*, a marriage which most probably took place in the Caucasus, where in forests both species abound. (See under Roach in the Bibliography.)

But damsons belong to a distinct species, *P istititia*, the bullace in its wild form. Damson plums were cultivated well before the Christian era in Damascus and are the ancestors of the French mirabelle, *P damascena*. A descendant of this tree is growing in our masseria; it makes an astonishingly delicious and perfumed jam. Its small blue plums are disregarded by our neighbours 'because their flesh is attached to the stone'. A Gascon confronted with this jam is reminded of French plums of bygone days. I imagine that the Crusaders, returning via Otranto and Brindisi from the Holy Land, stuffed their pockets with dried Damascus plums, discarding the stones en route. (The octagonal Crusader churches still stand in Ugento and Tricase.) Prunes stem from the same stock, by cultivation increasing in size.

CATALAN USES. There are untold Catalan dishes containing prunes, soaked for a brief hour and cooked so that they have a bite to them (in water with lemon juice and zest, or in wine), then added to the dish: veal stewed with prunes, pork fillet with prunes, eels with prunes, roast turkey stuffed with prunes, pine kernels and raisins. See also Rabbit with prunes and pine kernels (p 257). All are delicious dishes.

CILIEGIA MARASCA (or AMARENA) • morello cherry

Prunus cerasus (family ROSACEAE)

In southern Italy this tree, once planted, quickly produces its delicious fruits and is most beautiful in flower. Of light pendulous habit, it waves white wands of blossom in April.

CONSERVING.Pick the fruits a dark red for jam, and slightly less dark if you wish to preserve them in *grappa*. In this case cut their delicate stems to leave 1 cm (less than ½"), wipe them, prick each cherry twice with a needle, pack them in glass jars and pour into each jar a small quantity of sugar. Cover with Grappa Giulia and fasten the lids or cork the jars. The cherries colour the *grappa* and impart to it their taste. Served in glasses, the *grappa* with a few cherries, at the end of a meal. It is preferable to fill several small jars than one large one, as the intoxicating perfume quickly escapes, once opened. See also *Marmellata di ciliegie marasche* (p 308) and *Lingue di vitello in salsa di ciliegie marasche* (p 273).

PERSICO (the tree), PERSICA (the fruit) • 'wild peach'

Prunus persica (family ROSACEAE)
préssec (C) • rodákino (G)

The peach originated in China, came thence to Persia (Iran) and later to the Mediterranean, where it was regarded as a Persian fruit. Its ancestral wild form does not survive, but when the stone of a cultivated peach (*pesca*) germinates, up springs this 'wild' peach and bears its fruit (*persica*). This is the stock on which cultivated varieties of peach, and sometimes apricots, are grafted in Apulia.

The tree so resembles the almond, *P dulcis*, that it is difficult to distinguish it except when in flower (dark pink) or fruit.

In Catalonia, roast meat and roast game are accompanied by whole peaches, sometimes stoned and stuffed with lean pork (*pressecs farcits*). The wild peach lends itself to cooking, as it scarcely ever ripens. See page 311 for the use of these 'green' peaches in *la persicata*.

SORBO (the tree) and CORNIOLO (the fruit)
wild service tree

Sorbus torminalis (family ROSACEAE)
serva (C) • ciculi (Sal)

A thorny little tree, growing in the limestone maquis and favoured by shepherds. Its rather acid little fruit is made edible by macerating it in wine vinegar and sugar. Until recently in the Salento these fruits were prepared by greengrocers and sold in their shops in autumn. According to Robert Graves, *The White Goddess*, this is the 'apple' of the Thracian Orphic cult.

PINOLI • pine kernels of the stone pine

Pinus pinea (family PINACEAE)
pinyons (C) • pignólia (G)

The stone or umbrella pine produces very large cones in which, neatly packed in pairs, are the pine nuts. The cones only release their nuts when exposed to the heat of a fire. Each nut then has to be cracked open without damaging the little kernel (use a hammer and stand the nut on end), which explains why the kernels are expensive. If the Ligurian *pesto* makes the most poetic use of pine kernels in Italy, the Catalan *picada* (p 32) is equally a culinary inspiration. In *pâtisserie*, strewn on the surface of a cake and baked, or lightly pressed into Italian almond cakes, delicious *amaretti*, or Catalan *panellets*, they acquire a nutty flavour. But they have many culinary uses: see page 166 for *Espinacs amb panses i pinyons*.

A vehicle for other tastes: a handful stuffed inside Christmas turkeys and plump chickens, a pheasant, or little quails for roasting (*Guatlles amb panses i pinyons*), they absorb the flavour of the bird. They are used in cooking rabbit (*Conill a la catalana*), stewed with onions, tomatoes, bayleaf and salt pork; and with pig's trotters cooked for a fantastically long time (24 hours) in a slow oven. These are only a few of the dishes employing this culinary chameleon.

Most of the *pinoli* in commerce come from the pine woods along the coast between Viareggio and Pisa, playground of poets – Byron, Shelley and d'Annunzio. In Carrara they arrived once a fortnight, freshly extracted from the cone. The umbrella or stone pine is also at home in Apulia and forms part of the Christmas ritual. Wrapped in the kernel are to be found the tiny clasped fingers of *Il Bambineddu*, the Christ Child.

NOCCIUOLO • hazel nut

Corylus avellana (family CORYLACEAE)
avellana (C) • foundoúki (G)

The hazel was once the king-pin of English hedgerows. The destruction of the hedges provokes the most melancholy thoughts as does the disappearance of the tree and the wattles made from it. Looking back, the hazel in Irish lore was the Tree of Knowledge. That it is also the tree from which divining rods are cut is significant. Water divining remains a normal activity in the Salento, where the rods are sometimes made of vine. Here the hazel nuts come down from the Abruzzi, and appear on market stalls on feast days.

Hazels are cultivated in some regions of Catalonia. Whole hillsides are planted with them in the mountains behind Reus. Their nuts play a vital role, with almonds, in the manufacture of *torrons*, and are used in *romesco* (p 121).

NOCE (masc., the tree), NOCE (fem., the fruit) • walnut

Juglans regia (family JUGLANDACEAE)
nou (C) • karíthi (G)

This tree in its magnificence flourishes in the high valleys leading down from Benevento to the plain of Naples and furnishes the Sorrentine walnuts of commerce. These, unfortunately, instead of being sun-dried as in Apulia, are dried industrially, losing much of the flavour in the process. In the south, walnuts are regarded as vital winter fare rather than as festive treats. They are kept in large glazed earthenware jars and are brought out to end a meal while carrying on with wine.

See also *Pollo colla salsa di noci* (p 261); *pesto* made with walnuts instead of pine kernels (p 97); and conserve of green walnuts (p 310).

FICO D'INDIA • prickly pear, Indian fig

Opuntia ficus-indica (family CACTACEAE)
figa de moro (C) • frangósiko (G)

Native of Mexico naturalized in the Mediterranean where its impenetrable thickets are often used as boundary lines. Its broad 'stems' when young are chopped for goat fodder. Its orange fruits, ripening in late summer, grow on the edges of the stems and are covered with minute prickles, almost invisible. They taste best when still green, at early morning after rain. Or late in winter.

Pick at dawn, handle with caution. An adept with a knife, having used a figleaf to twist off the fruit, slices a circle from the top, makes four vertical incisions, then opens out the skin by deftly peeling it back. Eat at breakfast. The self-drying yellow flowers, carefully collected on a windless day and put in screw-top jars, are used in infusion for bronchial conditions. Can be preserved till Christmas by cutting the broad stems bearing their coral-coloured fruits, making a hole through each stem and hanging them on nails in a sheltered place, out of doors. Should you get pricked, apply olive oil immediately.

KAKI · persimmon

Diospyros kaki (family EBENACEAE)
caqui (C)

Another oriental intruder, a tree of great splendour in winter. The fruits, pale green when they first appear, turn to burning gold and remain on the tree long after its leaves have fallen. The landscape of the Tiber Valley is illuminated by them and so are the narrower valleys between Naples and Benevento in late autumn. They falsely recall the Golden Apples of the Hesperides.

A favourite winter fruit, eaten when very ripe, the sign being the cracking of the delicate skin. The Japanese sculptor, Inoué Yukichi, told me that in Japan they are left on the bough until there is a heavy frost, the soft luscious pulp becomes frozen, and they are eaten on the spot, iced. At home, cut them in half and eat with a spoon.

MELAGRANA · pomegranate

Punica granatum (family PUNICACEAE)
magrana (C) · ródi (G)

This fruit has a sculptural form unparalleled and colours of fire. The tree itself, *melagrano*, is insignificant with frail branches; it makes every effort to become a shrub and has to be reconciled to being a tree by frequent cutting back of shoots springing from the base.

There are several varieties: very sweet with carmine-coloured seeds; slightly sweet, with paler seeds; and acid, the seeds being almost white. The acid kind are best with fish and meat. Count Stolberg mentioned a variety in Sicily without kernels.

In Arab mythology the pomegranate plays the role of the apple in the Bible, i e it is the fruit of the earthly paradise. Packed with its innumerable faceted seeds it is an emblem of death and resurrection: the last indigenous fruit of autumn, it ripens at All Souls. At Paestum a fresco on the end wall of a Lucanian tomb shows two mourning women, tearing their hair, and two huge pomegranates hanging on long stalks between them. On Naxos these fruits were ritually hung from the roof-beam at the death of the year to protect the inmates.

USES. Eaten out of doors while walking; very refreshing, one sucks the delicious seeds and spits the kernels on the wayside. Crush them to produce a reviving drink. The juice of a rather acid pomegranate was used in certain sweet-sour dishes in mediaeval Catalan cooking, as was the juice of green grapes (*verjus*) and that of bitter oranges. See also *Llengues de porc amb salsa de magrana* (p 233).

MELA COTOGNA · quince

Cydonia vulgaris (family PUNICACEAE)
codony (C) · kydóni (G)

It is possible that *Cydonia* and related names derive from the town of Cydon in Crete. I have already referred to the superlative quinces of Naxos, which is very near to Crete. They are also splendid grown in the mountain valleys of northern Greece. See page 309 for *kydóni glikó*.

The *cotognata* mentioned in that recipe is industrially confected at Lecce, the fruit being made into a delicious paste by slow reduction and carefully packed in little wooden boxes. A similar preparation is the Catalonian *codonyat*. Quinces roasted whole sometimes accompany game and chicken in Catalonia. A slice or two of quince in autumn put into chicken stock gives an excellent flavour.

MORA DI GELSO · mulberry

Morus nigra (family MORACEAE)
móra (C) · moúra (G)

Mora is the fruit and *gelso* the tree. Fortunate are those to find this tree already growing in their garden. The mulberry attains to a very great age, like the fig, to which family it belongs. There is a species with white fruits, *Morus alba*, sweeter, of less substance. The fruits of both reach their perfection in Mediterranean areas, and are less acid than when grown in northern climates, their flavour inexplicable, refreshing. In August it is a delight to climb into this tree.

FICO · fig

Ficus carica (family MORACEAE)
figa (C) · síko (G)

A tree that survived the ice ages (others are: carob, myrtle, vine, oleander, plane, olive, lentisk and Judas tree). The milky juice the fig exudes was used as rennet to curdle milk in cheese-making. This explains the ever-repeated advice not to drink wine after eating figs. In any case a too enthusiastic indulgence produces a feeling of satiety and a swollen stomach.

EPHEMERAL FRUITS. The first crop appears mid-June (on the feast of San Giovanni), called *fiorone*, ripening from last year's buds. They are relatively insipid, large and juicy if it has rained; eaten with *prosciutto crudo* to begin a meal.

TRUE FIGS, much smaller, ripen in late August and later; no need to touch them, you know they are ripe when a bead of nectar appears at the opening of the fruit. Some taste of honey, and one kind tastes like raspberry jam. (See Norman Douglas's *Old Calabria*, p 67, for the many types of fig.)

USES. Best eaten from the tree, or gathered in the very early morning and set on a figleaf in a dish in pyramid form to eat at mid-day. Green, golden, purple, black. For drying, you pick them early, every other day, as they ripen in sequence. See *Fichi mandorlati* (p 307) and *Marmellata di fichi* (p 306).

ARANCIO AMARO · bitter (or Seville) orange

Citrus aurantium (family RUTACEAE)
taronja amarga (C) · nerántzi (G)

The bitter orange, a medicinal fruit indigenous to China and India, was introduced by the Romans to the Mediterranean from Arabia, and by the Arabs to Spain. The tree in fruit, laden, is an apparition as in a mediaeval painting.

The fruits are smaller than oranges and are, of course, the ones used in orange marmalade. Marmalade made with the freshly picked fruit has a more 'sparkling' taste than that of English marmalades: use 8 bitter oranges and 2 lemons to 1 kg (2¼ lb) sugar, and a freshly picked bayleaf.

The finely pared zest cut into little strips and prepared as an infusion (5-10% zest) is a balm to the stomach and revives appetite.

The juice and carefully pared zest, finely cut, is employed in the *Canard à l'orange* (mentioned on p 109) and in *Sauce bigarade*.

RUTA · rue

Ruta graveolens (family RUTACEAE)
ruda (C) · píganon (G)

A beautiful small shrub with fine-cut leaves, bluish. Called 'herb of grace', I discovered, because the seeds when developed are deeply incised in the form of a cross.

Rue grows wild in Apulia; in gardens it has an overpowering smell. Strangely enough, it belongs to the same plant family as the orange and other citrus fruits. A sprig of rue put in a bottle of *grappa* (p 223) improves the taste and reduces the alcohol's effect on the heart.

CARRUBO (the tree) and CARRUBA (the pod)
carob, locust-bean

Ceratonia siliqua (family FABACEAE)
garrofa (C) · xilokérato (G)

This biblical tree which occurs where soil is poor in upland wastes in Calabria, in stony deserts in Catalonia, on impoverished hillsides in Greece, is a singular sign of Providence operating in the desert. It bears very large pods, the colour of burnt umber when ripe in autumn, which are sweet in taste and velvety in texture, with a vanilla flavour.

These are said to be the 'locusts' eaten by St John the Baptist. You munch them and spit out the shiny seeds.

Of particular interest to me, these seeds provided the original 'carat' weight of jewellers. The pods are sold on market stalls in winter in the Veneto. In the Salento you pick your own. A pod or two enter into the infusion of *macchia* plants used to swill out the wine barrels, before filling them again at the *vendemmia*.

GINEPRO (the bush) and GINEPRA (the berry) · juniper

Juniperus communis (family CUPRESSACEAE)
ginebró (C) · árkevthos (G)

Wild juniper thrives on calcareous soils, on chalk downland, on the slopes of the Apuanian mountains, in oak woods in Tuscany and on the foothills of the Alps, and in the wild mountains of Greece.

The blue-black fruits, used to flavour gin, are also responsible for the aroma of Ginepro, one of the best Italian liqueurs.

USES IN COOKING. They have a tenderizing effect when pounded with a few allspice and peppercorns and applied to pieces of beef before cooking them *en daube*. Indispensable when cooking pork, wild boar or hare.

MIRTO, MORTELLA · myrtle

Myrtus communis (family MYRTACEAE)
murtró (C) · mirtiá (G) · murtedda (Sal)

A limestone shrub which can become a tree, another survivor of the ice ages; it grows by the sea, was once sacred to Aphrodite and is a symbol of death. It has exquisite white flowers and purple-blackish fruits which one eats in autumn when walking through the maquis. The fragrant leaves and seeds are much used in Sardinian cooking.

The ancient Romans made myrtle wine by immersing the ripe fruits in *mosto* (fermenting grape juice) at vintage time, leaving it to ferment, and then decanting it. The fruits were also used in Roman cooking, poetically enough in relation to wild boar, also a death symbol – being hunted in the dying year when fruits the myrtle.

Use the ripe fruits to stuff little quails (p 255).

LENTISCO · lentisk

Pistacia lentisca (family ANACARDIACEAE)
llentiscle (C) · stingu (Sal)

Just as blackberries are the 'mother of forests', so the lentisk is mother of the limestone wilderness. The whole shrub has an acrid pungency, often carried on the wind.

The Romans used the small red berries, which grow in clusters and turn black, ground in the mortar with other aromatics in cooking, as they also used the bitter seeds of rue and those of myrtle. The Sards in prehistoric times extracted their oil by grinding the seeds in hollows in the rocks, as did the island inhabitants of Pantelleria. (Carlo Maxia: lecture, 1973 on 'Piety and Sacrificial Altars' at Cagliari.)

CORBEZZOLO (the tree) and CORBEZZOLA (the fruit)
strawberry tree

Arbutus unedo (family ERICACEAE)
arboç (C) · koúmaron (G)

This evergreen grows tall in Tuscan woods, but in the south more often remains a shrub; it bears pale waxy flowers in clusters in autumn, simultaneously with rich scarlet-orange fruits. These fruits are edible *en passant* and a delight to birds. Used in Catalonia for liqueurs.

In the Salentine dialect the name of the tree is *urmeculu*.

CISTO · rock-rose, cistus

Cistus spp (family CISTACEAE)
mucchiu, mucchia (Sal)

Of the many kinds of cistus, *C salviaefolius*, *C albidus* and *C monspeliensis* predominate in the Salento. The plants grow with great vitality in the southern *macchia* (maquis), and under them several species of *Lactarius* (p 214), locally called *mucchiareddi*. This collective dialect name certainly derives from their connection with the cistus.

If you turn to the little book called *The Twelve Healers* by the great physician Edward Bach, you will find Rock Rose as the rescue remedy – a specific against terror. We made the decoction in fresh spring water in a glass bowl (it should be crystal) in April when the flowers bloom. But it was only in August that we realised the connection between terror and the cistus: when the fire dragon serpents through the landscape, it devours the *macchia* and consumes the rock rose. Just as the venom of the snake is used as an antidote to snake-bite, so the plant in danger is the specific against fear, in this case of fire.

We made the decoction: we never take it. Terror gave place to action when the hillside some years ago was swept by fire. And when the black ash, a mantle, had blown away, we discovered that the neighbouring fields were littered with delicately worked flints, flint arrow-heads, obsidian blades. Picking them up we began to realise that the deserted hill overlooking the Ionian had for millennia been inhabited, if sporadically, by craftsmen and that at our door lay 40,000 years of prehistory, unwritten and unread.

BIBLIOGRAPHY

LIST OF ILLUSTRATIONS

INDEX

Bibliography

In my introduction I wrote: 'Living in the wild, it has often seemed that we were living on the margins of literacy. This led to reading the landscape and learning from people'. So, you may well ask, why this formidable bibliography?

I confess I have always been devoted to the written word and to the study of languages, and books have always formed part of our baggage. The weed from which I have drawn the honey is the traditional knowledge of Mediterranean people; the books cited can be regarded as the distillation of this knowledge. Like Gertrude Stein I write 'for myself and strangers' and wish to share my enthusiasm for both with them.

In composing this bibliography I have been greatly helped by the poet and historian Marcus Bell.

Part I
(works referred to in the text)

ABATANGELO, L., *Chiese-Cripte e affreschi italo-bizantini di Massafra*, Cressati, Taranto, 1966.

AESCHYLUS, *Prometheus and Other Plays*, translated into English by Philip Vellacott, Penguin, 1985.

ALIGHIERI, DANTE, *La Commedia di Dante Alighieri*, first printed at Jesi, Marche, 1472. Translated into English by D. Sayers, Penguin, 1985.

ANATI, EMANUEL, *Le Statue-Stele della Lunigiana*, Jaca Books, Milan, 1981.

ANDREWS, KEVIN, *The Flight of Ikaros*, Weidenfeld and Nicolson, London, 1959. Reprinted by Penguin, 1984.

ANONIMO TOSCANO, see Faccioli, E.

ANONIMO VENEZIANO, see Faccioli, E.

APICIUS, *De Re Quoquinaria*, 1st and 2nd printed editions by Le Signerre, Milan, 1498.
    De Re Coquinaria, edited by Barbara Flower and Elizabeth Rosenbaum under the title *The Roman Cookery Book*, Harrap, London, 1958. Contains the recipes and complex bibliographical details, with line drawings by Katerina Wilcynski.
    Les Dix Livres de Cuisine d'Apicius, traduits du latin . . . et commentés par Bertrand Guégan, René Bonnel, Paris, 1933.

ARCHESTRATUS (493-439 BC), 'Hedypatheia', a poem on good food. In the original Greek in *Corpusculum Poesis Epicae Graecae Ludibundae*, vol 1, edited by Paul Brandt, Teubner, Leipzig, 1888; in Italian translation in *I Frammenti della Gastronomia di Archestrato raccolti e volgarizzati*, Domenico Sciná, Palermo, 1823.

ARISTOPHANES, *The Plays*, 2 vols, translated into English by Patric Dickinson, Oxford University Press, London, 1970.

ARTAUD, ANTONIN, *Les Tarahumaras*, in Tome IX of the author's complete works, Editions Gallimard, 1971. Translated by Helen Weaver as *The Peyote Dance*, Farrar, Straus and Giroux, New York, 1976.

ARTUSI, PELLEGRINO, *La Scienza In Cucina E L'Arte Di Mangiar Bene*, Casa Editrice Marzocco, Florence, c 1890. More than 50 subsequent editions include one edited by Piero Camporesi, Einaudi, Turin, 1974.

ATHENAEUS (*fl* 3rd century AD), *Deipnosophistae*, 7 vols, translated into English by Dr C. B. Gulick, Loeb Classical Library, 1927-41.

BACH, EDWARD, *The Twelve Healers*, Stanhope Press, Rochester, Kent, 1933.

BINI, GIORGIO, *Pesci Molluschi Crostacei del Mediterraneo*, with line drawings, FAO, Rome, 1965: a catalogue of fish, molluscs and crustaceans with their Mediterranean names and Latin nomenclature.

(IL) BREVIARIO DI PAPA GALEAZZO, edited by Michele Paone, Congedo Editore, Galatina, 1973.

CARÊME, ANTONIN, *L'Art de la Cuisine Française au 19ᵐᵉ Siècle*, Paris, 1835. With magnificent engravings.

CARTWRIGHT, JULIA (Mrs Henry Ady), *Beatrice d'Este*, J. M. Dent, London, 1899 and since.

CHAUCER, GEOFFREY, *The Miller's Tale*, in *The Canterbury Tales*, Caxton, London, 1475-80. *The Works*, edited by F. N. Robinson, Oxford, 1985.

CLUSIUS, CAROLUS, *Rariorum Plantarum Historiae*, Liber IV, Antwerp, 1601.

CONGEDO, R., *Salento: Scrigno d'Acqua*, Martina Franca, 1984. The most interesting work on the Salento published in recent years.

CONGRÉS CATALÀ DE LA CUINA, issued by the Generalitat de Catalunya, Department of Commerce and Tourism, Barcelona, 1982: a summing up of a 2 year investigation into the Catalan culinary tradition.

COTTON, CHARLES, *Scarronides or Virgil Travestie, A mock-poem on the 1st and 4th Books of Virgil's Aenaeis*, 1664. Subsequent editions include the 13th with woodcuts by Thomas Bewick, J. Galton, London, 1804.

CRATEVAS (*fl* 1st century BC), Greek doctor, author of the first treatise on medicinal plants. A manuscript of his treatise, illustrated with precise representations of the plants described, existed at Constantinople until the 17th century and served as a model for subsequent treatises.

CULPEPER, NICHOLAS (1616-1654), *The English Physician*, London, 1652. *Culpeper's English Physician and Complete Herbal*, arranged by Mrs C. F. Leyel, Arco, London 1961.

CUMMINGS, E. E., *Complete Poems: 1910-1962*, edited by G. J. Firmage, Granada, London, 1981.

DAVID, ELIZABETH, *Italian Food*, drawings by Renato Guttuso, Macdonald, London, 1954, and since 1967 in Penguin.
'Mad, Bad, Despised and Dangerous' (on the aubergine), in *Petits Propos Culinaires*, n° 9, Prospect Books, London, 1981.

DAVIDSON, ALAN, *Mediterranean Seafood*, with beautiful line drawings, 2nd edition, Allen Lane and Penguin, 1981. The vital handbook for identification of fish, crustaceans, molluscs together with a gold-mine of fish recipes and a challenging bibliography.

DAVIS, IRVING, *A Catalan Cookery Book*, edited by Patience Gray, with 12 copper engravings by Nicole, published in a limited edition of 165 copies by Lucien Scheler, 19 rue de Tournon, Paris VIᵉ, 1969.

DE NOLA, ROBERT (MESTRE ROBERT), *Libre del Coch*, edited by Veronika Leimgruber, Curial Edicions Catalanes, Barcelona, 1977. The first recorded printing of this celebrated work was in Catalan at Barcelona in 1520.
  A copy of the first among many Castilian versions translated by Ramon de Petrus, Toledo, 1525, is in the British Library. The work is thought to have been written and circulated in manuscript when Robert de Nola (Mestre Robert) was cook to King Ferdinand of Naples 1458-94. For bibliographical details see pp 10-11 in *El què hem menjat* by Josep Pla (below).

DE VRIES, HERMAN, *Natural Relations I – die marrokanische sammlung*, Institut für Moderne Kunst, Nürnberg, and Galerie Mueller-Roth, Stuttgart, 1984. Invaluable plant bibliography including information on the 1610 version of Dioscorides' *Kräuterbuch* (reprinted, Grünwald, 1964); Tabernaemontanus' *Neu Vollkommen Kräuterbuch*, Frankfurt-am-Main, 1588-91; and a work by A. Maurizio, *Die Geschichte unsere Pflanzennahrung von den Urzeiten bis zur Gegenwart*, Berlin, 1927.

DICKENS, CHARLES, *Pictures from Italy*, London, 1846. Also (ed D. Paroissien) Andre Deutsch, London, 1973.

DIOSCORIDES (*fl* 1st century AD), *De Materia Medica*, this herbal was first published by Aldus, Venice, 1499. An illustrated codex of the 14th century is in the Biblioteca del Seminario, Padua. An English translation was made by John Goodyer in 1655, but not published until Robert Gunther's limited edition of 1934, which was reprinted by Hafner, New York, 1968.

DOLCI, DANILO, *Racconti Siciliani*, Einaudi, Turin, 1973.

DOUGLAS, NORMAN, *Old Calabria*, Martin Secker, London, 1915, and Peregrine Books, 1962.

DUPIN, PIERRE, *Les Secrets de la Cuisine Comtoise*, with woodcuts, dedicated to Colette, Librairie E. Nouvry, Paris, 1927.

ESPRIU, SALVADOR, *Formes i Paraules*, Edicions 62, Barcelona, 1975. Poems inspired by Apel.les Fenosa's bronzes, with photographs of them.

Formes et Paroles, French translation by Max Pons, Éditions de la Barbacane, Paris, 1977.

Forms and Words, English translation by J. L. Gili, Dolphin Book Company, Oxford, 1980.

FACCIOLI, E. (editor), *Arte della Cucina*, Edizioni Il Polifilo, Milan, 1966. A collection of medieval culinary manuscripts including those by the 'Anonimo Toscano', the 'Anonimo Veneziano' and *Libro de Arte Coquinaria* by Maestro Martino.

FENOSA POÉTIQUE, an issue of *SUD, revue littéraire*, devoted to the sculptor and his work and including the quotation from Daniel Abadie (n° 18, 1971, published from 11 rue Peyssonnel, 13003 Marseilles). (A major work on Fenosa is: *Apel.les Fenosa* by Raymond Cogniat, Tudor Publishing Company, New York, c 1970.)

FERNALD, M. L. and KINSEY, A. C., *Edible Wild Plants of Eastern North America*, revised edition, Harper, New York, 1958.

FONT I QUER, PIUS, *Resultats del Pla Quinquennal Micòlogic a Catalunya, 1931-35*, Institut Botànic de Barcelona, 1937.

Una Historia de Fongs, Collectanea Botánica, Barcelona, 1959.

El Dioscórides renovado, Labor, Barcelona, 1979.

FORME OF CURY, late 14th century English cookery manuscript in the British Library, reprinted and edited in *Curye on Inglysch* by Constance B. Hieatt and Sharon Butler, E.E.T.S., Oxford University Press, 1985.

FUCIGNA, AUDA, *'l Cararin*, Pontremoli, 1965. A collection of sayings and poems in Carrarese dialect with Italian translations.

GERARD, JOHN, *The Herball or General Historie of Plantes*, first published in 1597. Also, facsimile reprint of the 1633 edition by Dover Publications, New York, 1975.

GIOVENE, ANDREA, *L'Autobiografia di Giuliano di Sansevero*, Rizzoli, Milan, 1967. Translated into English as *The Book of Giuliano Sansevero*, 3 vols, Penguin, 1972, 1977. These 3 vols cover only 4 of the 5 original Italian vols; a translation of the whole work is due to be published by Quartet Books, London, in Autumn 1986.

GISSING, GEORGE, *By the Ionian Sea*, Chapman and Hall, 1901. Reprinted by Richards Press, London, 1956.

GOIDANICH, G. and GORI, G., *Funghi e Ambiente, Una Guida per l'Amatore*, Edagricole, Bologna, 1981. A good Italian source of reference on mushrooms. Professor Goidanich is President of the Agrarian Faculty at Bologna University and of the Unione Italiano della Micologia.

GOLDSMITH, OLIVER, *An History of the Earth and Animated Nature*, 8 vols with copper plates, London, 1774. Republished, with hand-coloured steel engravings, frequently in the 19th century up to 1876.

GRAY, PATIENCE and BOYD, PRIMROSE, *Plats Du Jour*, illustrated by David Gentleman, Penguin, 1957.

GRAVES, ROBERT, *Greek Myths*, 2 vols, Penguin, 1955 and since.

The White Goddess, Faber and Faber, London, 1946 and since.

GREWE, RUDOLF, 'Catalan Cuisine, in an Historical Perspective', a paper in *National and Regional Styles of Cookery, Oxford Symposium 1981*, Prospect Books, London, 1981.

GRIGSON, GEOFFREY, *The Englishman's Flora*, with woodcuts, Paladin, London, 1975.

GRIGSON, JANE, *Charcuterie and French Pork Cookery*, Michael Joseph, London, 1967.

HATTON, RICHARD G., *Handbook of Plant and Floral Ornament from Early Herbals*, Dover Publications, New York, 1960, with superb wood and copper engravings.

HESIOD (*fl* end of 7th century BC), *Works and Days* first printed (with Theocritus) 1493. English translation by Richard Lattimore, University of Michigan Press, 1959.

HILLS, LAWRENCE D., *Comfrey the Herbal Healer*, Henry Doubleday Research Association, Bocking, Essex (undated).

HOMER, *The Odyssey*, first printed in Florence, 1488. English translation by E. V. Rieu, Penguin, 1985.

HORACE, *Odes and Epodes*, translated by C. E. Bennett, Loeb Classical Library, 1986.

HOURMOUZIADES, G., ASIMAKOPOULOU-ATZAKA, P., MAKRIS, K. A., *Magnesia*, Athens, 1982. Includes an account of the earliest neolithic habitations at Sesklo and Dimini in Thessaly c 7500 BC.

JACOBSEN, T. W., '17,000 Anni di Preistoria Greca', a paper in *Viaggio nel Tempo* (an issue of *Le Scienze*, the Italian edition of *Scientific American*), Milan, 1977.

JARRY, ALFRED, *Ubu Roi*, edited by Maurice Saillet, Livre de Poche, Paris, 1962.

JONSON, BEN, *The Alchemist* (1616), edited by F. H. Mares, Manchester University Press, 1979.

KETTNER, AUGUSTE with DALLAS, E. S., *Kettner's Book of the Table*, Dulan & Co, London, 1877. Reprinted by Centaur Press, London, 1968.

KROPOTKIN, P. A. *Memoirs of a Revolutionist*, London and Boston, 1899. Reprinted, edited by C. Ward, Folio Society, London, 1978.

LENORMANT, FRANÇOIS, *La Grande Grèce, Paysage et Histoire*, 2 vols, Paris, 1881.
À travers l'Apulie et la Lucanie, Paris, 1883.

LIBRE DE SENT SOVÍ, edited by Rudolf Grewe, Editorial Barcino, Barcelona, 1979. This is the first accurate printed version of 'El Manuscrit de *Sent Soví*', an anonymous, undated (believed to be early 14th century), collection of Catalan recipes.

LONDON, GEORGE and WISE, HENRY, *The Compleat Gard'ner*, London, 1699. An English version of Jean de la Quintinie's *Le Parfait Jardinier*. The authors drew on John Evelyn's translation, published in 1693, but 'compendiously abridg'd, and made of more use'.

LOUDON, JOHN CLAUDIUS, *An Encyclopaedia of Gardening*, engravings on wood by Branston, London, 1822. A new edition was published in 1835.

LUZIO, A. and RENIER, R., 'Delle Relazioni di Isabella d'Este Gonzaga con Lodovico e Beatrice Sforza', in *Archivio Storico Lombardo*, vol XVII, Società Storica Lombarda, Milan.

MABINOGION, THE FOUR BRANCHES OF THE, translated by G. and T. Jones, Everyman Classics, Dent, 1985.

MAESTRO MARTINO, *Libro de Arte Coquinaria*, see Faccioli, E.

MAIRE, RENÉ, *Fungi Catalaunici*, La Junta de Ciències Naturals, Barcelona, 1933.

MALATESTA, ERRICO, *L'Anarchia*, 1890. *L'Anarchia*, edited by A. M. Bonanno, Edigraf, Catania, 1969.

MATTIOLI, PIERANDREA (1500-1577), *Commentarii in sex libros Pedacii Dioscoridis*, with woodcuts, 1544.

MAUBLANC, A., *Les Champignons de France*, vols XXII and XXIII of *L'Encyclopédie Pratique du Naturaliste*, 3rd edition, Paul Lechevalier, Paris, 1946. Reissued in 1974. Colour plates of watercolour drawings by J. Boully and M. Porchet. An invaluable work.
Champignons Comestibles et Vénéneux, 2 vols, 6th edition, revised by Viennot-Bourguin, Éditions Lechevalier, Paris, 1976.

MCGEE, HAROLD, *On Food and Cooking*, Charles Scribner's Sons, New York, 1984, and George Allen & Unwin, London, 1986.

MENNIS, SIR JOHN and SMITH, JAMES, *Musarum Deliciae*, 1656. Reprinted in 2 vols, London, 1874, with title *Facetiae*.

MONTAGNÉ, PROSPER, *Larousse Gastronomique*, Paris, 1938. Translated into English by Nina Froud, Patience Gray, Maud Murdoch and Barbara Macrae Taylor, Hamlyn, London, 1962.

MORARD, CLEMENT-MARIUS, *Manuel Complet de la Cuisinière Provençale*, with copper plates, Marseilles, 1886.

MORYSON, FYNES, *An Itinerary*, London, 1617. Reprinted in 4 vols, Maclehose and Sons, Glasgow, 1904.

MOZART, W. A., *The Letters*, translated by M. M. Bozman and edited by Hans Mersmann, Dover Publications, New York, 1985.

NEAPOLITAN FÊTE BOOKS: Examples can be seen in the Print Room of the British Museum, London; particularly *Narrazione delle Solenni Reali Feste fatte Celebrare in Napoli da Sua Maestá Il Re delle Due Sicilie Carlo Infanta di Spagna, Duca di Parma, Piacenza etc Per la Nascita del suo Primogenito . . .*, engravings by G. Vasi, after drawings by Vincenzo Ré, Naples, 1749. Case 164 c 22.

See also *The Bourbons of Naples, 1734-1825* by Harold Acton, Methuen, London, 1956 and the same author's *The Last Bourbons of Naples, 1825-1861*, Methuen, 1961.

NELSON, DAWN and DOUGLAS, 'Chuño and Tunta', a paper in *Food in Motion, Oxford Symposium Documents 1983*, Vol 1, Prospect Books, London, 1983. An interesting account of Inca methods of potato storage.

ORIOLI, G., *Adventures of a Bookseller*, privately printed by the author, Florence, 1937.

OVID, *Metamorphoses*, translated by Mary Innes, Penguin, 1955. See particularly Book XV, lines 336-47, for reference to Pythagoras.

OXFORD SYMPOSIUM DOCUMENTS, 1981 (National and Regional Styles of Cookery); 1983, 2 vols (Food in Motion); 1984 and 1985, 1 vol (Cookery: Science, Lore and Books), all published by Prospect Books.

PARKINSON, JOHN, *Theatrum Botanicum*, 1640.

PARTRIDGE, ERIC, *Shakespeare's Bawdy*, Routledge, London, 1947.

PASCUAL, RAMON, *El libro de las setas (fungi)*, with recipes by Mercè Sala, Pol.len Edicions, Barcelona, 1985.

PAZ, OCTAVIO, *The Labyrinth of Solitude*, Allen Lane, London, 1967.

PERRY, CHARLES, 'The Oldest Mediterranean Noodle: A Cautionary Tale', in *Petits Propos Culinaires*, n° 9, Prospect Books, London, 1981. 'Notes on Persian Pasta', in *Petits Propos Culinaires*, n° 10, 1982. 'Buran: 1100 Years in the Life of a Dish', in *Journal of Gastronomy*, vol 1, American Institute of Wine and Food, Santa Barbara, 1984.

'(LE) PETIT TRAITÉ DE 1300', an early French manuscript published by Pichon and Vicaire in their edition of Taillevent (see VIANDIER).

PETRONIUS (PETRONIO ARBITRO), *Cena Trimalchionis. Il Satiricon*, Italian translation by Piero Chiara, Mondadori, 1967. *Satyricon*, English translation by J. P. Sullivan, Penguin, 1985.

PHILLIPS, ROGER, *Mushrooms and Other Fungi of Great Britain and Europe*, Pan Books, 1981. *Wild Food*, Pan Books, 1983.

PLA, JOSEP, *El què hem menjat*, full page colour photographs by F. Català Roca, Edicions Destino, Barcelona, 1981. Described by the author, who died in 1981, as 'a digression on food in relation to cooking'. A definitive and nostalgic work, it awaits translation.

PLATINA (Bartolomeo Sacchi), *De honesta voluptate*, Venice, 1475. The first European work on diet. This work was translated into French in 1505 and frequently reprinted. An English translation has been published in the Mallinckrodt Collection of Food Classics, vol 5, Mallinckrodt Chemical Works, St Louis, Missouri, USA, 1967.

PLINY, *Natural History*, 10 vols, Loeb Classical Library, 1967.

POLUNIN, OLEG, *Flowering Plants of the Mediterranean*, with colour photographs and line drawings, 2nd edition, Chatto and Windus, 1972.

QUÉLET, L. and BATAILLE, F., *Flore Monographique des Amanites et des Lépiotes*, Masson, Paris, 1902.

RABELAIS, *Gargantua and Pantagruel* (1532), 2 vols, Everyman Library, Dent, London, 1985.

RAMSBOTTOM, JOHN, *Mushrooms and Toadstools*, Collins, London, 1953 and 1972.

REBOUL, J.-B., *La Cuisinière Provençale*, Marseilles, 1895, and many subsequent editions.

ROACH, F. A., *Cultivated Fruits of Britain*, Basil Blackwell, Oxford, 1985.

ROGGERO, SAVINA, *I Segreti dei Frati Cucinieri*, Mondadori, Milan, 1979.

ROHLFS, GERHARD, *Vocabolario dei dialetti salentini (Terra d'Otranto)*, with illustrations, 3 vols, 2nd edition, Congedo Editore, Galatina, 1976. This magnificent work was originally printed by the Bavarian Academy of Sciences, the first volume appearing in 1956.

ROSS, JANET, *The Land of Manfred*, 1889. This book was translated into Italian by Ida De Nicolo Capriati, Valdemare Vecchi, Trani, 1899. Reprinted by Lorenzo Capone Editore, Cavallino di Lecce, 1978.

SALA, M. and PASCUAL, R., 'La Micologia a Catalunya', a paper in *Congrés Català de la Cuina* (see above).

SALAMAN, R. N., *The History and Social Influence of the Potato*, Cambridge University Press, 1949, and reprinted with new introduction by J. G. Hawkes, 1985.

SCAPPI, BARTOLOMEO, *Il Cuoco Secreto di Papa Pio Quinto*, 1570. The first Italian cookery book.

SCHAUENBERG, PAUL and PARIS, FERDINAND, *Guide des Plantes médicinales*, Delachaux and Niestlé, Neuchâtel, Switzerland, 1969.

SMOLLETT, TOBIAS, *Travels through France and Italy*, 1766. Reprinted in World's Classics, Oxford University Press, 1985.

SOPHOCLES, *Oedipus Rex*, translated and edited by R. D. Dawe, Cambridge University Press, 1985.

SOYER, ALEXIS, *The Gastronomic Regenerator*, Simpkin and Marshall, London, 1846.

STEIN, GERTRUDE, *The Autobiography of Alice B. Toklas*, Bodley Head, 1933. Reprinted by Penguin, 1966, 1977.

STENDHAL, *Souvenirs d'Égotisme*, published posthumously by Le Divan, Paris in 1892, and then in 1927 and 1950. Reprinted in *Oeuvres Intimes*, vol II, Gallimard, 1981.
Correspondance, Tome III, Bibliothèque de la Pléiade, 1968. Particularly item 1704, a letter to M. Thiers, Président du Conseil etc, on *La morue*.

STERNE, LAWRENCE, *Tristram Shandy*, 1760. Everyman Classics, Dent, London, 1985.

STOBART, TOM, *The Cook's Encyclopaedia*, Batsford, 1980. Also in Papermac, Macmillan, 1982.

STOLBERG, COUNT F. L., *Travels through Germany, Switzerland, Italy and Sicily*, translated by Thomas Holcroft, 4 vols, 2nd edition, London, 1797. Vols III and IV for Apulia and Sicily.

STUART THOMPSON, S., *Flowering Plants of the Riviera*, with coloured plates, Longmans, London, 1914.

SWIFT, JONATHAN, *Gulliver's Travels*, 1726. Everyman Classics, Dent, London, 1985.

THEATRUM SANITATIS, a codex describing the therapeutic properties of plants, with exquisite paintings, conserved in the Biblioteca Casanatense, Rome, 14th century.

THEOPHRASTUS (372-287 BC), *Enquiry into Plants*, translated by Sir Arthur Hort, 2 vols, Loeb Classical Library, 1916.

THOUSAND AND ONE NIGHTS, THE, A Plain and Literal translation of the Arabian Nights' Entertainment, by R. F. Burton, 16 vols, Kamashastra Society, Benares, 1885-8.
Tales from the 1001 Nights, translated by N. J. Dawood, Penguin, 1973.

TOMA, GIUSEPPE, *Riviviscenze classiche nella Grecia Salentina: I Rami Bendati dei Supplicanti del'Edipo Re*, privately printed, Maglie, 1980.

TRELAWNEY, EDWARD JOHN, *Recollections of the Last Days of Byron and Shelley*, Oxford University Press, 1906. Reprinted, edited by J. E. Morpurgo, Folio Society, London, 1952.

VERGA, GIOVANNI, *I Malavoglia*, 1881. Reprinted in the 'Oscar' series, Mondadori, 1978.
Translated as *The House by the Medlar Tree* by Eric Mosbacher, Greenwood Press, London, 1985.

VEYRIER, HENRI, *Encyclopédie de la Divination*, Madrid, 1973.

(LE) VIANDIER, a 14th century cookery manuscript by Taillevent (Guillaume Tirel) in the Bibliothèque Nationale, Paris, edited by Pichon and Vicaire, 1892. Reprinted recently by Daniel Morcrette, Luzarches, France.

VIOLA, S., *Piante medicinali e velenose della flora italiana*, Edizione Artistiche Maestretti, Istituto Geografico De Agostini, Novara, 1965.

VIRGIL, *The Aeneid*, translated by W. F. J. Knight, Penguin, 1985.
The Eclogues, translated by G. Lee, Penguin, 1985.

VITTORINI, ELIO, *Conversazione in Sicilia*, first published as *Nome e Lagrime*, Parenti, Florence, 1941. Reprinted by Einaudi, Turin, 1966, 1975. Translated by Wilfrid David, Drummond and David, London, 1948.

XERVOS, CHRISTIAN, *La Naissance de la Civilisation en Grèce*, 2 vols, and *Les Cyclades* 1 vol, Cahiers d'Art, Paris, 1959.

Part II

Books for further reading: those not mentioned in the text, but which interested readers may wish to consult, have been arranged in convenient groups.

CATALONIA

COOKERY

AGULLÓ, FERRAN, *Llibre de la cuina catalana*, Barcelona, 1933, reprinted in facsimile by Edició Alta Fulla, Barcelona, 1978.

BALLESTER, PERE and Pons, Pedro, *De re cibaria*, Cocina, Pastelería, Repostería menorquinas, Mahón, 1923. Valuable for its precise explanation of Minorcan culinary practices in the early 20th century.

CAMBA, JULIO, *La Casa de Lúculo o el arte de comer*, Nueva fisiología del gusto. First published in Madrid, 1929, now available in paperback Coleccíon Austral. ('A cookery book for intelligent people' according to Josep Pla.)

(LA) CUINA DE L'AVIA, La llibreta de cuina d'una barcelonina de finals del Segle XIX, Edicions de la Magrana, (no precise date). Reissued Empar Sabata, Barcelona, 1979.

(LA) CUINA DE L'EMPORDANET, Unió d'associacions d'hosteleria de Costa Brava Centre (Recipes from their first gastronomic exhibition, 1984).

CUNILL DE BOSCH, J., *La Cuyna Catalana*, Barcelona, 1907.

(LA) CUYNERA CATALANA, Reglas utils, facils, seguras y economicas per cuynar bé, Barcelona, 1851. Facsimile reprint, Edició Alta Fulla, Barcelona, 1980.

PENYA, PERE ALCÀNTARA, *La cuyna mallorquina*, Felanitx, Reus, 1905. The subtitle, translated, concludes, 'which for the convenience of those persons who wish to cook well what is cheap and live to eat, an amateur publishes in order to eat to live.'

PUIGPELAT, DOLORES LLOPART, *El Rebost* (Adobs, conserves, confitures i licors), Edició Alta Fulla, Barcelona, 1979.

REGAS, GEORGINA, *La Cuina de festa major*, e altres plats de la Lola de Forxá, Edició La Gaya Ciència, Barcelona, 1981.

VIDAL, C. A., *Cocina selecta Mallorquina*, 7th edition, published by the author, 1969.

REFERENCE WORKS

DICCIONARI ANGLÈS-CATALÀ, CATALÀ-ANGLÈS, by Salvador Oliva and Angela Buxton, Enciclopèdia Catalana, Barcelona, 1983-6. Excellent.

DICCIONARI CATALÀ-ANGLÈS, ANGLÈS-CATALÀ, Jordi Colomer, Editorial Pòrtic, Barcelona, 1981.

GILI, J. L., *A Catalan Grammar*, Dolphin Book Company, Oxford, 4th edition, 1974.

GREECE

COOKERY

CHANTILES, VILMA LIACOURAS, *The Food of Greece*, Avenel Books, New York, 1979.

PARADISIS, CHRISSA, *The Best of Greek Cookery*, Efstathiadis Brothers, Athens & Thessaloniki, 1974.

SALAMAN, RENA, *Greek Food*, Fontana, 1983.

TSELEMENTÉS, N., *Odigós Mageirikis*, 9th edition, Athens, 1948. A 19th century classic. It has been translated as *Greek Cookery*, by D. C. Divry, published at New York, 1950.

ART AND INSPIRATION

ANDREWS, KEVIN, *Athens Alive*, Hermes Publications, Athens, 1979. Throw away all tourist guides and get this book.

L'ART DES CYCLADES DANS LA COLLECTION DE N. P. GOULANDRIS, Catalogue issued by Les Éditions de la Réunion des Musées Nationaux, Paris and in English by British Museum Publications, London, 1983.

See also *Les Cyclades* under Xervos, Christian in Part I.

See also *Les Cyclades* under Xervos, Christian in Part I.

MILLER, HENRY, *The Colossus of Maroussi*, 1941. Reprinted by Penguin, in association with Heinemann, 1963.

SCULLY, VICTOR, *The Earth, the Temple and the Gods*, Yale University Press, 1962 and 1979.

ITALY

Cookery

BONI, ADA, *Il Talismano della Felicità*, Rivista *Preziosa*, Rome, c 1932. Frequently reprinted since. Translated as *The Talisman Italian Cook Book* by Mattilde La Rosa, W. H. Allen, London, 1953.

CAMINITI, M., PASQUINI, L., QUONDAMATTEO, G., *Mangiari di Romagna*, 2nd edition, Garzanti, Milan, 1961.

CARNACINA, L. and VERONELLI, L., *La buona vera cucina italiana*, 2nd edition, Rizzoli Editore, Milan, 1970.

CORRENTI, PINO, *Il Libro d'Oro della Cucina e die Vini di Sicilia*, Edizione Mursia, Milan, 1970.

DA MOSTO, R., *Il Veneto in Cucina*, Martello, Milan, 1969.

DI CORRATO, RICCARDO, *Le delizie del divin porcello*, Idealibri, Milan, 1984.

DELLA SALDA, A. G., *Le Ricette Regionali Italiane*, La Cucina Italiana, Milan, 1967.

FRANCESCONI, JEANNE CARÒLA, *La Cucina Napoletana*, Fausto Fiorentino, Naples, 1965.

SADA, L., *Puglia in Bocca*, Edizione Chronus, Bari, 1977.

VITTORE, F. *et al*, *Puglia a Tavola*, Edizione Adda, Bari, 1979.

Archaeology, Travel, Tradition

ALLEN, N., *Stone Shelters*, Massachusetts Institute of Technology, 1969. A study of the *trulli* of Locorotondo, Alberobello etc.

D'ANDRIA, FRANCESCO, *Itinerari Archaeologici: Puglia*, Newton Compton, Rome, 1980.

DE FERRARIIS, ANTONIO (IL GALATEO), *Liber de Situ Iapygiae*, Basle, 1558. Reprinted, Naples, 1855.

DE GIORGI, *La Provincia di Lecce, Bozzetti di Viaggio*, 1888. Of fundamental interest for an understanding of the Salento.

DE SAINT-NON, RICHARD, *Voyage Pittoresque de Naples et de la Sicile*, 5 vols in folio, Paris, 1786. A very rare work in an edition limited to 150 copies. The magnificent engravings are by Fragonard, De Saint-Non and others. Apulia is described in vol III.

FARANDA, LAURA, *Le Tradizioni Popolari in Puglia*, Casa Editrice Anthropos, Rome, 1983. An illuminating little book.

FUMO, PIO, *La Preistoria delle Isole Tremiti: Il Neolitico*, Edizione Enne S. R. L., Via Petrella 22, Campobasso.

GRAY, CORINNA, *Rustic Structures*, Downhill Press, Compton Abbas, 1984. With drawings of the *pagghiari* and *llame* of the Basso Salento.

GUIDO, MARGARET, *Southern Italy: an archaeological guide*, Faber and Faber, London, 1972.

RADMILLI, A. M., *Piccola Guida della Preistoria Italiana*, G. C. Sansoni Editore, Firenze, 1975 *et seq.*

SWINBURNE, HENRY, Travels in the Two Sicilies, with engravings, London, 1783.

PLANT REFERENCE

CONOSCERE LA NATURA ITALIANA, vols 1-6, L'Istituto Geografico De Agostini S.P.A., Novara, 1984. Vols 7-11 in preparation.

COUPLAN, FRANÇOIS, *Plantes Sauvages Comestibles*, Hatier, Paris, 1985. 50 edible weeds, illustrations in colour, valuable notes (photographs of sorrel and oregano are accidentally transposed). Includes this warning: for certain recognition of plants and knowledge how to use them, books are not sufficient. The author recommends those interested in the subject to get in touch with: L'Institut de Recherches sur les Propriétés de la Flore, 37 Rue Charles-Michels, 91740 Pussay, France, who organize courses of plant study in Europe.

FLORA EUROPEA, Edited by T. G. Tutin *et al,* 7 vols including index, organized under plant families, Cambridge University Press, 1964-80.

HEINZ, H. J. and MAGUIRE, B., *The Ethno-biology of the !ko-bushman,* Occasional papers n° 1, Botswana Society, Gaberone, 1974. Concerns the botanical knowledge and plant lore of the !ko People.

ICONOGRAPHIA FLORAE ITALICAE , published between 1895 and 1904 and reprinted since.

NEGRI, G., *Erbario Figurato,* Edizione Hoepli, Milan, 1960.

PELIKAN, W., *L'Homme et les Plantes Médicinales,* Éditions Triades, 4 Rue Grande-Chaumière, Paris.

STARENKYJ, DANIELE, *Le Bonheur du Végétarisme,* Principes de vie et recettes, Orion, Quebec, 1977. 10th edition, 1984.

VON FÜRER-HAIMENDORF, CHRISTOPH, *Tribes of India,* Delhi, 1982.

WHEAT, MARGARET, *Survival Arts of the Primitive Paiutes,* Reno, Nevada, USA, 1967.

List of Illustrations

These are by Corinna Sargood. All were drawn specially for this book, except for those marked with asterisks, which come from the same artist's *Rustic Structures* – see under GRAY (SARGOOD) in Part II of the Bibliography.

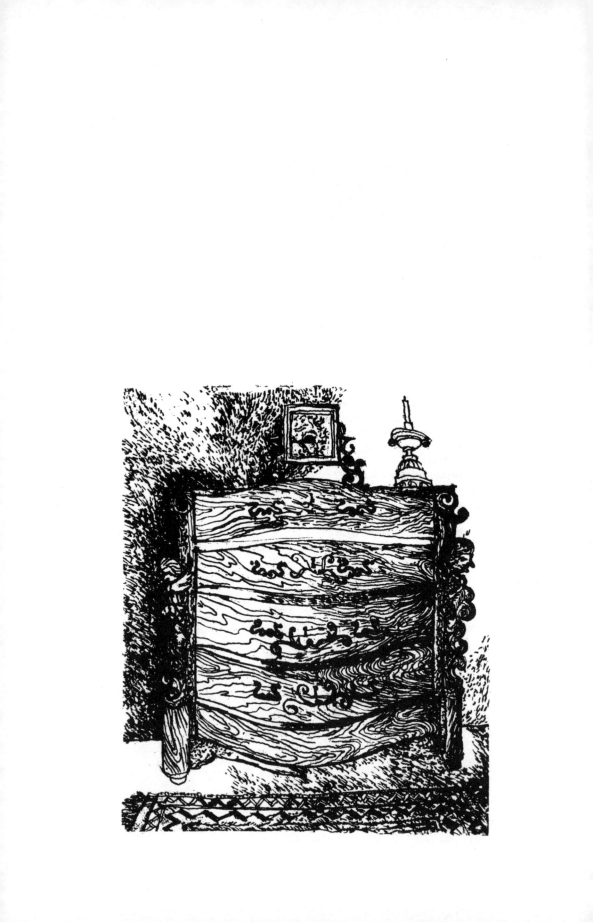

Index

The titles of all full recipes are printed in capitals in English and in the original language. The English names, principal foreign-language names, and scientific (Latin) names of the principal foodstuffs described are given; also places, people and themes.